To Baroness Liz Barker

Dear Liz

Everyone loves a good cartoon
— and this book commemorates 75
momentous years of Israel's existence

with all good wishes
    Colin Shindler

the Lib Dem Friends of Israel

London 2023

Israel

Since its establishment in 1948, the state of Israel has not ceased to be a unique and controversial entity: vehemently opposed by some, and loyally supported by others. In this novel and original study, Colin Shindler tells the history of Israel through the unusual vehicle of cartoons – all drawn by different generations of irreverent and contrarian Israeli cartoonists. Richly illustrated with a cartoon for every year since Israel's establishment until 2020, the book offers new perspectives on Israel's past, politics and people. At once incisive and hilarious, these cartoons, mainly published in the Israeli press, capture significant flashpoints, and show how the country's citizens felt about and responded to major events in Israel's history. A leading authority on Israel Studies, Shindler contextualises the cartoons with detailed timelines and commentaries for every year. Sometimes funny and sometimes tinged with tragedy, *Israel: A History in 100 Cartoons* offers a new, visually exciting and accessible way to understand Israel's complex history and, in particular, the Israel–Palestine conflict.

Colin Shindler is Emeritus Professor at the School of Oriental and African Studies, University of London. He became the first Professor of Israel Studies in the UK in 2008 and was the founding chairman of the European Association of Israeli Studies (EAIS) in 2009. He has published twelve books and his most recent publications include *Israel and the European Left: Between Solidarity and Delegitimisation* (2012) and *The Rise of the Israeli Right* (2015).

Israel

A History in 100 Cartoons

Colin Shindler

School of Oriental and African Studies,
University of London

CAMBRIDGE
UNIVERSITY PRESS

Shaftesbury Road, Cambridge CB2 8EA, United Kingdom

One Liberty Plaza, 20th Floor, New York, NY 10006, USA

477 Williamstown Road, Port Melbourne, VIC 3207, Australia

314–321, 3rd Floor, Plot 3, Splendor Forum, Jasola District Centre, New Delhi – 110025, India

103 Penang Road, #05–06/07, Visioncrest Commercial, Singapore 238467

Cambridge University Press is part of Cambridge University Press & Assessment, a department of the University of Cambridge.

We share the University's mission to contribute to society through the pursuit of education, learning and research at the highest international levels of excellence.

www.cambridge.org
Information on this title: www.cambridge.org/9781107170131

DOI: 10.1017/9781316756027

First published 2023

Printed in the United Kingdom by TJ Books Limited, Padstow, Cornwall

A catalogue record for this publication is available from the British Library.

ISBN 978-1-107-17013-1 Hardback

For my cousin Zelda Harris, and in memory of
my friend Sylvia Becker, who both fought so courageously for
many years to secure the emigration of Jews from the
Soviet Union

Contents

vii

The Cartoonists Featured

Yehoshua Adari (1911–66)
Born in Poland, immigrated to Palestine in 1932, contributed to *HaYarden*, *Herut*, *HaBoqer*, *Ha'aretz*

Arnon Avni (1957–)
Member of Kibbutz Nirim, graduate of Bezalel, contributor to *HaDaf HaYarok*

Noah (Birzowski) Bee (1916–92)
Born in Warsaw, immigrated to Palestine in 1934, contributed to *Ha'aretz*, *HaBoqer*, *Jerusalem Post*, author of several books, left for the USA, contributor to the Jewish Telegraphic Agency

Amos Biderman (1952–)
Member of Kibbutz Kfar Glikson, daily cartoonist for *Ha'aretz*, contributor to *Kol Ha'Ir*, Dosh Prize 2002

Shay Charka (1977–)
Contributor to *Makor Rishon*, *Otiot*, book illustrator, comic book author

Shlomo Cohen (1943–)
Graduate of Bezalel, daily cartoonist for *Israel Hayom*, contributor to *HaOlam Hazeh*, *Hadashot*, *Yediot Aharanot*, written many books

Zach Cohen (1983–)
Graduate of Shenkar College, daily contributor to *Calcalist*, illustrator and animator

Itamar Daube (1975–)
Graduate of Bezalel, contributor to *Yediot Aharanot*, head of illustrations and animation programme at Shenkar College, Senior Vice-President Creative of US media channel *babyfirst*

Eyal Eilat (1964–)
Graduate of Haifa University, contributor to *Walla News*, *Yediot Aharanot*, Schocken Books, illustrator of children's books

Ya'akov Farkash (Ze'ev) (1923–2002)
Born in Budapest, participant in death marches in 1944, Buchenwald inmate, interned by the British on Cyprus, immigrated to Palestine in 1947, started with *Ma'ariv* in 1953, given a weekly page in *Ha'aretz* in 1963

Kariel Gardosh (Dosh) (1921–2002)
Born in Budapest, immigrated to Israel in 1948, started with *Ma'ariv* in 1953, contributor to *Ha'aretz Shelanu*, creator of national symbol, Srulik

Avi Katz (1949–)
Born in Philadelphia, graduate of UC Berkeley and Bezalel, contributor to *Davar*, *Jerusalem Report*, children's book illustrator

Shmuel Katz (1926–2010)
Born in Vienna, interned in labour camps in Hungary and Slovakia, immigrated to Palestine in 1947, founder of Kibbutz Ga'aton in 1948, contributor to *Al Hamishmar*, *Davar*, *Ma'ariv*, Dosh Prize 2006

Michel Kichka (1964–)
Born in Liège, contributor to *L'Arche*, *Regards*, 'Cafe Telad' on Channel 2, lecturer at Bezalel

Ya'akov Kirschen (1936–)
Born in New York, freelance cartoonist for *Playboy*, immigrated to Israel in 1973, originator of 'Dry Bones' strip in *Jerusalem Post*

Dani (Lucien) Levkovitz (1927–2002)
Born in Paris, interned on Cyprus where he attended art courses, immigrated to Israel in 1948 and fought at Latrun, followed Moshe Sneh into the Communist party, contributor to *Kol Ha'am* 1954–61, worked for educational television as illustrator and animator

Moshik Lin (1950–)
Graduate of Bezalel, lecturer at Ben-Gurion University, contributor to *Davar*, *Ma'ariv*, *Iton 77*, children's book illustrator, Dosh Prize 2011

Guy Morad (1975–)
Graduate of Bezalel, contributor to *Yediot Aharanot*, book illustrator, comics creator

Arie Navon (1909–96)
Born in Dunaivtsi, Ukraine, contributor to *Davar*, creator of first children's characters, Jerusalem Prize 1941, 1944, Israel Prize 1996

Meir Ronnen (Mike) (1926–2009)
Born in Melbourne, graduate of the Royal Melbourne College of Art, cartoonist for *Sunday Telegraph*, immigrated to Israel in 1949, contributor to *Yediot Aharanot*, *Jerusalem Post*

Yosef (Rosenberg) Ross (1911–91)
Born in Antwerp, immigrated to Palestine in 1935, contributor to *Ashmoret*, author of many books

Shlomo (Helmut) Sawady (1917–2003)
Born in Berlin, contributor to *HaBoqer*

Dudy Shamai (1969–)
Contributor to *Ma'ariv*, Channel 1, illustrator of children's books

Friedel Stern (1917–2003)
Born in Leipzig, graduate of the Academy of Visual Arts, Leipzig, immigrated to Palestine in 1936, contributor to *Bamahaneh*, book and map illustrator, Dosh Prize 2004

Yoni Wachsmann (1975–)
Graduate of Bezalel, head illustrator for *Calcalist*

Preface and Acknowledgements

Most people appreciate a political cartoon. It gives a voice to the powerless and brings a smile to the face. The unexpected and the unimaginable evoke a respect for the cartoon creator, quietly beavering away at a sketch board.

Politicians, however, either detest cartoonists or are deeply flattered to be the focus of attention. More than one public figure has been known to arduously create a collection of their published images.

Historians, on the other hand, are allowed a window of observation into the past to view what may have been a popular perception of an episode or a noted figure.

Those who appreciate cartoons often single out one or two favourites which are particularly meaningful. For me, it is the remarkable cartoon of David Low which was published in the London *Evening Standard* in June 1940. It depicted a British soldier, standing on the White Cliffs of Dover, enveloped by threatening waves, but waving an angry fist at the Luftwaffe, high above in a black sky. Low drew this after the fall of Paris and the lightning conquest of much of Europe by the Nazis. Low's defiant caricature followed the retreat from Dunkirk and preceded the expected invasion of the British Isles. The cartoon's caption said it all. 'Very Well: Alone!' Low captured the national resolve of the British when the United States remained neutral and the Soviet Union was a fellow traveller of the Nazi state.

For me, there is another aspect to this cartoon. It is that of the outsider – and history's outsiders were the Jews. This is the underlying theme of this book, which depicts Jews as stiff-necked and contrarian rather than as the proud and compliant members of a community. It also explains why Jews were disproportionately represented as members of the fraternity of cartoonists and satirists.

The book's central focus is, of course, as its title states, a history of Israel which builds on sections about the rise of Zionism and the struggle for independence in 1948. It views Israel, not as an international pariah, but as the dissident of the nations – a revolt against the place allocated to the Jews by the international community.

In one sense, it is represented by Arie Navon's caricature of a traditional 'Iudaea Capta' coin of Vespasian or Titus after the fall of Jerusalem in the year 70 CE. This shows a standing Roman soldier looking down upon a seated, but dejected and weeping Jewess. The obverse, however, is not the head of one of the Flavian emperors, but instead that of an Israeli kibbutznik, wearing a kova tembel hat, bearing the inscription 'Iudaea Libera'. The establishment of a Hebrew republic in the Land of Israel in 1948 symbolised a fundamental transition in the flow of Jewish history. Navon's cartoon was entitled 'From Occupation to Liberation'.

This book begins with an exploration of depictions of Jews during the nineteenth century, drawn to amuse the reader. These were often superficial in their racism, but they were precursors for the demonisation of the Jews which proliferated in Hitler's Germany and Stalin's Soviet Union. While those regimes have passed into a well-deserved oblivion, the persecution of cartoonists in general has continued unabated in today's authoritarian states. Neither have anti-Semitic tropes from the past been laid to rest. While some cartoonists have wished to criticise Israeli policies, they often forget that a majority of Israelis just happen to be Jews – and this sometimes tips over into unintended anti-Semitic stereotypes. On the other hand, the country with the largest population of Jews in the Muslim world, Shi'ite Iran, has not been reticent to exhibit Holocaust denial in the guise of cartoon contests.

Even so, there have been marvellous depictions of the seemingly intractable Israel–Palestine imbroglio by both Israelis and Palestinians. Those outside the Middle East often attempt to reduce the complexity of this struggle into an attractive simplicity – and this does not always work. Even so, a few years ago, the British artist 'Banksy' produced a Christmas card cartoon which showed a bewildered and bemused Joseph and Mary, barred from entering Bethlehem by an Israeli army roadblock.

This book looks at political and cultural figures such as Ben-Gurion, Weizmann and Jabotinsky who were active in the Yishuv, the Jewish settlement in Palestine before 1948, and in the Jewish Diaspora. This leads on naturally to cartoons during the last years of the British Mandate and the first years of the state of Israel. However, the bulk of this work looks at the history of Israel, year by year, from 1949 until 2020.

Each year consists of four pages: a cartoon with an explanation, a timeline of that year and two pages of narrative which relate to the main events of that particular year.

This book features a hundred cartoons by solely Israeli cartoonists and finishes in 2020. However, the world moves on – as must cartoonists. Therefore this work does not include the fall of Benjamin Netanyahu and his replacement by the Bennett–Lapid administration, a pantomime horse of eight disparate parties sitting in an ideologically diverse coalition.

So this work is not a full-blown history of Israel – there are many detailed histories including my own rendition which can be consulted. Neither is it an art book of brilliant sketches which utilises the history of Israel as little more than a vehicle. Yet both are present in this hybrid, which hopefully will open a window for many on recent Jewish history and the onward odyssey of a state of the Jews. This unusual approach will provide food for thought for further exploration.

Why then select one specific cartoonist for a specific year – and not another one? My first port of call was to select a cartoon which illustrated a central event in that year rather than the cartoonist. For example, the depiction of Netanyahu as a haughty Roman emperor, reflecting on his conduct during the 2015 election, would have been a wonderful choice. Yet, as I have discovered, there is an abundance of insightful cartoons from a plethora of brilliant caricaturists which could easily have been chosen. In such a book, however, only one can be chosen for each year – and it becomes almost a question of personal choice. There could have been as many parallel histories, featuring different cartoonists and cartoons, as there are readers. My choice implies no judgement on those which have been omitted. There is an immense number of brilliant cartoons out there.

Another question emerges from the choice of cartoon: why this event and not another one to characterise a particular year? Again, it is not easy to make a decision, but hopefully other events are mentioned in both the timeline and the narrative.

The restriction of space in such a work essentially produces a snapshot history of a year. There are therefore borders in terms of detail and explanation. I did not have the luxury of explorative meandering into a particular episode, but I have tried my best to be as comprehensive as possible.

I delved into the press reportage of the time and checked the reports for their accuracy. This was often a difficult exercise. An Israeli government minister would tender his or her resignation, but this might only become official some forty-eight hours later. So which date should register the event?

Indeed, access to relevant information was made more difficult by being unable to travel and to visit archives during the pandemic. All this became heavily time-consuming. Despite the corroding addiction of social media, the internet, however, was a boon during this period. The digitised newspaper collection of the Yishuv and the state of Israel in the National Library of Israel was an enlightening discovery. It allowed me to identify the date and place of publication of several cartoons. However, it is still a work in progress. For example, *Ma'ariv* starts in 1948, but finishes in March 1991 with a few months added for good measure for 2020.

There are occasional lacunae where I have been unable to locate the details surrounding the publication of a cartoon.

It has proved difficult to find the date and place of publication of Yosef Ross's English-language cartoons for the period 1945–8 – although he published his Hebrew-language work in the daily *Hatsofeh* after 1949. One explanation is that the British authorities censored unfriendly caricatures during the final years of the Mandate.

I was fortunate to be in contact with the following cartoonists and to utilise their work in this book: Amos Biderman, Shay Charka, Shlomo Cohen, Zach Cohen, Itamar Daube, Eyal Eilat, Avi Katz, Michel Kichka, Ya'akov Kirschen, Moshik Lin, Guy Morad, Dudy Shamai and Yoni Wachsmann.

I would also like to thank the families of many cartoonists who have since passed on: Gideon Ross (Yosef Ross); David Navon (Arie Navon); Sarah Levkovitch (Dani Levkovitz); Nili Praiz (Yehoshua Adari); Naomi Farkash ('Ze'ev'); Daniella, Nancy and Miki Gardosh ('Dosh'); Dorit Katz, Yael and Roi Khenin (Shmuel Katz); Michal Safdie ('Mike').

My thanks also to the Israeli Cartoon Museum in Holon for drawing my attention to the wonderful work of figures such as Arnon Avni, Noah Bee, Shlomo Sawady, Friedel Stern and many others.

My thanks also to my good friend Amira Stern of the Jabotinsky Institute for her expertise in identifying specific cartoons, featuring Jabotinsky, from the 1930s.

I am grateful to the Israel National Library, Archives Department, for their help in accessing the Dosh Archive. The Library's Hebrew newspaper website proved to be an excellent tool for locating dates of publication.

I am deeply indebted to Hila Zahavi who is in charge of the archive at the Israeli Cartoon Museum. During the difficult time of the pandemic, I could not have completed this book without her expertise, help and good will. She answered all my questions and provided everything that I requested. She was a pleasure to work with.

I am also indebted in a broader sense to the Cartoon Museum itself. It is a marvellous institution which I first visited many years ago. It is a revelation to all Israelis who visit, both adults and children, and indeed to anyone who is interested in Israeli history.

I am deeply indebted to Ari Roth and his colleagues at the Israel Institute for their support in this work. The Israel Institute has valiantly supported academics who teach Israel Studies internationally - it has really put Israel Studies on the map as a genuine discipline in academia.

I would also like to thank Maria Marsh and Natasha Whelan of Cambridge University Press for smoothing the way and for their willingness to find solutions to the most insoluble of problems.

The eighteen months of isolation during repeated lockdowns allowed me the space to complete this project. This work would not have seen the light of day if it was not for my wife, Jean, my best friend and inspiring life partner.

I have tried to use a transliteration of other languages which is consistent. However, where familiarity occasionally trumps convention, then I have utilised the former. Of course, any errors of fact and interpretation are entirely my own.

Introduction:
Jews: Caricatures, Cartoons, Comics

Rebels with a Cause

Caricatures, cartoons and comics reflect the age-old human desire to be independent in thought and action. Cartoons challenge subservience and deference – and acknowledge that the master in his underwear looks really ridiculous. As Orwell succinctly pointed out in *Animal Farm*: 'All animals are equal, but some animals are more equal than others.'

Cartoons also record history. They provide a snapshot of an event or an episode that often reflects popular feeling at the time. They are an invaluable adjunct of historical research.[1]

While caricatures go back to antiquity, Annibale Carracci (1560–1609) is reputed to have developed it in more modern times and realised its potential to reveal and indeed shock. He said that 'a good caricature, like every work of art, is more true to life than reality itself'.[2]

Pompous politicians often worry about reputational damage and a downward swing in the polls if they are constantly lampooned. Others revel in the brilliance of the cartoonist in depicting their flaws and foibles as well as their achievements.

Hannah Arendt pointed out in 1967 that 'truth and politics are on rather bad terms with each other' and that no one had ever counted truthfulness among the political virtues.[3] Cartoons therefore bring out the fears and insecurities of authoritarian leaders. They 'capture the bias, prejudice and suspicion often sanitised from other mass media content'.[4] Throughout history, cartoonists have been murdered, imprisoned and exiled because they stoke the fires of dissidence.

In the UK, James Gillray attacked sympathisers of the French Revolution such as Charles James Fox and his Whig supporters. In February 1805, he mocked Britain and France for literally carving up the globe in *The Plumb-Pudding in Danger (or State Epicures Taking un Petit Souper)*, in which the newly crowned Napoleon Bonaparte and Prime Minister William Pitt were depicted eagerly dissecting a plum-pudding-shaped world.[5] Although figures such as William Hogarth had depicted the vagaries of life in eighteenth-century Britain in works like the brilliant *A Rake's Progress*, it was only the French Revolution at the end of that century and the European Enlightenment that truly liberated caricaturists to ply their trade in puncturing the high and mighty in political cartoons.[6]

1

---

[1] Richard Scully and Marian Quartly, 'Using Cartoons as Historical Evidence', in *Drawing the Line: Using Cartoons as Historical Evidence*, ed. Richard Scully and Marian Quartly (Clayton, Victoria 2009) pp. 1–13.
[2] E. H. Gombrich and E. Kris, *Caricature* (London 1940) pp. 11–12.
[3] Hannah Arendt, 'Truth and Politics', *The New Yorker* 25 February 1967.
[4] Ilan Danjoux, *Political Cartoons and the Israeli–Palestinian Conflict* (Manchester 2012) p. 1.
[5] See Tim Clayton and Sheila O'Connell, *Bonaparte and the British: Prints and Propaganda in the Age of Napoleon* (London 2015).
[6] See David Alexander, *Richard Newton and English Caricature in the 1790s* (Manchester 1998).

Yet this still brought threats and intimidation to those who challenged the established order. Honoré Daumier, a republican, was repeatedly imprisoned for his caricatures of the nineteenth-century Orléanist monarch Louis Philippe. Even so, the advance of technology brought with it the introduction of mass-circulation newspapers and journals. *La Caricature* started in Paris in 1830, *Punch* in London in 1842 and *Simplicissimus* in Berlin in 1896. *Le Canard Enchaîné* remarkably began publication at the height of World War I.

Cartoons and caricatures acted upon the public imagination in nineteenth-century France. The competing regimes, Bourbon, Orléanist, Bonapartist and Republican, fought for dominance whenever there was a whiff of revolution. A cartoon, like the head on a coin, could be a subtle method of propaganda. Conversely a satirical cartoon which distorted the figure of a leader in caricature and held him up to ridicule was clearly a weapon of social criticism. Charles Philipon depicted the head of Louis Philippe as gradually morphing into a pear! *La Poire* subsequently led to censorship of some cartoons by his regime.

A clever caricature can also be a catalyst to quite easily release pent-up anger at a particular political scenario. As the writer Joseph Conrad succinctly commented in his 1915 novel *Victory*: 'A caricature is putting the face of a joke on the body of a truth.'

In more modern times, cartoonists have continued to pay for their ingenuity and biting wit. In 2006 in Belarus, the cartoonist Oleg Minich was given the choice of five years in prison or exile from the country for insulting President Aleksandr Lukashenko.

Héctor Germán Oesterheld, an originator of graphic novels and comics in Argentina, fell foul of the military dictatorships that held power during the post-Peronist period in the 1970s. A supporter of the Cuban Revolution, he was also a member of the Montoneros underground. Jorge Videla staged a military *coup d'état* in 1976 in the name of Christian civilisation – and many opponents, including a disproportionate number of Jews, were murdered. Between 1976 and 1983, it is estimated that as many as five thousand political inmates were tortured, drugged and undressed to be sent as unwilling passengers on 'death flights' from which they would be dropped far out to sea. Inhabitants of the Paraná delta, north of Buenos Aires, reported 'bodies falling out of the sky'. The babies of executed parents were handed over to 'good' military families.

Oesterheld 'disappeared' when this Argentinian junta took power. He was never seen again – and neither were his daughters, Diana, Beatriz, Estella and Marina. One grandson, born in prison, was rescued by Oesterheld's wife. She became one of the *Abuelas de Plaza de Mayo* (the grandmothers of the Plaza de Mayo) who continue to search for the stolen children of the murdered.

In the Arab world, cartoonists have often run into trouble when depicting leaders in authoritarian societies. In Algeria, Ali Dilem was sentenced to a year in prison and a 50,000 dinar fine in February 2006 for drawing the ancestors of President Abdelaziz Bouteflika in a less than flattering light. Dilem had previously also been the subject of a fatwa issued by Islamists and angry threats from army chiefs.

Naji al-Ali, a Palestinian illustrator, was shot in the head in London in 1987 outside the offices of the Kuwaiti paper that he worked for. In 2008, Baha Boukhari, the chief cartoonist for *al-Ayyam* in Gaza, drew attention to the sycophantic behaviour of those around the Hamas leader, Ismail Haniya. All depicted in his cartoon bore the image of Haniya's face. Boukhari was sentenced to six months' probation and a fine of $270. In 2011, Ali Ferzat was attacked by Bashar Assad's security police in Syria; both his hands were broken as a warning.[7]

---

[7] For a recent list of cartoonists who have been the victim of repression, see Victor S. Navasky, *The Art of Controversy: Political Cartoons and their Enduring Power* (New York 2013) pp. 201–9.

In Turkey, Recep Erdoğan was elected prime minister for the first time in 2003, before later becoming president, and since then has repeatedly sued cartoonists for their perceived misdemeanours. Erdoğan has been depicted as a horse (Sefer Selvi), a dog (Michael Dickinson) and a cat (Musa Kart). As Turkish courts do not make their records public, the number of lawsuits which Erdoğan has filed is unknown.[8]

Cartoons also prepare the ground for revolution and record its stages such as the denouement of the Egyptian president, Hosni Mubarak, during the 25 January Revolution in 2011.[9] Cartoons always achieve new zeniths of popularity during the course of unpopular wars waged by democracies. As early as 1954, the British cartoonist Vicky was illustrating an article about the leader of the Communist insurgents in Vietnam, Ho Chi Minh, following the defeat of the French at Dien Bien Phu.[10]

Figures such as Hugh Haynie (*Courier Journal*, Louisville), Guernsey Le Pelley (*Christian Science Monitor*), Pat Oliphant (*Denver Post, Washington Star*), Bill Mauldin (*Chicago Sun-Times*) and many other notable cartoonists continued to deconstruct the policies of successive American administrations in dealing with the war in Vietnam. Herbert Block (Herblock) won three Pulitzer prizes and shared a fourth for his caricatures. The flip-flop policies of Lyndon Johnson on Vietnam and Richard Nixon on Watergate provided ample material for American cartoonists.

On the other hand, cartoons were also utilised during times of war to uphold public morale and to mobilise public support for the conflict.[11] During the 1930s, the Nazis extended this to peacetime and were particularly adept at mobilising support under the direction of Josef Goebbels. Anti-Nazi cartoonists therefore posed a potent threat to the regime, which was particularly sensitive to any ridiculing of the Führer. Goebbels conveyed his anger to the British foreign secretary, Lord Halifax, about David Low's cutting cartoons of Adolf Hitler in the London *Evening Standard*. These drew attention not only to the evil of Nazism but also to the mental instability of the Führer. Halifax's softly-softly approach failed to convince Low and the cartoonist took little notice of the admonitions of his editor at the *Evening Standard*, Percy Cudlipp. He responded by depicting Halifax's butler asking the good Lord in bed: 'Which backbone shall I lay out this morning, my Lord?'[12]

When war broke out, Low's name was placed on the *Sonderfahndungsliste GB* – in the Black Book of citizens to be arrested by the Gestapo if Operation Sea Lion, the German invasion of Britain, was successful in August 1940. Hitler's sensitivity to the power of art had no doubt been heightened through his failure twice to enter the Academy of Fine Arts in Vienna.[13] He also knew the value of art to move people and understood full well that Low's caricatures in conjunction with Churchill's rhetoric would stiffen British resistance to the Nazis. As early as 1926, he had referred to the ease of utilising a caricature as an instrument of propaganda in a chapter in *Mein Kampf* on the spoken word.

> One must also remember that of itself the multitude is mentally inert, that it remains attached to its old habits and that it is not naturally prone to reading something which does not conform with its own pre-established beliefs when such writing does not contain what the multitude hopes to find there. Therefore,

---

[8] Efrat E. Aviv, 'Cartoons in Turkey: From Abdülhamid to Erdoğan', *Middle Eastern Studies* vol.49 no.2 (2012) pp. 221–36.

[9] Rania Saleh, '"Let them Entertain Themselves": the Fall of the Mubarak Regime, Seen through Egyptian Political Cartoons', *Middle Eastern Studies* vol.54 no.3 (2018) pp. 494–520.

[10] *New Statesman* 8 May 1954.

[11] Eberhard Demm, 'Propaganda and Caricature in the First World War', *Journal of Contemporary History* vol.28 no.1 (1993) p. 167.

[12] *Evening Standard* 1 August 1938.

[13] Ian Kershaw, *Hitler, 1889–1936: Hubris* (London 1998) p. 48

some piece of writing which has a particular tendency is, for the most part, read only by those who are in sympathy with it. Only a leaflet or a placard, on account of its brevity, can hope to arouse a momentary interest in those whose opinions differ from it. The picture, in all its forms, including the film, has better prospects. Here there is less need of elaborating the appeal to the intelligence. It is sufficient if one be careful to have quite short texts, because many people are more ready to accept a pictorial presentation than to read a long written description. In a much shorter time, at one stroke, I might say, people will understand a pictorial presentation of something which it would take them a long and laborious effort of reading to understand.[14]

Goebbels too understood Hitler's appreciation and sponsored a travelling exhibition, *Der Ewige Jude* (The Eternal Jew), replete with cartoons. This was on display between November 1937 and January 1939 and was viewed by hundreds of thousands of citizens in Munich, Vienna and Berlin. Its central theme of anti-Semitism was then transferred to the silver screen as Fritz Hippler's film of the same name in 1940.

A Solitary Profession

Cartoonists were, by definition, outsiders. David Low's famous cartoon, 'Very Well: Alone!', published during the summer of 1940, captured this. It depicted a British soldier, standing on the White Cliffs of Dover, lapped by angry waves, waving a fist defiantly at the Luftwaffe in a black sky.[15] It, of course, reflected the grave situation after Hitler had overrun Europe, marched into Paris and was preparing for an invasion of the British Isles. It also described the solitary nature of the cartoonist, developed into a national perspective when Britain truly stood alone.

Cartoonists challenged the accepted order and therefore could never be fully trusted by any regime. On one level, they did not have the responsibility that comes with government. On the other, they were relatively free of the shackles of politics and often spoke out for the governed. They were not, however, free of the whims and demands of their employers – often all-powerful newspaper proprietors.

In 1929, Lord Birkenhead, a leading Conservative party politician and eminent member of several previous governments, had written to Lord Beaverbrook, owner of the *Evening Standard*, complaining that Low had published 'filthy and disgusting cartoons of me which were intended and circulated to do me deep injury'. Low had characterised him as 'Lord Burstinghead' owing to his overblown speeches.

In response, Beaverbrook told Birkenhead that he was out of touch:

> The new generation like the Low caricatures. For my part, Low outrages my feelings when he makes me crawl out from under the table or peep through the door. But I hold the view that a caricature cannot give good ground for complaint. Perhaps I am wrong, but I stick to it.[16]

The *Evening Standard*, in which David Low's cartoons were featured, was banned in Nazi Germany. Even Beaverbrook failed to get the ban lifted during a visit to Germany. While allowing

---

[14] Adolf Hitler, *Mein Kampf* (1926), vol. II, trans. James Vincent Murphy (1939), chapter 6: 'The Struggle of the Early Period: the Significance of the Spoken Word'; see https://hitler.org/writings/Mein_Kampf/mkv2ch06.html.

[15] *Evening Standard* 18 June 1940.

[16] A. J. P. Taylor, *Beaverbrook* (London 1972) p. 261.

editorial independence, Beaverbrook made an exception when he told Low to 'lay off Franco' in 1940, when Britain feared that Hitler would be given carte blanche by the Spanish dictator to march through Spain and conquer Gibraltar.[17]

While a cartoonist was clearly attracted to the very idea of an independent existence, this sometimes translated into radicalism. After all, the middle of the road was the location where people got knocked down by passing traffic. Many were attracted to the far Left or the libertarian Right.

David Low was irked by the British government's inability to stand up to Hitler. Under official pressure, he stopped his *Hit and Muss (in their axis)* cartoon strip of the dictators and unapologetically telescoped them into *Muzzler*. Yet even avid cartoon collectors such as Churchill complained about Low's independence and described him as 'a communist of the Trotskyist variety'.[18]

Yet clearly Low, while sympathising with the underdog, was not going to be straitjacketed by subservient ideology. This was apparent in his memorable cartoon 'Rendezvous',[19] which was drawn after the dissection of Poland by the Nazis and the Soviets in the wake of the Molotov-Ribbentrop pact. Over the dead body of 'Poland', Hitler bows to Stalin with the greeting: 'The scum of the earth, I believe?' To which Stalin responds, 'The bloody assassin of the workers, I presume?'

History's Outsider

Cartoonists as outsiders sided with the underdog, and during the 1930s, this was the persecuted Jew. Moreover it was made patently clear who was the persecutor and who was the persecuted – there was no need for explanation. Low himself had depicted Hitler setting fire to 'some inoffensive Jew' with an Olympic torch during the Berlin Games in 1936.[20]

Moreover, the Jew had been history's outsider. It did not matter whom he aligned himself with, he was marked out for special attention and individual treatment. The essay by Moses Leib Lilienblum, 'The Future of our People', which was written shortly after the discriminatory May Laws of 1882 and the first *aliya* – the first emigration of Jews from the Tsarist Empire to Palestine – captures the sheer absurdity of the situation, exemplified by a wry black humour.

> The opponents of nationalism see us as uncompromising nationalists, with a nationalist God and a nationalist Torah; the nationalists see us as cosmopolitans, whose homeland is wherever we happen to be well off. Religious gentiles say that we are devoid of any faith, and the freethinkers among them say that we are orthodox and believe in all kinds of nonsense; the liberals say we are conservative and the conservatives call us liberal. Some bureaucrats and writers see us as the root of anarchy, insurrection and revolt, and the anarchists say we are capitalists, the bearers of the biblical civilisation, which is, in their view, based on slavery and parasitism.[21]

Two events occurring within days of each other indicated the pathways through the twentieth century for the Jews. The October Revolution espoused the universalism within Jewish tradition to repair the world. This persuaded many Jews to declare their natural affinity

---

[17] Ibid. p. 435.
[18] Ibid. pp. 434–5.
[19] *Evening Standard* 20 September 1939.
[20] *Evening Standard* 25 July 1936.
[21] Moses Leib Lilienblum, *The Future of our People* (1883) quoted in Arthur Hertzberg, *The Zionist Idea: a Historical Analysis and Reader* (Philadelphia 1997) p. 173.

with the Left and to transcend their Jewishness. Their hallmark was often acculturation and assimilation.

The Balfour Declaration, on the other hand, promised a home for the Jewish people in Palestine and appealed to particularism in Jewish tradition. The Jews, it was argued, did not simply adhere to a specific religion but were actually a nation in exile with all the accoutrements of a people – history, culture, languages, literature and a religion. The Zionists of 1917 believed that Zionism was not wrong, but just different. It did not fit into the conventional theory of nations and nation-states.

Both universalism and particularism – and their hybrids – gave Jews a sense of belonging, which gave them a mission and an identity, and provided a structure.

As cartoonists, Jews were latecomers. As the focus of cartoonists, they were not. Many of the early cartoonists such as Honoré Daumier and Aubrey Beardsley conjured up anti-Semitic stereotypes. Ashkenazi Jews in late eighteenth-century London were characterised as purveyors of criminality by caricaturists such as Thomas Rowlandson. In 'Get money still and then let virtue follow if she will' of 1808, Rowlandson depicted three decrepit and grotesque Jews – as stereotypical Fagins. It is estimated that 60 per cent of Rowlandson's prestigious output was devoted to anti-Semitic caricatures.[22]

Racist imagery in Europe looked back to medieval times and viewed Jews as child murderers, blood drinkers, sorcerers, blasphemers and Christ-killers. Jews in the early twentieth century were often depicted as aged, bearded, ugly and religious, with bulging eyes and hooked noses. They were sometimes caricatured in zoomorphic terms – often as spiders at the centre of a web of conspirators. In January 1953, in Stalin's USSR, the Doctors' Plot depicted Jewish doctors as poisoners. Whether as capitalists or communists, they were seen as the puppet masters, controlling the world through others.

Jews were disproportionately represented in the various socialist movements that threatened Tsarism. For many, Russia was the homeland of death and destruction for Jews, characterised by pogroms and persecution. For several million, emigration to the United States, Palestine and Western Europe became the solution.

In established Jewish communities such as that in Britain, there was a liberal backlash against Russian anti-Semitism. Following the assassination of Alexander II in March 1881, the *Punch* cartoonist John Tenniel published 'A Cry from Christendom' which protested against the many attacks on Jews following the killing of the Tsar.[23] Alexander III, who succeeded his father, was much more hardline and continued to introduce oppressive measures against Jews in Russia. A cartoon in *Punch*, entitled 'The Alarmed Autocrat', showed an old, bent Jew bowing before a uniformed Tsar Alexander III, who retreats in horror, ordering his guards: 'Take him away! Take him away! He frightens me!'[24] Tenniel portrayed the persecuted Jew exotically as Shylock from *The Merchant of Venice*.[25]

In other countries, a similar struggle by the liberal intelligentsia was taking place. In France, there was the infamous case of Alfred Dreyfus and the defence by Emile Zola. In Austria, the

[22] Jeremy Smilg, *The Jews of England and the Revolutionary Era, 1789–1815* (London 2021) pp. 55–65.
[23] *Punch* 28 January 1882.
[24] *Punch* 13 June 1891.
[25] Dominic Williams, 'Punch and the Pogroms: Eastern Atrocities in John Tenniel's Political Cartoons, 1876–1896', *Revue d'Art Canadienne* vol.42 no.1 (2017) pp. 32–47.

populist Karl Lueger, known for his anti-Jewish comments, became mayor of Vienna despite the objections of Emperor Franz Josef. Both Hitler and Theodor Herzl, living in Austria, took note.

While the Bolsheviks initially combated traditional anti-Semitism, by 1926 Stalin began to use anti-Semitism against his rivals, Trotsky, Zinoviev and Kamenev. This paralleled the growing fear of Judeo-Bolshevism, stoked by many priests in the Catholic church in many European countries.

In a territorially shrunken Germany after the sudden defeat in 1918, the easy answer was to blame 'the stab in the back' by cosmopolitan Jews who owed no allegiance to the Fatherland. The War Ministry had actually conducted a survey of the 100,000 Jewish soldiers in the German forces during World War I. It found that 80 per cent of all Jews in the ranks were serving at the front. And, of these, 12,000 had been killed and 35,000 decorated for bravery. The results were never published and so the myth of Jews as shirkers, deserters and defeatists was born.

'The stab in the back' became a political instrument for more mainstream figures to build their political careers. It can be argued that even Hindenburg used it to divert attention from his own military failures during World War I.[26]

The post-war instability of the Weimar Republic encouraged the imagery of the scheming Jew which the far Right subsequently promoted assiduously during the inter-war years. The German minister of finance, Matthias Erzberger, was assassinated by a far Right group in August 1921. He was a victim of the ultra-nationalism that had ballooned in the immediate aftermath of the end of World War I. The humiliation of defeat and the prospect of a Communist uprising were also characterised by cartoonists on the far Right who often blamed the Jews for Germany's woes. The gradual character assassination in cartoons of figures such as Erzberger was no doubt a factor in his real assassination.

These difficult times also brought many German Jews into the world of caricatures and cartoonists. For many Jews, it was an escape from the ghetto and Jewishness. It was a world without boundaries where nascent fascism could be counteracted and conquered. It was paradoxically an extension to the richness of self-deprecating Yiddish humour – with the cartoonist cast in the role of a warrior in the fight against injustice. Puncturing the inflated and the pompous while spotlighting the absurdities of life appealed to the post-war Jew after 1918 – someone who often looked to Lenin and Trotsky for an answer to the problems of the world.

For some, it was the legacy of the stubborn Jew who, no matter how distant he or she was from their Jewishness, always stood on the margins and insisted on speaking out against the prevailing wisdom. In 1904, Ahad Ha'am, the Zionist thinker, wrote a remarkable essay about Moses. In it, he defined Moses neither as a warrior nor as a lawgiver, but as a prophet. He characterised today's prophet:

> He sees facts as they are, not through a haze of personal dispositions and tells the truth as he sees it . . . not because he has convinced himself by a process of reasoning that he is duty-bound to tell the truth, but because he can do no other. Truth-telling is the law of his nature, he cannot escape it even if he would.[27]

This perception which defined the Jew by his moral strength suited the budding Jewish cartoonist perfectly. While the freedom of cartooning appealed to the acculturated and the assimilated Jew rather than the traditional Jew, it also characterised that category of Jews who defined their Jewishness by escaping from it.

7

[26] Richard Sculley, 'Hindenburg: the Cartoon Titan of the Weimar Republic, 1918–1934', *German Studies Review* vol.35 no.3 (2012).
[27] Ahad Ha'am, *Moses* (1904) in Leon Simon, *Ahad Ha'am: Essays, Letters, Memoirs* (Oxford 1946) p. 105.

The Nazis and the Cartoonists

The difficulty was that the Jewish cartoonist could not escape who he was in Nazi Germany.

Many were suddenly confronted with an abrupt end to their careers when Hitler became chancellor on 30 January 1933. Non-Jewish cartoonists, on the other hand, had the choice of remaining and acquiescing in Nazi megalomania or going into exile and seeking work abroad. For Jews, there was no choice.

Max Liebermann became the president of the Berlin Academy of the Arts in 1920, but despite his attempt to acculturate, he had been described as 'the Jewish enemy within'.[28] When the Nazis came to power, his works were removed from public view.

The youthful Victor Weisz left Germany for Britain in 1935 and became a national institution as 'Vicky', famed as the deflater of politicians. In 1958 he famously drew Prime Minister Harold Macmillan as 'Supermac',[29] an ageing superhero who had told the British public that they had 'never had it so good!'

Vicky later recalled the atmosphere in January 1933, when Hindenburg appointed Hitler as chancellor. He went out from the offices of the *12 Uhr Blatt* into the street:

> Thousands of Nazi swastikas and old Nationalist black-white-red flags decorated the houses and enthusiastic Nazis were making their way to the centre of the city to see their Führer. They cheered him wildly as he drove to the Presidential palace. But there were those Berliners whose sullen, grim expressions spoke as loudly as the shouts of 'Heil Hitler'.[30]

The burning of the Reichstag, the end of freedom of the press and the Nazi takeover of *12 Uhr Blatt* ended Vicky's Berlin career. He reached Britain in October 1935.

Many German caricaturists followed Vicky out of Germany. They had been stalwarts of publications such as *Simplicissimus* and *Kladderadatsch*. Although both had moved to the Right, *Simplicissimus* had been a beacon of hope and enjoyment during the Weimar years; it was now transformed into a tool of Goebbels's propaganda machine.

Prague became a centre of opposition to the Nazis by German émigrés. In May 1934, an exhibition of anti-Nazi cartoons opened in the Czechoslovak capital. Hitler's appetite to reverse the Versailles Treaty and to recover lost German territory led to the Anschluss, the conquest of Czechoslovakia and a growing thirst for *Lebensraum*. Many cartoonists subsequently fled to Britain and the United States.

Arthur Szyk (Poland), Walter Trier (Czechoslovakia), Stephen Roth (Czechoslovakia) and Louis Mitelberg (Poland via Paris) managed to escape to the UK. Eric Godal, né Erich Goldstein, left Germany just a few weeks after Hitler's ascent to power and made his way to the United States. André François, né Farkash (Hungary), remained in Paris during World War II. Saul Steinberg (Romania) left for the United States in 1941. Fritz Behrendt, a student at the Amsterdam College of Arts and Crafts whose family had escaped from Germany to Holland, was imprisoned by the Gestapo, but managed to survive the war.

Such cartoonists interpreted their Jewishness in different ways. Arthur Szyk was a committed Zionist who illustrated the rise of Israel and its pioneering youth. John Heartfield was the son of the

---

[28] Mitchell B. Frank, 'Max Liebermann: Assimilation and Belonging', *Revue d'Art Canadienne* vol.45 no.2 (2020) pp. 97–110.
[29] *Evening Standard* 6 November 1958.
[30] Russell Davies and Liz Ottaway, *Vicky* (London 1987) p. 14.

Jewish socialist writer and activist Franz Herzfeld. He joined the newly founded Communist party in 1918 and settled in the German Democratic Republic fifty years later at the end of his life.

Jewish cartoonists who fled abroad were joined by many anti-fascist emigrés from different European countries. Josef Novák and Antonín Pelc managed to reach the United States but returned to Czechoslovakia after the war. Joseph Flatter left Austria in 1934 for London, but was subsequently interned as an enemy alien, but then became an official British war artist. George Grosz, Otto Dix and Max Beckmann were all associated with *Simplicissimus* during the 1920s. Grosz, a bitter anti-Nazi and Weimar caricaturist, had seen what was coming and left for the United States just a couple of weeks before Hitler became chancellor. Dix was conscripted into the Volksstrum, the makeshift people's militia formed to defend Germany at the end of the war, and survived the conflict. Beckmann went into Dutch exile and emigrated to the United States after the war.

Thomas Theodor Heine was one of the founders of *Simplicissimus* in Munich in 1896. He soon fell foul of the Kaiser and was imprisoned for several months. His Jewish origin proved to be an impediment in 1933 for the editors of *Simplicissimus*, who tried to accommodate the journal to the demands of the new regime. Heine eventually settled in neutral Stockholm where he died in 1948.

Others who remained often paid the price. Josef Čapek was arrested in 1939 and disappeared in Bergen-Belsen. František Bidlo died of typhoid in Terezin in May 1945 – on the very day after the formal end of the war.

Many Jews who had escaped from Nazism and found sanctuary in Britain and other countries appreciated the incisive attacks on Hitler by local cartoonists. Sigmund Freud, whose books had been burned by the Nazis, wrote to David Low, 'A Jewish refugee from Vienna, a very old man, personally unknown to you, cannot resist the impulse to tell you how much he admires your glorious art and your inexorable, unfailing criticism.'[31]

In Occupied Europe

Sometimes anti-fascist organisations published cartoons in their own journals to attack their opponents during the 1930s. In Paris, the Ligue Internationale contre l'Antisemitisme caricatured François de la Rocque, the leader of the Croix-de-Feu, for his Janus-like duplicity and the anti-Semitic colouring of his organisation.[32] On the other hand, in London Alexander Bowie drew many anti-Semitic cartoons, often featuring the Jewish East End, for the British Union of Fascists' journal, *Action*.

In occupied Europe, underground newspapers often carried cartoons. L. J. Jordaan's *De Robot*[33] which characterised the impervious, unstoppable Nazi war machine, appeared in the underground *De Groene Amsterdammer* after the invasion of Holland in 1940.

In contrast, assorted fascists, Nazi admirers and ultra-nationalists collaborated with the Germans in occupied Europe. Cartoonists were amongst them and they often drew hook-nosed Jews whom they depicted as part and parcel of Judaeo-Bolshevik subversion. Following Operation Barbarossa – Hitler's invasion of the USSR – high-ranking Soviet Communists who happened to be Jewish were the target for caricature. Stalin's commissar for foreign affairs, Maxim Litvinov, né Meir Walloch-Finkelstein, suddenly acquired exaggerated 'Jewish features' in *La Gerbe* in Paris.[34]

[31] Colin Seymour-Ure and Jim Schoff, *David Low* (London 1985) p. 118.
[32] *Le Droit de Vivre* 4 April 1936.
[33] Mark Bryant, *World War II in Cartoons* (London 1989) p. 38.
[34] La Dernière Croisade, *La Gerbe* 16 October 1941.

This French publication was pro-Nazi and regarded Operation Barbarossa as a pan-European crusade to destroy Communism – a modern-day version of past crusades to reclaim the Holy Land for Christendom.[35]

In occupied Holland, the fascist sympathisers Peter Beekman and Pieter Pouwels utilised anti-Semitism in their illustrations. Beekman, a supporter of the Nationaal-Socialistische Beweging in Nederland (NSB), featured prominently in *Volk en Vaderland*, an NSB weekly. Jews were viewed as either representing the elite or at the centre of a web controlling them from behind the scenes,[36] including everyone from Prince Bernhard to King George VI to Eleanor Roosevelt. The Jews were depicted as both greedy capitalists and devout Communists. The Princess Irene Brigade, a Dutch military force stationed in Wolverhampton in the United Kingdom, was depicted as a Jewish unit.

In Mussolini's Italy, anti-Jewish legislation was not introduced until 1938. However, Italy's alignment with Nazi Germany and eventual participation in the war allowed Mameli Barbara to suggest that Jews controlled the United States in the satirical magazine *Marc'Aurelio*. John Bull was similarly transformed into a Jewish stereotype to imply that the British were, in fact, fighting a Jewish war against Italy.

In the Soviet Union, Boris Efimov drew for *Pravda*, *Krokodil* and *Ogonyok*, but followed the latest twists and turns of Stalin's political whims such as castigating Trotsky and Bukharin during the period of the show trials. His brother Mikhail Koltsov, who had fought in the Spanish civil war, was shot as an English spy in February 1940. Boris Efimov was the son of a Jewish shoemaker, Haim Fridlyand, and had attacked Hitler through his cartoons as early as 1924.[37] Like many Jews in Stalin's USSR, Efimov preferred to conceal his Jewish origins for fear of discrimination and persecution.

In Nazi Germany itself, Julius Streicher published *Der Stürmer*. It was characterised by its crude but popular anti-Semitic cartoons. Many of these stereotypes were drawn by its in-house cartoonist, 'Fips', aka Philipp Rupprecht, who had worked for the magazine since 1925. Jews were depicted as sexual predators, financial exploiters, collectors of Christian blood, ritual murderers of German children[38] and anti-patriotic subversives. One cartoon in 1935 depicted a kosher butcher and his wife making sausages from rats.

In the August 1935 edition, Streicher wrote: 'The Jew is monstrosity incarnate … his soul is disjointed, inharmonious, debased. As the blood so the soul! The soul of the Jew is the sum of the bad qualities of other races.'[39]

In periodicals such as *Das Schwarze Korps* of the SS, members of the Jewish Brigade were depicted as weaklings who did not want to fight and bribers of non-Jews to take their place. Churchill was seen in Nazi publications sporting an armband bearing the insignia of the Star of David. Periodicals such as *Kladderadatsch* and *Lustige Blätter* often featured Jews as the puppet masters of the Allies.

Some cartoonists who stayed in Germany believed that they could retain their spirit of critical observation. Karl Arnold remained with *Simplicissimus* after 1933 and attempted to cope with its total change of direction under Nazi rule. He believed initially that Hitler would quickly be

---

[35] Roy Douglas, *The World War, 1939–1945: the Cartoonists' Vision* (London 1990) p. 93.

[36] Kees Ribbens, 'Picturing Anti-Semitism in the Nazi-Occupied Netherlands: Anti-Jewish Stereotyping in a Racist Second World War Comic Strip', *Modern Jewish Studies* vol.17 no.1 (February 2018) pp. 8–23.

[37] Stephen M. Norris, 'Laughter's Weapon and Pandora's Box: Boris Efimov in the Khrushchev Era', in *Cultural Cabaret: Russian and American Essays for Richard Stites*, ed. David Goldfrank and Pavel Lyssakov (Washington, DC 2012) p. 132.

[38] *Der Stürmer* (Nuremberg) May 1934.

[39] *Der Stürmer* no.32 August 1936, in *The Yellow Spot* (London 1936) p. 74.

replaced by just another of Hindenburg's numerous chancellors, taken from his 'Magic Factory'.[40] Others such as Oskar Garvens and Paul Weber continued to draw for publications which promoted anti-Semitic caricatures.

The war decimated Europe. It had lasted in reality from 1914 until 1945 with a hiatus in between. Hitler and his acolytes turned the friendly neighbour into a member of the *Einsatzgruppen* whose mission in life was to kill as many Jews as possible. Many wondered in hindsight how this could have happened. How could 'a down and out' from Linz have reinvented himself as the infallible, conquering hero of a new Germany – and sucked millions into blindly following him.

The Allies might have won the war, but the Jews certainly lost it. The British cartoonist Philip Zec – of Russian-Jewish parentage – summed up the fragility of victory in his VE Day cartoon for the *Daily Mirror*. A wounded British soldier is seen handing over a laurel wreath, representing peace in Europe. The caption reads: 'Here you are. Don't lose it again!'

Stalinism and the USSR

The post-war world was a period of renounced empires and a clash of ideologies. The wartime cooperation between the anti-Nazi powers fell apart within months rather than years. This initially led to the Berlin airlift and then to the full onset of the Cold War. Half of Europe had substituted one oppressor for another.

In the post-war period, Stalin directed a campaign against Jews in the USSR which led to the trial and execution of leading members of the Jewish intelligentsia in August 1952. This was followed by the Slánský trial in Czechoslovakia in November 1952 and the Doctors' Plot in January 1953. In both processes, Jews were represented throughout as the forces of evil, bent on undermining the benevolent wisdom of the leadership.

While the brutal nature of victimisation and deportation to the Gulag receded after Stalin's death in March 1953, anti-Semitic innuendo and discrimination against Jews continued. There even was an unofficial *numerus clausus* to prevent Jews from gaining access to universities. After all, Khrushchev had commented in 1958 that 'Jews never consider themselves educated enough' and always wanted to enrol at universities.[41]

The rise of the state of Israel in 1948 provided an alternative pathway for Jews. Although the USSR and the USA had joined together in recognising Israel, Stalin had hoped for a warm-sea harbour in Haifa or a socialist state sympathetic to the USSR. What he did not expect was the warm welcome which Soviet Jews extended to Golda Meir, the Israeli ambassador, when she attended the Jewish New Year service in a Moscow synagogue in the autumn of 1948. Jews turned out in their thousands to greet her – crowded on the streets, suspended from lampposts, hanging out of windows, shouting greetings in Yiddish to the emissary. It was perhaps the biggest unofficial demonstration since those of the oppositionists in the 1920s.

Many had written to Soviet officials requesting permission to leave for Israel to join surviving family members. Others took Stalin at his word and offered to put their military knowhow at the disposal of the state which was fighting a war of independence against a plethora of Arab armies. Stalin responded with arrest and incarceration. Externally the USSR supported Israel. Internally it did not. Requests for emigration were frowned upon and applicants often sentenced to years in strict-regime labour camps.[42]

---

[40] Karl Arnold, *Simplicissimus* 25 December 1932.
[41] *Le Figaro* 9 April 1958.
[42] See Mordechai Namir, *Shlichut B'Moskva* (Tel Aviv 1971).

While the gates of the Gulag were opened under Khrushchev and Stalin's crimes gradually condemned, Jews who wished to leave for Israel were still being placed on trial and sentenced during the 1950s. Anti-Semitism had not abated such that several Jews were accused of economic crimes in the 1960s.

In October 1963, the Ukrainian Academy of Science published Trofim Kichko's *Iudaizm bez prikas* (Judaism without Embellishment) which featured caricatures of hook-nosed Jews, wearing prayer shawls in synagogue and dipping their claw-like hands into pots of gold. This brought protests from the Western Left and in particular from Communist parties who had clearly undergone some retrospective examination of past Soviet history. Indeed, cartoons featuring Jews and Israel which appeared in the Ukrainian press during the 1960s bore an uncanny resemblance to those that had appeared in journals such as *L'vivs'ki visti* and *Krakivs'ki visti* during the German occupation.[43]

During the 1960s, the Soviet Union followed a policy of cultivating the developing world. This meant preferring nationalist regimes in the Arab world, such as Nasser's Egypt, and opposing social democratic Israel. Themes castigating the state of Israel appeared regularly in Soviet cartoons: Uncle Sam was controlled by Israel and Nelson Rockefeller in the United States was Jewish; there was no difference between Jews in the Middle East conflict and Nazis during World War II.

During and in the aftermath of the Six Day War in June 1967, Soviet cartoonists were deployed to depict Israeli soldiers as Nazi stormtroopers, backed by the long arm of American capital;[44] a goose-stepping Moshe Dayan kicking Hitler off his pedestal in order to take his place;[45] a skeletal hand emerging from a broken swastika to hand a baton labelled 'Genocide' to an Israeli soldier already dripping blood.[46] Israel's territorial expansion to almost four times its initial area during the war was compared in *Pravda* to Nazi expansionism in Eastern Europe decades before.[47]

The quick defeat of Egypt and Syria spurred on this Soviet display of rage and led to a breaking-off of diplomatic relations with Israel. Cartoons depicted Israel as now being on the wrong side of history and compared the Israeli military forces to the Americans in Vietnam and to the military junta that had taken over Greece.[48] Such tropes began to influence the far Left in Western Europe. Such imagery was therefore in place before the Jewish settlement drive on the West Bank and before the election of Menahem Begin's Likud party some ten years later.

In Poland, anti-Semitic imagery was similarly utilised in a power struggle within the Polish Communist party. Non-Jews were turned into Jews, leading figures were found to be controlled by their Jewish wives – and all were connected to the Zionists in Israel. This led to an exodus of often highly assimilated Polish Jews – the remnant who had survived the Shoah and thought that they had found a home in the Communist party in Poland – to Scandinavia in 1968.

In addition, Jews featured disproportionately in the dissident movements in both the USSR and the Eastern bloc. This allowed the Kremlin to invoke the idea that Jews were unpatriotic and unworthy. Publications such as Yuri Ivanov's *Ostorozhno sionizm* (Beware Zionism!) in

---

[43] Henry Abramson, "'This is the Way it Was': Textual and Iconographic Images of Jews in the Nazi-Sponsored Ukrainian Press of Distrikt Galizien", in *Why Didn't the Press Shout? American and International Journalism during the Holocaust*, ed. Robert Moses Shapiro (Hoboken, NJ 2003) pp. 537–56.

[44] *Kommunist Tadjikistana* 9 June 1967.

[45] *Kazakhstanskaya Pravda* 21 June 1967.

[46] *Bakinsky Rabochi* 23 June 1967.

[47] *Pravda* 4 July 1967.

[48] *Sovietskaya Estonia* 24 June 1967.

1969 accentuated the sense of discrimination. This gelled with the anti-Semitic inferences projected by anti-Israel cartoons.

The Star of David was associated in the USSR both with the synagogue and with the Israeli tank. As cartoons were driven by government policy, there was no inner restraint on the part of Soviet cartoonists to ensure that criticism of Israel did not tip over into criticism of Jews per se. 'Excused as satire and obscured as symbolism, cartoons reflect the biases and prejudices of their community'[49] – and the Soviet Union was no different.

When demonstrators protested in Red Square against the invasion of Czechoslovakia in 1968, the police attacked, screaming that they were all Jews.[50] Soviet intellectuals who spoke out in support of human rights in the USSR, such as Andrei Sakharov, Andrei Sinyavsky and Dmitri Shostakovich, regarded the malaise of anti-Semitism in their country as symbolic of all that was wrong in the Soviet Union.

Lenin had always believed that the answer to the Jewish problem in Russia was assimilation and disappearance. He was surrounded by many acculturated Jews and therefore had little contact with the Jewish masses. He knew nothing about Marxism–Zionism and the building of socialism in Palestine. Stalin's use of anti-Semitism since 1926 and the Nazi–Soviet pact of 1939 started a reappraisal for Soviet Jews. The invasions of Hungary in 1956 and Czechoslovakia in 1968 proved to be the final straw for many of them.

Many Jews in the literary and artistic world hid their identity behind traditional Russian names. The writer Samuil Abramovich Draitser became Emil Abramov. The satirist Grigory Kremer became Grigory Kroshin.[51] The only task of cartoonists who worked for satirical journals such as *Krokodil* was 'to ridicule things the state apparatus has proved wrong and worthy of criticism'.[52]

McCarthyism in the United States

In the United States in the 1950s, there was a similar but different involvement by cartoonists and satirists in political life. The McCarthy years tried to define patriotism by opposing Communism and persecuting liberals. The search for clandestine Communists was led by the House Committee on Un-American Activities. Of course, some Jews did indeed believe in Stalin, but a far greater number believed in liberalism and a tolerance of the other. US Jews – and their humour – cemented the existing ties between Jews and the profession of cartoonists.[53] After all, Jews had voted overwhelmingly for the Democrats since the 1920s and embraced Roosevelt's New Deal. The manic search for 'Reds under the bed' in the USA was paralleled by the discovery of 'Zionists under the bed' in the USSR. Both affected Jews – albeit in different scenarios.

Mad magazine first saw the light of day in August 1952. Many of its writers and cartoonists were left-wing Jews. It reflected the post-war humour, non-conformism and political individualism of Jewish New York. Many who worked at *Mad* were acculturated Jews who did not wish to advertise their Jewishness in the era of McCarthy. The anarchic dialogue in the magazine was peppered with Yiddishisms – sometimes real words, other times not, written sometimes in English,

---

49 Danjoux, *Political Cartoons and the Israeli–Palestinian Conflict* p. 11.
50 Abraham Rothberg, *The Heirs of Stalin: Dissidence and the Soviet Regime, 1953–1970* (London 1971) pp. 146–7.
51 Emil Draitser, *In the Jaws of the Crocodile: a Soviet Memoir* (London 2021) pp. 77–83.
52 Ibid. p. 117.
53 George M. Goodwin, 'More than a Laughing Matter: Cartoons and Jews', *Modern Judaism* vol.21 no.2 (May 2001) pp. 146–74.

other times in Yinglish. It subtly attacked McCarthyism and the antics of the House Committee who saw Jews as 'liberal outsiders'.

Such second-generation Jews came from poor immigrant backgrounds and often sided with the Left politically. Harvey Kurtzman edited *Mad* magazine between 1952 and 1956 and later recorded the remarkable evolution of US comics.[54] William Elder (Wolf William Eisenberg), Al Jaffee (Abraham Jaffee) and Al Feldstein (Albert Feldstein) were all associated with *Mad* magazine in its earliest days.

Several members of staff on the magazine had survived the Shoah and made their way to America. While Jews were formally not mentioned in *Mad* and Yiddishisms were essentially dissociated from Jewishness, there was a clear irritation at how Hollywood occasionally softsoaped Germany and the Germans during the period of the Shoah. Jewish victims became nondescript general victims.

Jewish food featured heavily in the magazine and its use often reflected Jewish uncertainty about acceptance in American society. In the third issue of *Mad* in early 1953, the parody 'V-Vampires' depicted the main character Godiva the Vampire, 'who pretended to eat blintzes and borscht but preferred blood'.[55]

In the shadow of the defeat of Nazism, superheroes were soon discovered to be Jewish in *Mad* magazine! The mild-mannered Clark Kent was actually a Jew. For non-Jews, this was a bizarre revelation which they eventually acclimatised to, but for American Jews at that time, it built on the very opposite belief that Jews were totally helpless and disempowered – and alienated from mainstream American society. Jerry Siegel and Joe Shuster brought Superman to the world's attention – significantly on the eve of World War II. Bob Kane (né Robert Kahn) followed with Batman. Indeed some found echoes within the Jewish liturgy and compared Superman to Moses.[56] Joe Simon (Hymie Simon) and Jack Kirby (Jacob Kurtzberg) brought forth Captain America. X-Men, the work of Kirby and Stan Lee (né Stanley Lieber), first appeared in September 1963. Lee revamped the Flash and the Justice League of America, and then brought the exploits of the Fantastic Four, the Black Panther and Spiderman to an appreciative audience.

While Lee is best known because of the proliferation of superhero films in recent years, he was just one of many Bronx Jews who distanced themselves from both their geographical and ethnic backgrounds.[57] Even so, Lee, dubbed 'the Jewish Walt Disney', was deemed worthy of inclusion in Yale's *Jewish Lives* series.[58]

Israel after 1948: Anti-Semitism and Anti-Israelism

Many non-Jewish cartoonists strongly identified with the Jewish survivors of the Shoah. As challengers of the established order, many were to be found on the Left. The difference for Jews was that they did not want to be defined by victimhood. In contrast, they believed now that they should stand up for themselves and be the forgers of their own destiny. Many Jews asked why, if the solidarity of the international working class was unbreakable, there were so few uprisings in support of persecuted Jewry.

---

[54] See Harvey Kurtzman, *From Aargh! to Zap! A Visual History of Comics* (New York 1991).
[55] Leah Garrett, '"Shazoom. Vas ist das Shazoom?": Mad Magazine and Post-War Jewish America', *Modern Jewish Studies* vol.16 no.1 (March 2017) pp. 57–79.
[56] Itay Stern, 'Where Moses Meets Superman', *Ha'aretz* 31 July 2015.
[57] J. Hoberman, 'Marvel's Ringmaster', *New York Review of Books* 19 August 2021.
[58] Liel Leibovitz, *Stan Lee: a Life in Comics* (Yale 2020).

The tragic reality in the Holy Land was that two national movements had arisen at essentially the same point in history with claims to the same territory. The proposed partition of Mandatory Palestine into Israel and Palestine, according to UN Resolution 181 in November 1947, was an inevitability. The British during their sojourn in Palestine believed that Jews and Arabs were little more than 'squabbling natives (who) had to be kept apart by poor, harried John Bull'.[59]

Even so, British censorship prevented the publication of acerbic and critical cartoons by artists such as Yosef Ross. By 1947, the British government returned the Mandate to the United Nations. In Britain itself, the Labour government of Clement Attlee had hoped to find a solution to the problem, but there were clearly differences of opinion even within the party. While Aneurin Bevan, the leader of the Labour Left, threatened to resign from the Attlee government over British conduct in Palestine,[60] cartoonists such as David Low and Leslie Illingworth began to discern the complex reality of the Israel–Palestine struggle and thereby distance themselves from the conflict. For Vicky, it was different. As an acculturated Jew, he was certainly ambivalent about Zionism, yet he could not forget what the Nazis had done even if he wished to. While he visited Israel in 1951 and published his sketches afterwards,[61] privately he favoured an assimilationist solution to the question of the Jews.[62]

The idea of 'the fighting Jew' affected ideological sensibilities: it was easier to cast the Jew as the victim of fascism, peacefully seeking a haven in the Holy Land. The very idea of the Jews as a nation in exile, returning to their ancient homeland from far-flung lands – as of right – did not fit into theory. The nascent, evolving Palestinian Arab nation, suppressed by British imperialism, was less problematic as it fitted the template of colonised peoples. The campaign of nationalist organisations such as the Irgun under Menahem Begin and Lehi under Natan Yellin-Mor, Israel Eldad and Yitzhak Shamir accentuated unease. Following the blowing up of the King David Hotel in Jerusalem in 1946, Illingworth drew two British soldiers carrying a stretcher – and written on the blanket concealing a body was 'World Sympathy with Zionism'.[63] Begin had defined the Irgun as an underground army, but it was also noted for its botched military operations in which civilians became 'collateral damage'. Lehi, on the other hand, embraced the principle of 'individual terror', taking its ideological cue from the Narodnaya Volya, which had employed assassination as a revolutionary tool in Tsarist Russia.

15

David Low had drawn a cartoon entitled 'Standing Room Only' in 1937, which drew attention to the proposal of the Peel Commission to partition Mandatory Palestine.[64] While David Ben-Gurion and Chaim Weizmann accepted the idea of partition, Golda Meir and Vladimir Jabotinsky rejected it. Paradoxically, Low's cartoon sided with the sceptics.

Ten years later, Low had moved away from his original position. The fighting in the Holy Land and the Irgun's activities had clearly disillusioned him. At the beginning of 1947, he drew 'The Dark Mirror' in which a 'Jewish terrorist' is seen peering into a mirror which reflects back 'the beast of anti-Semitism'.[65]

The armistice in early 1949 concluded with an independent state of Israel, the West Bank was occupied by Jordan and Gaza was seized by Egypt. It also produced a refugee problem of more than

[59] Jonathan Freedland, Introduction to the *Guardian* exhibition *Twice Promised Land* 2–30 July 2004.
[60] Michael Foot, *Aneurin Bevan, 1945–1960* (London 1975) p. 87.
[61] *Jewish Chronicle* 27 April 1951.
[62] Davies and Ottaway, *Vicky*, p. 105.
[63] *Daily Mail* 23 July 1946.
[64] *Evening Standard* 30 July 1937.
[65] *Evening Standard* 3 January 1947.

700,000 Palestinian Arabs who had fled or been expelled. Low compared the plight of the refugees to that of the Jews before World War II in a cartoon entitled 'There, yesterday were we'.[66]

Between 1949 and the Suez war of 1956, Israel refused entry to all those refugees who wished to return. In the summer of 1948, the Israeli cabinet had agreed this policy for fear of establishing a fifth column. Even after the end of hostilities in 1949, Israel's policy did not fundamentally change. The raids of fedayeen, often with Jordanian and Egyptian help, resulted in the deaths of Israeli civilians and the triumph of the hardline approach of Ben-Gurion, Moshe Dayan and Shimon Peres. This was in contrast to the questioning of the policy of automatic retaliation by Moshe Sharett. Low was critical of Israel's Operation Black Arrow which resulted in the killing of many Egyptian soldiers.[67] Sharett himself was appalled and realised that the raid would have far-reaching consequences.[68] Low was presciently critical on the eve of the Suez campaign in a cartoon entitled 'What is sown must come up'.[69]

The collusion of Israel with the imperial powers, Britain and France, agreed at Sèvres in 1956, enhanced the charge of the Left that Israel had crossed the ideological Rubicon and was therefore opposed to the principle of decolonisation. With the establishment of the Palestine Liberation Organisation (PLO) in 1964 and a growing national awareness on the part of the Palestinians, many cartoonists gradually shifted their sympathy towards the Palestinians.

Israel's conquest of the West Bank and Gaza during the Six Day War in 1967 led to a settlement drive. At first, security settlements were established at strategic points to impede any future invading Arab army. The victory in the war, however, awakened forgotten dreams of a Greater Israel among the Right, the National Religious and even some members of the Labour party, to incorporate the West Bank as Judaea and Samaria. As the Left fragmented and demanded change, the Right coalesced and supported the status quo – now understood as holding on to the conquered territories.

Spiritual fervour and messianism coloured the outlook of the succeeding generation of religious Zionists in the National Religious party (NRP). They moved from demanding religious rights from a secular government, such as the provision of kosher food, to espousing the demand to establish new settlements on the West Bank. The election of the Likud under Menahem Begin in 1977 cemented the approach of a new Israel.

The débâcle of Operation Peace in Galilee in 1982, in which Lebanon was invaded, and the subsequent killing of Palestinians in the camps at Sabra and Shatilla by the Christian Phalangists, brought opprobrium from many cartoonists. The change in the 1980s from a labour-intensive, controlled command economy to one based on neo-liberalism extinguished the ideal of a new type of society arising in Israel in the minds of many on the international Left. On the fiftieth anniversary of the founding of Israel, the *Guardian* newspaper in the UK proclaimed that 'in the 1970s, before it was fashionable to do so, we pioneered the argument that there must be justice for the Palestinians'.[70] Increasingly, the *Guardian* gave less space to the peace camps amongst both Israelis and Palestinians: it proved easier to provide polarised opinions from both sides. With the start of the al-Aqsa, or Second Palestinian, Intifada in 2000, from the *Guardian* standpoint, it was as if the Oslo Accords between Yitzhak Rabin and Yasser Arafat in 1993 had never been signed. The retaliatory attacks by the Israel Defence Forces (IDF), in an attempt to force an end to the Islamist suicide bombers, brought tremendous criticism – and this was reflected in many cartoons.

---

[66] *Evening Standard* 23 March 1949.
[67] *Guardian* 4 March 1955.
[68] Benny Morris, *Israel's Border Wars, 1949–1956* (Oxford 1993) pp. 324–34.
[69] *Guardian* 16 October 1956.
[70] *Guardian* 30 April 1998.

16

Misinterpretations and Ignorance

The problem for the critics of Prime Minister Ariel Sharon's policies in the early 2000s was that the Star of David, which signified the synagogue and Jewish communities around the world, also adorned an Israeli flag which flew from many an Israeli military vehicle. This lack of distinction and indeed of sensitivity, together with an absence of familiarity with the complexities of the Israel–Palestine conflict, led many cartoonists to dig a hole for themselves.[71] David Brown's cartoon in the *Independent* showed Sharon seemingly biting off the head of a baby. Its caption stated: 'What's wrong – you never seen a politician kissing babies before?'[72] This contrasted Sharon's desire for re-election in the upcoming national election in 2003 with his orders to the IDF to crush the al-Aqsa Intifada, to implement air attacks on overcrowded Gaza and to stage the incursion into Jenin in Operation Defensive Shield.

David Brown used as his model for the cartoon Goya's *Saturn Devouring his Son*. For Jews, it conjured up instead a medieval anti-Semitic imagery of Jews imbibing Christian blood. Moreover, Sharon was not kissing babies, but eating them.

This unintentional tipping over from criticism of an Israeli government policy into a classic depiction of anti-Semitism – albeit a misinterpretation – marked a lack of awareness, but did not prevent Brown's cartoon from being awarded 'Political Cartoon of the Year' at the end of 2003. Cartoonists had almost a duty to offend, but were there any red lines that should be drawn?

Les Gibbard also walked into 'an emotional minefield' when he published a cartoon of Begin and Sharon in the *Guardian*[73] in 1982, following the killing of Palestinian men, women and children in the refugee camps outside Beirut by the Christian Phalangists, allies of the Israeli invading forces. Amidst a pile of dead bodies, Begin is seen holding out his hands in bewilderment, while Sharon, in party dress on top of a tank, proclaims 'Happy New Year!' The caption reads: 'We did not know what was going on . . .' The implication that the Israelis were mounting a cover-up after a crescendo of international criticism was accompanied by an implied comparison between Israeli Jews and German Nazis. The cartoon also implied that since the massacre coincided with the Jewish New Year, Rosh Hashanah, the celebration of this religious festival was similar to the secular New Year and somehow tied to the deaths of the Palestinian civilians.

Again, a lack of awareness led a concerned cartoonist to drive at full speed into a dead-end street. It suggested that the complexity of the Israel–Palestine conflict was difficult for the reductionist approach of many a cartoonist. It was not as clear-cut a situation as British Tommies or American GIs confronting Nazi stormtroopers.

Similarly the Portuguese illustrator António Moreira Antunes was perplexed at accusations of anti-Semitism after publication of his cartoon of a blind President Trump, sporting a skullcap, being led by his guide dog, Benjamin Netanyahu, in the *New York Times* (15 April 2019). The dog's collar was emblazoned with a Star of David. For some Israelis and Jewish organisations in the USA, it conjured up anti-Jewish tropes from the past.[74]

The absence of context has caused contemporary cartoonists many problems since those who read these creations may see something else. Yet even within the coterie of Jews who identify with the state of Israel, there are differences between Jews who have settled in Israel and those who

17

---

[71] Jerome Bourdon and Sandrine Boudana, 'Controversial Cartoons in the Israel–Palestine Conflict: Cries of Outrage and Dialogue of the Deaf', *International Journal of Press/Politics* vol.21 no.2 (2016) pp. 188–208.

[72] *Independent* 27 January 2003.

[73] *Guardian* 20 September 1982.

[74] *Jerusalem Post* 3 May 2019.

remain in the Diaspora over what is and what is not anti-Semitic when attacking Israeli politicians.[75]

In Israel itself, there has often been disagreement between what is overtly anti-Semitic and what is a criticism of politicians and policy. In October 2014 Amos Biderman drew Netanyahu as the pilot in the cockpit of an aircraft which was flying towards a tower, adorned with the American flag.[76] The self-evident comparison with the hijackers of 9/11 in New York brought forth an agitated protest from the Israeli Foreign Ministry. *Ha'aretz*, however, defended its cartoonist. It stated that 'it reflected the current state of mistrust between Prime Minister Netanyahu and the Obama Administration'.[77]

A profoundly different controversy arose in the summer of 2018 when the cartoonist Avi Katz was dismissed from the *Jerusalem Report* – probably at the behest of the *Jerusalem Post* management – for a cartoon which offended the elite in the Likud and employed pigs to represent them. While this was internationally criticised as another breach in the wall of freedom of speech, the *Jerusalem Post* editorial stated that the cartoon was 'reminiscent of anti-Semitic memes, used against Jews in history'. It also trumpeted its patriotism: 'We, a Zionist newspaper, cannot accept this demeaning analogy.'[78]

Katz's cartoon was based on an Associated Press (AP) photograph of a selfie by the controversial Likud MK, Oren Hazan, with triumphant party representatives, huddled around Netanyahu after the passing of the controversial Nation-State Law. Avi Katz drew the Likudniks in exactly the same position in exactly the same clothes as in the photograph – but as pigs! The caption was, of course, taken from George Orwell's *Animal Farm*: 'All animals are equal, but some are more equal than others.' This was plainly a nod to the broad accusations that the Nation-State Law made Israeli Arabs second-class citizens.

The relevance to Orwell's pigs was glossed over. Instead it was the notion that pigs are not kosher that prevailed.

Yet the Israeli cartoonist Ze'ev had similarly depicted a squabbling Menahem Begin and Ariel ('Arik') Sharon as pigs around a table in a cartoon in August 1980.[79] It also featured Rabin as a donkey, Peres as a horse, Shamir as a piglet and Ezer Weizman as a camel. The cartoon depicted Sharon's anger at not being appointed minister of defence following Weizman's resignation. Begin took over the post himself as Sharon was both feared and unpredictable. Hanging on the wall behind Begin and Sharon was a framed statement which read: 'All ministers are equal, but some are more equal than others.'

The leader of the National Religious party, Yosef Burg, was also depicted as a pig – while wearing a *kipa*, a skullcap. He was anxiously drawing attention to another framed picture which depicted 'Arik' Sharon as 'Aricus Caesar', a Roman soldier, crossing the Rubicon. Begin's fellow architects of the Camp David Agreement in 1979, Anwar Sadat and Jimmy Carter, peer through the windows in bewilderment at this spectacle.

While all this also caused protests, it did not result in the dismissal of Ze'ev. The liberal *Ha'aretz* in 1980 proved more tolerant than the illiberal *Jerusalem Post* in 2018. It also perhaps reflected the profoundly different times. In 2018, Netanyahu was at the height of his power during the Trump era. In addition, the *Jerusalem Post* was an English-language newspaper, directed also at

---

[75] *Guardian* 29 January 2013.
[76] *Ha'aretz* 30 October 2014.
[77] *Ha'aretz* 31 October 2014.
[78] *Jerusalem Post* 31 July 2018.
[79] *Ha'aretz* 15 August 1980.

the Jewish Diaspora. The very idea of conjuring up leading Israeli politicians as pigs may have proved more offensive to a broad Diaspora audience, emotionally connected to Israel and cognisant of the heritage of 'pigs' in Jewish tradition.

Ducks also caused a problem. In September 1991, the Disney Corporation sued the Israeli cartoonist Dudu Geva for appropriating the figure of Donald Duck without permission. Geva argued that his creation was entirely different, but was fined 9,000 shekels. Many artists viewed this as an example of cultural Americanisation and symbolic of 'the broader relationship between artists and power'. A decade later Geva's duck was celebrated as an official symbol of Tel Aviv.[80]

Given the differences between communities in Israel, Left and Right, religious and secular, non-Zionist ultra-orthodox and religious Zionist, a dispute took place in 2007 between Mizrahim and Ashkenazim. The spiritual leader of the Mizrahim in Israel, Ovadia Yosef, took umbrage at what he perceived to be an 'anti-Semitic' cartoon, disparaging his flock. It appeared in the Ashkenazi, non-Hasidic weekly, *Yated Ne'eman*.[81]

In Germany, the 85-year-old veteran cartoonist Dieter Hanitzsch drew a cartoon for *Süddeutsche Zeitung* at the time of Neta Barzilai's triumph at the Eurovision Song Contest in the summer of 2018.[82] It depicted Netanyahu holding a missile emblazoned with a Star of David and a background at the Eurovision Song Contest. The 'V' in Eurovision was replaced by a Star of David. Hanitzsch, who was no racist, intended to depict Netanyahu as an opportunist who would exploit any situation to his benefit, but he was summarily dismissed by the *Süddeutsche Zeitung*.

This incident not only depicted German ultra-sensitivity to questions of anti-Semitism in the aftermath of the Shoah, but also asked whether Germans, specifically, and other non-Jewish cartoonists could direct their ire at an Israeli politician. Netanyahu was exceptional in that he was disliked in Europe for his cavalier attitude in arenas of political trust. It was well known that in Israel itself, Netanyahu was being investigated on several charges by the Israeli police and his moral conduct in high office was the subject of weekly protests.

Jews in the Arab Mirror

Arab cartoonists were faced with the difficulty that a majority of Israelis just happened to be Jews. The dilemma was one of how to criticise Israeli actions without appearing to be anti-Jewish.

The use of the Star of David and the bearded, orthodox Jew wearing a skullcap, however, often proved to be a signifier for Israelis in cartoons in the Arab press. Jews were also seen to be rich. At the onset of the Arab Revolt in 1936, *Filastin*, an Arabic-language daily in Mandatory Palestine, published a cartoon entitled 'Jewish Money Talks'.[83] In addition, there were often the tropes that appeared in both Nazi and Soviet cartoons[84] – Jews at the centre of a spider's web of influence, as blood-drinking vampires and child murderers, as controllers of international finance and of America, and comparisons between the Israeli presence in the West Bank and Nazi-occupied Europe, and between Warsaw in 1945 and Jenin in 2002. Mentions of the Tsarist forgery *The Protocols of the Elders of Zion* reoccurred in Arab, and especially Islamist, media.

---

[80] 'Duck Fights: Walt Disney vs Dudu Geva and the Politics of Americanisation in Late Twentieth Century Israel', *Journal of American Studies* (2022) pp. 1–29.

[81] *Ha'aretz* 16 October 2007.

[82] *Süddeutsche Zeitung* 15 May 2018.

[83] *Filastin* 19 June 1936.

[84] Joseph S. Spoerl, 'Parallels between Nazi and Islamist Anti-Semitism', *Jewish Political Studies Review* vol.31 no.1/2 (2020) pp. 210–44.

In April 2002, the IDF entered Bethlehem as part of Operation Protective Shield – in retaliation for the killings at the Park Hotel in Netanya as guests sat down for the Passover meal. Israeli troops laid siege to the Church of the Nativity in Manger Square after Palestinian militants fled there. This induced a spate of cartoons identifying the Palestinians as Jesus on the Cross,[85] with captions such as 'Do not kill him twice!'[86] and 'Father, forgive them because they know what they do ...'[87] Giorgio Forattini similarly depicted the Israelis as Christ-killers in the liberal Italian daily *La Stampa*.[88] All this conjured up the ancient imagery of the Jews as deicides, promulgated by the Church Fathers.

The role of Palestinian Islamists in the al-Aqsa Intifada and in the Hamas takeover of Gaza in 2007 pointed to a growing Islamisation of the conflict. This communicated to the international Muslim community beyond the Arab world. In addition, periodic flare-ups between the IDF and Hamas, such as in 2009, 2014 and 2021, promoted the Palestinians as a cause célèbre to many Muslims. This also coincided with the rise of both al-Qaeda and ISIS (or Islamic State).

Following the murder of Theo van Gogh in Amsterdam, the Danish daily newspaper *Jyllands-Posten* published twelve cartoons of the Prophet in September 2005. Many Muslims considered them blasphemous and insulting. While the situation provided fertile territory for Islamists to expand their influence amongst Muslims, it was also accompanied by violence and anger directed against Denmark.[89] It led to attacks on Danish embassies in Syria, Lebanon and Iran. Al-Qaeda advocated a boycott of Danish goods, while Saudi Arabia recalled its ambassador from Copenhagen. One politician in Uttar Predesh in India called for the beheading of the cartoonists. In Pakistan, the Islamist party Jamaat-e-Islami offered a $10,000 reward for killing a cartoonist. Six people were killed when the Danish Embassy in Islamabad was stormed in June 2008.

In Iran, Mahmoud Ahmadinejad was in power and the Danish cartoons provided him with an opportunity to erase from human consciousness the perception of the Shoah, which ostensibly offered a raison d'être for the existence of Israel. Iran broke off diplomatic relations with Denmark and at Ahmadinejad's behest, an International Holocaust Cartoon Exhibition was organised by the daily *Hamshahri*. While this was geared to questioning the Shoah as a historical event, Ahmadinejad also attempted to question modern Germany's responsibility for it and its reparations agreement with Israel. Why should the Germans have feelings of guilt toward Zionists? Why should the costs of the Zionists be paid out of their pockets? If people committed crimes in the past, then they should have been tried sixty years ago. Why must the German people be humiliated today because a group of people committed crimes in the name of the Germans during the course of history?[90]

In February 2008, the Danish police prevented an assassination attempt directed at Kurt Westergaard, the cartoonist who drew the 'Bomb in the Turban' cartoon. In 2009, a scholarly work by Jytte Klausen of Brandeis University about the cartoons controversy was due to be published by Yale University Press – except that Yale thought it best that the controversial cartoons be omitted in the name of preventing further violence.

In Paris in 2012, the satirical weekly newspaper *Charlie Hebdo* published the cartoons – and a court held that this did not incite race hatred. Republican France upheld secular values and refused

---

[85] Joël Kotek, *Cartoons and Extremism: Israel and the Jews in Arab and Western Media* (London 2009) pp. 43–6.
[86] Boukhari, 7 April 2002, Arabia.com.
[87] Stavro Jabra, *Daily Star* 4 April 2002.
[88] *La Stampa* 3 April 2002.
[89] See David Keane, 'Cartoon Violence and Freedom of Expression', *Human Rights Quarterly* vol.30 no.4 (2008) pp. 845–75.
[90] *Der Spiegel* 30 May 2006.

religion a role in public life – and there was no law against blasphemy. *Charlie Hebdo* attacked and insulted priests as well as rabbis and imams.[91]

Some Algerians who settled in France had been influenced by FIS, the Islamic Salvation Front, and its struggle to overthrow the Algerian regime. The availability of satellite television and the increasing influence of the internet and social media assisted in the growth of Islamism in France. The invasion of Iraq and the al-Aqsa Intifada in Israel provided local Islamists with foreign causes. Islamism also brought with it a growing anti-Semitism such that several French Jews moved to London or emigrated to Israel.

In January 2015, twelve people were killed at *Charlie Hebdo*'s offices by brothers Saïd and Chérif Kouachi, French-born sons of Algerian immigrants – one of whom had declared his desire to attack Jewish targets. This was followed by an attack by an associate of the brothers on a kosher supermarket, Hypercacher, in which four Jews were killed.

The cover of the next issue of *Charlie Hebdo* showed the Prophet in tears, carrying a placard which stated: 'Je suis Charlie'. This defiant illustration in the face of a mass killing undercut the Kouachi brothers' core beliefs. It indicated that the Prophet himself not only opposed the killing of the cartoonists, but by implication also criticised their brand of Islamism. In September 2020, *Charlie Hebdo* republished the Danish cartoons.

The Rise of Zionism

Zionism was just one solution among numerous answers to the age-old conundrum that was the 'Jewish problem'. Some like the fathers of Marx and Disraeli chose conversion. Others chose assimilation and disappearance – as did a multitude of Jewish revolutionaries who had emerged from closeted ghettos. Still others wished to preserve the Jewish national heritage – some within religious tradition, others outside it, often within socialist parameters. Many believed in a territorial solution in a plethora of geographical locations. Zionism projected one such solution: the Zionists believed in a return to the ancient Jewish homeland, Israel, then a backwater under the control of the Ottoman Turks.

Zionism arose in the penumbra of European nationalism and the advent of the nation-state. The early Zionists were therefore highly influenced by the French Revolution and its desire and motivation to overthrow the *ancien régime* and create a new order. Max Nordau spoke of 'the great men' of the French Revolution at the first Zionist Congress in 1897.

The Zionist movement quickly fragmented into different political factions, but they looked to different periods of the revolutionary era and to different figures. Ben-Gurion and Yitzhak Tabenkin looked to Robespierre and Danton while Jabotinsky preferred Mirabeau. While Zionism was to some extent a revolt against Judaism, religious tradition provided the backdrop to the emergence of the movement. Many drew their inspiration from the annals of Judaic history.

Zionist factions were influenced by recent history and the revolutionary national movements of the nineteenth century including the Italian Risorgimento and Irish Republicanism. Many located Jewishness within the advance of Bolshevism in Russia after 1917. Some Zionists therefore switched to the here-and-now of Communism in the 1920s and found biblical universalism there rather than within Marxist-Zionism. Moreover, many felt that they needed to prove themselves ideologically and turned on their former comrades in the Zionist movement in the USSR which was gradually being suppressed. Zionists in the newly established Soviet Union were sentenced to long periods in the Gulag.

21

[91] Jane Weston, 'Bête et méchat: Politics, Editorial Cartoons and Bande dessinée in the French Satirical Newspaper, *Charlie Hebdo*', *European Comic Art* vol.2 no.1 (2009) pp. 109–29.

The French Revolution also fragmented Judaism into several new interpretations. There were many other religious leaders who followed the views of the Hatam Sofer who simply wanted to rebuild the ghetto walls after Waterloo and defined themselves as 'authentic' followers of Judaism. Indeed Shneur Zalman of Lyady preferred the autocratic traditional rule of the anti-Semitic Tsar Alexander to that of the French invader in 1812.[92] After all, Napoleon had originally promoted the secularism of the French revolutionary republic. This approach of the Hatam Sofer and ultra-orthodoxy meant standing against Zionism and not forcing 'God's hand' to return the Jews to the Holy Land. The Lubavitcher Rebbe of the time accused the Zionists of replacing the Torah with nationalism.

At its outset, the Zionist movement was led by the socialists rather than by the nationalists and the religious. This placed emphasis on the creation of a new society as well as settling a new land. This defined Zionism as different from the imperialist inclinations of the great empires. Zionists did not arrive in Palestine in great conquering armies, but as impoverished workers carrying pitchforks and hoes, willing to build a new Promised Land.

Zionism also arose in the early nineteenth century when nationalism had assumed a progressive approach. European nationalism, however, gradually moved to the Right with the desire to colonise the world and built grandiose empires.

Zionism was spiritually and culturally indigenous to Palestine, but Zionists remained outside in a widely dispersed Diaspora. This posed a difficulty for European socialists who had no theoretical mechanism for understanding national liberation movements that existed outside the territory that they wished to liberate. Zionism was different and possibly unique. Was it therefore also wrong?

The other fundamental problem for Zionism was that it occurred at approximately the same time as the rise of Arab nationalism. The Arabs too wished to free themselves from the Turks and to decide their own destiny. Both Zionist Jews in the Diaspora and the Arabs of Palestine ultimately had claims over the same territory. The inevitable armed clashes followed, with partition of the land the obvious solution.

Cartoonists for Zion

Cartoonists who supported Zionism were undoubtedly affected by the heavy burden of Jewish history and the possibility of changing its course to forge a different future. Zionism, however, was a displaced national liberation movement, dispersed around the world and working towards emigration – as well as liberation. There were therefore many cartoons that appeared in the journals of different factions of the Zionist movement as well as in Jewish newspapers which catered for the general reader in a plethora of languages. This included specifically Jewish languages such as Yiddish and Ladino as well as English, French and German. Many illustrators would come to hear Ben-Gurion or Jabotinsky pronounce on the latest developments – and proceed to sketch them as they were in full flow.

For journals, such major figures would serve a political purpose. Thus, at the time of the Tarpat disturbances in 1929, Jabotinsky was depicted, dressed in his Jewish Legion British army uniform, sword in hand, in front of the Western Wall in Jerusalem, the outer wall of the Second Temple which was destroyed by the Romans in the year 70 CE. All of this resonated with those who closely followed events in 1929 and believed that the Jews should defend themselves against Arab attacks. Jabotinsky was also depicted wearing a blood-red cloak over his uniform which resembled a talit (a prayer shawl), presumably reflecting the holiness of the Western Wall. Yet

Jabotinsky himself was never religious: once he even organised a meeting of his aides without realising that it was Yom Kippur.

In a broader context, art was at the disposal of the Jewish national movement to create the imagery to further its goals and to attract new supporters. At the opening of the fifth Zionist Congress in Basel in 1901, both Max Nordau and Martin Buber promoted Jewish art as part and parcel of national rebirth – an essential part of cultural Zionism.[93] This was integral to a broader move by Chaim Weizmann's newly formed Democratic Fraktion. This essentially opposed the continual demand of religious Zionists and their rabbinical mentors to control education and propaganda within the movement. The orthodox suspected that an uncontrolled Zionist culture would be the first step on the slide towards secularism. The 'cultural question' therefore became an ongoing, sharp controversial debate between Weizmann and his allies and the rabbis.[94]

Even so, this espousal of a Jewish national art actually attracted many religious Zionists such as Hermann Struck, who argued that culture and religion were not in opposition to each other. This led to the establishment of the Bezalel Academy of Arts and Design by Boris Schatz in Jerusalem in 1906. It was named after Bezalel ben Uri, the artisan of the mishcan (the Tabernacle) which housed the Ark of the Covenant during the forty-year-long Israelite wandering in the desert before entering Canaan.

The Democratic Fraktion also attracted many young liberals who were opposed to Theodor Herzl's cultivation of 'the rich and the powerful, Jewish bankers and financiers' as well as the Kaiser and the Turkish Sultan.[95] One of those attracted to Weizmann's standard was the artist Ephraim Moses Lilien, who was opposed to the conservatives within the Zionist movement and indeed to the bourgeois values of Theodor Herzl himself. At the fifth Zionist Congress in 1901, Lilien organised an exhibition of Jewish artists and earned Buber's public praise for his art and his endeavour to challenge conventional views.

The socialist Lilien had embraced the Jugendstil movement, an art nouveau opposition to neo-classicism, and he contributed to several avant garde and modernist periodicals. In opposing the middle-class values of Herzl and his followers, Lilien celebrated 'sexuality and physicality as well as the life of the working man' and promoted 'the rejuvenation and potential freedom of the Jewish people – a rejuvenation, as it were, of the Jewish body as well as the Jewish body politic'.[96]

Lilien thereby portrayed Herzl as Moses, as the Assyrian emperor, as the very embodiment of 'male Jewishness' and the concrete projection of Nordau's *Muskeljudentum* (Muscular Judaism) in contrast to the imagery of the ghetto weakling.

Cartoons therefore reflected the highs and lows of the Zionist movement, the flaws and foibles of its main actors and the advance of the Hebrew press during the inter-war years. Children's works were often a starting point for cartoonists. In the 1930s in Palestine, Itzhak Yatziv, the editor of *Davar l'Yeladim*, asked Arie Navon to illustrate a story accompanied by rhyming text in Hebrew by Leah Goldberg. This gave rise to the character of Uri Muri, a sabra, native of the Jewish settlement in Palestine, the Yishuv. Other cartoon characters for children appeared who were fighting the Nazis in the late 1930s on the eve of World War II.[97]

---

[93] See Gilya Gerda Schmidt, *The Art and Artists of the Fifth Zionist Congress, 1901: Heralds of a New Age* (New York 2003).

[94] Jehuda Reinharz, *Chaim Weizmann: the Making of a Zionist Leader* (Oxford 1985) pp. 65–91.

[95] Chaim Weizmann, *Trial and Error: the Autobiography of Chaim Weizmann* (New York 1949) p. 52.

[96] Michael Stanislawski, *Zionism and the Fin de Siècle: Cosmopolitanism and Nationalism from Nordau to Jabotinsky* (Berkeley 2001) p. 100.

[97] Galit Gaon, 'How to Write Comics in Hebrew: the Early Years, 1935–1975', in *Israeli Comics (Part 1): the Early Years* (Holon 2008) pp. 6–11.

The Shoah was the great leveller. Several of Israel's cartoonists after 1948 carried the memory of the anti-Semitic cartoons in *Der Stürmer* and their role in dehumanising Jews. This produced a subconscious block on demonising Arabs during the early years of Israel's existence.

In addition, some cartoonists were survivors of the Shoah and many had to learn a new language, not being fluent in Hebrew: this produced problems in providing captions. Of the 'Hungarian Mafia' at *Ma'ariv* – Tommy Lapid, Ephraim Kishon, Kariel Gardosh and Ya'akov Farkash – all, apart from Kishon, had lived in the Hungarian ghettos at the end of the war in Budapest and in part owed their lives to the heroism of the Swedish diplomat Raoul Wallenberg. Ranan Lurie, a veteran of the Irgun, attacked Ernest Bevin in *Yediot Aharanot* and then contributed to *Bamahane*, the IDF weekly. In the United States, he drew cartoons for *Life Magazine*, the *New York Times* and *Newsweek*.[98]

Some were stopped from entering Palestine by the British navy and subsequently interned in detention camps in Cyprus. Ze'ev Ben-Zvi (1904–52) and Naftali Bezem (1924–2018) organised art classes for the internees and subsequently became cartoonists and caricaturists in Israel. Some cartoonists during the dying days of the British Mandate were unable to publish their frequently acerbic drawings because of censorship laws. Instead they often found American publications willing to publish them.

The first Israeli cartoonists, however, reflected the euphoria of the re-establishment of a Hebrew republic after two millennia of exile. Arie Navon brought the cartoon character 'Mr Israel' to public attention to record the events of the first years of the new state. He also looked back to Jewish history. He took the theme of the Iudaea Capta coins, minted by Vespasian and his two sons, Titus and Domitian, to commemorate the victory over the Jews in the decade after 70 CE, the year of the destruction of the Temple in Jerusalem. These coins were also designed to reflect the power and durability of the Flavian dynasty to the ordinary Roman citizen.

Navon reimagined the two sides of the coin. On one side was the traditional 'Iudaea Capta' image with the Roman centurion standing guard over a seated weeping Jewess. On the obverse was the head of a young Israeli, wearing the kova tembel hat of the kibbutznik; the words 'Iudaea Libera' were inscribed around the edge of the coin. From defeat and enslavement in 70 to liberation and freedom in 1948.

In December 1949 during the Festival of Hanukah, Navon similarly depicted the move of the Knesset from Tel Aviv to Jerusalem in the manner of the Arch of Titus in Rome. Instead of defeated and exhausted Jews carrying the Menorah into captivity, Ben-Gurion and his cabinet were carrying it back to Jerusalem.[99]

Recording the History of Israel

In the 1950s, Dosh (Kariel Gardosh) introduced the child-like 'Srulik', kova tembel, sandals and short trousers to the Israeli public in *HaOlam Hazeh*. Srulik seemed to embody the aspirations and enthusiasm of the new state, evolving into a national symbol and even featuring on an Israeli stamp.

Once again events were noted in children's sections of the press. Navon and Uriel Ofek introduced 'Sa'adia', the Yemenite boy who flies to Jerusalem on a magic carpet. This reflected Operation Magic Carpet which brought Jews from Yemen, Aden, Djibouti, Saudi Arabia and Eritrea in a series of airlifts between June 1949 and September 1950.

[98] *Ha'aretz* 21 August 2017.
[99] *Davar* 16 December 1949.

Avigdor Luizada's character 'Daring Dan' appeared in the children's section of the religious Zionist paper, *HaTzofeh*. This reflected fighting the Arab foe – and all the Israelis were depicted as religious.

Israeli politicians were lampooned by their political rivals in cartoons. The General Zionists during the 1955 election campaign depicted Herut's Menahem Begin as sporting a 'fascist' armband. The word on the armband read 'Herut' – Begin's party – while a childish Begin was seated on a rocking horse, labelled 'demagoguery'.[100] The electoral outcome a few days later showed an increase of seven seats for Herut and a decrease of seven seats for the General Zionists.

The desire for a better world for all its citizens reflected the work – and wishful thinking – of Pinhas Sadeh and Elisheva Nadel. They introduced Dr Joseph K. in *Ha'aretz* in 1960. The good doctor discovered that the radiation from the atomic plant at Dimona caused the local ants to turn into giants. Moreover, the bodies of these ants contained a chemical cure for cancer. Receiving Ben-Gurion's approval, Joseph K. approaches Kennedy and Khrushchev to end the Cold War in return for the cure for cancer. He similarly resolves the conflict with Egypt by approaching Nasser.

Israel's politics have changed profoundly since the early years of rebirth and wonder. It expanded its territory almost fourfold after the Six Day War of 1967 and thereby clasped the poisoned chalice of the West Bank and Gaza – and their populations of Palestinian Arabs. In 1977, Israel moved from the Left to the Right with Menahem Begin's victory, such that the Likud has remained the dominant party in power while Labour has now diminished to a single figure representation in the Knesset.

Since the Camp David Agreement between Egypt and Israel in 1979, the far Right has emerged and established a permanent presence in Israeli politics, forming part of numerous government coalitions. There has been a normalisation of relations with several countries in the Arab world – Egypt, Jordan, UAE, Morocco, Sudan – and no major wars with Arab states. The leaders of rejectionist states such as Gaddafi and Saddam Hussein have disappeared from the scene.

There has not been a peace treaty with Lebanon. Instead there was a war with Hezbollah in Lebanon in 2006. This conflict reflected an ongoing proxy conflict with Hezbollah's mentor, Iran, which subsequently established a military presence in Syria during the course of the country's civil war.

While the signing of the Oslo Accords in 1993 between Yitzhak Rabin and Yasser Arafat was greeted with great expectations, the hope for a conventional peace did not materialise – more a situation of 'no war'.

Palestinian nationalists in the West Bank were challenged by Palestinian Islamists in Gaza. Palestine has been split into two parts, the West Bank and Gaza. While the Jewish settlements on the West Bank have proliferated, the takeover of Gaza by Hamas in 2007 resulted in a state of siege by Israeli military forces. Ditching its belief in suicide bombers, Hamas has instead developed long-range and sophisticated missiles in the workshops of Gaza and through smuggling routes, often starting in Iran. These missiles have been fired during periodic clashes with the Israel Defence Forces, who have responded with air attacks on a crowded Gaza.

Israel also moved from a regulated command economy in the 1980s to a globalised free enterprise philosophy. This was accentuated by the advance of a dot.com technology which produced a plethora of young entrepreneurs. Israel's newly found prosperity also brought in its wake corruption and great disparities between the haves and the have-nots in the country. While Zionism was supposed to create a new society unlike the ones the pioneers had left behind, by the

25

---

[100] *Ma'ariv* 24 July 1955.

1990s, the Israeli economic model resembled that of Western Europe. Prime ministers and presidents, instead of being revered, found themselves convicted by courts and sent to prison.

This ongoing voyage of discovery as Jewish history advanced brought forth a richness of possibilities for many aspiring cartoonists – from Navon's 'Mr Israel' and Dosh's 'Srulik', to the detailed presentations of Ze'ev[101] and the strips of Ya'akov Kirschen's 'Dry Bones', to the animated illustrations of Amos Biderman in the twenty-first century.

The advent of social media in all its inanity often produced a tipping over of anti-Zionism into anti-Semitic tropes. Sometimes it was through ignorance, other times through ideological blindness, and still others through sheer racist malice. Moreover, the far Right in Israel believed that anti-Zionism and anti-Semitism were one and the same, while the far Left in Europe believed that anti-Zionism could never be anti-Semitic.

When the Iranian daily *Hamshahri* organised a cartoon competition in the name of 'free speech', to essentially cast doubts on the reality of the Shoah and its legacy, it provoked an Israeli Anti-Semitic Cartoons Contest which was designed to exceed the Iranian one in total absurdity.

The broad rise of anti-Semitism generally provoked reactions to this developing scenario from figures such as Fritz Behrendt in Holland and Will Eisner in the United States. Eisner wrote a graphic novel about the Tsarist forgery *The Protocols of the Elders of Zion*. Writers such as Arie Stav[102] and Joel Kotek[103] have published collections of anti-Jewish cartoons. Yet others believe that pushing the boundaries of humour is a radical act.[104] For many Jews, the Shoah remains a no-go area.

The brilliance of Israeli cartoonists was finally recognised by the establishment of the Israeli Cartoon Museum in Holon – a joint venture between the local municipality and the Israeli Cartoonists Association. Its voluminous archives, publications, exhibitions and educational work will serve the cartoonists of the future well.

In today's era of 'alternative facts', 'fake news', unhinged imaginations and vested interests, art – and especially the political cartoon – attempts to impede the blurring of fiction and reality, to puncture Orwellian 'doublethink'. As Gideon Ofrat says, 'Could it be that even in the era of post-truth, art has no choice but to tell the truth? Could it be that in an age when culture seems to be losing its hold on truth, art may be the last space unable to say "yes" to a lie?'[105]

Today's cartoonists carry a heavier burden in the age of social media than their predecessors, but they still speak truth to power. The tradition continues.

---

[101] 'Ze'ev: Eyewitness with a Smile' at the National Museum of Cartoon Art, London, April–May 1994.

[102] Arie Stav, *Peace, the Arabian Caricature: a Study in Anti-Semitic Imagery* (Tel Aviv 1999)

[103] Joël and Dan Kotek, *Au nom de l'antizionisme: l'image des Juifs et d'Israël dans la caricature depuis la seconde Intifada* (Brussels 2003).

[104] Louis Kaplan, '"It Will Get a Terrific Laugh": On the Problematic Pleasures and Politics of Holocaust Humor', in *Hop on Pop: the Politics and Pleasures of Popular Culture*, ed. Henry Jenkins, Tara McPherson and Jane Shattuc (Durham, NC 2002) pp. 343–56.

[105] Gideon Ofrat, *Art and Lie* (Haifa 2017).

Zionism: Ideology and the Building of the State

On Zionism

Zion: Lieder des ghetto. Drawn by Ephraim Moses Lilien (1903).

The New World

Dress me, dear mother, in splendour, a coat of many colours
And at the break of dawn lead me to work.
My land lies wrapt in light as in a prayer shawl,
The houses stand forth like frontlets
The asphalt roads we laid with our own hands
Branch out like the thongs of phylacteries.
Thus does a graceful city
Offer up morning prayers to the Creator
And among the creators, your son Abraham,
Poet–roadbuilder in Israel.[1]

Avraham Shlonsky. Drawn by
Noah Bee (1939).

---

[1] *Amal* by Avraham Shlonsky. English translation by Robert Mezey in Howard Schwartz and Anthony Rudolf, eds., *Voices within the Ark: Modern Jewish Poets* (New York 1980) p. 176.

Avraham Shlonsky wrote this poem, *Amal* (Toil), in the 1920s, the halcyon days of Zionist pioneering. Emigrating to a Palestine under the British Mandate, he came at the tail-end of the third *aliya* (the third wave of modern Jewish immigration to Palestine, 1919–23), bringing with him the liberating vision of the October Revolution. For Shlonsky, the meaning of Zionism was not only building a new land, but also creating a new society – unlike the one he had left behind.

Like his contemporary Uri Zvi Greenberg, he had wandered through the ravaged landscape of Eastern Europe, devastated by civil war, by Red against White, by reactionary nationalism – and by mass killings of its Jewish communities. Up to an estimated 150,000 Jews went to their deaths in the massacres in Ukraine between 1918 and 1920.[2]

Like Greenberg, he began to write for the weekly *Hapoel Hatzair* and moved to Tel Aviv. However, Zionists in the new Soviet Union began to inhabit prison cells owing to the oppressive campaign of Jewish Communists – many of whom were former Zionists and who were now determined to build a new Jerusalem in Moscow. Those who managed to emigrate to the Yishuv, the Jewish settlement in Palestine, in the mid-1920s were astounded to discover that the reality of Soviet Communism in 1925 had not dissipated the romantic idealism of 1917.

David Ben-Gurion, a central figure in the Yishuv, actually gave eulogy for Lenin when the Soviet leader died at the beginning of 1924. While he opposed Communism and saw it as a rival attraction to Marxism–Zionism, he appreciated Lenin's ability to make the revolution with very few resources. He wrote that Lenin's 'penetrating gaze perceives reality as through a clear prism, impeded by no formula, proverb, phrase or dogma. For this man has been blessed with the ingenious ability to look life in the eye, to articulate matters neither in concepts nor in words, but rather in the basic terms of reality.'[3]

While Shlonsky kept the faith and remained a left-wing socialist, Greenberg moved to the Right, joined Vladimir Jabotinsky's Revisionists in 1928 and embraced a militant nationalism.

Like Greenberg, Shlonsky had come from a traditional Jewish family who were Habad Hasidim. Yet both did not embrace the anti-Zionism of the Lubavitcher Rebbe who was Habad's spiritual mentor. While Shlonsky's father was interested in Ahad Ha'am's cultural Zionism, his mother was a fervent supporter of the revolutionary movement in Tsarist Russia. Shlonsky wrote and spoke Hebrew at an early age and studied in the Herzliya High School in the Yishuv before World War I.

Shlonsky's poem *Amal* reflects not only the pioneering passion of the early Zionists, but also the transition between 'exile and return', between dispersion and the 'altneuland' that was being constructed. It compares the Zionist builder who greets the new day with determination and the belief of the traditional Jew who recites shaharit (morning prayer), wearing tefilin (phylacteries) on head and arm and a talit (prayer shawl) over the shoulders. The biblical allusions to Joseph's coat of many colours[4] and to God's envelopment in light[5] stand out.

The poet Leah Goldberg interpreted Shlonsky's *Amal*:

> Kirya (city) in old Hebrew usually designates Jerusalem but in modern usage, a new town or settlement.
>
> The town prays to the creator, but it is not God, creator of the old world, but man, the creator of the new.
>
> This Abraham is a new Abraham: poet, roadbuilder.[6]

31

[2] Howard M. Sachar, *Dreamland: Europeans and Jews in the Aftermath of the Great War* (New York 2002) p. 18.

[3] David Ben-Gurion, *Yoman*, vol. I (Tel Aviv 1971) p. 201; English translation in Israel Kolatt, 'Image and Reality', in *David Ben-Gurion: Politics and Leadership in Israel*, ed. Ronald W. Zweig (London 1991) p. 18.

[4] Genesis 37:3.

[5] Psalm 104:2.

[6] Lea Goldberg, in *The Modern Hebrew Poem Itself*, ed. Stanley Burnshaw, T. Carmi and Ezra Spicehandler (Cambridge, MA 1989) p. 76.

Leah Goldberg in 1954. Drawn by Arie Navon (1982).

The Old World

Zionism arose as an offshoot of European nationalism in the aftermath of the French Revolution. Its backdrop was the rich literature of the Bible and the travails of Jewish history.

The Napoleonic period brought the Jews in from the periphery. The ghetto walls were broken down by the revolutionary armies and Jews were given an opportunity to become citizens and comrades. While anti-Judaism lingered, it was gradually transformed into modern anti-Semitism by the advent of the nation-state. All these forces persuaded many young Jewish thinkers to conclude that the Jews were not simply the adherents of a religion, but a nation in exile – a dispersed nation with a history, literature, culture, language and a religion. Hebrew became more than the language of the Bible.

In the aftermath of Waterloo, Jewish intellectuals were forced to return to the ways of the *ancien régime*, but the French Revolution and the Napoleonic period had opened up new vistas for looking at the present and into the future. This reversion particularly affected Jews who lived in Central Europe.

Nachman Krochmal was one of this first generation of emancipated Jews. The Jews were defined by their monotheism, selected by God for specific tasks. The history of the Jews was not Judaic history, the history of the rabbis, but Jewish history, the history of the people. Moreover, the civilisation of the Jews including religion was dynamic and not static.

> Man is a social animal and man's achievements express themselves in collective entities, possessing a common denominator. Society, the nation (*uma*) are the subjects of history. History is the story of these cultural entities and this heritage common to groups of human beings is what creates culture. Following Herder and Hegel, Krochmal calls these cultural entities, *ruah ha-uma* – the spirit of the nation.[7]

Yet the return of the Bourbons and the entrenchment of the old monarchies of Europe also meant the return of discriminatory legislation directed at Jews after 1815. The Jews had seen what was possible – what other life could be lived – during the revolutionary period. This longing was supplemented in the nineteenth century by the Jewish Enlightenment, the Haskalah, and the proliferation of a spectrum of Jewish identities, positioned across a scale stretching from the rebuilding of the ghetto walls by the ultra-orthodox to the embrace of Christianity through conversion. The nineteenth century promoted the search for national liberation amidst a demand for social justice. Jews often found themselves in the forefront of these movements for change.

However, nationalism had moved from the Left to the Right during the course of the nineteenth century. Moreover, the Jewish question had become an issue, often aided and abetted by the Catholic church which spurned any notion of liberalism.

In France, the political turmoil of the nineteenth century – the Bourbons and the Orléanists, Bonapartism and Republicanism, the defeat of the Communards – led to reaction and to anti-Semitism. In the aftermath of the defeat by the Prussians in 1870, overtly nationalist movements such as Boulangerisme attracted popular support. These gathered anti-Semitism in their onward march – of which the Dreyfus Affair was the cause célèbre of this period. Political philosophers such as Gustav le Bon and Georges Sorel paved the way for nationalist ideology in Europe in the twentieth century – and Jewish reaction to it.

In Eastern Europe, the oppression and discrimination enacted against Jews was keenest in the Pale of Settlement at the periphery of the Tsarist empire. Many solutions to the Jewish problem consequently emerged.

This was symbolised in the emergence of three possible responses in the year 1897/8. There was the establishment of the Russian Social Democratic Labour Party (RSDLP), a forerunner of the Bolsheviks which advocated a disappearance into the host Russian people. In contrast, the Bund proclaimed national-cultural autonomy in areas where Jews were concentrated and the building of a socialist society. Finally there was the Zionist answer which put forth the idea of a Jewish homeland where Jews would control their own territory and their own destiny.

A territorial solution to the Jewish problem, however, suggested many possible locations for settlement, but clearly the one territory which commanded both Jewish and Christian attention was the biblical homeland of the ancient Israelites – now a backwater province of the Ottoman Empire, housing an impoverished, religious Jewish minority.

33

---

[7] Shlomo Avineri, *The Making of Modern Zionism: the Intellectual Origins of the Jewish State* (London 1981) p. 15.

The Zionist Answer

During the nineteenth century, the Zionist solution gained traction in its various forms. Thus Moses Hess, friend of Marx and a Left Hegelian, outlined the principles of socialist Zionism. Yehuda Alkalai and Zvi Hirsch Kalischer, believers in the Haskalah, developed religious Zionism. All had come of intellectual age in the aftermath of the French Revolution. Alkalai and Kalischer lived in multi-ethnic areas and discerned the parallel evolution of local nationalisms. The Risorgimento of the Italians influenced both Hess's *Rome and Jerusalem* and Alkalai's *Drishat Zion*.

Zionism found its central calling amongst the impoverished traditional Jews of the Pale of Settlement. The pogroms which followed the assassination of Tsar Alexander II catalysed the first emigration of young Jews to Palestine in 1882.

Theodore Herzl. Drawn by Hermann Struck (1915).

Theodor Herzl, founding father of modern Zionism, was indifferent to these developments in the 1880s and even disparaged and ridiculed his fellow Viennese Jews. He viewed himself as being far from Jewishness, an assimilationist – until he was awakened by growing anti-Semitism in the 1890s. In particular, he was concerned by the political campaigns of the nationalist Karl Lueger and his dalliance with anti-Semitism which eventually earned him election as mayor of Vienna in 1895.

This event was a central factor in Herzl's growing awareness of his Jewishness and his search for a solution to the Jewish problem. The situation persuaded him to write *Der Judenstaat* (The State of the Jews) and to eventually establish the World Zionist Organisation (WZO) with Max Nordau.

After failing to persuade many influential Jewish leaders who presided over European Jewry, Herzl and Nordau instigated the staging of the first Zionist Congress which took place in Basel in 1897.

Herzl propagated a Viennese bourgeois Zionism – and many opposed him. To them, from the assimilated to the ultra-orthodox, from the well-to-do philanthropist to the poor socialist worker, Zionism seemed to be utopian and unachievable – the stuff of dreams. Other solutions to the Jewish problem seemed more realistic.

Even so, Herzl's magnetism and zeal for his cause attracted many to his standard. In addition his non-political General Zionism had hardly lasted a year when factions began to appear within the movement. This development pitted public ownership against private enterprise, the devoutly secular against the traditionally religious, democrats against autocrats. At the root of much of this was the nature of this break with the previous two millennia of Diaspora history: to what extent should there be a continuity of the Jewish culture of the past?

In one sense, Herzl reflected the sense of hopelessness that many Jews felt in *fin de siècle* Russia and Poland. Whichever path they followed, it would be frowned upon.

In an article entitled 'The Future of our People' in 1883, Moses Leib Lilienblum delineated the fatalism of the Jewish predicament. Lilienblum wrote his essay in the context of a spate of pogroms between 1881 and 1884, following the assassination of Tsar Alexander II in March 1881. Pogroms took place mainly in Ukraine; the worst occurred in the provinces of Kiev, Kherson and Ekaterinoslav. The official approach was that Jews only had themselves to blame for the outbreaks of violence.

> Officialdom accuses us of circumventing the laws of the land – that is, of course, the laws directed specifically against us ... Musicians like Richard Wagner charge us with destroying the beauty and purity of music. Even our merits are turned into shortcomings: 'Few Jews are murderers,' they say, 'because Jews are cowards.' This, however, does not prevent them from accusing us of murdering Christian children.[8]

Ahad Ha'am and Other Opponents

The Zionist Congresses were also the location of East meeting West, deeply acculturated Jews such as Herzl meeting highly knowledgeable ones such as Ahad Ha'am. The latter was highly disparaging about the former – 'a king of the Jews' who knew little about the ongoing struggle for Zionism and the day-to-day hardships of the Jews of Russia and Poland.

Ahad Ha'am opposed Herzl's version of Zionism because of its pragmatic populism and its bypassing of the intellectual traditions of the past. Unlike Herzl, who came of age with the rise of Imperial Germany, Ahad Ha'am was a liberated son of the shtetl who favoured Moses and Maimonides as well as John Stuart Mill and Herbert Spencer. In addition to the problem of the Jews, Ahad Ha'am was interested in the problem and future of Judaism. For him, it was a specifically Jewish state that mattered and not simply a state of the Jews – like any other state. Herzl flirted with Argentina and Uganda as the location for the future state. For Ahad Ha'am, it was always Palestine. Moreover, Hebrew, 'the handmaiden of the Haskalah', rather than Yiddish or German, provided a self-evident focus of Palestine as a spiritual centre.

[8] Quoted in Arthur Hertzberg, ed., *The Zionist Idea* (New York 1969) pp. 173–4.

Ahad Ha'am differentiated between the Jews of Western Europe and the *ostjuden* of the East. For the former, it was the challenge of assimilation and acculturation on an individual basis. For the *ostjuden*, it was the gradual disappearance of Judaism which thereby threatened the collective with non-existence. For Ahad Ha'am, a return to historic Palestine meant a reconstruction of a new society and a resurrection of a Jewish culture.

Ahad Ha'am's opposition to Herzl's outlook had been crystallised years before in a rebuke to acculturated French Jews in his essay *Slavery in Freedom*. The essay formulated his views on the Jews of Western Europe. He argued that it was not simply Judaism that had accounted for the inexplicable survival of the Jews and moreover, he criticised those in Western Europe who put this forward as an explanation. In doing so, 'they tie themselves up in a hopeless tangle of paradoxes and sophistries, thereby proving that they are simply driven to take this line because they are afraid that they may lose their civil rights if they admit that the Jews are a separate nation'.[9]

Ahad Ha'am did not have problems with identity and argued that he knew full well why he should remain a Jew. He boldly cherished his freedom to say so.

> I can say exactly what I think about traditional ideas and beliefs without being afraid that I may thereby cut myself adrift from my people. I can even adopt 'the scientific heresy that bears the name of Darwin' without any danger to my Judaism. In a word, I belong to myself and my opinions and feelings are my own. And this freedom of the spirit – scoff who will – I would not exchange or barter for all the civil rights in the world.[10]

Ahad Ha'am was revered by Hebrew poets such as Haim Nahman Bialik and by Zionist diplomats such as Chaim Weizmann. When Herzl died at the age of forty-four in 1904, many Jews sat 'shiva' for him for the traditional seven days of mourning in recognition of his contribution. Weizmann emerged eventually as his successor and attempted to forge a synthesis between the views of Herzl and Ahad Ha'am.

The Socialist Zionists

While Weizmann led one faction, the Democratic Fraktion, Nahman Syrkin was the first to develop a socialist direction within the Zionist movement. He was the author of *The Jewish Problem and the Socialist Jewish State* in which he argued that emancipation in the nineteenth century had not emerged from a genuine understanding of the social and economic foundations of Jewish society. Syrkin believed that the interrelationship of Jews and non-Jews within transactional capitalism was a source of ongoing tension. In the age of the nation-state and rising nationalism, this was also a source of a new anti-Semitism – different from the anti-Judaism of the past. The entry of Jews – no matter how assimilated or acculturated – into the middle class was often resented. Jews were outsiders, vulgar and motivated by a lust for money – so the anti-Semitic refrain went.

Syrkin was also aware of anti-Semitism on the Left which often equated capitalism with Judaism and Jewishness. Some sections of the French Left were ambivalent about defending Dreyfus. Syrkin was particularly critical of acculturated, bourgeois Jews who had disowned their Jewishness to rise in

---

[9] Ahad Ha'am, letter to Rabbi Eude Lolli of the University of Padua, 11 April 1898, in Leon Simon, *Ahad Ha'am: Essays, Letters, Memoirs* (Oxford 1946) p. 261.

[10] Ahad Ha'am, 'Slavery in Freedom', *HaMelitz* 10–12 February 1891. Translated from the Hebrew by Leon Simon, 1912.

socialist movements. He argued that Jewish workers were doubly oppressed – as a nation and as a class. Zionism therefore was a national liberation movement for all, regardless of their class.

He also dwelled on the non-conformity of the Jews throughout history – a stiff-necked people. Jewishness was the moral protest of the Jews. In May 1901, he appealed to Jewish youth to build a Jewish socialist society in Palestine by following the path of cooperative colonisation.

> The closer Zionism approaches fulfilment, the nearer the problems of colonisation press, the more obvious the necessity for socialist Zionism becomes. The reactionary bourgeois Zionists seek colonisation on a capitalist basis. In doing so, they doom Zionism to death. At the very outset of the movement, they introduce those class interests and social conditions which will destroy Zionism.[11]

In *fin de siècle* Europe, Marxism was beginning to fragment and open to new interpretations. In 1905 Ber Borokhov wrote *The National Question and the Class Struggle*. Socialist Zionism had coalesced as Poale Zion groups in several Diaspora countries, but it was formally founded as a party in Palestine in October 1906. Borokhov's writings influenced the party from the outset and *The Communist Manifesto* was translated into Hebrew. A Jewish proletariat in Palestine was seen as participating in the international struggle of the working class to establish global socialism.

Borokhov attempted a synthesis of Marxism and Zionism – and based it on the abnormality of the situation of the Jews in that its class structure resembled an inverted pyramid. In 'Our Platform', he argued that the Jewish problem could not be resolved solely through migration. Borokhov commented that 'the Jewish nation in exile has no material possessions of its own and it is helpless in the national competitive struggle'.

> The capitalist economy has reached the stage where no revolutionary changes are possible without the participation of the working masses and especially of the organised sections of the proletariat. The emancipation of the Jewish people will be brought about by Jewish labour – or it will not be attained at all. The labour movement has only one weapon at its command – the class struggle … Proletarian Zionism is possible only if its aims can be achieved through the class struggle; Zionism can be realised only if proletarian Zionism can be realised.[12]

Both Syrkin and Borokhov understood that it was important to build a workers' command economy in Palestine. In parallel, A. D. Gordon of the non-Marxist Hapoel Hatzair developed 'the religion of labour' – the personal redemptive value of manual labour. This too brought Jews of all classes back to the soil and gave rise to the first kibbutz. Gordon wanted to build a new Jewish society in Palestine – and not one which was simply another offshoot of the Diaspora.

The October Revolution

Several thousand Jews came to Palestine during the second *aliya* – the decade before the outbreak of World War I, after the Kishinev pogrom and the death of Herzl. Figures such as David Ben-Gurion, Yitzhak Tabenkin, Berl Katznelson, Yitzhak Ben-Zvi, Manya Yanait and Israel Shohat were revolutionary socialists who had decided to make the revolution in Palestine and not in Tsarist Russia or Poland. They were the builders of the state of Israel during the next sixty years.

---

[11] Nachman Syrkin, *An Appeal to Jewish Youth*, May 1901, in *Jewish Frontier* December 1935.
[12] Ber Borochov, 'Our Platform', in Ber Borochov, *Class Struggle and the Jewish Nation*, ed. Mitchell Cohen (London 2020) p. 75.

The October Revolution and the triumph of Lenin's Bolsheviks was a tremendous challenge to the labour Zionists. There was great enthusiasm for what had been achieved in Russia, coupled with disdain for the ruthlessness in achieving it. Ben-Gurion and Tabenkin, advocates of Borokhov's Marxism–Zionism, were enthralled, while Katznelson was extremely wary. In an anonymous article, Katznelson quoted Dostoyevsky's Ivan Karamazov, saying that 'if the world's happiness is to be achieved at the expense of an infant's tear, then I wash my hands of happiness and of the world and I return my bond to my creator'. Katznelson asked why was Russia waging war 'steeped in blood'?[13]

Berl Katznelson. Drawn by Noah Bee (1939).

[13] Berl Katznelson, 'From Afar', *Kuntres* 1 July 1919 in Anita Shapira, *Berl: The Biography of a Socialist Zionist* (Cambridge 2009) p. 106.

The October Revolution appealed to the universalism within Jewish teachings. The Balfour Declaration, which occurred virtually simultaneously, appealed to the particularism within Jewish tradition. It stated:

> His Majesty's Government view with favour the establishment in Palestine of a national home for the Jewish people and will use their best endeavours to facilitate the achievement of this object, it being clearly understood that nothing shall be done which may prejudice the civil and religious rights of existing non-Jewish communities in Palestine, or the rights and political status enjoyed by Jews in any other country.

Katznelson closely observed the Russian civil war, the mass killing of Jews in Ukraine and the Marxist–Leninist society which was evolving. The very idea of an international workers' order appealed to many. Indeed some hoped that Trotsky and the Red Army would advance to Palestine. Instead the revolution was halted at the gates of Warsaw and by several failed revolts in Germany. While many Jews were attracted to different elements in both Communism and Zionism, Lenin insisted on adherence solely to the Communist party – there could be no federated parties lingering on the periphery. In August 1920 the Comintern put forward its twenty-one conditions for joining at its second congress.

39

Chaim Weizmann and David Ben-Gurion in 1944. Drawn by Arie Navon (1982).

This growing polarisation confronted the members of Poale Zion when they met in Vienna at their first world conference after World War I. It brought together those who had stayed in Russia during the war and experienced the revolution and those who remained outside. Indeed the central issue on the table was Moscow or Jerusalem, reflected in a resolution to join the Comintern. The movement effectively split. However, twenty years before, Lenin had argued that 'the idea of a separate Jewish people which is utterly untenable scientifically is reactionary in its political implications'. He disparaged the very idea of Jewish nationality, which is 'in conflict with the interests of the Jewish proletariat'. Lenin, who was unaware of figures such as Syrkin and Borokhov, framed the Jewish question simplistically as 'assimilation or separateness'.[14] Many Zionists, however, became ardent Communists in the early 1920s and their zeal for a new Soviet civilisation was often manifested in their attacks on their former colleagues in Russia who had not renounced Zionism.

Zionists under the British Mandate

Poale Zion morphed into Ahdut Ha'Avoda and then combined with the remnant of Hapoel Hatzair to form Mapai in 1930. Those who still believed in the October Revolution existed as the fringe Left Poale Zion or eventually coalesced as the Palestine Communist Party. David Ben-Gurion, first as secretary of the Histadrut (the Labour Workers' Federation) and then as head of the Jewish Agency, became a central political force in leading the Yishuv (the Jewish settlement in Palestine) to statehood. In this, he worked closely with the liberal General Zionist Chaim Weizmann.

Religious Jews essentially took their lead in politics from the labour Zionists. After all, many socialists who had moved away from a religious lifestyle and belief had been educated in a religious environment. They therefore shared a common knowledge with those who remained religious.

In Eastern Europe, the advent of Zionism had caused deep rifts in the fabric of Judaism. Families were often divided. The adherents of the Lubavitcher Rebbe and the Satmar Rebbe were passionate anti-Zionists, believing that the Torah had been replaced by nationalism.

Many followed the teachings of the nineteenth-century sage the Hatam Sofer and felt that there should be no human intervention in forcing God's hand to return the Jews to their ancient homeland. Others who remained observant followed the proto-Zionist ideas of Alkalai and Kalischer – and drew attention to Nahmanides's journey to medieval Palestine. Both backed up their views with commentary from the Jewish liturgy.

Although religious Jews were comparative latecomers to enter the Zionist tent, they extrapolated their ideological views back to ancient times – before the French Revolution and the development of European nationalism.

While messianism was ever-present, it was never high up on the agenda of the first religious Zionists who lived in Eretz Israel – the Land of Israel. They worked with the Marxists to ensure that they could live a religious Jewish lifestyle – the building of synagogues, no work on Shabbat (the Jewish sabbath), the provision of kosher food, the celebration of Rosh Hashana and the observance of Yom Kippur.

[14] Vladimir Ilyich Lenin, *Iskra* 22 October 1903.

This mode of co-existence with atheistic kibbutzniks was fortified by the example of the Ashkenazi Chief Rabbi, Avraham Yitzhak Kook, who regarded them as instruments of the Holy Will to gather in the exiles and return the Jews to the Land of Israel. Each kibbutznik was thus a carrier of the holy sparks which would reclaim the Land and rebuild Jerusalem – even if they denied it. The ideological dedication of the founders was paralleled by the evolution of a Hebrew culture in Palestine, carried by Eliezer Ben-Yehuda, Rachel Blaustein, Shai Agnon, Uri Zvi Greenberg and Yosef Haim Brenner. Many of these new Hebrew poets looked back to both the persecution of the past and their amazement at being in the Land of Israel in the present. Shaul Tchernichovsky wrote:

> Kingdoms blossom and kingdoms sink into death and the borders of states grow blurred and then sharp –
> here on their beds they stand like headstones
> on the back of a strange great past, forgotten forever,
> faded away even out of poems and legends.[15]

Labour Zionists. From right to left: Yitzhak Ben-Zvi, Moshe Sharett and Ya'akov Zerubavel. Drawn by Arie Navon (1938).

41

---

[15] Saul Tchernikovsky, 'Man is Nothing But', translated by Robert Mezey and Shula Starkman, in *Voices within the Ark: Modern Jewish Poets*, ed. Howard Schwartz and Anthony Rudolf (New York 1980) p. 193.

Shaul Tchernichovsky. Drawn by Noah Bee (1939).

The Zionist Right

In Palestine, Uri Zvi Greenberg gradually became disillusioned with labour Zionism. He and his family had been the victims of a mock execution in Lemberg. Such memories had been instrumental in his embrace of the far Right.

He spoke of 'My God the Blacksmith' in a poem.

> Each wound which time has cut in me opens like a crack for Him
> And emits in sparks of moments the pent-up fire.[16]

---

[16] Uri Zvi Greenberg, 'With My God the Blacksmith', in *The Modern Hebrew Poem Itself*, ed. Stanley Burnshaw, T. Carmi and Ezra Spicehandler (Cambridge, MA 1989) p. 76.

Greenberg, together with Abba Ahimeir and Yehoshua Hirsch Yevin, moved from the Left and joined Vladimir Jabotinsky's new Revisionist Zionist movement in 1928. One central factor had been their reaction to labour Zionist attitudes towards the new Soviet Union.

The third *aliya* in 1919 had included many who had borne witness to the enthusiasm in the first flush of the Bolshevik Revolution. Those who came at the end of the third *aliya* perceived the Soviet reality differently and several had seen the inside of Soviet prisons simply because they were Zionists. Amongst the leaders of the Yishuv, such as members of Ahdut Ha'Avoda, however, there still existed an idyllic solidarity with Lenin's upheaval. Many former Soviet Zionists therefore constituted the nucleus of the Revisionists.

Jabotinsky himself was a Russian man of letters, a writer of feuilletons and plays – a man who could write and speak a dozen languages, but who felt most at home in Russian. As a young man in Italy, his articles in the Odessa press indicated an individual who was opposed to Italy's imperialist adventures. Back in Russia, he wrote for the socialist paper in Italy, *Avanti* and kept company with progressives and intellectuals.

Jabotinsky was well acquainted with the views of Lenin and the *Iskra* collective as well as the Bund. He also took issue with Russian liberals who proposed assimilation and acculturation as a solution to the Jewish problem. His conversion to Zionism brought with it a criticism of the utopianism of the Left. In 1908 he wrote:

43

Vladimir Jabotinsky.

> Long ago I had a strong sense of the beauty in the sovereignty of a free person, who has no label on his forehead, who owes nothing to anybody on earth, whose attitude to members of his own people is the same as to members of another people, the sovereignty of a man who moves according to his own will and not of others. I still see its beauty. But for myself I have given it up.[17]

Jabotinsky's disillusionment became more pronounced after Bolshevik rule in Russia became permanent. He felt strongly about censorship in the press and theatre, the closing of cultural institutions, the stifling of different views and the growing suffocation of intellectual endeavour. He moved from a non-socialist position to an anti-socialist one. By 1925, he had founded the Revisionist Zionist movement in the Latin Quarter in Paris – and promised a return to Herzlian Zionism to challenge labour Zionism. By April 1927, he was writing articles entitled 'We, the Bourgeoisie'.[18]

Militant and Military Zionism

Yet Jabotinsky's initial nuanced approach was being pulled in two directions, by the labour Zionists, on one side, and the maximalists within the Revisionist movement, on the other. The latter was led by Abba Ahimeir who increasingly confronted Jabotinsky's belief in England and its parliamentarianism. He had penned a series of articles entitled, 'From the Notebook of a Fascist' and referred to Jabotinsky as 'Our Duce'[19] – much to Jabotinsky's disgust. This was long before Mussolini's anti-Jewish legislation in 1938. Even so, Ahimeir welcomed the growth of authoritarian regimes across Europe. He wrote: 'The national dictatorship is striking roots without claiming any victims. It is absurd to speak of Italian fascism as a murderous regime.'[20]

The maximalists within the Revisionist movement began to cultivate the youthful followers of Jabotinsky, inspired by his rhetoric and writings. Jabotinsky had established a youth group, Betar, in Riga, at the end of 1923 and it grew more militant as time progressed. In Palestine, this was fuelled by the lack of progress towards a state of the Jews and was reflected in the Shaw Commission and the Passfield White Paper in 1930. It was perceived as a failure of Zionist diplomacy in negotiations with the British.

In addition, the Tarpat disturbances of 1929 had led to the killing of Jews by their Arab neighbours. This subsequently resulted in a split in the Hagana, the Yishuv's self-defence force, and the emergence of a more militant group, 'Hagana Bet' – or the Irgun Zvai Leumi.

---

[17] Vladimir Jabotinsky, 'Your New Year', *Odesskie Novosti*, 3 January 1908, in Shmuel Katz, *Lone Wolf: a Biography of Vladimir Ze'ev Jabotinsky*, vol. I (New York 1996) p. 75.
[18] Vladimir Jabotinsky, 'We, the Bourgeoisie', *Rassviet* 17 April 1927.
[19] Abba Ahimeir, 'On the Arrival of our Duce', *Doar Hayom* 10 October 1928.
[20] Abba Ahimeir, 'Rome and Jerusalem', *Ha'am* 8 May 1931.

גוליבר בין הגמדים...

Vladimir Jabotinsky is holding his plan to evacuate Polish Jews to Palestine and, being attacked by his many Polish Jewish ideological opponents, is depicted as Gulliver surrounded by unworthy Lilliputians. At the top left, the Jewish Communists are firing at him from a boat called *Emes* ('Truth' in English; 'Pravda' in Russian) and flying the hammer and sickle. At the bottom left, the Bundist leader, Henryk Ehrlich, is shooting. At the bottom right, Yitzhak Gruenbaum, the radical Zionist leader, is using a bow and arrow. Above him is Sholem Asch, the novelist, who wrote an article in the Warsaw daily *Haynt*, opposing Jabotinsky's evacuation plan. The name of the newspaper is written on the cannon. Noach Pryłucki, the Folkspartei politician and editor of *Der Moment*, is bent over the top of the evacuation plan. Drawn by Yehoshua Adari (*Kav L'Kav* 1 January 1937).

In Poland and Eastern Europe, where most of Jabotinsky's supporters were living, the authoritarian culture of the host regimes was influential. The growth of anti-Semitism and the increasing power of the National Socialists in Weimar Germany fortified the idea of Zionist militancy.

In Palestine, Avraham Stern and David Raziel adhered to this militant camp. In Poland, the youthful Menahem Begin and Yitzhak Shamir joined Betar. Jabotinsky fell out with his long-time colleagues in the Revisionist movement at the Katowice Conference in 1933 and found himself, then in his fifties, allied with young militants. Whereas he inspired young Jews to stand up for themselves, but to refrain from embarking on military adventurism, his acolytes did not appreciate Jabotinsky's subtlety. 'Learn to Shoot'[21] became an edict in Jabotinsky's rhetorical canon, but his disciples took it a stage further and actually acted upon it. Jabotinsky therefore never embraced the model of Irish Republicanism as the way forward for Zionist activism. Yitzhak Shamir, however, adopted 'Michael Collins' as his *nom de guerre.*

The third World Conference of Betar took place in Warsaw in September 1938. It was the location of a profound difference of views between the young Begin and the elder statesman, Vladimir Jabotinsky. Begin espoused maximalism and military Zionism, while Jabotinsky ultimately believed in England despite a militant Zionist colouring. Jabotinsky told the audience that Begin's speech and the applause that it had received were like 'the squeaking of a door with no sense and no benefit'. Jabotinsky walked out, but Begin's rhetoric and proposals had won the day. The youth of Betar graduated to become the fighters of the Irgun.[22]

In the years before his death, Jabotinsky's mixed messages to different Zionist audiences left him isolated and fighting ideological battles on several fronts. His remaining years were thus ones of managing his supporters as the storm clouds gathered in the Europe of the 1930s.

On the declaration of war in September 1939, Jabotinsky immediately proclaimed his support for Great Britain. Avraham Stern was not so sure and concluded that since Nazi Germany was 'the enemy of my enemy', it made sense to contact the German Legation in Beirut. David Raziel disagreed and split from his long-time colleague and friend in order to work for the British. Begin, who had escaped from Poland to neighbouring Lithuania in the wake of the Nazi invasion, argued that 'the enemy of my enemy' was not automatically my friend. Begin was subsequently arrested by Soviet forces after the invasion of Lithuania, sentenced to eight years and imprisoned in the Gulag. A year later, he left the USSR with General Anders's forces and subsequently decamped in Palestine where he resumed his political activities.

In late 1943, Begin became commander of the Irgun Zvai Leumi and launched 'The Revolt' against the British in early 1944 when the war was still ongoing. Up until the declaration of the state of Israel in May 1948, Begin continued to implement his doctrine of military Zionism through the vehicle of the Irgun in a conflict with the British forces in Palestine.

---

[21] Vladimir Jabotinsky, 'Afn Pripitshek', *Haynt* 16 October 1931.
[22] Colin Shindler, *The Rise of the Israeli Right: From Odessa to Hebron* (Cambridge 2015) pp. 165–71.

Before Israel:
the Road to 1948

The Road to 1948

The Aftermath

Consider that this has been:
I commend these words to you.
Engrave them on your hearts
When you are in your house, when you walk on your way
When you go to bed, when you rise:
Repeat them to your children.
Or may your house crumble,
Disease render you powerless,
Your offspring avert their faces from you.[1]

So wrote Primo Levi after he had returned from his imprisonment by the Nazis. The poem was addressed to those 'who live secure in your warm houses'. While the Jews of the United States and the United Kingdom had suffered hardship and austerity, they remained at liberty. Thousands fought in the Allied armies to defeat Nazism. In the weeks before VE Day, the British and the Canadians had liberated Bergen-Belsen and the Americans had taken control of Dachau. While there were no gas chambers to carry out mass extermination in these camps, the landscape of bestiality was shown to London cinema audiences. The images of stacked dead bodies and living emaciated ones shocked all. While British soldiers wearing handkerchiefs on their faces shovelled the bodies into pits, the stench of death permeated those who bore witness – even on the silver screen. The Allies may have won the war, but the Jews certainly lost it.

It also brought into sharp relief the refusal to grant the Jews a homeland before the war. The Peel Commission in 1937 had proposed a two-state solution. The Palestinian Arabs opposed it as did many in the Zionist camp – especially the religious and the Revisionists. The possibility of a Jewish homeland before the Shoah became one of the great 'what ifs' of twentieth-century history.

This led to increased support for the Zionist movement which had been working towards the establishment of a Hebrew republic in Palestine for more than half a century. Jews increased their donations to the cause while many former soldiers came to the conclusion that they should place the skills learned in wartime at the disposal of the Zionists. Many Jews therefore became involved in the struggle for Israel between 1945 and 1948 in whichever sphere their expertise lay – in financial acumen, in political influence, in military affairs.

The Revisionist Zionist leader, Vladimir Jabotinsky, had once spoken of the Jews operating like a machine to secure a state. Anti-Semites had often drawn attention to a mythical web of Jewish conspirators. At this point in their history, Jews did not care what others thought. A natural

---

[1] From Primo Levi, 'Shema', translated by Ruth Feldman and Brian Swann, in *The Collected Poems of Primo Levi* (London 1976).

caution and reticence was thrown to the winds. The mass extermination of the Jews had cast away all reservations and doubts, and perhaps truly for the first time, the Diaspora did act as a whole towards a defined goal – a state of the Jews in Palestine.

The revelations affected Jews everywhere. In the Soviet Union, Jewish Red Army soldiers began to petition Stalin to be allowed to fight for Israel. He had them arrested and sent to spend long years in the Gulag. Yet in the spring of 1947, he switched the USSR's allegiance from the Arabs to the Jews. The Kremlin hoped to replace Britain as the central power in the Middle East and to make use of the country's deep-sea harbours. Stalin enacted a policy of internal repression of Jews in the USSR while externally supporting the Zionists in the international corridors of power. During Israel's war of independence, Stalin authorised the Czechs to supply ammunition and war materiel in general to the Israelis. American Jewish pilots were trained to fly German Messerschmitts to fight the British Spitfires of the Egyptians. The new state of Israel significantly did not opt to join the British Commonwealth of nations.

50

...נואם ווייצמן

After 1945, many felt that the time for meaningful negotiations with the British had passed. The liberal anglophile Chaim Weizmann is seen here as merely the mouthpiece of the British. Drawn by Yehoshua Adari (1 August 1937) (Adari 1945).

לקראת אפנת הסתיו...

The British prime minister, Neville Chamberlain, is trimming 'the Balfour Declaration' on Chaim Weizmann as part of 'the autumn fashions'. This pre-war image indicates Britain's rowback from the terms of the Balfour Declaration of 1917 and the promise of a Jewish home in Palestine as the storm clouds gathered in Europe in the late 1930s. Britain began to realise that oil supplies from the Arab world were crucial to fighting the Nazis. Drawn by Arie Navon (1938).

51

Entry into Palestine

In 1939, on the eve of war, a British White Paper proposed placing an annual ceiling of fifteen thousand on the number of Jews allowed into Palestine. This ruling was kept in place even as Jews attempted to escape from the Nazis at the beginning of World War II. The *Patria* was a refugee ship carrying Jews escaping from Nazi-occupied Europe at the beginning of the war. In November 1940 the Hagana attempted to disable the ship and thereby prevent its passengers from being deported to Mauritius because their number would have exceeded the annual limit for immigration. Instead the ship was holed and it sank in Haifa harbour with more than 250 people lost.

Just over a year later, in February 1942, a Soviet submarine torpedoed the *Struma*, another ship which was bringing Jews from Romania en route to Palestine. Negotiations between the Turks and the British ended in an impasse and the refugees were refused the opportunity to disembark. Instead the ship was permitted to drift in the Bosphorus, where it sank with the loss of nearly 800 people on board.

After 1945 the White Paper was not abrogated. Jews in Palestine remembered these tragedies and were deeply opposed to the actions of the Royal Navy in preventing Holocaust survivors from reaching Palestine. Many ships were turned back and their passengers interned in camps on Cyprus. While the UN publicly debated the question, Jews in Palestine were deeply sceptical about their deliberations.

International Recognition of Israel and Palestine

Many who believed that the establishment of a state of the Jews was not a good thing were unable to fit Zionism into a theoretical framework – and since Zionism was different, it must therefore also be wrong. The Zionists believed instead that they were returning to their Land. They were coming 'as of right and not on sufferance'.

The new British Labour government refused to abrogate the restrictions on immigration despite the revelations of the Shoah. The announcement of 'no change in immigration' is made here by the writer George Lichtheim in the *Palestine Post*. The *Patria* is seen here to be the first of the many refugee boats that were attempting to reach the shores of Palestine. Drawn by Yosef Ross (*Ashmoret* 17 April 1947).

Hugh Dalton, the incoming chancellor of the exchequer, told the Labour party conference in 1945 that he hoped for 'a happy, free and prosperous Jewish state in Palestine'. The British prime minister, Clement Attlee, and his foreign secretary, Ernest Bevin, were not so sure. There was resentment in the Zionist camp that both Bevin and the US secretary of state, George Marshall, believed that the problem of survivors in displaced persons' camps in post-war Europe could be solved by advising Jews to rebuild their lives in their countries of origin – countries where their families had been exterminated, often with the collaboration of neighbours. Even Winston Churchill, in a speech in the House of Commons in 1946, thought that this idea should be considered.

In November 1945, an Anglo-American Commission of Inquiry into finding a solution to the problem of Zionist Jews and Palestinian Arabs was established. It recommended that a hundred thousand Jews, the persecuted remnant that had survived the Shoah, be granted emigration permits for Palestine. It further proposed a federated, unitary state with Jewish and Arab provinces under the British Mandate, the mode of government of which would be decided later. It further argued that neither side should be allowed to dominate the other. Both sides opposed the commission's recommendations. The Arabs were vehemently opposed to any notion of partition.

One member of the commission was the Oxford academic and Labour Member of Parliament Richard Crossman. Like former Liberal prime minister David Lloyd George, he had been brought up in a religious home and was acquainted with the biblical geography and history of the Holy Land. He had visited Nazi Germany several times before the war and had now seen the camps, filled with survivors, after the war.

In Jerusalem, Crossman met Ben-Gurion, whom he described as 'a Pickwickian cherub'. Ben-Gurion had read Crossman's book on Plato and objected to his labelling of Plato as 'a fascist'. At a reception at the Mufti of Jerusalem's villa, Crossman discerned the problem between Arabs and Jews in social rather than political terms:

> It was a magnificent party, evening dress, Syrian food and drink, and dancing on the marble floor. As far as I could see, the party was 50:50 Arab and British. It is easy to see why the British prefer the Arab upper class to the Jews. The Arab intelligentsia has a French culture, amusing, civilised, tragic and gay. Compared with them, the Jews seem tense, bourgeois, central European or even German.
>
> As we motored back, a British official said to me: 'There are two societies in Jerusalem, not three. One is Anglo-Arab and the other is Jewish. The two just can't mix.'[2]

ALT-NEUER ZEUGE.

The Anglo-American Commission of Inquiry reported in April 1946. Its findings displeased both Attlee and Bevin. It was published on the anniversary of the publication of Theodor Herzl's *The Jewish State* (1896). Here the book is positioned in a symbolic central place for the assembled delegates to ponder its meaning. Drawn by Yosef Ross.

[2] Richard Crossman, *Palestine Mission: a Personal Record* (London 1947) p. 123.

The Morrison–Grady Plan was instituted to examine how the proposals of the Anglo-American Commission would be implemented. Both sides opposed virtually every suggestion. There was no unanimity of thought between Zionist Jews and Palestinian Arabs. There was also a sense that every review, every proposal, every White Paper by the British had been governed by British national interests. Bevin then proposed a five-year British trusteeship. This too was rejected. The lack of progress to find a meaningful solution always ended in deadlock.

By February 1947, Britain handed the problem back to the newly formed United Nations. Within weeks it had established the UN Special Committee on Palestine (UNSCOP). The eleven-member delegation visited Palestine, but the Arab Higher Committee refused to engage with it. In September 1947, the UNSCOP delegation put forward its majority proposal to partition Palestine, with Iran, India and Yugoslavia dissenting. The Zionist Jews accepted partition, the Palestinian Arabs did not.

This was translated into UN Resolution 181. The dispersion of the Jews at this time became an asset. It allowed for the international canvassing of the hesitant and the undecided. All of this happened in the shadow of the Shoah – a message and understanding which conveyed itself to the most far-flung of Jewish communities. The vote was supported at the UN General Assembly by both superpowers, most European states and many Latin American countries. Thirty-three voted in favour, thirteen against, with ten abstentions and one absentee. The Arab world and Muslim countries voted against. The United Kingdom abstained. Historically this was a window of opportunity for the Zionists. It took place before the era of decolonisation and before the developing world joined the United Nations. It also took place before Stalin performed a volte-face and embarked on an anti-Zionist policy externally and an anti-Semitic one internally in the USSR.

A few days after the vote, a financially strapped Britain announced the end of the Mandate by mid-May 1948 and its subsequent withdrawal from Palestine.

By 1947, a plethora of proposals had achieved little in resolving this clash of two national movements. The Palestinian Arabs saw themselves as an anti-colonial movement, while the Zionist Jews viewed their claim to be in Palestine 'as of right and not on sufferance' after the Shoah. Drawn by Yosef Ross.

U.N. - COOPERATION

There was great suspicion that many of those involved in the UN deliberations on Palestine in 1947 were closet anti-Semites. Sir Alexander Cadogan had described Soviet diplomats as 'a most stinking creepy set of Jews'. Ernest Bevin, a former right-wing trade union leader and now British foreign secretary, believed that the surviving Jews should return to their communities of origin. Haj Amin al-Husseini, the Mufti of Jerusalem, had spent the war years in Berlin, cultivating the Nazi elite. Hence he is called 'the Mufti of Berchtesgaden' in this image. Drawn by Yosef Ross (1947).

55

Israel's War of Independence and the Nakba

The UN vote in favour of partition and a two-state solution was accepted by the Zionists and opposed by the Palestinian Arabs. The absolutism of the Arab side was reflected in attacks on Jewish communities in the Arab world. This zero-sum game immediately ignited a civil war between the two sides.

Many Jews felt that it was a question of kill or be killed. This sentiment was made more concrete by pronouncements by Arab leaders and in the media. Azzam Pasha, the secretary-general of the Arab League, spoke in apocalyptic terms of 'a war of extermination'.

Although the Arab side was slightly bigger in terms of conventional forces, the Zionist Jews began to succeed militarily in early 1948, at which time 75,000 Arabs fled Palestine. This developed into a flood with the fall of major Arab centres such as Haifa and Tiberias. The killing of more than a hundred civilians by the Irgun Zvai Leumi and Lehi at the village of Deir Yassin became an instrument in the Arab media assault. The broadcasts, however, unnerved many Palestinian Arabs in that they feared they too would suffer the same fate. This accelerated the Arab exodus from Palestine. When Ben-Gurion proclaimed the state of Israel in mid-May 1948, it was estimated that between 200,000 and 300,000 Arabs had departed.

In the aftermath of the Shoah, many Jews in Palestine felt that if they were overrun by Arab armies, no quarter would be given. The Jews were haunted by the ghosts of the past. If they failed on the battlefield, there would be a repetition of recent history.

Moshe Sharett, the future foreign minister of Israel, later declared that his calmness on signing the Declaration of Independence was a clever deception. He felt 'as though he was standing on a cliff with a gale blowing up all around him and nothing to hold on to except his determination not to be blown over into the raging sea below'.[3]

The Israelis were driven by a historical imperative. The Jews had been enslaved by their Roman conquerors some two thousand years before. The Temple had been destroyed, Jerusalem burned down and the Menorah, the symbol of the ancient Jewish state, taken to Rome. In 1948, it was Jewish force of arms that was retrieving that symbol in a war of liberation.

Within hours of the Declaration of Independence, five Arab armies, representing several countries in the Arab world, invaded the new state of Israel on different fronts. The goal was to reach Tel Aviv on the coast and to lay siege to Jerusalem inland. Ceasefires, the delivery of Czech arms and the arrival of mainly Jewish volunteers allowed the Israelis to regroup and retrain. The Arab armies were pushed back and Jerusalem's siege was lifted.

The Zionist Jews fought Palestinian Arabs in a civil war until May 1948. Five Arab armies invaded after Israel's Declaration of Independence and were confronted by the Israel Defence Forces. Large numbers were killed in the battle with the Jordanians for the Old City of Jerusalem. At Kfar Etzion, Arab irregulars killed its defenders after they had surrendered. Drawn by Yosef Ross.

The flight of the Arabs surprised many. In Benny Morris's words, the Palestinian refugee problem was 'born of war, not by design, Jew or Arab'.[4] In parallel, there was a desire to maximise this exodus. This was a factor in the expulsion of Palestinian Arabs by Ahdut Ha'Avoda military figures such as Yigal Allon, Moshe Carmel and Yitzhak Rabin. There was also a desire to secure militarily important strategic locations and to disarm hostile fighters.

[3] Golda Meir, *My Life* (London 1975) pp. 74–5.
[4] Benny Morris, *The Birth of the Palestinian Refugee* (Cambridge 1988) p. 286.

In all, another 300,000 left at this time. Overall a total of 600,000–760,000 Palestinians had become refugees by the war's end in early 1949. The Palestinian Arabs called it the Nakba – the Catastrophe. The Zionist Jews called it the 'War of Independence'.

Yigal Allon in 1979. Drawn by Arie Navon (1982).

57

A month after the declaration of the state, the Israeli cabinet resolved to bar the return of those Palestinian Arabs who had left – in theory at least until the conflict was over. Guiding this approach was the fear that the returning Palestinian Arabs would constitute a fifth column, determined to destroy the state from within.

While Israel had prevented the attempt by five Arab armies to overrun the country, there was still no peace, only a state of no war: an armistice amidst periodic acts of terror.

The Jews saw in their salvation the dream of a progressive Hebrew republic, a state of the Jews for which they were prepared to fight – despite opposition from Arab nationalists and the oil lobby in the USA and Europe. In 1948, Israel's makeshift civilian conscripts won a war for independence, but the price had been heavy. More than six thousand had been killed – one per cent of the entire population – and more than fifteen thousand were injured.

The Ingathering of the Exiles

The early years were ones of the ingathering of the exiles. There were no more quotas imposed by the British. Now Jews could come to Israel as of right, according to the Law of Return.

A campaign 'to gather in the exiles' from Europe was strongly promoted to those who had survived the Nazi extermination. It also extended to the rescue of Jews in the Arab world who were identified as a fifth column.

In 1948 only 6 per cent of Jews, some 650,000 people, lived in Israel. By 1951, through emigration, this figure had almost doubled:

1948	101,828
1949	239,954
1950	170,563
1951	175,279[5]

During the first decade of Israel's existence, a million Jews emigrated there – 48 per cent from European countries and 52 per cent from non-European states. The bulk came from Eastern Europe – countries which had become part of Stalin's fiefdom after 1945, countries where there were often show trials of Jewish leaders and subsequent imprisonment. They were also countries where assimilated Jewish Communists were turned into Zionist spies – as during the Slánský trial in 1952. Some governments put a price tag on members of their Jewish community. Israel subsequently 'bought' Jews from Romania.

Of the emigrants, 130,000 were Shoah survivors who ended up in displaced persons camps in Europe. Others had been apprehended by the British and placed in internment camps on Cyprus.

More than half a million came from Arab countries, Turkey and Iran. In Iraq, many were essentially dispossessed and forced to leave in 1950. This Jewish community had dwelled by 'the rivers of Babylon' for some two and a half thousand years, ever since the time of Nebuchadnezzar.

After the Suez campaign, Nasser served notice on large numbers of Egyptian Jews that they should leave the country within a specified period.

More than 800,000 Jews were forced to leave Arab countries – and Israel was unable to cope with such an influx. Food, housing and employment were major problems for the new state. Many immigrants were housed in tent cities in adverse conditions.

Few Jews left North America. Ben-Gurion compared American Jews to those Babylonian Jews who did not return to ancient Israel with the prophets Nehemiah and Ezra two and a half thousand years before. While expressing solidarity with Israel, most American Jews regarded themselves as builders of the American republic – and at home.

Moreover, there was a growing resentment among the Mizrahim, immigrants from North Africa and the Islamic world. Unlike the Israeli elite of mainly European Ashkenazi origin, the Mizrahim had lived in different Jewish societies which had historically been little influenced by the Haskalah, the Jewish Enlightenment. Although Jews had been founder members of the Communist parties in Egypt and Iraq, the traditionalist Mizrahim were far removed from the world of the Ashkenazi socialist kibbutzniks.

---

[5] Arie Lova Eliav, *Refuge*, vol.14 no.6 (November 1994).

Israel and its Politics

The left-wing political party Mapam regarded itself as the Soviet Union's representative in Israel. One of its components, Hashomer Hatzair, had published the works of Stalin in Hebrew – but bound in red leather. The Mapai party, to the right of Mapam and led by Ben-Gurion, was the leading political force in establishing the state. Ben-Gurion was fearful of Soviet influence in Israel even though the USSR had recognised the state despite a history of imprisoning Zionists. Ben-Gurion ensured that the Palmach, which was associated with Mapam, was dissolved. Here a watchful Marx keeps an eye of the ideological debate that is taking place. Yehoshua Adari (*Herut* 24 April 1959).

The Provisional Council was formed as a governing executive following Israel's Declaration of Independence in May 1948 and was a temporary measure due to the ongoing war with the Arab states. It acted as a temporary provisional government until the first election in January 1949 when hostilities were drawing to a close. The Provisional Council became the Knesset, Israel's parliament of 120 seats. There was no constitution because religious Jews felt that it existed already – as the Torah.

There was no mention of God in the Declaration of Independence, only a reference to the Rock of Israel – a constructive ambiguity that could be interpreted positively by both the religious and the secular. David Ben-Gurion was seen as the builder of the state and destined to become its first prime minister, with the displaced Chaim Weizmann as the ceremonial president.

Menahem Begin addresses an election rally of his supporters in Moghrabi Square, Tel Aviv, in January 1949. Accompanied by multitudes of police, two supporters hold a banner in front of Begin, bearing the Irgun slogan, 'Only Thus'. The map includes Israel, the West Bank and the state of Jordan – as Begin's party, Herut, did not recognise the first partition of Palestine in the 1920s. Ze'ev (unknown place of publication), 18 January 1949.

The Zionist Right was essentially represented by Menahem Begin and his Herut movement. Many came from Poland where Begin led the Betar youth movement and was associated with the maximalists of Jabotinsky's Revisionist movement. Arriving in Palestine in 1942, Begin became the leader of the Irgun Zvai Leumi at the end of 1943. He embarked on the path of parliamentary politics by transforming the Irgun into Herut in 1948.

Both the official Revisionists and the post-Jabotinsky Lehi of Natan Yellin-Mor, Israel Eldad and Yitzhak Shamir were rivals for the same ideological space. With Jabotinsky, Stern and Raziel all dead, Begin projected himself as the undisputed leader of the Zionist Right and expected Herut to perform extremely well in the forthcoming election for the Knesset. He believed that Herut would pose an ideological alternative to the socialism of the main parties.

The culture of the Right was centred on the leader and his dominance. Menahem Begin was an incendiary speaker at rallies and meetings. His socialist opponents suggested that he based his style on pre-war authoritarian leaders.

A History of Israel: 1949-2020

1949

An observant Jew, dressed in a prayer shawl, is casting his vote in the first Israeli election for the Provisional Assembly in January 1949.

The caption is a section from the traditional 'Shehecheyanu' blessing in which the reciter thanks God for having lived to see this day.

Yosef Ross

3 Jan	Italian steamer sails from Genoa with Czech Jews
4 Jan	Yehuda Karni, Hebrew poet and Yiddish writer, dies in Tel Aviv aged 65
7 Jan	Israeli shoot down five RAF reconnaissance aircraft
7 Jan	Operation Horev under Yigal Allon comes to an end
12 Jan	Talks between Israel and Egypt open on Rhodes
13 Jan	2,725 Jewish displaced persons arrive in Haifa
25 Jan	Twenty-one lists take part in elections for the Constituent Assembly
30 Jan	Ernest Bevin finally announces UK de facto recognition of Israel
31 Jan	USA grants de jure recognition of Israel
1 Feb	First El Al flight to New York via Rome
1 Feb	Military governorship of Jewish West Jerusalem returned to civilian rule
11 Feb	Last inhabitants of British internment camp on Cyprus leave
11 Feb	Natan Yellin-Mor given eight years in prison for terrorism by Acre military court
11 Feb	Amnesty for all political prisoners approved
12 Feb	Hassan al-Banna, founder of the Muslim Brotherhood, assassinated
14 Feb	First meeting of the Knesset takes place
15 Feb	Nine hundred Jewish refugees from Shanghai arrive at Haifa
16 Feb	Chaim Weizmann elected president in Knesset vote 83–15
21 Feb	Exchange of Arab and Israeli prisoners begins
24 Feb	Armistice agreement signed with Egypt
5 Mar	Operation Uvda begins in the southern Negev
8 Mar	Ben-Gurion presents coalition government for Knesset vote of confidence
23 Mar	Armistice agreement signed with Lebanon at Rosh Hanikra
3 Apr	Armistice agreement signed with Jordan on Rhodes
17 Apr	Meir Bar-Ilan, leading religious Zionist, dies in Jerusalem aged 69
27 Apr	Lausanne Conference opens to resolve disputes with Arab states
4 May	Israel celebrates first Independence Day with 200,000 new immigrants
11 May	Britain abstains when Israel becomes 59th member of United Nations
12 May	Israel signs Lausanne Protocol as the basis for territorial discussions
20 July	Armistice agreement signed with Syria at Hill 132 near Mahanayim
17 Aug	The remains of Theodor Herzl reburied in Jerusalem
8 Sept	Knesset passes act to conscript men and unmarried women 47–13
8 Nov	Operation Magic Carpet, the airlift of more than 40,000 Jews from Yemen, begins
9 Nov	Yigael Yadin appointed IDF Chief of Staff after Yaakov Dori
10 Dec	UN General Assembly votes 38–14 to internationalise Jerusalem
13 Dec	The Mossad, headed by Reuven Shiloah, established

Israel's war of independence and the Palestinian Nakba moved towards its close at the beginning of the year. Even so, there was fighting in Kfar Saba and Israeli cities were still being bombed by Egyptian aircraft. At the end of December 1948, the IDF, under the command of Yigal Allon, conducted Operation Horev to drive out Egyptian forces from the Negev and 'the Faluja Pocket'. Egyptian airfields were attacked and undamaged Spitfires removed. The head of the IDF, Yigael Yadin, warned the Egyptians not to use gas as a weapon in attacks on Jewish settlements.

Operation Horev began with a diversionary attack on Gaza, but it earned criticism from both the USA and the UK. The British were unsure about the extent of the operation and whether they believed Ben-Gurion's assurances. Reconnaissance aircraft, four Spitfires and a Tempest, were sent up and promptly shot down by the Israelis. Two pilots were killed and others captured.

Britain stationed fighters and bombers in Jordan while military preparations were made in Malta and Cyprus. The Israeli fear was that the British would invoke the Anglo-Egyptian Treaty of 1936 and intervene militarily. On the diplomatic front, Aubrey Eban attacked the British at the United Nations, while *The Times* in London implied that there were Soviet citizens flying 'Red Planes' in Sinai. The British cabinet finally decided to recognise Israel in mid-January despite Ernest Bevin's delaying tactics. It then allowed the inhabitants of the internment camps in Cyprus to leave for Israel. Britain later abstained on the vote to allow Israel to join the United Nations. Even so, the BBC instituted a Hebrew service at the end of October. Following the Israeli election at the end of January, many countries began to recognise Israel and to sign trade agreements.

Operation Horev was followed by Operation Uvda in March to cement Israeli sovereignty over the southern Negev. Separate negotiations to agree armistices began between Israel and Egypt, Lebanon, Jordan and Syria. Iraqi forces positioned in the Nablus–Tulkarem–Jenin triangle withdrew without any agreement.

A standing army was maintained in readiness for any future conflict and it included dogs. In January, the army advertised its desire to recruit 'Boxers, Alsatians, Dobermans and Airedale terriers under three years old and at least 20 inches tall'. In September the Knesset passed a universal conscription act that enlisted men and unmarried women into the armed forces, which caused protest from the religious and Arab parties.

The ingathering of the exiles proceeded apace, with many new settlements being established. An objective of fifty-one new settlements was set for the first six months of the year. Jews were brought from Eastern Europe, while Yemeni Jews left Rashid camp just outside Aden. In Bucharest, hundreds of Jews wishing to apply for permits jammed the streets outside the building which housed the Israeli Legation. In Turkey, a Spanish Jew, Abraham Meyer, was deported for encouraging Jews to emigrate to Israel. In mid-January, the SS *Bulgaria* left Varna with 4,592 passengers, while the SS *Galilah* left Constanza with 1,310. A few weeks later, 900 refugees from Shanghai arrived in Haifa on the SS *Negba*. Ships were often stopped en route to Israel. The British freighter *Richard Borchard* was stopped by the Egyptians 110 km off Haifa, and the SS *Tampa*, carrying 500 passengers, was detained in Crete while checks were carried out for men of military age.

There were still many refugees in displaced persons camps in Germany who wished to leave for Israel. In addition to 8,000 in Berlin, there were many Jews remaining in the US Zone (65,000), British Zone (10,000), French Zone (1,000) and Soviet Zone (1,700).

As the conflict ended, the dire economic situation became more apparent. The Israeli pound was devalued amidst austerity measures. In mid-February, Israel secured the first tranche of $35 million from the US Export–Import Bank at an interest rate of 3.5 per cent, with repayments starting after three years. The new government instituted an austerity plan. Daily food rationing was introduced in May at 360g bread, 58g sugar and 25g meat per person, while only twelve eggs could be used each month.

The first election for the Constituent Assembly took place at the end of January and Ben-Gurion's party, Mapai, won an overwhelming victory with forty-six seats. However, in order to form a blocking majority of sixty-one in the 120-seat Knesset, Mapai had to negotiate with other parties to establish a coalition government. The electorate also elected a motley collection of fringe parties, including those representing the Yemenite community, the Womens' International Zionist Organisation and the Democratic List of Nazareth. The right-wing Herut movement of Menahem Begin and the Communists were deemed to be beyond the political pale. Begin had expected forty seats instead of fourteen. Chaim Weizmann defeated the Right's candidate, Yosef Klausner, to become president.

A political amnesty allowed Natan Yellin-Mor to escape an eight-year prison sentence for terrorism as a leader of Lehi and he was able to take his seat on behalf of the Fighters' party. Arieh Altman, the chairman of the official Revisionists, resigned after electoral annihilation. Ben-Gurion was also wary of Mapam, a left-wing Zionist but pro-Soviet party, which had been formed from Hashomer Hatzair, Ahdut Ha'Avoda and remnants of Left Poale Zion at the beginning of 1948. Following the election, Mapam became the second largest party with nineteen seats, but Ben-Gurion was avowedly suspicious of its fondness for the Kremlin. Mapam regarded itself as Stalin's representatives in Israel rather than the official Communists. Ben-Gurion labelled Mapam as 'Israel's Yevsektsia' after the Jewish sections of the Soviet Communist party. He admired Lenin for his ability to make a revolution with few resources, but was a fierce anti-Communist because of the ideological opposition of Marxism–Leninism to Zionism.

Instead Ben-Gurion formed an alliance with the four religious parties, the United Religious Front of the National Religious and ultra-orthodox, which had won sixteen seats in the election. The ultra-orthodox parties Agudat Yisrael and Poale Agudat Yisrael did not regard themselves as 'Zionists'. They were joined by the Progressives and the Sephardim in creating a coalition of more than seventy seats. Mapam and the General Zionists refused to enter the government. At the Herut party conference in July, Menahem Begin attacked UN Resolution (UNR) 181 and the partition of Palestine. Begin condemned not only the partition of 1947, but also the very first partition of Palestine in the early 1920s which led to the establishment of TransJordan under the then Emir Abdullah. Begin wanted to reclaim 'the East Bank' from Abdullah and often berated Ben-Gurion for not invading Jordan. He condemned the lack of a constitution and called for the introduction of an economy based on free enterprise.

The Lausanne Conference, convened by the UN Conciliation Commission in Palestine and attended by Israel and its neighbouring Arab states, took place between April and September. In May, Israel was elected 37–12 as a member of the United Nations. The following day, it signed the Lausanne Protocol which essentially recognised the proposed borders of UNR 181. While Israel wanted a broad framework agreement, the Arab states concentrated on the Israeli conquest of territory beyond the borders of UNR 181 in November 1947. They also argued for the right of return of more than 700,000 refugees and compensation for lost property, which Israel opposed. The Arab states also proposed the internationalisation of Jerusalem – a corpus separatum – a solution previously rejected.

Despite pressure from the Truman White House to make concessions, Ben-Gurion argued that Israel had been established through the conflict with both the Palestinian Arabs and its neighbours – and not through UNR 181 and the proposed partition of Palestine.

A few weeks after signing the Lausanne Protocol, Israel proposed a return of 100,000 Palestinian Arab refugees, but not to their deserted homes. At the same time, Israel proposed the annexation of Gaza. By December, Ben-Gurion argued for moving the capital of Israel to Jerusalem, but the Israeli cabinet voted against it. The 1949 Armistice Demarcation Line, the Green Line, became the effective border between Israel and the West Bank.

The 1950s

The 1950s was a decade of nation building. The war of independence had ended in the spring of 1949 with a disproportionate loss of life. The slogan on the bus reads 'The Ingathering of the Exiles'. It is passing the roadside stone marking the first million inhabitants – the second million is in sight further along the road.

Yosef Ross (*HaTsofeh* 25 November 1949)

After the conflict with the Palestinian Arabs and the Arab world, there was little infrastructure initially to cope with the influx of immigrants. Instead tent cities arose until sufficient housing had been built. The reparations agreement with West Germany and US support in part allowed Israel to keep afloat economically.

Most immigrants came from the Islamic world and the Communist bloc where they had suffered persecution and often induced expulsion. It was also a clash of cultures. The conservative Mizrahim from North Africa reacted to the secular socialist Israelis and the acculturated Europeans. Many were sent to recently established new settlements rather than to urban areas and cities such as Tel Aviv and Jerusalem.

The United States provided a polar attraction for Jews wishing to leave their countries of birth. Some immigrants went first to Israel and then left for the United States at a later date.

The decade marked a distancing from Israel by the Soviet Union after recognition in 1948. Increasing anti-Semitism, the refusal to allow Soviet Jews to leave for Israel and the Kremlin's embrace of the Arab world led Ben-Gurion to align Israel with the West and to seek the collusion of the imperial powers Britain and France during the Suez campaign in late 1956.

1950

Operation Magic Carpet brought tens of thousands of Jews from Yemen, Aden and surrounding areas on 'the Wings of Eagles' in a remarkable airlift.

The immigrants are flying in on magic carpets from the Arab world while overworked employees at the Ministry of Immigration are busy running a carpet shop.

Arie Navon (*Davar* 2 December 1949)

23 Jan   Knesset resolution proclaims Jerusalem as Israel's capital

10 Feb   Religious parties protest about inhibiting camp religious education

11 Feb   UK releases £15 million in frozen Israeli assets

17 Feb   Mossad's Reuven Shiloah meets King Abdullah in Jordan

24 Feb   Israeli–Egyptian armistice agreement regards Gaza as a neutral zone

28 Feb   Airport opened in Eilat

11 Mar   Kol Zion l'Golah begins broadcasting in Yiddish, English and French

14 Mar   Iran extends de facto recognition to Israel

14 Mar   Knesset passes 'Absentee Property Law', allowing for confiscation

26 Mar   Hannah Szenes, freedom fighter and poet, is reburied on Mount Herzl

4 Apr   UN Trusteeship Council advocates Jerusalem as a corpus separatum

24 Apr   Jordan formally annexes West Bank

1 May   May Day conflicts between Mapai, Mapam and Communists

16 May   Twenty-four-hour strike of government doctors for higher wages

18 May   Planning begins for Operation Ezra and Nehemiah to save Iraqi Jews

20 May   Near East Air Transport brings first Iraqi Jews to Israel

25 May   Israel excluded from arms purchase by USA–UK–France agreement

13 June   Gradual Basic Law compilation to form Israeli Constitution

13 June   Joint Israeli–Jordanian patrols of demarcation line begin

21 June   Ship carrying Yemeni Torah scrolls arrives at Eilat

25 June   Khalsa transit camp becomes town of Kiriat Shemona

25 June   Israel reluctantly supports UN resolution on North Korean invasion

5 July   Law of Return, allowing Jews to emigrate to Israel, passed in Knesset

5 July   Minister of justice advocates abolition of capital punishment

8 July   Police and army search village of Tireh for infiltrators

17 July   Conference of Israeli Ambassadors takes place

1 Aug   Law passed allowing death penalty for Nazi war criminals

1 Aug   Water pipeline to Eilat inaugurated

4 Aug   Shopkeepers protest against new rationing law

7 Aug   General strike against government austerity programme

23 Aug   Jacob Blaustein and Ben-Gurion publicly agree on US Jewish allegiance

24 Sept   Army radio Galei Zahal starts broadcasting

24 Sept   Operation Magic Carpet, carrying Yemeni and Adeni Jews, completed

15 Oct   Cabinet resigns, caretaker government of seven Mapai ministers

30 Oct   Jack Gerling becomes non-party minister in new Ben-Gurion coalition

1 Nov   Knesset approves new Ben-Gurion coalition 69–42

14 Nov   General Zionists' vote increases dramatically in municipal elections

While the armed conflict between Israel and the Arab states had formally ended in 1949, Ben-Gurion warned at a rally in Ein Harod in May that there would be a second round. The Egyptians installed military structures on the islands of Tiran and Sanafir at the southern entrance to Aqaba, allowing for the potential blocking of maritime passage to Eilat. The Egyptians told the US Embassy in Cairo that they had no intention of interfering with shipping.

The IDF conducted a military campaign against Palestinian Arab infiltrators – those who wished to return to their homes as well as those who wished to attack Israeli targets. In October, the IDF moved 2,500 Arabs from Ashkelon to Gaza – some had returned after a cessation of hostilities. Following the Armistice Agreement with Jordan, joint patrols began in June, but Gaza was regarded as a neutral zone. In July, more than a hundred infiltrators were located at Abu Ghosh, while police and army personnel imposed a curfew on Tireh before searching the village.

At the beginning of the year, a foreign policy debate took place in the Knesset in which Herut, Mapam and the Communists all voiced opposition to any pact with Jordan's King Abdullah. Reuven Shiloah's negotiations at the king's winter palace at El Shunah in February were nullified by subsequent opposition. In April, the Knesset approved an 'Absentees Property Law' in which Arab property could be confiscated. Jordan formally annexed the West Bank, an act which was recognised by the UK. Herut organised a demonstration in Tel Aviv's Mograbi Square to protest against the Jordanian annexation since they regarded the West Bank as Judaea and Samaria, part of the Land of Israel. Menahem Begin opposed both partitions of historic Palestine and regarded Jordan as 'the East Bank'.

In contrast, 'the ingathering of the exiles' gathered pace. Jews were brought from Iraq in May, following the desire of the Nuri al-Said government to effectively strip them of their Iraqi nationality, deprive them of their assets and expel them to Israel, Some sixty thousand Jews registered to leave Iraq in 1950. A bomb in the El-Dar El-Bayda coffee shop in Baghdad in April heightened Jewish fears that there would be a repeat of the Farhud, a pogrom in the city in June 1941 in which almost two hundred Jews were killed. The Jewish arrivals in Israel were both Zionists and non-Zionists, including many members of the Iraqi Communist party.

The ingathering of the exiles was legalised by the Law of Return which permitted any Jew to return to Israel and claim Israeli citizenship. Ben-Gurion argued that it had been 'granted by Jewish history'. The government focused on the emigration of Jews from Eastern Europe – especially Poland, Romania and Hungary – rather than the Soviet Union. Even so, Ben-Gurion did appeal for the emigration of Soviet Jewry in May to mark the twenty-fifth anniversary of the founding of Kibbutz Afikim.

The Black Years of Soviet Jewry were marked by arrests and imprisonment. Soviet newspapers characterised Jews as 'rootless cosmopolitans'. The original names of assimilated Jews were published next to their contemporary Russified ones. Polina Zhemchuzhina, Foreign Minister Vyacheslav Molotov's Jewish wife, was divorced on Stalin's suggestion and sent into internal exile.

Such officially inspired anti-Semitism and the tarring of Jewish Communists as 'Zionists' persuaded Ben-Gurion and many in Mapai that Israel's future lay with the West and not in continuing with its non-aligned status. While Israel became the first country in the Middle East to recognise Mao's Communist regime in China, it also reluctantly supported the UN resolution which condemned North Korea's invasion of the south. This marked the widening gap between Foreign Minister Moshe Sharett's advocacy of maintaining a non-alignment policy, supported by many Diaspora Jewish organisations, and Ben-Gurion's support for a pro-American direction. It also indicated the ideological gap with the pro-Soviet Mapam, which argued for recognition of North Korea over its neighbour to the south.

The impoverished Jews of Yemen were brought to Israel in Operation Magic Carpet via an airlift from the British Crown colony of Aden. They were joined by a much smaller number of Jews who had lived as traders in surrounding Muslim countries – Saudi Arabia, Eritrea and Djibouti. Adeni Jews also left, having experienced a pogrom in the aftermath of the passing of UNR 181 in November 1947.

The strain of so many new immigrants meant that the Israeli government was forced to institute *ma'abarot* – tent cities for newcomers where conditions were basic. Many Yemenite children fell ill and they died in considerable numbers in the ma'abarot. This gave rise to the belief that they had been abducted and handed over to childless Israeli couples. Around 170,000 new immigrants arrived in 1950, of whom 93,000 lived in ma'abarot. This happened in parallel with new settlements being established. While there was an economic crisis such that austerity measures had to be instituted, there was also a political crisis. In February, the leaders of the religious parties sent a letter to Ben-Gurion alleging that religious rights in the ma'abarot were being hampered. At an extraordinary meeting of the cabinet, designed to discuss the matter, ministers from the religious parties refused to attend. This set in train a year-long series of threats of resignations and the holding of new elections. In parallel, Ben-Gurion negotiated with the secular parties, Mapam, the Progressives and the General Zionists, which offered the prospect of alternative coalitions.

Ben-Gurion also had ideological struggles with political forces further to the Left. On May Day, there was a dispute between Mapai and the pro-Soviet Zionists of Mapam. In Ramla, there were clashes between supporters of Mapai and local Communists. In Jerusalem, Communists marched on the Jewish Agency building, carrying portraits of Stalin. In January, the trial of journalists involved with the Communist daily *Kol Ha'am* was scheduled to begin.

Ben-Gurion argued that he wanted both private enterprise and public control within the economy: 'Neither full capitalism nor full socialism'. During a May Day speech, he claimed that the Jewish worker was characterised neither by the ideology of Marx nor by the philosophy of Ahad Ha'am: Marx because he linked the Jews with a sole concern for money and Ahad Ha'am as he argued that cheap Arab labour was necessary.

The pressure on the economy led to austerity measures being implemented together with a rationing regime. Between March 1949 and February 1950, $62 million had been spent on importing food. Tighter measures in June now restricted the meat eater to 500g per month. Citizens were allowed 1kg of sugar each month and could buy only one pair of shoes and one suit annually. This led to an outcry from shopkeepers and traders generally. A general strike ensued in August in which the only shops that were open were those run by the Histadrut and the Axa Textile factory, which were guarded by police. The Ministry of Supply opened special canteens which supplied milk products.

All this led to the resignation of Ben-Gurion and his government and its re-establishment when Pinhas Rosen of the Progressives was unable to form an alternative. The municipal elections in November indicated a fall in the vote share for Mapai (37.2 to 26.9 per cent) and a remarkable increase for the General Zionists (from 7.3 to 25.2 per cent) who had strongly supported the cause of the small shopkeeper and private enterprise in general. In Tel Aviv, the General Zionists achieved an 8 per cent lead over Mapai.

73

1951

The wave of immigration produced a proliferation of tent cities – ma'abarot – where new immigrants were housed. This dire situation, deemed to have been caused by bureaucratic delay, resulted in increasing frustration. The sense of powerlessness is captured in the caption, the Latin legal term 'Bis dat . . . qui cito dat!' It broadly translates as 'someone who gives immediately without hesitation, it is as if he has given twice'.

Yosef Ross

1 Jan Tel Aviv Stock Exchange opens for trading

4 Jan Yehuda Leib Maimon resigns over religious education in ma'abarot

4 Jan Contract for loan of $35 million from US Export–Import Bank signed

11 Jan Defence minister Ben-Gurion prolongs military rule

5 Feb General Zionists defeat government in Knesset vote 49–42

6 Feb IDF attack Arab village of Sharafat with civilian casualties

7 Feb IDF attack on Falama, north-east of Kalkilya

13 Feb Seventy thousand metal plant workers go on symbolic strike

14 Feb New cabinet formed after ma'abarot crisis

16 Feb Sharett calls for alternative to proportional representation elections

19 Feb Demonstrations against visiting British general, Brian Robertson

20 Feb Mapai central committee supports Arab right to vote 19–14

26 Feb Agreement with USA for technological aid and cooperation

1 Mar Work begins on enlarging the port of Haifa

12 Mar Israel asks four powers for $1.5 billion for plundered Jewish property

25 Mar Israel resumes work to drain Huleh swamp and to divert River Jordan

4 Apr Seven soldiers killed by Syrian forces in al-Hamma in the DMZ

2 May Battle with Syrian army after it enters DMZ

8 May Ben-Gurion meets President Truman at White House

15 May Brit HaKanaim radicals arrested before disruption of IDF conscription of women law

19 May Education minister David Remez dies in office aged 64

25 June Immunity granted to members of the Knesset (MKs) despite Ben-Gurion's objections

20 July King Abdullah of Jordan shot dead at al-Aqsa mosque in Jerusalem

30 July General Zionists triple their vote in second election

20 Aug Menahem Begin sends Herut a letter of resignation

21 Sept Five Israelis killed in bedouin attack on Sodom–Hatzeva road

27 Sept Chancellor Adenauer tells Bundestag that he is willing to negotiate on reparations

8 Oct Ben-Gurion forms coalition of Mapai and religious parties

11 Oct Egged bus company becomes a nationwide franchise

16 Oct IDF blow up flour mill near Qalkilya

20 Oct IDF attacks eastern suburb of Gaza in Operation Yegev

4 Nov US aid to Israel of nearly $65 million

19 Nov Knesset votes 85–11 for second term for President Chaim Weizmann

29 Nov Helmut Schacht, Hitler's economics minister, in stopover at Lydda airport

4 Dec Leah Feistinger abducted from Bayit V'Gan, raped and killed

6 Dec Adenauer accepts responsibility for reparations in Goldmann discussion

At the beginning of the year, the minister of religion, Yehuda Leib Maimon, resigned from the government only to retract his resignation a few days later. Maimon was in dispute over the provision of religious education to mainly Yemenite children who had been brought to Israel in Operation Flying Carpet. The critical report of a commission headed by Judge Gad Frumkin was rejected by Ben-Gurion.

Discrimination against the Jews in Iraq deepened. More bombings against Jewish targets took place. They had gradually been forced out of the professions and dismissed from government positions. The departure of the Jews from Iraq was welcomed because it also meant the exodus of many Jewish Communists who ironically rejected Zionism. The government of Nuri al-Said now froze all the assets of the emigrating Jews. Such measures were prepared clandestinely and banks were closed to prevent Jews accessing their money. Jews were essentially stripped of their economic and civil rights in Iraq. In March, an airlift of Iraqi Jews, initially to Cyprus en route to Israel, began as part of Operation Ezra and Nehemiah. By the end of the year, 120,000 Jews had left the country.

In the Warsaw bloc, the Kremlin proceeded with laying the ground for show trials of members of the Jewish Anti-Fascist Committee. The Jewish journalists Shmuel Persov and Miriam Zheleznova, who wrote for *Eynikayt*, had already been executed. At the end of 1951, investigations into the Kremlin physicians – many of whom were Jewish – was initiated. This evolved into the basis of the Doctors' Plot.

A disproportionate number of leading Jewish Communists were arrested in Czechoslovakia during 1951. Many were questioned in prison by often anti-Semitic interrogators. This culminated in the arrest of the party's former secretary-general, Rudolf Slánský, in November. Many were accused of being part of a Zionist conspiracy, in advance of a show trial in Prague.

Two amendments to the Compulsory Education Law of September 1949 appeared to give prior authority to the minister of education to register a child for one of the four school systems – General, Histadrut Workers, Mizrahi national religious and Aguda ultra-orthodox. However, both main religious movements retained labouring wings – Hapoel Hamizrahi and Poalei Agudat Yisrael. Ben-Gurion understood the central problem as being one of jurisdiction over these labouring wings – the labour movement or the religious parties? Mizrahi and the Aguda did not trust the Ministry of Education and insisted that there should be supervisors allocated to each school system so that they had control over the situation. Despite repeated attempts to resolve the question, there was a stalemate. In a Knesset vote in February, the General Zionists supported the religious bloc of parties, won the vote and effectively passed a vote of no confidence in Ben-Gurion. The cabinet resigned and an election was called for the end of July.

In addition, there was opposition to Ben-Gurion's intention to conscript religious women into the armed forces, and the religious parties held demonstrations in Jerusalem. While they could serve in agricultural settlements, social welfare agencies and military offices, Ben-Gurion told Chief Rabbi Herzog that no exemptions would be made. The religious kibbutz movement, Hakibbutz Hadati, supported Ben-Gurion's proposal.

On a 75 per cent turnout in the election, the General Zionists increased their vote from 5 per cent to 16.4 per cent and gained thirteen seats. Mapai lost one seat, but retained its position as the party of government which would lead the next coalition. Both Mapam on the Left and Herut on the Right lost seats. Menahem Begin resigned as chairman of the Herut movement, contemplating a return to the legal profession, only for it not to be acted upon by his colleagues. Mapam was beginning to suffer from its devoutly pro-Soviet approach when Jews were being arrested and incarcerated in the USSR. Some kibbutzim had broken away and joined Mapai. In October, after some fifty-five meetings with other parties, Ben-Gurion presented a new coalition which was once again solely composed of Mapai and the religious bloc.

Mapai did pass laws on Equal Rights for Women, Fallen Soldiers' Families, Hours of Work and Rest, and Annual Leave. Some Muslim judges opposed the Equal Rights for Women legislation as it prohibited polygamy.

Mapai projected plans to attain a population of two million within four years and to establish 560 new rural settlements. However, the continuing austerity had led to increased support for the General Zionists who represented small businesses. The Korean War had also affected the economy such that the black market thrived and there was a shortage of foreign currency. The government secured generous loans from the United States, but it also began to argue for reparations for Nazi crimes from the two Germanys. West German Chancellor Konrad Adenauer accepted the principle and negotiated with Nahum Goldmann, representing the Conference on Jewish Material Claims against Germany. In an appeal to the four occupying powers in Germany, Israel stated that restitution for plundered Jewish property would amount to $1.5 billion.

At the end of the year, there was an inter-union dispute. The Seamen's Union wanted to form a separate and independent union outside the Histadrut. This coincided with the expansion of the port at Haifa which handled 86 per cent of all imports into Israel. Many seamen went on strike and the union instructed the crew on the SS *Artza* not to allow Histadrut volunteers on board. The union further appealed to crew on foreign merchantships not to aid the Histadrut volunteers. When the *Negba* arrived in Haifa, carrying four hundred immigrants from North Africa, the crew went on strike on landing and twenty-seven were arrested. Sixty striking crew members on the SS *Galila* refused a police request to leave the ship. A hundred and fifty seamen stormed a Haifa prison in an attempt to free the *Negba* crew members.

At the beginning of the year, the IDF conducted a retaliatory policy against often unaffiliated criminal gangs which would attack Israeli civilians. In February the IDF attacked the village of Sharafat, south of Jerusalem, killing three women and five children, in retaliation for a murder and rape. At a cabinet meeting a couple of days later, Pinhas Rosen criticised the killing of civilians. Diaspora Zionists such as Norman Bentwich and Leon Simon were similarly critical of the raid on Sharafat and condemned the lack of an inquiry. An attack on the village of Falama, north-east of Qalkilya, took place a few days later.

In April and May, there were clashes with Syrian forces in the demilitarised zone (DMZ) between the two countries which had been established in 1949. Israel had resumed work on draining the Huleh swamps and diverting the waters of the Jordan. At the beginning of April, seven Israeli soldiers were killed in the DMZ and in May, an armed conflict took place in the area between the two sides.

Ben-Gurion conducted a libel action against *Kol Ha'am*, the Communist party's daily newspaper, because it alleged in an article in October 1949 that he had committed 'treason against the nation and the working class'. The newspaper was critical of Ben-Gurion's order to withdraw from the Suez Canal area in December 1948. Yitzhak Sadeh, one of the founders of the IDF, testified that this had prevented a total defeat of Egyptian forces. At the end of July, the court found in favour of Ben-Gurion, fined *Kol Ha'am* $420 and ordered it to publish the court's judgment in three consecutive issues of the paper.

77

1952

An aged grandfather, an observant Jew, takes his grandson to a monument for the six million who died in the Shoah – and explains the fate of European Jewry.

Hiding behind his back is a receipt for $1.5 billion. This reflects the controversial decision to negotiate with the West German government for reparations for the Shoah.

Yosef Ross

1 Jan	Nineteen-year-old girl attacked and killed In Beit Yisrael in Jerusalem
6 Jan	Six killed in IDF attack on Beit Jala
9 Jan	Knesset votes 61–50 to support the negotiations for a reparations agreement
22 Jan	UN Israeli delegates walk out protesting at hanging of two Jews in Baghdad
12 Feb	Government authorises continued military rule in Arab areas
13 Feb	Three different rates of exchange to the Israeli pound introduced
13 Mar	David Bergmann appointed head of Atomic Energy Commission
25 Mar	Begin asks for recall of delegation at The Hague reparations talks
4 Apr	Israel demands $3 billion from Germany at Hague Tribunal
14 Apr	Two killed in attack on Israeli vehicle near Hatzeva
5 May	Zionist Organisation Status Law introduced in Knesset
8 May	Trial of Soviet Jews begins in the USSR
29 May	Early Hebrew writer Peretz Smolenskin reburied in Jerusalem
14 July	Five Israeli watchmen killed by bedouin at Timna
25 June	Levi Eshkol appointed deputy prime minister in cabinet reshuffle
26 June	Haim Cohen appointed minister of justice
13 July	Eliezer Kaplan, former finance minister, dies aged 61
23 July	Free Officers Movement, led by Mohamed Naguib, seizes power in Egypt
11 Aug	King Talal of Jordan abdicates in favour of his son, Hussein
12 Aug	Thirteen Soviet Jews executed in the cellars of the Lubyanka
14 Aug	David Zvi Pinkas, communications minister, dies in King David Hotel
20 Aug	Yitzhak Sadeh, founder of the Palmach, dies in Tel Aviv aged 62
27 Aug	Ben-Gurion receives Knesset approval to buy arms from the West
8 Sept	Cabinet approves Reparations Agreement of $715 million
10 Sept	Adenauer and Sharett sign Reparations Agreement in Luxembourg
18 Sept	Yitzhak Meir Levin resigns; Agudat Yisrael leaves government coalition
5 Oct	Bomb attempt against Foreign Ministry by Dov Shilansky foiled
9 Oct	Moshe Dayan and Hassan Jadid resume Israeli–Syrian talks
9 Nov	Chaim Weizmann, first president of Israel, dies in Rehovot aged 77
20 Nov	Slánský trial begins in Prague
6 Dec	Czechoslovakia demands Israel recall its ambassador, Arieh Kubovy
7 Dec	Mordechai Maklef becomes Chief of Staff of IDF
8 Dec	Yitzhak Ben-Zvi elected second president of Israel in Knesset vote
19 Dec	Hapoel Hamizrahi and Mizrahi ministers resign from government
22 Dec	New government formed including General Zionists and Progressives
30 Dec	Arab workers admitted to Histadrut Trades Union department

At the beginning of the year, the Knesset debated the government's desire to move forward with negotiations with West Germany about reparations for Nazi war crimes conducted against the Jews. This sensitive issue divided the Knesset. While the General Zionists, Herut, Mapam and the Communists were vehemently opposed, many parties including some in the ruling Mapai had similar misgivings. A Gallup poll, published in *Ma'ariv*, indicated that 80 per cent were opposed to any negotiations with Adenauer's Germany.

Ben-Gurion's position was that Israel was entitled to inherit the property of annihilated communities and the heirless as the Jewish remnant was now represented by those living in Israel. Although hardly mentioned, a central reason was to prevent an economic crisis.

During the debate, an emotional Menahem Begin called Ben-Gurion 'a hooligan' and was asked to withdraw by the Knesset Speaker, Yosef Serlin. Begin refused and the session was adjourned. Begin then addressed a large rally in Jerusalem's Zion Square. He compared the situation to the civil war which had broken out in ancient Israel between the tribe of Benjamin and the tribe of Levi, resulting in the virtual extermination of the Benjaminites at the battle of Gilbeah. He then joined a march on the Knesset by many of his irate followers – only to be met by the deployment of tear gas and water hoses, rings of barbed wire and a circle of fire from lit paraffin. In the mêlée, both police and protesters were injured.

When the debate resumed in the Knesset, Begin withdrew the accusation of 'hooligan'. Ben-Gurion went on the offensive, calling Begin 'a hysterical clown' and lumping together the right-wing Herut with the Communist party. He said that 'the profane fascist ideology in its various forms, from left and right, an ideology of imposing a minority will by terror, will not succeed. It will not be permitted to ruin the nation's freedom and sovereignty.' Shmuel Mikunis, representing the Communist party, termed the West German government 'the successor to Hitlerism' and called for peace with East Germany.

Yitzhak Gruenbaum, a representative of Polish Jewry in the Sejm in the 1920s and now a political leader in Israel, condemned Ben-Gurion's move and argued that it would lead inevitably to diplomatic relations with West Germany. The left-wing Zionist Zivia Lubetkin, who had fought in both the Warsaw Ghetto Uprising in 1943 and in the Polish Revolt in 1944, argued at a Mapam meeting that Ben-Gurion's proposal was 'a desecration of the memory of the six million'.

After three days of debate, the Knesset gave its approval to Ben-Gurion and Sharett to proceed with the negotiations, 64–51. The religious bloc split, with the National Religious supporting the government, while Agudat Yisrael and its labouring wing abstained. The Knesset voted 56–47 to exclude Begin from its deliberations until after the Passover break. When Ben-Gurion was awarded the Bialik Prize shortly afterwards by the Tel Aviv Municipality, the representatives on its council from Herut, Mapam and the Communists protested by walking out of the proceedings. Negotiations with West Germany began in The Hague in May.

Dov Shilansky, who had emigrated to Israel aboard the *Altalena* and was a follower of Menahem Begin, was arrested when he attempted to bring a bomb in a suitcase into the building of the Foreign Ministry. As someone who had survived the Shoah, Shilansky wanted to protest about the reparations negotiations with West Germany. He was sentenced to two years' imprisonment.

Sharett's attempt to maintain a non-aligned approach between the superpowers became increasingly difficult. The ongoing Korean War and the need for US economic support soon made it impossible, but it was the deepening of Stalin's attacks on Soviet Jewry, mirrored by characterisations of Jewish Communists in Eastern Europe as agents of Zionism, that provided the death-knell to Israel's desire to remain unaligned.

The Black Years of Soviet Jewry had resulted in the arrests and incarceration of many well-known Jewish poets and writers such as Itzik Feffer, David Bergelson, David Hofshteyn and Peretz

Markish. All had been associated with the Jewish Anti-Fascist Committee and some had welcomed the establishment of the state of Israel. Many Jewish writers had wished to develop a flowering of Jewish culture in Yiddish in the USSR. Several who had lived abroad were suspect. Bergelson had lived in Weimar Germany and Markish in pre-war Poland. Leon Talmy had spent a few years in the USA before the revolution, while Ilya Vatenberg had graduated from a New York law school. The medical director of the Botwin Clinical Hospital, Boris Shimeliovich, was included together with the director of the Institute of Physiology of the Academy of Sciences, Lina Shtern. Still others were loyal Communists, such as Solomon Bregman who had been a party member since 1912, while Solomon Lozovsky had joined in 1901. They had been opposed to Zionism all their lives. Many had been awarded medals for bravery during World War II. The trial began in early May and concluded when the thirteen defendants were sentenced to death. Bregman was taken ill during the trial and died a few months afterwards. Lina Shtern was given three and a half years in a labour camp, followed by another five years in exile. In mid-August, all the other defendants were executed and their property confiscated.

At the end of 1951, Mordechai Oren, a prominent figure in the pro-Soviet Mapam and an editor of *Al Hamishmar*, had been arrested in Prague after attending a trades union conference in East Berlin. Oren, together with Shimon Orenstein, found themselves caught up in the investigation which led to the Slánský trial of mainly Jewish Communists in November. Oren confessed at a show trial that he was an agent for British intelligence and was sentenced to fifteen years' imprisonment. The interrogations of the defendants in the Slánský trial were replete with anti-Semitic innuendo and there were accusations in the trial itself that these Jewish anti-Zionists had in fact been working for the state of Israel. Ten of the thirteen defendants were Jews. Eleven defendants were hanged.

The Slánský trial and the arrest of Oren widened the deepening schism within Mapam into actual splits. Kfar Szold, Givat Haim and other Mapam kibbutzim transferred their allegiance to Mapai. Ben-Gurion and Sharett strongly condemned the proceedings in Prague in speeches to the Knesset. Some considered banning the Communist party in Israel. The Communists defended the Czechoslovak party's conduct. Mapam tried to follow a middle path in defending Oren's innocence while projecting itself as 'an integral part of the world revolutionary camp, headed by the USSR'. This eventually led to a three-way split between the Stalinists, the anti-Stalinists and a reformist Mapam.

The Kremlin itself attempted to draw attention away from the trial and executions by highlighting the plight of Julius and Ethel Rosenberg in the United States.

Chaim Weizmann's death persuaded Ben-Gurion to ask Albert Einstein to become Israel's second president. Einstein's refusal led to a four-way contest for the presidency in December, with Yitzhak Ben-Zvi emerging victorious on the third ballot with sixty-two votes. The question of religious education led to the resignation of Agudat Yisrael from the government in September and Hapoel Hamizrahi in December. Ben-Gurion was able to restructure his coalition by excluding the ultra-orthodox religious parties and replacing them with the General Zionists and the Progressives.

The problem of infiltrators continued. Four hundred were killed during the year, including seventy-eight in March alone. Forty-two Israelis were killed and fifty-six injured. In January, two Arabs were abducted in Jordan, brought to the abandoned village of Walaja and killed by an IDF patrol.

81

1953

The accusation that Jewish doctors attempted to poison the leaders of the Kremlin in the Doctors' Plot both unnerved and infuriated the Israeli public. Former members of Lehi responded by delivering bombs. The 'bouquets' of bombs are addressed to both the Soviet and Czech envoys in Tel Aviv together with the Israeli Foreign Ministry. The attached note states 'With Love, Israel'. An astonished 'Mr Israel' looks out from the window.

Arie Navon (*Davar* 13 February 1953)

4 Jan	Egyptian ship, *Samir*, with supplies for Arab refugees, seized
6 Jan	Sharett and Reuven Barkat attend first Asian Socialist Conference
13 Jan	Doctors' Plot begins in the USSR with anti-Semitic press campaign
17 Jan	Moshe Sneh forms pro-Soviet Left Socialist faction within Mapam
28 Jan	Mapam expels Sneh and his followers
7 Feb	Ralph Bunche arrives in Israel, carrying message from leading Egyptians
9 Feb	Malchut Yisrael plants bomb at Soviet Legation in Tel Aviv
12 Feb	Soviet Union breaks off diplomatic relations with Israel
4 Mar	Naftali Herz Imber, who wrote the words to *Hatikvah*, reburied in Jerusalem
24 Mar	Compulsory Tax Law passed by Knesset
4 Apr	After Stalin's death, the Kremlin discovers charges against doctors are groundless
20 Apr	Independence Day Parade includes British Centurion tanks
20 Apr	Rabbinical student and his niece killed in Jerusalem
20 Apr	First Israel Prizes awarded to nine people from different disciplines
13 May	US secretary of state, John Foster Dulles, visits Israel
17 May	Reprisal attacks on two villages in Operation Viper on the Tracks
25 May	Four General Zionist ministers resign over flying red flags from schools
26 May	Brit HaKanaim members stopped from bombing Education Ministry
26 May	Grenade attacks on homes in Beit Nabala, Deir Tarif, Beit 'Arif
9 June	Grenade attack on home in Tirat Yehuda
10 June	Grenade attack on home in Mishmar Ayalon
20 July	USSR restores diplomatic relations with Israel in post-Stalin era
11 Aug	Operation Vengeance and Reprisal launched against Jerusalem villages
12 Aug	Knesset votes to approve State Education Law
19 Aug	Yad Vashem, a Holocaust Remembrance Authority, established
20 Aug	Knesset passes law separating judiciary from executive
25 Aug	Thirteen Malchut Yisrael members sentenced from one to twelve years
27 Aug	Knesset agrees rabbinical courts' jurisdiction over marriage and divorce
27 Aug	Five killed in Jordan in attempt to visit Petra
7 Sept	Attempt to blow up ships in Haifa carrying German goods
12 Oct	Mother and two children killed in attack on home in Yehud
14 Oct	Ariel Sharon leads attack on Qibya in which dozens of civilians are killed
24 Oct	Halakhic authority Hazon Ish dies in Bnei Brak aged 74
2 Nov	Official announcement that Oren sentenced to 15 years in Czechoslovakia
25 Nov	Mapai central committee endorses Sharett as next prime minister
6 Dec	Ben-Gurion officially resigns as prime minister

83

The Black Years of Soviet Jewry culminated in the Doctors' Plot of January 1953. The press campaign, arrests, imprisonment and general persecution of Soviet Jews since 1948 reached its nadir when senior doctors – the majority of whom were Jewish – were charged with attempting to poison the leaders of the Kremlin. In the USSR, the composer Mieczysław Weinberg and the leading diplomat Ivan Maisky were arrested. Jewish communal leaders in Hungary and East Germany were arrested. Ana Pauker, Romania's former minister of foreign affairs, was arrested in February.

Many Jews were dismissed from their jobs amidst a rising tide of anti-Semitic innuendo and a rumour that Stalin was planning to expel all Jews living in the western reaches of the USSR to remote locations in the country.

The charge of Zionism and betrayal of the Soviet motherland was a recurring feature in the press. Many Israeli leaders still had relatives in the USSR. Siblings often chose different ideologies, one Communism, the other Zionism. Chaim Weizmann's sister, whom he had not seen for forty years, was arrested. All this created fear and disgust within Israel. Moshe Sharett extracted a rebuke for the Soviet Union at the first Asian Socialist Conference in Rangoon. A few days later, he denounced the Doctors' Plot in the Knesset. This was regarded as incitement by the Kremlin and 'a blood libel' by the Communist party in Israel.

This rift deepened when Malchut Yisrael, composed mainly of former Lehi and Irgun members, bombed the courtyard of the Soviet Legation in Tel Aviv in February. The wife of the Soviet ambassador was slightly injured. The security of the courtyard, however, was controlled by legation personnel and Soviet Ambassador Yershov refused entry to police who were investigating the incident. A few days later, the USSR broke off diplomatic relations with Israel and demanded the withdrawal of the Israeli Legation from Moscow. Ben-Gurion's report to the Knesset on the matter was approved 79–16.

Meanwhile, the moderate allies of Sharett who had opposed Ben-Gurion were now leaving politics – in particular, with the passing at the end of 1952 of the first president, Chaim Weizmann, known as 'the prisoner of Rehovot' after the town where he lived, ill and partially blind, after his sidelining by Ben-Gurion.

Members of Malchut Yisrael, who had also been responsible for at least three attacks on Czechoslovak diplomats in Israel after the Slánský trial, were arrested, tried and sentenced at the end of August. A few weeks later, six of the thirteen sentenced, mainly minors, were freed by the acting minister of defence, Pinhas Lavon. The leaders, Yaakov Heruti and Shimon Bachar, were given ten and twelve years respectively for membership of a terrorist organisation.

Following Stalin's death in March, diplomatic relations between the two countries were eventually resumed and there was an end to the campaign against Soviet Jews, but the entire episode brought to a head the simmering divisions within Mapam. The party's visiting representative, Mordechai Oren, had been sentenced to fifteen years' imprisonment in Prague. He had been brought as a witness in the Slánský trial. Mapam's initial stand was to proclaim Oren's innocence, but simultaneously to laud the Communist bloc. The Doctors' Plot finally persuaded Mapam to denounce the persecution of Soviet Jews. Moshe Sneh and two other MKs disagreed and formed the Left Faction within Mapam in January. Mapam expelled them a few weeks later. Other MKs and kibbutzim considered breaking with Mapam and joining Ben-Gurion's Mapai. The Ahdut Ha'Avoda component of Mapam, led by Yitzhak Tabenkin, was also considering secession and reverting to its original independent status.

Those who subscribed to the Reparations Agreement were also a target for reprisal. In mid-April, the violinist Jascha Heifetz was attacked outside his hotel after a concert in which he had played a sonata by Richard Strauss – who was regarded as a fellow traveller with Nazism. His hand was injured and he cancelled his last concert in Israel. Letter bombs were also sent to Konrad Adenauer.

Sharett was also concerned about the incoming US Republican administration of President Eisenhower. The new secretary of state, John Foster Dulles, who had previously been sympathetic to Israeli aspirations, commented that 'the US would not become an Israeli prisoner'.

Contact between Israel and the new military regime of Neguib and Nasser in Egypt was maintained via the Paris Embassy. In February, the UN diplomat Ralph Bunche brought a message from Egyptian foreign minister, Mahmud Fawzi, and two others, suggesting a back channel. Nasser wanted Israeli and US Jewish assistance in forcing a British evacuation of the Suez Canal area. He also wanted help to develop the Egyptian economy. At this stage, Nasser was seen as winning the power struggle within the Free Officers' administration. The increasing number of attacks on Israeli civilians and the opposition of Ben-Gurion made it difficult for Sharett to develop such possibilities.

At the beginning of the year, General Moshe Dayan negotiated with the Syrian Colonel Hassan Jaddid about the demilitarised zone between the two countries and water rights concerning the River Jordan.

In 1953, twenty-seven Israeli soldiers were killed. Two watchmen were abducted from Mevo Betar and killed. Two members of the IDF were killed near Tel Mond. Grenades were often thrown into civilian homes. In June, homes were attacked in Tirat Yehuda and Mishmar Ayalon. On 26 May, apartments in Beit Nabala, Deir Tarif and Beit 'Arif were attacked. While there were reprisal attacks by the Israelis, the killing of a mother and her young children in October in Yehud by a grenade provoked a planned assault on the village of Qibya a few days later.

One hundred and thirty troops, of whom a third were the elite Unit 101, commanded by Major Ariel Sharon, took part and forty-five houses were blown up, with fifty to sixty civilians killed in cellars and attics. Sharon reported that ten to twelve had been killed, whereas the Jordanians stated sixty-nine. The incident led to tremendous international criticism including by the Jewish Diaspora. Ben-Gurion's false assertion that no IDF troops were involved – although two-thirds of the Israelis present in Qibya were part of the paratroopers' 890th Battalion – widened the increasing gap between Ben-Gurion and Sharett. Indeed, when Ben-Gurion decided to resign at the end of the year, he suggested to the Mapai political committee that his successor should be Levi Eshkol and not Moshe Sharett.

Ben-Gurion's new government had included the General Zionists who favoured private enterprise and tighter economic control. Many price controls on basic foodstuffs, petrol and electricity were lifted. This led to rifts in the cabinet between Mapai ministers and their General Zionist colleagues. At the end of May, four General Zionist ministers resigned in the aftermath of the Doctors' Plot because of the raising of the red flag and the singing of the *Internationale* on 1 May in schools for those parents who desired it. A compromise was reached a few days later and the General Zionists returned to the government coalition.

In May, the legal adviser to the government was critical of Malkiel Gruenwald who had made defamatory accusations against Rudolf Kasztner, then spokesman for the Ministry of Commerce and Industry, regarding his conduct in Hungary during the war.

85

1954

The attack on a bus on the Beersheba–Eilat road took place at Ma'ale Akrabim (Scorpions' Pass) and eleven passengers were killed. The poisonous tail of the scorpion is dripping blood.

The pied piper is dressed in military uniform and wears a United Nations armband. This reflected public anger in Israel that the United Nations was less than effective in preventing infiltrators from entering Israel and demonstrated a reluctance to condemn such atrocities in the Security Council.

Arie Navon (*Davar* 26 March 1954)

26 Jan   Knesset approves fifteen-member Sharett cabinet 75–23

7 Feb   Defence Ministry relaxes freedom of movement restrictions in Galilee

14 Feb   Security guard killed at Moshav Marseya near Beit Shemesh

20 Feb   Egyptians kidnap Israeli bedouin at Nitzana

17 Mar   Eleven killed in bus attack at Ma'ale Akrabim, south of Beersheba

28 Mar   Nine killed in retaliatory attack led by Sharon on Nahalin

6 Apr   Remains of Baron Edmond de Rothschild brought to Israel

23 May   Romanian immigrants' hunger strike against show trials in Bucharest

26 May   Attack, led by Sharon, on West Bank village of Khirbet Jinba

28 May   Attack on West Bank village of Nazlot Isa

18 June   Attack on West Bank village of Zeita

27 June   Infiltrators from 'Azzan kill farmer at Ra'anana

29 June   Two policemen killed in Syrian attack in Galilee

2 July   Military intelligence activates Jewish network in Egypt

14 July   Bombs planted in US Information Centres in Cairo and Alexandria

23 July   Arrest of network members in Egypt

29 July   Seventeen killed when light aircraft crashes at Kibbutz Ma'agan air display

16 Aug   Capital punishment abolished by Knesset 61–33 except for Nazi crimes

22 Aug   Four MKs exit Mapam to form Ahdut Ha'Avoda Knesset faction

28 Aug   Guard killed at Moshav Ramat Raziel

1 Sept   890th Battalion launches retaliatory attack on Beit Liqya

4 Sept   Egyptians kill tractor driver near Kibbutz Ruhama

28 Sept   Merchant ship *Bat Galim* impounded by Egyptians in Suez Canal

19 Oct   UK and Egypt sign agreement on British withdrawal from Canal Zone

1 Nov   Left faction dissolves, Moshe Sneh joins Maki (Communist party)

3 Nov   Tel Aviv Savidor central railway station opens

14 Nov   Nasser succeeds Naguib as Egyptian president

17 Nov   Hebrew poet and editor Yitzhak Lamdan dies aged 55

6 Dec   First issue of Ahdut Ha'Avoda's *Lamerhav* daily newspaper

8 Dec   Five Israeli soldiers captured inside Syria

11 Dec   Trial of 11 Jews begins in Cairo

As Israel's second prime minister, Moshe Sharett had difficulty in forming a coalition, eventually taking fifty-one days. The Progressives refused to join any government until the threshold to gain a Knesset seat had been raised to 4.2 per cent. Such a threshold would have eliminated the smaller parties. Ben-Gurion, now living a spartan life in Sde Boqer in the Negev desert as an example to other Israelis, suggested a provocative 10 per cent threshold.

The General Zionists and the religious parties were at odds with each other. Mapam decided to remain outside the coalition because it suspected Sharett's pro-Western orientation. Even so, Sharett's coalition accounted for seventy-five MKs.

The differences between the General Zionists and the religious parties continued into government over the raising of pigs and the sale of pork in Israel. Chief Rabbi Unterman argued in January that the religious parties should refuse to join any government coalition until a ban had been passed by the Knesset. The towns of Netanya, Tiberias and Safed had independently already banned the sale of pork.

The left-wing party Mapam continued to disintegrate with the secession of Ahdut Ha'Avoda and the publication of *Lamerhav*. Moshe Sneh and Adolf Berman finally decided to join Maki (the Communist party).

Although there had been correspondence between Nasser and Sharett via unpublicised meetings of officials from both sides in Paris, the hope for a peaceful reconciliation began to diminish with remarkable effect. Earlier in the year, Nasser had formally displaced Neguib in Egypt. In Syria, the pro-Western Shishakli government was overthrown in a *coup d'état*.

Sharett and Levi Eshkol favoured cuts in military spending. This provoked a reaction from the minister of defence, Pinhas Lavon, and the IDF Chief of Staff, Moshe Dayan – who, together with Shimon Peres, now regularly met Ben-Gurion at Sde Boqer.

Ben-Gurion, however, was arguing that the Arab states were preparing for another round of conflict. He became increasingly critical of Sharett and his consideration of 'international sensitivities' to the extent of writing an article in *Davar*. Sharett's policy of self-restraint was in essence an attempt to reverse the negative publicity over the attack on Qibya by Ariel Sharon's force some months before. Sharett argued for a policy of not retaliating against Jordanian villages from where many infiltrators originated.

Infiltrators from both Jordan and Egyptian-controlled Gaza had become a growing concern with attacks on Israeli civilians. In March, an attack on an Egged bus travelling from Eilat to Tel Aviv killed eleven passengers in the Ma'ale Akrabim pass. This proved to be very much a breaking point in terms of the relations between Ben-Gurion and Sharett. The outrage in Israel, however, strengthened the hand of the *bithonistim*, the security lobby, who demanded a military retaliation in each case and a more aggressive approach. Sharett authorised a limited operation against the village of Nahalin. Ben-Gurion himself threatened to resign from Mapai. This further divided the party into antagonistic factions.

Unit 101 had merged into the 890th Battalion, an elite unit now utilised for retaliatory actions and led by Major Ariel Sharon. West Bank villages which were deemed responsible for sending forth infiltrators were attacked. This approach often ended in confrontation between Israeli and Jordanian official forces. In Gaza, Egyptian forces were sent into Israeli territory as well as supervising general infiltration. On the Syrian border, there were similar clashes.

Plans were formulated to permit the Druze minority to join the IDF while the Arabs of Israel were given greater freedom of movement.

The Lavon affair began in early July when a network of young Jews was activated in Egypt. Its task was to plant incendiary devices in the US Information Centres in Cairo and Alexandria to create the impression that the Egyptian regime was incapable of providing security and stability, and was generally inefficient. This campaign of sabotage was designed to undermine the negotiations between the UK and the Egyptians which had started in April with a view to withdrawing British forces from the Canal Zone area within twenty months. It was finally agreed that a number of bases would remain for a period of seven years and that if Egypt was attacked, then Britain would have the right to intervene.

On 23 July, one member of the network, Philip Natanson, was arrested by the police, tortured and forced to supply the names of other members who were promptly apprehended as well. Thirteen members were arrested, six of whom were directly connected to a unit which theoretically operated under the joint control of the Mossad and Israeli military intelligence. The Israeli operative Avraham Dar, aka John Darling, had established the network a few years previously. Both Dar and Avri Elad, an Israeli agent who had been turned by Egyptian intelligence, were able to escape while two others, Yosef Carmon and the Israeli intelligence agent Max Binett, committed suicide.

The 'Mishap' or 'esek bish' proved catastrophic for the ruling elite of Mapai. Controversy broke out over the question of who exactly had initiated Operation Suzannah. Sharett himself knew nothing about the operation or indeed the network. Was it Pinhas Lavon, the minister of defence, or Binyamin Gibli, the head of military intelligence? Both had their supporters. Sharett only learned about the affair when it was over. He instinctively blamed Lavon, who, it was said, was planning similar operations in other Arab capitals. Sharett had been kept in the dark by Lavon, Dayan and Gibli. Ben-Gurion regretted making Lavon minister of defence. In contrast, Moshe Dayan, the head of the IDF, opposed Sharett because he wanted a more aggressive military approach against Arab infiltrators. Shimon Peres, director-general of the Defence Ministry, manoeuvred to prevent himself becoming the scapegoat for the affair. The trial began in December. Both Sharett and Ben-Gurion believed that Pinhas Lavon bore responsibility for the affair.

Prime Minister Sharett was worried that any public fallout and any open political division would affect Mapai's chances in the 1955 election. He therefore deliberated on dismissing Lavon and instead instructed Supreme Court Justice Yitzhak Olshan and the former IDF Chief of Staff, Yaakov Dori, to lead a public committee of inquiry. This was in addition to private investigations by both Mapai and the intelligence services. The British Labour Member of Parliament Maurice Orbach went to Cairo several times at the end of the year to carry messages between the Israelis and the Egyptians.

Since there had been positive contacts between the Israelis and the Egyptians, Sharett agreed to test Nasser's resolve and goodwill regarding the blockading of Israeli vessels and Israel-bound ones in the Suez Canal. At the end of August, the UN Security Council argued for the free passage of shipping through the Suez Canal, but a few weeks later, the *Bat Galim*, which had sailed from Eritrea, was impounded by the Egyptians at Port Tewfik. Its ten crew members were arrested, interrogated and accused of killing two fishermen. They were released in December.

This was augmented by the Soviet Union's turn towards supporting the Arab states as part of its approach to cultivating the developing world in an era when decolonisation appeared to be on the horizon. The French had been defeated by the Viet Minh at Dien Bien Phu. At the United Nations, the Soviet Union stopped a draft resolution by New Zealand from going forward – this endorsed Israel's freedom of navigation through the Suez Canal.

89

1955

Ben-Gurion's Mapai emerged as the largest party in the 1955 election. Here (on the right) the ordinary worker is being vigorously canvassed for his vote. Each party leader approaches the somewhat bewildered worker carrying the Hebrew letter of the party in the election. Ben-Gurion's Mapai, Begin's Herut, Meir Ya'ari's Mapam and others all rush towards the worker, who somehow manages to avoid the ensuing mêlée among the feuding parties.

Despite attempts to ban the Communist party, the worker casts his vote (on the left) for the party, indicated by the Hebrew letter kuf. The Communists won six seats in the election.

The caption read: 'From Metulla to the Red Sea, every worker votes "kuf".'

Dani Levkovitz (*Kol Ha'am* 22 July 1955)

2 Jan Two hikers killed in the Judaean desert

12 Jan Olshan and Dori report to Sharett the findings of investigation of the Lavon affair

18 Jan Two immigrants killed at Moshav Agur

24 Jan Two tractor drivers killed near Kibbutz 'Ein Shlosha

31 Jan Moshe Marzouk and Shmuel Azar executed in Egypt

21 Feb Defence minister Pinhas Lavon resigns, succeeded by Ben-Gurion

28 Feb Operation Black Arrow commences with attack on Gaza

4 Mar Meir Har-Zion conducts revenge killing of innocent bedouin

24 Mar Grenades thrown at wedding party kill one woman and injure ten

29 Mar USSR and USA censure Israel at UN Security Council

3 Apr Ben-Gurion defeated in cabinet vote to invade Gaza

18 Apr Israel prevented from attending Bandung Conference of the non-aligned

30 May Shelling of kibbutzim Nirim, Kissufim and 'Ein Shlosha

22 June Trial verdict implies Rudolf Kasztner served Nazis

19 July Yarkon–Negev pipeline inaugurated at Rosh Ha'Ayin

20 July Mapai largest party in election; General Zionists lose ground to Herut

23 July Bomb thrown into home of Israel Rokach, Tel Aviv mayoral candidate

27 July Bulgarian MiG jets shoot down El Al flight 402 with loss of 51 passengers

7 Aug Bar-Ilan University founded

22 Aug Border clash with Egyptians in Mefalsim area

29 Aug Four farmers killed near Moshav Beit Oved

31 Aug Operation Elkayam opens with attack on Khan Yunis police

1 Sept Two Egyptian jets shot down over Yad Mordechai

11 Sept IDF attack on Khirbet al-Rahwa police station

12 Sept Straits of Tiran blockade tightened

19 Sept Town of Dimona founded

20 Sept IDF occupies Nitzana (al Auja) in DMZ

22 Sept Two Israelis killed in attack on Safed–Haifa bus

27 Sept Nasser announces Czech–Egyptian arms deal

4 Oct Tractor driver killed neat Moshav Gilat

25 Oct France approves sale of Mystère 4 fighters to Israel

28 Oct Operation Egged attack on Kuntilla results in 12 Egyptians killed

2 Nov Operation Volcano attacks Egyptian bases at al Sabha and Wadi Siram

2 Nov Ben-Gurion presents new government for Knesset approval

10 Dec Syrian forces open fire on Israeli fishing boats

11 Dec Operation Olive Leaves attack on Syrian bases at Sea of Galilee

Despite clandestine Israeli approaches as well as public international ones to Nasser, two defendants in the trial of young Egyptian Jews for sabotage in the 'Mishap' affair were sentenced to death. At the end of January, Moshe Marzouk and Shmuel Azar were executed. Although this was often explained by arguing that Nasser was unable to withstand the internal political pressure – even though the efforts at sabotage were amateurish and caused no deaths – there was public outrage in Israel. It initiated a deterioration between the two sides which further sharpened the division in the cabinet between those who worked for diplomatic solutions and military restraint and those who believed in a more aggressive approach and retaliation.

The inquiry into the Lavon affair by Olshan and Dori was inconsequential in that it could not be established who had given the order to activate the network to carry out sabotage – Lavon or Gibli. The deaths of Marzouk and Azar did lead to the resignation of Pinhas Lavon who, as minister of defence, assumed overall responsibility. Even the resignation was a prolonged affair, with Eshkol and Aranne opposing it and Sharett and Golda Meir demanding it – all while Lavon continued to protest his innocence. This deepening division within Mapai led to Ben-Gurion's return to government as minister of defence and his espousal of a policy of retaliation and reprisal against Arab attacks on Israeli civilians. In 1955, forty-eight Israelis were killed, whereas only seven had been killed the year before.

The increase in skirmishes weakened Sharett's ability to seek diplomatic solutions and to curtail reprisal raids, led by Ariel Sharon. It simultaneously strengthened Ben-Gurion's approach and allowed the Chief of Staff, Moshe Dayan, to plan military action, whereas only a few months before he had submitted his resignation.

At the end of February, Operation Black Arrow took place in which an assault on Gaza resulted in the killing of thirty-eight Egyptians. This led to widespread condemnation internationally. The British withheld the delivery of Centurion tanks, while the USA and USSR censured Israel at the UN Security Council. This further diminished the ability of Israeli diplomats to explain their government's approach.

After an attack on a wedding party at Patish at the end of March, Ben-Gurion proposed the conquest of Gaza to the cabinet. Sharett and his allies opposed Ben-Gurion, who lost the vote 9–4 with two abstentions. Further attacks on Israeli citizens – hikers, tractor drivers, farmers, fishermen – eroded Sharett's support in cabinet.

At the beginning of March, Meir Har-Zion, a key member of the 890th Battalion and friend of Ariel Sharon, took three paratroopers with him into the West Bank, and killed five innocent bedouin in revenge for the murder of his sister on a hiking trip a few weeks before. Sharon had provided them with food and driven them to the border. The incident provoked widespread debate in Israel. Har-Zion refused to cooperate with the police and was not placed on trial. Within a short time, he had returned to army duty. Sharett condemned what had happened, but it symbolised the deepening rift with Ben-Gurion.

Sharett's coalition began to dissolve before the election. Judge Halevi's ruling in the trial of Malkiel Gruenwald after a nine-month recess, that Rudolf Kasztner had indeed served the purposes of the Nazis in Hungary and bore responsibility for the killing of Jews from Cluj, was greeted with much criticism. Halevi asserted that Kasztner, a Mapai activist, had sold his soul to the devil. The outcome of the Kasztner trial subsequently became a political weapon in the hands of political opponents on the Right on the eve of the election. The General Zionists refused to support the government in a vote of confidence, while the Communists pointed to a 'Nazi–Zionist' collaboration. Sharett resigned so as to form a temporary government coalition without the General Zionists.

The election results for the third Knesset indicated a loss of approximately a third of the seats of the General Zionists to Menahem Begin's Herut. Mapai lost five seats mainly due to the secession of Ahdut Ha'Avoda from Mapam and its resurrection as an independent party. Ben-Gurion resumed his leadership as prime minister and Sharett reverted to his long-held position as foreign minister.

At the end of August, the IDF mounted an assault on Khan Yunis in Gaza. This followed several attacks on Israeli citizens in Yad Mordechai, the Ashkelon area, Rishon l'Zion and Rehovot. Sharett agreed to Operation Elkayam which resulted in further Egyptian casualties. Two Egyptian aircraft were shot down.

A few weeks later, in September, Nasser announced a multimillion-dollar arms deal, ostensibly with Czechoslovakia. It included T-34 tanks, MiG-15 fighters and Ilyushin Il-28 bombers. This fortified Ben-Gurion's view that another war was on the horizon. Sharett had hoped that Israel would remain above the Cold War, especially after the demise of Stalin.

The arms deal was the culmination of Egypt's striving to maintain a non-aligned status, but also to play one superpower off against the other. Nasser's goal was to build up Egypt's armed forces and to aid anti-colonial movements such as the FLN in Algeria. He therefore strongly opposed the Baghdad Pact between Iraq, Iran, Turkey and Pakistan which supported the Cold War status quo and the containment of the USSR in the region. He also encouraged the infiltration campaign of the fedayeen into Israel and the attempt to oust King Hussein in Jordan.

In the post-Stalinist era, Khrushchev and Bulganin had embarked on a policy of embracing the emerging states of the developing world. The barring of Israel from attending the conference of the non-aligned in Bandung because of Egyptian and Arab opposition increased Israel's isolation internationally. Despite Nehru's best efforts, the choice was starkly between Israel and the many Arab states – which signalled their refusal to attend if Israel was invited. Sharett's frosty meeting with the Soviet foreign minister, Molotov, in Geneva at the end of October was another sign of the USSR's embrace of the developing world. A few weeks later, Khrushchev publicly commented that ever since the beginning of its existence, Israel had threatened its neighbours.

The arms deal therefore cancelled out Israel's power of deterrence and made a war far more likely. The nightmare of Soviet heavy bombers attacking Israeli cities became a reality. At the end of October, Ben-Gurion instructed Dayan to make preparations to capture the Straits of Tiran. The Israeli approach was to prevent the build-up of Soviet arms and the acquisition of know-how before a critical point had been reached.

The British too were concerned since they worried that the Suez Canal would fall into Soviet hands and thereby threaten a stranglehold on a lifeline of trade.

The USA simply wanted to limit Soviet influence and believed that an Israeli–Arab rapprochement would calm the situation in the Middle East. Both Project Alpha about sharing the waters of the Jordan and Project Gamma about a solution to the Palestinian Arab refugee question came to nothing. In addition, the Americans were reticent about supplying arms to Israel in violation of the Tripartite Agreement of 1950. This limited arms sales to both Israel and the Arab states.

Israel embarked on a process of gradual escalation of retaliatory attacks in order to provoke the Egyptian military. Operation Yarkon took place against the Egyptians in June, and at the end of the year, Israel launched Operation Olive Leaves against Syria following its mutual defence pact with Egypt.

1956

Nasser's blockade of the Straits of Tiran to Israeli shipping was a major factor in the outbreak of war in the Suez campaign.

Israel's capture of the islands of Tiran and Sanafir allowed Israeli shipping to continue to trade with the outside world. The lifting of the symbolic barrier between the two islands permits vessels to sail through the Gulf of Aqaba to the port of Eilat.

Shmuel Katz (*al Hamishmar* 7 January 1957)

23 Jan UN's Dag Hammarskjöld makes first visit to Israel

1 Mar French foreign minister, Christian Pineau, lifts arms embargo

1 Mar King Hussein dismisses Glubb Pasha and other foreign officers

29 Mar Captured Golani Brigade soldiers swapped for Syrian prisoners

5 Apr Gaza shelling kills 58 civilians and injures 100

11 Apr Instructor and three students killed in attack on Shafir synagogue

12 Apr Four Egyptian jets enter Israeli airspace

23 Apr Peres signs arms deal with French

23 Apr Four water company workers killed on Beersheba–Eilat road

29 Apr Ro'i Rottenberg from Nahal Oz killed

30 Apr Eisenhower states that USA will not sell arms to Israel

1 May Eshkol approves founding of city of Ashdod

8 May Austria and Israel establish diplomatic relations

12 May Mordechai Oren released by Czechs and flies to Zurich en route to Israel

6 June Three research institutes agree to form Tel Aviv University

10 June Hapoel Hamizrahi and Mizrahi unite to form the National Religious party (NRP)

18 June Sharett announces his resignation in cabinet

23 June Egyptians (99.9 per cent) elect Nasser as president in referendum

11 July Mustafa Hafez, Egyptian director of fedayeen operations, killed in Gaza

25 July French arms begin to arrive in Israel

26 July Egypt nationalises Suez Canal

16 Aug Four killed in attack on Eilat bus

12 Sept Three Druze guards killed by fedayeen at Ein Ofarim

23 Sept Attack on archaeology gathering at Ramat Rachel kills four

25 Sept Operation Lulav reprisal raid on village of Husan

10 Oct Military attack on Qalkilya kills 18 Israelis, injures 68

22 Oct British, French and Israelis meet clandestinely at Sèvres

25 Oct Egyptians, Syrians and Jordanians unify military forces

29 Oct Border police kill 48 civilians at Kafr Qasim

29 Oct Operation Kadesh, the Suez war, begins in the south and in Sinai

2 Nov IDF breaks through Egyptian lines to capture Gaza

4 Nov Expulsion and arrests of Egyptian Jews initiated by Nasser's government

5 Nov Egyptian forces at Sharm el-Sheikh surrender to IDF

6 Nov British prime minister, Anthony Eden, announces ceasefire

12 Nov Dozens of civilians killed during screening operation in Gaza

21 Dec British and French military forces leave Egypt

24 Dec Israeli forces begin withdrawal from Sinai

95

Although there had been no fatalities during the first three months of the year, the broad instability on Israel's borders caused the first major clash with the Egyptians in April. Israeli troops came under fire when the IDF attempted to return a flock of sheep that had wandered across the Gaza border. The IDF responded with attacks on Deir al-Balah and Bani Suheila which in turn were followed by Egyptian attacks on kibbutzim near the Gaza border. The IDF then began to shell central Gaza, which resulted in the killing of fifty-eight civilians and a hundred injured. This initiated a five-day offensive by fedayeen infiltrators who attacked Ashkelon and nearby kibbutzim. They were able to reach Rehovot and instigate grenade attacks on civilian homes and attacks on bus and train passengers, water company workers and synagogue worshippers. A bus carrying teachers and pupils was attacked at Moshav Shafir.

Ben-Gurion prepared for war and several brigades were mobilised. Sharett voted against this in cabinet, but Ben-Gurion was given the go-ahead to launch retaliatory strikes if necessary. Cairo stopped the raids into Israel.

In mid-April, a UN-sponsored ceasefire came into play. However, the reaction to the killing of Ro'i Rothenberg, the head of security at Kibbutz Nahal Oz, at the end of April, personified the mindset of Ben-Gurion, Dayan and Peres at this juncture. At Rothenberg's funeral, Dayan's fatalistic speech symbolised the situation that Israelis now faced: 'Let us not drop our gaze lest our arms be weakened. That is the fate of our generation – to be ready and armed, tough and harsh.'

A couple of months later, the Egyptian colonel Mustafa Hafez, who controlled the fedayeen infiltration from Gaza, was killed by a book bomb. Three days later, Lieutenant Colonel Mahmud Salah ad Din Mustafa, a military attaché at the Egyptian Embassy in Amman, similarly received a book, the biography of Field Marshal von Rundstedt, one of Hitler's most loyal commanders – and was killed when it was opened.

The French, however, had lifted their arms embargo and began to deliver war materiel to the Israelis, following negotiations with Peres. This was followed by further agreements at Chantilly and at Paris St Germain. The Eisenhower administration and Whitehall continued to withhold any arms sales to Israel. Both the USA and the UK strongly wanted to maintain a presence in the Middle East and to contain Soviet influence.

There was growing military cooperation between the Egyptians, the Jordanians and the Syrians. The young King Hussein had dismissed 'Glubb Pasha' (his British military adviser, Sir John Glubb) and other British military personnel and appointed Jordanians in their place. In September, raids from Jordanian territory increased tremendously. Nasser began to promote even more vigorously the cause of Arab nationalism in the Middle East. All this was augmented by attacks on Israeli locations and IDF reprisals.

In September, five hundred Israeli officials and archaeologists who had gathered at Kibbutz Ramat Rachel were attacked by an Arab Legion gunner, with four archaeologists killed and sixteen injured. A girl was killed at Moshav Aminadav and so was a tractor driver near Kibbutz Ma'oz Haim in the Beit Shean Valley. Operations Gulliver, Yonatan and Lulav were launched by the IDF in September, followed by Operation Shomron in October.

Ben-Gurion's desire to pre-empt any Egyptian attack brought him into conflict with his predecessor and current foreign minister, Moshe Sharett. The execution of two of the participants in the Lavon affair the previous year was seen as a turning-point in Sharett's fortunes. Indeed Sharett had originally agreed that Yigael Yadin would pay a secret visit to Cairo to initiate a dialogue. The Czech arms deal had further reduced Sharett's ability to block Ben-Gurion's policies in cabinet. On becoming prime minister once again, Ben-Gurion wanted to replace Sharett with Golda Meir as foreign minister in order to follow a policy defined by the inevitability of war.

Ben-Gurion proposed that Sharett should become Mapai secretary-general and threatened to resign if this did not happen. Sharett resisted for several months and finally resigned in June.

Despite UN Secretary-General Dag Hammarskjöld's efforts to find a compromise, the slide to war began properly in July with the American refusal to fund the building of the Aswan Dam and Nasser's formal nationalisation of the Suez Canal.

The clandestine meeting of the British, French and Israelis at Sèvres in late October led to a military collusion by the three powers to remove Nasser's threat to impede traffic in the Suez Canal. The deception called for Israel to advance into Sinai towards the Canal in Operation Kadesh. Israel and Egypt would then be asked to withdraw to a distance of ten miles from the Canal area. Israel would comply, but Egypt would not relinquish its control since this was the raison d'être for nationalising the Canal in the first place.

Britain and France would subsequently intervene at a later stage to eliminate the Egyptian presence from the Canal area in Operation Musketeer. The central aim was therefore to restore foreign dominance of the Canal, but also for Israel to ensure its right to use an international waterway by wresting control over the Straits of Tiran. Ben-Gurion also voiced ideas about rearranging the Middle East, such as extending Israeli control up to the Litani River in Lebanon and creating a Christian Maronite state.

Haifa was shelled by Egyptian warships while Israeli fighter aircraft were effective in combating the Soviet-supplied MiGs of the Egyptians. Israeli forces raced through Sinai to secure Sharm el-Sheikh and thereby end the Egyptian refusal to allow Israeli and often Israel-bound vessels to utilise the Straits of Tiran.

The IDF also invaded Egyptian-controlled Gaza to ensure that fedayeen infiltration came to an end. Many fled to the West Bank where Jordanian soldiers disarmed them. Within a couple of days, Israel had captured Gaza. Even so, the Israeli offensive had provoked fedayeen attacks near Kibbutzim Erez and Brur Hayil, as well as on Givat Brenner and Moshav T'lamim. The IDF killed large numbers of civilians as well as fedayeen in refugee camps. On the Lebanese border, there were attacks on Kibbutz Ma'ayan Baruch and on the Syrian border near Moshav Mishmar HaYarden. Fedayeen targeted water pipelines near Sha'ar HaGai in the Jerusalem Corridor.

On the same day that the Suez campaign opened, Israeli border police killed forty-seven Arabs including women and children on the outskirts of Kafr Qasim. Apparently the villagers knew little of a new curfew order and were shot down when they returned from the fields. Israeli intellectuals and members of the Communist party publicised the incident. Eleven members of the border police and its commander were sentenced to prison terms.

Although Israel had been militarily successful, both superpowers opposed the Suez war. Britain and France soon realised that they were no longer the epitome of imperial might and under American pressure were forced to evacuate Egypt. Bulganin sent Ben-Gurion a very bellicose letter which accused the state of 'sowing hatred amongst the Eastern peoples' and placed a question mark over Israel's very existence as a state. Eisenhower, on the other hand, demanded that Israel withdraw to the armistice line.

While Ben-Gurion prevaricated about Israeli departure from Sinai and Gaza, he bowed to the inevitable and slowly began to withdraw. His stand was strongly opposed by his political opponents, especially Menahem Begin and his Herut party.

97

1957

Rudolf Kasztner was shot by former members of Lehi for his alleged collaboration with the Nazis in wartime Hungary in order to secure the release of 1,600 Jews on a train to Switzerland. Kasztner died from his injuries several days later.

The revolver that killed Kasztner is the same shape as the Hebrew letter 'daled', followed by the letters 'yod' and 'final nun', producing the word for 'judgement'.

The caption read: 'A judgement like this in Israel?'

Arieh Navon (*Davar* 6 March 1957)

5 Jan   Eisenhower Doctrine on Middle East sent to US Congress

6 Jan   Tel Aviv stops pork consumption

15 Jan   Court martial of border police involved in Kfar Qasim killings

15 Jan   Herut vote of no confidence defeated 63–11, with 8 abstentions

22 Jan   Israel completes withdrawal from most of Sinai

9 Feb   Demonstration in Tel Aviv against US demands for total withdrawal

1 Mar   Israel agrees to leave Gaza and Sharm el-Sheikh

4 Mar   Rudolf Kasztner shot in Tel Aviv by Ze'ev Eckstein

5 Mar   Home of Gaza mayor, Rashid el Shawa, bombed; he leaves for Israel

7 Mar   Israel withdraws from Gaza

15 Mar   Rudolf Kasztner dies of his injuries

17 Mar   English abolished as one of three official languages

18 Mar   Four hikers en route to Petra killed by bedouin

16 Apr   Two guards killed at Kibbutz Mesilot

24 Apr   Egypt reopens Suez Canal

10 May   Strike at ATA textile factory

20 May   Vehicles travelling along Eilat–Beersheba road attacked

4 June   Knesset supports Ben-Gurion's endorsement of Eisenhower Doctrine

24 June   One killed when Syrians attack Kibbutz Gadot

9 July   Seven border guards injured in Syrian attack on Kibbutz Beit Guvrin

22 July   Egyptians arrest Israeli journalist on board Danish vessel

6 Aug   One killed in Syrian attack on Kibbutz Tel Katzir

8 Aug   Five prisoners escape from Tel Mond prison

12 Aug   Ben-Gurion government to protest openly about Soviet anti-Semitism

18 Aug   ATA strike ends after 14 weeks

17 Sept   Unexploded shell kills 15 children in the village of Sandala

17 Sept   Peres agreement with French for nuclear reactor at Rishon l'Zion

24 Sept   Egyptians apprehend fishing trawler *Doron* and its crew

1 Oct   Mann Auditorium opens in Tel Aviv

3 Oct   French–Israeli agreement for construction of Dimona nuclear reactor

28 Oct   Yitzhak Ben-Zvi re-elected president after Yosef Yoel Rivlin withdraws

29 Oct   Psychiatric patient throws grenade into Knesset, injuring ministers

3 Nov   Institute of Negev Research formally opens in Beersheba

24 Nov   One killed in Syrian attack on Kibbutz She'ar Yashuv

10 Dec   Knesset passes financial compensation bill for injured border settlers

31 Dec   Ben-Gurion resigns over disclosure of Dayan's Germany visit in *Lamerhav*

In the aftermath of the Suez war, Israel finally agreed to leave Egyptian territory. During the conflict 172 soldiers had been killed and 817 injured. One hundred tanks and large amounts of ammunition had been taken from the Egyptian forces. Ben-Gurion's government held out against the UN and the USA on a complete withdrawal until its freedom of navigation had been guaranteed in the region. It originally wished to maintain a presence in Sharm el-Sheikh to ensure free passage through the Straits of Tiran at the mouth of the Gulf of Aqaba.

The Suez Canal was closed until March. Nasser remained in control of it and in the Arab world was seen as the victor.

Despite Ben-Gurion's original claim that Israel had won a great victory, he was unable to resist international pressure for a complete withdrawal. Mass demonstrations in Israel, supported by all the major parties, proved to be of no avail. Ben-Gurion proposed alternative solutions such as a treaty, guaranteeing free passage, to be agreed by Israel, Egypt, Jordan and Saudi Arabia. In the end, Israel accepted US guarantees to ensure the freedom of navigation of its vessels in the Gulf of Aqaba.

In mid-January, Herut proposed a vote of no confidence in the government for its compliance with the UN resolution to leave Egyptian territory. Menahem Begin argued that stationing UN forces on the two islands in the Straits of Tiran would be insufficient to secure freedom of passage in the Gulf of Aqaba. Begin was supported by only ten other MKs – sixty-three opposed and there were eight abstentions.

The immediate post-Suez period did indicate Nasser's acceptance of the right of passage through the Straits of Tiran without Egyptian intervention, thereby confirming that Operation Kadesh had achieved this central objective. Yet there were exceptions. *The Doron*, a fishing trawler, was seized by the Egyptians in September and its crew held for several months before release. Ben-Gurion, however, had been forced to withdraw the IDF from two strategic locations, Sharm el-Sheikh and Gaza.

In Gaza, Israel had created a network of councils, but there was undoubtedly opposition to any permanent Israeli presence. This emanated mainly from Islamist groups despite Nasser's banning of the Muslim Brotherhood in Gaza. The cooperation of the mayor of Gaza was frowned upon such that his home was bombed. He and his family fled and were allowed to enter Israel. Israelis who lived in border settlements close to Gaza were particularly angry at the outcome of Operation Kadesh and the Israeli withdrawal since they had expected a greater level of security and this had not materialised.

In the aftermath of the Doctors' Plot and Stalin's demise in 1953, any hope for an improvement of relations with the USSR disappeared because of the Suez crisis. There was a constant fear in the White House that the Soviets would intervene in support of the Egyptians – and this would be the precursor to World War III. The periodic criticism of Israel was also a factor in the Kremlin's support for decolonisation, the end of empire and the consequential expansion of Soviet influence in the developing world. It was also a distraction from the Soviet invasion of Imre Nagy's Hungary and the suppression of the Hungarian Revolution. It also allowed Khrushchev to emerge as the major Soviet leader, winning a power struggle with his rivals.

Britain and France were forced to withdraw under pressure from both superpowers. Bulganin had threatened the use of Soviet missiles. The implicit threat of British financial collapse resulting from the American action and the Saudi-initiated oil boycott led to Prime Minister Eden's resignation at the beginning of January. Soviet threats to fire missiles at Israel profoundly contrasted with its stand in 1947 and 1948. The Kremlin's hostile reaction to Israel's participation in the Anglo-French collusion resulted in the recall of the Soviet ambassador to Israel from Tel Aviv and the suspension of oil supplies to Israel. It also placed the final nail in the coffin of non-alignment which had been articulated by Moshe Sharett during the previous decade. In June, the USSR delivered three submarines to Egypt. In October, Ben-Gurion had expressed concern about the supply of Soviet arms to Syria. With the humiliation of Britain and France during the Suez campaign, Ben-Gurion formally declared in November that he would not endorse any policy which embraced neutrality. Moreover, he wished to ensure the flow of American arms and political support in any future conflict.

Nasser further utilised the Suez crisis to impose an authoritarian regime on Egypt, leading to mass arrests, state censorship and the suspension of civil rights. Egyptian Jews were subject to arrest and detention, the sequestration of their businesses and property and the stripping of their Egyptian nationality. In late 1956, hundreds of Jews were incarcerated in Jewish schools in Cairo and Heliopolis. Assets were confiscated and professionals barred from employment as lawyers, teachers and doctors. Between the end of November 1956 and the end of June 1957, 20,200 were forced to leave Egypt.

The Hungarian Revolution and the Polish Uprising in 1956 had catalysed mass defections from Communist parties worldwide and Israel was no exception. However, the Eisenhower Doctrine in early January caused great consternation on the Israeli Left.

In a message to Congress in early January, Eisenhower had argued that any country in the Middle East could request US economic and military aid if it was threatened by armed aggression. This was directed against the spread of Soviet influence in the region and 'international Communism' generally. Any acceptance was opposed by members of Mapam and Ahdut Ha'Avoda who were part of Ben-Gurion's coalition. They still wanted a policy of non-alignment and feared becoming too close to the Americans. All this led to a cabinet crisis and the potential fall of the government. At the beginning of June, after a long correspondence between Tel Aviv and Washington, the Eisenhower Doctrine was endorsed in a Knesset vote. While the Communists voted against, it was the large number of abstentions that attracted attention. The thirty-nine abstentions included the MKs from Mapam and Ahdut Ha'Avoda, but also from Herut and the General Zionists. It was a development which united both nationalists and internationalists. The abstentions from the Left averted a government collapse.

The Czech–Egyptian arms deal, the Suez crisis, the hostility from Arab nationalists and threats from the Soviet bloc all pushed Ben-Gurion to accelerate and develop Israel's nuclear programme for both peaceful and non-peaceful purposes, both overtly and covertly. At the secret Sèvres meeting in October 1956 which resulted in the Suez campaign, Shimon Peres secured French agreement to construct a nuclear reactor at Dimona and the supply of uranium to it. In October 1957, Peres signed both technical and political agreements to proceed with the Dimona project.

The saga of the Kasztner affair came to a sorry conclusion when Ze'ev Eckstein along with Lehi veterans shot Kasztner outside his home in Tel Aviv. Eckstein was said to be originally a plant of the Shin Bet (Israel's internal intelligence agency) in Israel Eldad's Sulam group. Kasztner survived for another ten days and then died of his wounds. The Shin Bet had withdrawn the bodyguard that it had provided for Kasztner shortly before. For many years afterwards, questions remained about Kasztner's killing.

101

1958

The question 'Who is a Jew?' divided secular Israelis from religious ones. The former believed that a public embrace of belonging to the Jewish nation was sufficient, whereas the latter believed that Jewish status could only be transmitted through being born of a Jewish mother.

The government crisis over the issuing of identity cards brought this question to a head. Ben-Gurion is seen as preserving his coalition by placing the question of 'Who is a Jew?' into the cold freezer.

Friedel Stern

2 Jan	Natan Alterman wins the Bialik Prize for *City of the Dove*
7 Jan	Three men convicted of the murder of Rudolf Kasztner
7 Jan	Ben-Gurion presents new government to the Knesset
27 Jan	Fishermen from the trawler *Doron* released by Egyptians
1 Feb	Egypt and Syria agree on the formation of the United Arab Republic
4 Feb	Leaks on French willingness to supply uranium to Israel
12 Feb	Knesset passes Basic Law defining the role and function of the Knesset
14 Feb	Iraqi–Jordanian federation formed by its Hashemite monarchies
23 Mar	Twelve thousand Hebrew manuscripts received from Moscow's Central Lenin Library
23 Apr	Israel celebrates the tenth anniversary of its establishment
24 Apr	Five thousand soldiers participate in a military parade at Givat Ram, Jerusalem
15 May	Cost of living index at 272 compared with 100 for September 1951
26 May	Jordanian attack on Mount Scopus kills four Israeli policemen and a UN observer
25 June	NRP ministers resign in dispute over the 'Who is a Jew?' issue
14 July	Iraqi monarchy overthrown in military coup, led by Abd al-Karim Qasim
15 July	US marines land in Lebanon and British paratroopers go to Jordan
31 July	Violence in Shateh prison results in 11 inmates and 2 guards dead
3 Aug	Haredi protest at opening of mixed swimming pool in Jerusalem
3 Aug	Cabinet refuses to request the transfer of Jabotinsky's remains from USA
4 Aug	Amos Hakham of Jerusalem wins first National Bible Contest
13 Aug	Nazzer Naashif first Arab to be appointed as District Officer of Nazareth
9 Oct	Britain sells Israel its first submarine, HMS *Springer*
15 Oct	Habima, Israel's national theatre, to be subsidised by the state
16 Oct	Eight border police members sentenced for Kfar Qasim massacre
17 Nov	Syrian militants kill the wife of the British air attaché
23 Nov	Moses Hess, founding father of Zionism, to be reinterred in Israel
3 Dec	Prolonged Syrian shelling of Jewish settlements in the Galil
10 Dec	West Germany pays Israel half of the reparations agreed in 1952
20 Dec	Israeli Mystère shoots down an Egyptian MiG-17 over Israeli territory
31 Dec	Dag Hammarskjöld arrives in Israel and meets Ben-Gurion for talks

The tenth anniversary of the founding of the state of Israel was commemorated, according to the Hebrew calendar, at the end of April.

With the exodus of Palestinian Arabs in 1948 – flight from the war and selective expulsion – the demographic balance changed dramatically. In 1948, the new state of Israel possessed 806,000 inhabitants. By 1958, the total population was approaching 2 million – some 1.8 million Jews and 200,000 Arabs, including some 47,000 Christian Arabs. The Druze community which served in the Israel Defence Forces and in the police numbered 31,000.

While the attendance of Arab children at school had increased from 48 to 71 per cent, only five Arabs and Druze were among the 428 graduates from the Hebrew University. This included the first Arab woman, Huda Nashif, to receive a degree in Israel.

There was an influx of Jews from Poland – 'the Gomulka *aliya*' – and Romania in the post-Stalinist thaw. Polish Jews who had fled to the USSR before 1939 were now allowed to return to Poland and from there they were permitted to emigrate to Israel.

The anniversary was also marked by the opening of new totemic buildings in Jerusalem which symbolised the onward progress and permanence of the state of the Jews: the development of Binyamei Ha'Uma, the completion of the Givat Ram campus of the Hebrew University, the building of Hechal Shlomo, the seat of the Chief Rabbinate, the laying of the cornerstone of the new Knesset building.

Ben-Gurion in his independence day message stated that Jews from seventy-nine countries had emigrated to Israel and described it as a melting pot for the Diaspora: 'Tribes of various tongues, separated by time and space, distant by hundreds of years and thousands of miles, are mixed together in Israel into one nation that once again speaks Hebrew.'

The decade had also produced a *yerida* – a departure from Israel: 63,000 Jews had left Israel legally while several thousand tourists had not returned.

Recent immigrants, representing different Diaspora communities, were invited to light symbolic beacons on the tenth anniversary while members of the diplomatic corps attended a reception by the president, Yitzhak Ben-Zvi. Fifteen members of a West German parliamentary delegation were deliberately not invited by Ben-Zvi, but instead met Prime Minister Ben-Gurion separately – a reminder of the sensitivity in dealings with Germans in the post-Nazi era.

Five thousand soldiers participated in a parade in Jerusalem which demonstrated Israel's military prowess while 250,000 spectators watched. Many heads of foreign missions attended in their private capacity – for fear that their attendance might be construed as recognition of Jerusalem as Israel's capital while one half of the city was in Jordanian hands. In the Old City of Jerusalem, tanks and heavy equipment were on display to signal Jordan's intention to resist any alteration of the status quo. A month later, UN observer Lieutenant Colonel George A. Flint, chairman of the Israel–Jordan Mixed Armistice Commission, and four Israeli policemen were killed during a clash on Mount Scopus in Jerusalem.

There were several interchanges between Syrian and Israeli military forces as a reaction to Syrian shelling of Israeli settlements from the Golan Heights. The political union between Egypt, Syria and, a few weeks later, Yemen to create the United Arab Republic (UAR) was viewed in Israel as Nasser's first step in forging a hostile pan-Arab unitary state. There were also fears that Nasser would proclaim Gaza, then under Egyptian control, as an independent Palestinian state which would also join the UAR. The Marxist party Ahdut Ha'Avoda asked the Israeli government to review its security situation if Lebanon was also integrated into the UAR. The pro-Western Hashemite regimes in Iraq and Jordan responded within a few days by forming a federation. Israel was concerned about both Soviet military support for the UAR and the possibility that Iraqi troops could now gain access to the Jordanian–Israeli border.

The overthrow of the Iraqi monarchy and the killing of its king, the royal family and prime minister put an end to the short-lived federation with Jordan. The military coup of Abd al-Karim Qasim was based on the Egyptian model of the Free Officers' Revolt of 1952. It was staged on the pretence of Iraqi military units moving to Jordan to fortify the Hashemite federation. This encouraged Sunni Muslims in Lebanon to demand that their country should also join the UAR.

This pan-Arab development was perceived as a threat to Western interests in the region and persuaded President Eisenhower to respond to the plea of the Maronite Christians in Lebanon for US assistance in the form of Operation Blue Bat. Britain's Harold Macmillan similarly authorised the transportation of two thousand troops to Jordan. Owing to poor Israeli–British relations, it was only American pressure which persuaded Ben-Gurion to allow the British to overfly Israel.

Early in the year, Ben-Gurion reconstituted the government coalition after a row with Ahdut Ha'Avoda which had publicised the hitherto clandestine arms purchasing visit of Moshe Dayan, head of the IDF, to West Germany. The right-wing opposition, Herut and the General Zionists, attacked Ben-Gurion in the Knesset over such contact – yet their internal negotiations to secure unity as a credible electoral opposition floundered. Herut objected vehemently to the refusal of Ben-Gurion and the government later in 1958 to request the return of the remains of the Revisionist Zionist leader Vladimir Jabotinsky from New York where he had died from heart failure in August 1940.

The issuing of new identity cards by the Ministry of the Interior led to a coalition crisis over the question 'Who is a Jew?' Status governed marriage, divorce and burial. However, the evolution of Jewish history produced different understandings of Jewish identity. For some, it remained rooted in biblical history, but for others, it originated at a much later date during the Haskalah, the Jewish Enlightenment, and the period after the French Revolution. Many in Israel considered themselves secular Jews, while many in the Diaspora defined themselves as non-orthodox. This fragmentation of identity was reflected in discussions around the Law of Return (1950) and the Citizenship Law (1952).

The crisis prompted by the issuing of new identity cards pitted the minister of the interior, Ahdut Ha'Avoda's Yisrael Bar-Yehuda, against Haim-Moshe Shapira, the minister for religious affairs – this was a bastion of the National Religious party (NRP). In March, Bar-Yehuda instructed his civil servants to accept at face value any applicant who had applied for a new identity card. Bar-Yehuda argued that anyone who defined him- or herself as a Jew and did not practise any other religion should be granted an identity card. Haim-Moshe Shapira and his NRP deputy at the Ministry of Religious Affairs, Zerach Warhaftig, argued that this contradicted Halakhah (Jewish religious law), which stated that a Jew was someone born of a Jewish mother.

Ben-Gurion attempted to resolve the problem by establishing an inter-ministerial committee, but with no success at resolution. The NRP, which held eleven Knesset seats, instructed its ministers, Shapira, Warhaftig and the minister of posts, Yosef Burg, to resign from government. A no-confidence vote in the government failed 60–41 in the Knesset. However, the Religious bloc was supported by Menahem Begin's Herut and by Peretz Bernstein's General Zionists. Ben-Gurion appointed the former Chief Rabbi of Tel Aviv, Ya'akov Moshe Toledano, as the new minister of religious affairs.

The trade deficit was estimated at $300,000 and Israel depended heavily on contributions from Diaspora Jewry, loans from the United States and reparations from West Germany. The average Israeli wage was $138.75 per month. Government expenditure increased while unemployment fell.

105

1959

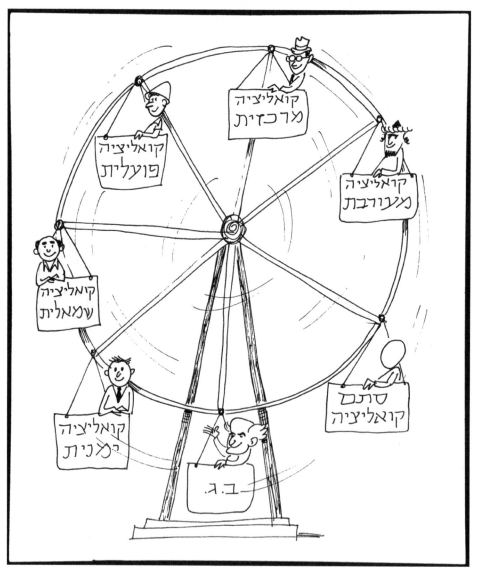

Ben-Gurion, in the lowest chair, is seen as a passenger in the circus carnival coalition ride following the national election – a coalition that can have various compositions. The other passengers depict the possibilities for coalitions: Labour, Centrist, Leftist, Rightist or 'Just a coalition'. The 'Mixed' coalition implies including the religious parties since the passenger is wearing a kipa and sporting peyot.

Shlomo Sawady (*HaBoqer* 11 December 1959)

28 Jan   Yosef Sprinzak, first Knesset Speaker, dies aged 73

25 Feb   Romania stops exit permits for Jewish emigrants to Israel

8 Mar   Amnon Keren, Israel diplomat in Bucharest, declared *persona non grata*

1 Apr   'Night of the Ducks' mobilisation, revealed as army exercise, creates panic

8 Apr   Knesset passes Holocaust Day observance law on 27 Nissan annually

12 Apr   Seven new American-owned ships are added to the Arab League blacklist

21 Apr   First pilot plant for saline water research in Israel opened in Beersheba

27 Apr   Two hikers shot and killed near Masada

28 Apr   Egyptian MiG-17s forced to turn back after flying over southern Israel

5 May   Members of armies that fought Nazism take part in a Holocaust Day march

5 May   French Super-Mystère fighter jets and Vautoure bombers acquired by Israel

1 June   Israel granted temporary membership of GATT

7 June   Huge swarm of locusts invade a central area of the Negev

7 June   Delek and Isratom form company for peaceful use of nuclear power

21 June   Hammarskjöld recommends integration of Arab refugees into Middle East

1 July   Knesset approves the arms agreement with West Germany 57–45

5 July   Ben-Gurion submits his resignation to President Ben-Zvi

9 July   Monument unveiled to Shlomo Ben-Yosef, first Jew hanged by the British

9 July   Wadi Salib disturbances of Mizrahim begin in Haifa

25 July   Chief Rabbi Isaac Herzog dies in Jerusalem aged 70

29 July   Knesset defeats religious law motion to determine Jewish identity

17 Aug   Israel's population increased by 55,718 in 1958 to a total of 2,031,672

3 Sept   West Germany to equip its new Panzer divisions with Uzi machine guns

5 Oct   Jews in Lebanon and Syria arrested for attempting to leave for Israel

6 Oct   Carmelit underground railway opens in Haifa

14 Oct   Cabinet discusses sudden decision by Renault to end operations in Israel

22 Oct   Israel's first joint Arab–Jewish bank is formally established

1 Nov   Gershon Agron, mayor of Jerusalem, dies aged 66

3 Nov   Ben-Gurion's Mapai wins 47 seats in national election

4 Nov   Egyptian MiGs penetrate 18 miles into Israeli airspace

16 Dec   New Israeli government coalition formed from five parties

16 Dec   Israel's first submarine, the *Tanin*, enters Haifa harbour

17 Dec   Moshe Dayan and Abba Eban appointed ministers in government

28 Dec   The number of immigrants for 1958 expected to exceed 24,000

107

Twenty years after the start of World War II, Israelis still felt strongly about any association with Germans and Germany. In early January, a showing of a German film about Israel, entitled *Paradise and Pressure Cooker*, had to be cancelled for fear of protests – regardless of its very positive approach to the country.

In August, the Israel Medical Association rejected a request by a local travel agent for the organisation to act as the host for a group of German doctors who were expected to tour Israel. The raison d'être for this rejection was the role that German doctors had played in the Nazi extermination of European Jews.

On Yom HaShoah (Holocaust Commemoration Day) in May, thousands marched in silence through Tel Aviv, with black-edged Israeli flags at half-mast. One banner read: 'Eternal Glory to the Sanctified'.

In an interview with the daily *Ha'aretz* to mark the Jewish New Year, Ben-Gurion held the entire generation of Germans responsible for the crimes of Nazism, but absolved their sons and daughters. He said that while he would be ready to visit Germany for reasons of state, he would not choose Germany for a holiday. He argued that the sale of Israeli arms to Germany was essentially 'an act of revenge' against the Nazis. Ben-Gurion further made a distinction between Adenauer's West Germany and the Communist GDR: 'East Germany's people are murderers and scoundrels because they feel no responsibility for what was done.'

Ben-Gurion refused to respond to an East German professor regarding a book about Spinoza – even though 'this professor is a man of sterling character'. Ben-Gurion said publicly that if the inquiry had come from a professor in Switzerland, 'I would have written willingly.'

In February, it was announced that the German reparations for the coming fiscal year would amount to $62.5 million.

Although the general election had been scheduled for November and it was a foregone conclusion that Ben-Gurion's Mapai would comfortably emerge as the biggest party, the question of arms sales to West Germany became a major bone of contention for parties of the Left.

Mapam and Ahdut Ha'Avoda refused to support Ben-Gurion over the sale of grenade launchers, worth $3 million – an agreement concluded in October 1958. Ahdut Ha'Avoda's Yigal Allon said that the deal was 'an abomination'. Ben-Gurion argued that it was a question of cabinet collective responsibility and met members of the religious parties as well as the General Zionists to indicate to his left-wing opponents that he could form a coalition with alternative partners. He then told a conference of his own party that if he did not receive complete support, he would retire once again to Sde Boqer. The Israeli Right, led by Menahem Begin's Herut, said that the deal desecrated the memory of the six million Jews who had perished during the Shoah. Rabbi Mordechai Nurock commented that the deal amounted to 'a vote of confidence in neo-Nazi Germany'.

The division was clear when the Knesset rejected a vote of no confidence by the Communist party 57–5, with 37 abstentions. In July, Ben-Gurion tendered his resignation and a caretaker government was formed under his leadership.

The probable outcome of the election was signalled by the results of the election for the Histadrut, the General Workers' Confederation, when Mapai won 55.42 per cent of the vote. Their left-wing opponents could only muster some 30 per cent.

Ben-Gurion's Mapai gained another seven seats to achieve forty-seven mandates in the new Knesset. By the year's end, Mapai had increased its percentage of the vote and formed a government coalition, encompassing 86 seats of the 120-seat Knesset.

Ahdut Ha'Avoda lost a third of its seats and the Communists a half. This move reflected the final disillusionment with Soviet Communism after the invasion of Hungary. Ben-Gurion had originally wanted a joint list of Israel's three left-wing parties, but this dispute over relations with West Germany scuppered that possibility. It also marked the permanence of the Right when Herut emerged as the second largest party. In the run-up to the general election, the cabinet voted to abolish military government in border areas populated by Arabs. Herut strongly opposed this measure.

The General Zionists, however, suffered a setback when they lost five seats, which made them more susceptible to Begin's advances. Even so, a joint list of the Right did not materialise when the more liberal General Zionists rebuffed the proposals of Herut.

Herut gained two seats and this was in part due to Begin's cultivation of the Mizrahim. In July, there had been a serious disturbance at Wadi Salib in Haifa, ostensibly between the local community and the police. Parked cars were set on fire and shops attacked.

In reality, it reflected the antagonism between Mizrahi civilians and Ashkenazi police officers. The riots spread to Jerusalem, Tiberias and Beersheba. This brought to the surface the differences between the Ashkenazi elite and the newly arrived Mizrahi immigrants who felt disparaged and discriminated against, and highlighted the very different societies from which Jews had emigrated.

The principal targets of the protesters in Haifa were significantly the offices of Ben-Gurion's Mapai and the Histadrut. Although Jews had been disproportionately represented in the Communist parties of Iraq and Egypt, the Jewish Enlightenment and the advance of socialism were weaker in the Maghreb compared with Eastern Europe. The differences in understanding 'Jewishness' and subsequently Zionism came to the fore in all these disturbances. The worldview of many Mizrahim was different from that of the Ashkenazim.

A fundamental difference was the place of religion. Judaism was a pillar of Mizrahi identity whereas many Ashkenazim defined themselves as secular. One of the leaders of the Wadi Salib demonstration, David Ben-Hanish, made the protesters swear on the Hebrew Bible in a synagogue that they were not opposed to the state of Israel and their public dissent would be non-violent.

There were also numerous clashes within Israel's Arab population. Many were due to differences between Nasser supporters and Communists.

A new recruit to Mapai was the former IDF Chief of Staff, Moshe Dayan, who projected a different vision of the future and ignited a generational conflict.

The Histadrut was quick to condemn Dayan's call for a wage freeze and for 'efficiency dismissals'. Dayan referred to Histadrut officials as 'those who for twenty years had been sitting on the fifth floor'. The Histadrut's daily newspaper, *Davar*, subsequently published a cartoon showing Dayan as a small boy throwing stones against the windows of the Histadrut building: the caption read 'naughty boy'.

Another newcomer to Mapai was the former UN ambassador, Abba Eban, who was highly critical of Dayan's retaliatory policy of 'hostility for hostility'. This had been provoked by Dayan's downplaying of diplomatic efforts designed to resolve the problem of Nasser's repeated attempts to prevent Israeli shipping and those involved in trading with Israel from using the Suez Canal.

The Norwegian ship SS *Sekvic* was refused fresh supplies of water at Port Sudan and prohibited from loading cargo for Europe. In April, another ninety-seven ships were added to the Arab League's blacklist. The United Arab Republic's 'War Spoils Court' endorsed the confiscation of cargoes taken in February from a West German ship and a Liberian freighter which were carrying goods through the Suez Canal from Haifa, Israel.

109

The 1960s

The most notable event of the 1960s was Israel's remarkable victory during the Six Day War in 1967. Its territory expanded almost fourfold after defeating its neighbours, Egypt, Jordan and Syria. Its conquest of the West Bank – biblical Judaea and Samaria – resonated with religious and nationalist Jews. It provided strategic depth if an Arab army decided to invade. This also provided the raison d'être for establishing the first settlements on the West Bank.

Many Palestinian Arabs fled to Jordan and other parts of the Arab world after Israel's military victory. It was also the beginning of an armed struggle by Palestinian groups such as Fatah and the Popular Front for the Liberation of Palestine. The Six Day War saw for the first time members of the Right sitting in an Israeli cabinet. The National Religious party was also moving to the Right owing to the increasing influence of its Young Guard.

In this cartoon, Ben-Gurion is depicted as Moses, displaying the tablets on Mount Sinai. Ben-Gurion was regarded as the founding father of Israel – someone who was almost infallible. Yet he had a capacity to fall out with many of his colleagues. including Moshe Sharett. Here Srulnik is depicted as looking up to heaven – from where Sharett's diary is tumbling down. Finally published in 1968, the diary revealed a different interpretation of events and a sharp criticism of Ben-Gurion's policies.

Dosh (*Ma'ariv* 5 November 1965)

1960

אחרי, בבקשה!

Yekusiel Yehuda Halberstam, the Klausenburger Rebbe, a heroic figure of spiritual resistance during the Shoah, emigrated from Brooklyn to Kiriat Sanz, near Netanya, in Israel. This occurred during a period of decreased emigration, especially from the United States, amidst Ben-Gurion's often barbed jibes about the situation.

Holding a lighted candle, emitting 'the commandment of emigration to Israel', the non-Zionist Rebbe addresses the reticent Zionist leaders of the Dispersion.

The caption alludes to the command of an Israeli officer to his men in battle: 'Follow me, please!'

Arieh Navon (*Davar* 1 January 1960)

3 Jan NRP interior minister cancels predecessor's instructions on 'Who is a Jew?'

5 Jan Bedouin paid compensation for previous year's drought

19 Jan Two Israeli Arabs sentenced to 12 and 7 years for working for Lebanon

24 Jan UAR bans films of Edward G. Robinson for pro-Israel sympathies

1 Feb Continuing Syrian shelling of Israeli settlements near the border

15 Feb Finance minister Eshkol announces relaxation of foreign currency controls

17 Feb President Eisenhower reiterates his rejection of US arms sales to Israel

21 Mar Turkey and Israel sign a $32 million trade agreement

23 Mar Chief Rabbinate opposes projected Billy Rose sculpture garden in Jerusalem

27 Mar Education minister Aranne resigns over support for independent teachers' association

28 Apr Border police officer demoted for killing two Jordanian infiltrators

11 May Eleven letters written by Bar Kokhba discovered in a cave near the Dead Sea

23 May Ben-Gurion announces that Adolf Eichmann is under arrest in Israel

6 June Hassidic conference marks 200th anniversary of Baal Shem Tov's death

15 June Kurt Sitte, Technion nuclear physics professor, arrested on espionage charges

16 June Israeli nuclear reactor at Nabi Rubin, south of Tel Aviv, goes into operation

21 June Yossele Schumacher, disguised as a girl, taken from Israel to Switzerland

28 June Religious Affairs Ministry announces plans to publish the Quran

10 July Religious affairs minister, Yaacov Moshe Toledano, aged 79, marries 25-year-old

14 July Jerusalem monument unveiled to commemorate centenary of Herzl's birth

17 July Poalei Agudat Israel's leader joins the cabinet as minister of posts

23 July Shah of Iran formally extends recognition to Israel

31 July Abba Eban appointed minister of education

9 Aug Knesset passes a child adoption law, limiting rabbinical court jurisdiction

5 Sept Oil field discovered at Negba, near Heletz site

14 Sept Supersol Company opens the first supermarket in Jerusalem

28 Sept Prime Minister Ben-Gurion's office resurrects the Lavon affair

25 Oct Seven Israeli Arabs sentenced in Haifa for working for Syrian intelligence

8 Nov John Kennedy elected president of the United States

13 Nov Oil pipeline from the Red Sea to Haifa Bay completed

Ben-Gurion's announcement in May that Adolf Eichmann was being held in Israel after being kidnapped in Argentina was received in stunned silence by members of the Knesset. Amongst the population and within the Jewish world, it recalled fading memories and intense emotions.

Eichmann had been responsible for presiding over the deaths of millions. He had promoted himself within the Nazi elite as an expert on the Jewish question. After the Anschluss, he had supervised the office for Jewish affairs in Vienna. During that pre-war period, the imperative had been to make certain that as many Jews as possible left the Reich. With the Final Solution agreed upon, Eichmann took on a more lethal understanding of the Jewish problem.

Once it became clear that Germany would lose the war, Eichmann transformed his persona into a lowly nondescript worker and was able to escape to Argentina.

One reason for the kidnap was Ben-Gurion's desire to ensure that the memory of the Shoah was conveyed to the new generation of Israeli youth. It was also directed at the non-Jewish world, especially those countries which had gained independence from the colonial powers.

The question of relations with Germany was always a sensitive one – as were Wagner concerts. Already that year, a Yemenite dance troupe had turned down an invitation to perform in West Germany and there was a public debate about whether to replace the term 'German murderers' by 'Nazi murderers' in the proposed new standard prayers. It also led to an ongoing diplomatic incident with Argentina – from where the Nazi war criminal had been kidnapped.

In a letter to the Argentinian president, the official Israeli response was that Eichmann had left Buenos Aires voluntarily, but did not give any legal basis for his abduction. The Israeli government expressed its regrets if 'the group of Jewish volunteers' had broken Argentinian law or violated its sovereignty. Unfortunately Ben-Gurion had already announced that Eichmann had been abducted by Israel's security service.

114

Despite a handwritten letter from Eichmann expressing his willingness to go to Israel, a furious Argentina demanded his repatriation. The press and public opinion in Israel were strongly opposed, citing the fact that Argentina had previously refused requests from West Germany and Yugoslavia to extradite ex-Nazis.

A federal judge in Buenos Aires also pointed out that a fifteen-year statute of limitations had just expired and ruled that another probable war criminal, Jan Durcansky, could now not be extradited to Czechoslovakia.

Argentinian nationalists viewed this as a cause célèbre and interpreted the Eichmann affair in a purely legalistic fashion while relegating the moral justification for a trial in Israel. Argentina subsequently brought its grievance against Israel to the UN Security Council.

The Israeli ambassador in Argentina, Arieh Levavi, was declared *persona non grata*. Yet in January 1944, Eichmann had instructed that all Argentinian Jews living under Nazi rule should be sent to Bergen-Belsen. Gradually Israeli–Argentinian diplomatic relations were repaired through back-channel negotiations and a new envoy to Buenos Aires appointed.

At the end of September, the Prime Minister's Office announced that the Lavon affair was to be re-examined by a special commission, led by Judge Haim Cohn. This was based on a recent civil trial which implied that perjured testimony had been given at the 1955 investigation. Lavon believed that this vindicated his protestations of innocence. He had always argued that false testimony had been given by the officers involved – and supported by members of the defence establishment as a means of forcing his resignation as minister of defence. A separate parliamentary committee investigation was also carried out.

The resurrection of the Lavon affair split both the cabinet and the ruling Mapai party. Lavon was accused by Ben-Gurion and Shimon Peres as being zealously critical of the IDF when minister of defence. Factions developed, based not on ideology, but on support for or opposition to Lavon.

While Lavon regarded himself as vindicated, Ben-Gurion then established a seven-member ministerial committee to further investigate the case. In December, it reported that a senior officer and a reservist bore responsibility, that Lavon did not give the order and the event took place without his knowledge. Ben-Gurion refused to accept the report and abstained in a cabinet vote on it.

The decrease in the vote for Ahdut Ha'Avoda allowed Ben-Gurion to restore the Ministry of the Interior to the National Religious party. The new minister, Haim-Moshe Shapira, immediately reversed the instructions given by the former holder of the office, Yisrael Bar-Yehuda. Shapira instructed his civil servants to define a Jew as 'a person born of a Jewish mother who does not belong to another religion, or one who has converted in accordance with religious law'.

The year 1960 saw the arrest of Kurt Sitte, accused of transferring material to the Soviet bloc, and the passing of the Israel Lands Act, which ensured that state territory remained in Israeli hands. It was also the year of the US election – a contest between the Democrats' John F. Kennedy and the Republicans' Richard M. Nixon. Kennedy argued for a new approach towards Middle East peace and that 'guns and anti-Communist pacts and propaganda and the traditional piecemeal approach are not enough'. He strongly supported the right of Israeli shipping to pass through the Suez Canal unhindered.

During the pre-election debate, Nixon and Kennedy differed profoundly on how to confront the Arab boycott and the discriminatory measures invoked by several Arab states against American Jews and enterprises which conducted business with Israel.

Kennedy argued that he would implement the amendments to the Mutual Security Act, which would allow the withholding of aid from countries engaging in economic warfare against other recipients of American aid. Nixon, however, pointed out that Kennedy's proposal would be counter-productive. It would be unlikely that any US government would impose such sanctions. A remarkable 82 per cent of American Jews voted for Kennedy. While Ben-Gurion greeted Kennedy's election in November with visions of 'human liberties, world peace and fraternity', the construction of a second nuclear reactor with the aid of France worried the Americans. Kennedy was concerned that Israel's nuclear programme was not solely directed towards peaceful purposes. The US State Department hinted that it might seek inspection of Israel's nuclear facilities.

While Syria continued to mount attacks against Israel, King Hussein of Jordan argued that Arab leaders were using 'the Palestine Arab refugees as pawns for selfish political purposes'. His central opponent was Brigadier Qasim of Iraq who had overthrown the Hashemite monarchy. At an Arab League meeting in Cairo in February, supporters of Qasim argued for the establishment of a state of Palestine incorporating the Jordanian-occupied West Bank, the Old City of Jerusalem, Gaza and parts of Israel – headed in all likelihood by Haj Amin al-Husseini, the Mufti of Jerusalem. Qasim instructed his compatriots to donate one hour's pay to a fund for a Palestinian state.

Qasim later proposed the establishment of a Palestine Republic Army which would liberate Palestine from 'the Jewish usurpers'. During a speech to the United Nations, Nasser stated that the Arab world was not reconciled to 'the loss of Palestine'.

King Hussein was enmeshed within this net of political rivalry between Nasser and Qasim. When the Jordanian premier, Hazza' al-Majali, was assassinated in August, Israel moved its troops up to the border with Jordan.

115

1961

ישראל

א״כמן גדולה

חטרנספורט האחרון

The trial of Adolf Eichmann, one of the major architects of the Final Solution, began in Jerusalem in April and heard harrowing testimonies from survivors of the Shoah. He was sentenced to death in December.

The Mossad tracked him down in Argentina, kidnapped him and brought him to Israel.

The cartoon alludes to the bolted cattle-wagons that transported Jews 'to the East' – to concentration and often extermination camps. It depicts an imprisoned Eichmann arriving in Israel.

The caption reads: 'The Final Transport'.

Arieh Navon (*Davar* 27 May 1960)

12 Jan   Mapam's Aharon Cohen goes on trial on espionage charges

23 Jan   Workers strike for a half-hour symbolic protest against price increases

31 Jan   Ben-Gurion resigns because of inquiry exoneration of Pinhas Lavon

1 Feb   Adolf Eichmann indicted on 15 charges

17 Feb   Veteran socialist Zionist Manya Shochat dies aged 81

15 Mar   US Export–Import Bank authorises $25 million credit for Israel

16 Mar   Remains of David Raziel, former head of the Irgun, reinterred in Jerusalem

2 Apr   Begin welcomes admission of Herut's trade union affiliate into Histadrut

11 Apr   The trial of Adolf Eichmann opens in Beit Ha'am in Jerusalem

13 Apr   Israelis observe a two-minute silence on Yom Ha'Shoah

18 Apr   Eichmann trial prosecutor, Gideon Hausner, completes a nine-hour speech

25 Apr   General Zionists and Progressives merge to form the Liberal party

30 Apr   Schools reopen after a 55-day strike by teachers

14 May   Haredim protest outside a Petah Tiqva theatre over Shabbat performance

18 May   Military analyst Israel Beer charged with spying for the Soviet Union

23 May   Knesset approves changes in election law to hinder splinter parties

30 May   Israel's nuclear programme discussed by Ben-Gurion and Kennedy in USA

29 June   Yaacov Sharett, First Secretary of the Moscow Embassy, expelled from the USSR

5 July   Shavit-2 rocket launched for meteorological purposes

7 July   Israel Shochat, founder of Hashomer, dies aged 75

15 July   Haredim stone hospital bus despite dispensation for Shabbat travel

30 July   Cornerstone for Israel's second deepwater harbour laid at Ashdod

31 July   Millionth immigrant arrives since the establishment of the state in 1948

15 Aug   Israel's fifth election takes place in 2,600 polling stations

23 Aug   Ben-Gurion's Mapai emerges as the largest party despite losing five seats

19 Sept   Large-scale demonstration by Israeli Arabs over killing of five youths

10 Oct   12 per cent income tax loaned to government to pay cost of immigrant absorption

15 Oct   Boycott of the sale of Lucky Strike and Pall Mall cigarettes in Israel lifted

27 Nov   Ben-Gurion states that Israel cannot ignore South Africa's apartheid

15 Nov   Eichmann sentenced to death by hanging by Jerusalem District Court

15 Nov   Martin Buber argues that Eichmann's sentence should be life imprisonment

Ben-Gurion began the year by going on holiday and leaving an unsent letter of resignation. He had reacted strongly to the exoneration of Pinhas Lavon by the cabinet, based on the unanimous findings of a ministerial committee that the former defence minister's instructions in 1954 had been forged. Ben-Gurion demanded a reversal of the ministerial committee's decision, the resignation of Lavon as secretary-general of the Histadrut and a further judicial inquiry. Abba Eban and Moshe Dayan supported Ben-Gurion, while Golda Meir, Pinhas Sapir and Levi Eshkol were loath to reverse a cabinet vote. A twelve-hour meeting of the Mapai secretariat ended in total deadlock at 4 a.m.

Lavon resigned under pressure, but Ben-Gurion's stand had antagonised many. The Progressives, Mapam and Ahdut Ha'Avoda all refused to serve in a government headed by him. New elections became likely rather than a new coalition.

The election was set for 15 August and Lavon's name was not on the list of Mapai candidates. Yet a month before the election, the cabinet reaffirmed its decision to absolve Lavon of all responsibility for 'the security mishap' in 1954.

In mid-August, Israelis voted for fourteen party lists. Mapai received forty-two seats, losing five. Both the Communists and the new Liberal party, formed by the merger of the General Zionists and the Progressive party, gained seats. Menahem Begin's Herut remained at seventeen seats – only three extra compared with the first election. In addition, Begin's cultivation of the General Zionists seemed to have failed. However, the bitterness generated by the Lavon affair continued: it took almost three months to form a new government under Ben-Gurion.

At the end of January, the Knesset passed amendments which provided special arrangements for the forthcoming trial of Adolf Eichmann. During the third reading, a clause was added which revived a law from the period of the British Mandate. This provided for the implementation of death sentences by hanging. Capital punishment had been abolished with the exception of treason during times of war and for Nazi crimes.

Eichmann's indictment listed seven counts of crimes against humanity, four against the Jewish people, one war crime and three charges of belonging to Nazi organisations. This was in accordance with the Nazi and Nazi Collaborators Punishment Act of 1950.

Eichmann's role in coordinating deportations from all corners of the Reich to the extermination centres after the Wannsee Conference was at the forefront of charges directed at him. He was charged with not only 'enslaving, starving, deporting, persecuting and incarcerating Jews in ghettoes and concentration camps under inhuman conditions of humiliation, starvation, overcrowding and torture', but also deporting half a million Poles and 14,000 Slovenes to make way for German settlers. The West German War Crimes Office stated that some 80,000 Germans had taken part in the mass murder of Jews.

In an interview in *Yediot Aharonot*, Ben-Gurion commented that Eichmann's personal fate was unimportant, but the world should be reminded of the extermination programme carried out against the Jews. 'The heavy burden of the Nazi holocaust' rested not only on the shoulders of the Germans, but also on England, 'which could have saved those Jews who fled toward Israel but were not permitted to land here".

In a long dramatic opening speech, the Attorney-General, Gideon Hausner, began by stating that he was not alone. 'With me are six million prosecutors. But they cannot rise to their feet and point an accusing finger towards the man who sits in the glass booth and cry out "J'accuse!".' Hausner described Eichmann as a new kind of killer – one who worked from behind a desk. His accomplices were 'neither gangsters nor men of the underworld, but the leaders of a nation – including professors and scholars, robed dignitaries with academic degrees, linguists, educated persons, the "intelligentsia"'.

Listing the fate of Jewish communities, country by country, Hausner related individual examples of the murder of a third of all Jews. He also paid tribute to specific individuals – such as the Swedish diplomat Raoul Wallenberg – and resistance groups – the French Maquis, the Yugoslav partisans, the Belgian underground – who tried their best to rescue Jews.

Hausner's nine-hour-long opening speech gripped Israel's citizens. Within a month of the commencement of the trial, 15,000 Israelis had visited the courtroom, while another 30,000 had followed the proceedings on a large closed-circuit television screen.

Survivors provided the bulk of testimonies. Itzik Remba, the editor of the Herut daily, criticised the testimonies of Zivia Lubetkin and Abba Kovner, Jewish resistance fighters in Eastern Europe, for playing down the role of Betar and right-wing movements in general. Two witnesses with a Nazi past were given immunity so that they could testify.

On 13 December, Hausner demanded the death penalty for Eichmann, a defendant who 'does not deserve mercy'. The Jerusalem District Court's guilty verdict was reflected in a widespread approval in the Israeli media and rejected any suggestion that he should not receive the death penalty. In a final statement to the court, Eichmann blamed 'the political leaders' of Germany. 'My only guilt was my discipline, my obedience, my adherence to my oath. I never persecuted Jews from any desire on my part.'.

President Ben-Zvi had the ability to commute the sentence to life imprisonment. While many people wrote to urge him to allow the sentence to stand, several members of the Israeli intelligentsia argued that Eichmann should not be executed. These included Avigdor Arikha, Yehuda Bacon, Leah Goldberg, Zwi Werblowsky, Helena Kagan, Natan Rotenstreich and Gershom Scholem.

The German Jewish poet Nelly Sachs similarly argued that Eichmann should not be hanged. Martin Buber, the philosopher, originally from Germany, argued that his sentence should be commuted to life imprisonment. Herut members on Tel Aviv Council argued that Buber should now not be awarded the municipality's award for literature for his work *Hidden Light*. The ceremony went ahead a few days after the end of the trial.

Others feared that any execution would give rise to a new wave of anti-Semitism, while yet others suggested that Eichmann should be transferred to Poland for execution.

In November, a split opened up between Israel and the Jewish community in South Africa when Israel voted in favour of censuring a speech by South Africa's foreign minister, Eric Louw. Israel then supported other states in condemning apartheid, labelling the system as 'reprehensible and repugnant'. Israel, however, did abstain on a Pakistani motion to stop selling arms to South Africa. It also opposed expelling South Africa from the UN.

In part this was due to both genuine support by Ben-Gurion and Golda Meir's cultivation of newly independent African states. Prime Minister Verwoerd, however, responded strongly and asked whether Israel was genuinely against the idea of separate development. Why not merge, therefore, with the surrounding Arab states into one single state? Verwoerd made such comments in a letter to a supporter – and ominously pointed out that many South African Jews favoured the Progressives rather than his own National party. In the Knesset debate, both Herut and Agudat Yisrael, while rejecting apartheid, condemned Israel's approach at the UN. Ben-Gurion responded that 'we would not have been true to ourselves, to our moral heritage and to our position in the family of nations if we had not joined in this protest'.

1962

Eight-year-old Yossele Schumacher was kidnapped by his grandparents, Breslaver hasidim, because they were concerned that he would not be brought up in a religious environment. He was hidden in Israel, smuggled out to Europe, brought to New York and finally settled with a religious household in Brooklyn. The Mossad conducted a worldwide search to find him and he was finally located in September 1962.

Schumacher's mother, Ida, is depicted here, bewildered and anxious, looking for her son in a forest of seemingly indifferent hasidim.

Arie Navon (*Davar* 9 February 1962)

1 Jan	Meir Amit appointed head of military intelligence
9 Jan	Aharon Cohen sentenced to five years by Haifa court for espionage
14 Jan	Israel Beer sentenced to ten years by Tel Aviv court for espionage
23 Jan	Health Ministry rejects doctor's request to test birth control pill on patient
30 Jan	Israel supports UN call to Portugal to relinquish power in Angola
1 Feb	Chief Rabbinate's day of prayer for Soviet Jewry
6 Feb	Marc Chagall speaks at dedication of 12 stained-glass windows at Hadassah
9 Feb	Eshkol announces devaluation of Israeli pound late on Friday afternoon
27 Feb	Knesset votes 39–23 to ban pig-farming in Israel
8 Mar	El Al planes grounded in pilots' dispute over hours in the cockpit
8 Mar	Syrians open fire on Israeli police patrol boat on Lake Kinneret
29 Mar	Supreme Court panel reject request for new witnesses in Eichmann appeal
16 Apr	Verwoerd regime withdraws right of local Zionists to transfer funds to Israel
29 Apr	National Water Council agrees annual flow of 225,000 litres from Kinneret
30 Apr	Oscar Schindler welcomed in Israel by 300 former workers from his factory
2 May	Frank Sinatra arrives in Israel to give seven concerts
14 May	Israel Prize for education awarded to Joseph Bentwich
1 Jun	Adolf Eichmann is hanged at Ramla prison
1 July	Yossele Schumacher, abducted three years ago, located in New York
1 July	Robert Soblen, convicted in the USA as a Soviet spy, deported from Israel
10 July	Yehuda-Leib Maimon, first religious affairs minister and Mizrahi leader, dies aged 86
21 July	Egyptians display new Soviet missiles during Revolution Day parade
5 Aug	Removal of government subsidies produces a doubling of the price of bread
12 Aug	Tel Aviv square named after actor Solomon Mikhoels, murdered by Stalin
22 Aug	Giora Josephtal, housing minister and Mapai leader, dies aged 50
3 Sept	Malaya follows Indonesia in refusing to issue visas to Israeli athletes
4 Sept	El Al carries first aid shipments to Tehran for earthquake victims
26 Sept	Israel acquires Hawk ground-to-air missiles from USA
7 Nov	Eleanor Roosevelt, long-time supporter of Israel, dies in New York aged 78
28 Nov	Yossele Schumacher abduction trial opens in Jerusalem
6 Dec	Supreme Court rejects Brother Daniel's application to be considered a Jew
19 Dec	First monarch to visit Israel, Mwambusta IV of Burundi, arrives in Jerusalem

121

Aharon Cohen and Israel Beer were sentenced to terms of imprisonment for passing information to Soviet diplomats in Israel. Both had been members of Mapam, the Marxist–Zionist pro-Soviet political party. Cohen, who was the party's Arab affairs expert, often met Soviet diplomats outside the gates of his kibbutz, Sha'ar Ha'amikim. He was accused of 'unauthorised contacts with foreign agents' rather than spying and sentenced to five years' imprisonment.

Meir Ya'ari, the Mapam leader, defended Cohen as 'not a spy and not a traitor to Zionism'. Israel Beer similarly identified with Mapam and had been close to Moshe Sneh. When Sneh broke with Mapam, formed the Left faction and then joined the Communist party, Beer moved to the Right and joined Mapai.

Beer's story had been ostensibly that he was a Viennese social democrat and Spanish civil war veteran who arrived in Palestine in October 1938. He became a lieutenant colonel in the IDF, an academic and a valued Defence Ministry employee, close to Shimon Peres. He became an official historian of Israel's war of independence and head of the department of military history at Tel Aviv University. Despite his background history being proved false by his interrogators, he never revealed his real identity or admitted to working for the Soviet bloc. He was found to have passed classified information to Vladimir Sokolov at the Soviet Embassy in Tel Aviv. On appeal, his sentence was increased to fifteen years.

The cases of Cohen and Beer arose as a result of the crisis in international Communism after the death of Stalin, Khrushchev's revelations at the twentieth party congress and the invasion of Hungary in 1956. The KGB was particularly interested in the development of the nuclear facility at Dimona. This led to the arrest of Kurt Sitte, a Czechoslovak nuclear physicist at the Technion, and his subsequent trial and imprisonment.

At the end of the year, the trial opened which dealt with the abduction of eight-year-old Yossele Schumacher. He and his family had immigrated to Israel from the USSR in 1958. The family, however, had tremendous difficulties in settling into their new country. Yossele's maternal grandfather, Nachman Shtarkes, a Breslover hasid who had suffered in Stalin's Gulag, was asked to look after the boy while the parents attempted to secure a foothold in Israeli society. The frustrations of the boy's father, Alter Schumacher, grew and he threatened to return to the USSR.

Shtarkes believed that the secular father was returning the boy to godless Communism, and following consultation with Jerusalem's Chief Rabbi, Zvi Pesach Frank, a ruling was obtained so as to prevent him from leaving Judaism. For the next two and a half years, Yossele was separated from his parents in Holon and taken first to a yeshiva in Rishon l'Zion, then to the village of Kommemiut, run under the auspices of the haredi party, Poalei Agudat Israel. Ruth Blau, a French convert to Judaism, chaperoned the boy and took him on false papers to Switzerland – to Moshe Soloveichik's yeshiva in Lucerne. Yossele then travelled to France and Britain before being looked after by a Satmar hassidic family in the Williamsburg area of Brooklyn.

The Mossad had great difficulty in infiltrating the haredi world, and at Ben-Gurion's insistence, began to divert more and more resources to find the child – deflecting funds from the search for the Nazi doctor Josef Mengele in Latin America. Yossele was eventually located by the FBI in Brooklyn in the summer of 1962 and returned to Israel. The boy's grandfather had spent two years in prison in Israel for adamantly refusing to disclose his grandson's whereabouts.

Yossele's 23-year-old uncle, Shalom Shtarkes, had falsely denied any involvement in the abduction and was sent to Brixton prison in London before being extradited to Israel. On Yossele's return, the Israeli government dropped all proceedings against those involved, except for Shalom Shtarkes, who was eventually sentenced to three years for kidnapping plus another two for perjury. Ben-Gurion's overriding desire was to secure national unity in Israel and avoid an overt eruption of the *Kulturkampf* between religious and secular. Shalom Shtarkes was pardoned a few months after the trial's conclusion.

A strike by six thousand public sector engineers, chemists, architects and agronomists was supported by a four-hour stoppage by doctors. Pressure on the government was increased by a rolling strike by engineers who worked in the electric power industry. West German engineers were brought in by AEG to operate the Haifa power plant.

Twelve thousand teachers who had just agreed a pay increase with the Ministry of Education came out on a one-day strike in support of the engineers. Although a stoppage of government lawyers was averted, a state of emergency was declared by the cabinet. The engineers eventually voted 14–13 to accept the government offer of a pay increase of 7 per cent and return to work.

Such industrial unrest was exacerbated by the government's decision to devalue the currency. One dollar was now worth three Israeli pounds instead of 1.8. Increasing prices and conflicting government statements created chaos in the marketplace. Mortgages increased by two-thirds. The cost of staple foods rocketed. The governing Mapai party advocated a wage freeze – a policy welcomed by the Manufacturers Association, but condemned by major parties to the left of Mapai. While the government hastened to alleviate the effect of devaluation on Israeli workers, such as by cutting the price of diesel for vehicles, this did not prevent the bus cooperatives from asking for higher fares.

Post office workers came out on strike, bringing communications to a halt. El Al pilots refused to work more than eight hours a day. Jerusalem's sanitation workers went on strike while Haifa's dockers maintained a go-slow.

Ben-Gurion was concerned about the build-up of Soviet-supplied arms in Egypt and wished to maintain Israel's qualitative edge. To ignore it was 'a dangerous complacency', given Egyptian bellicosity and repeated threats to destroy Israel. In 1962, the USSR decided to send to Egypt missiles originally intended for Cuba. A nuclear reactor was being built with Soviet assistance and Israeli intelligence estimated that Nasser would be able to produce nuclear weapons within a decade. Israel's standing army numbered 43,000, while the combined forces of Egypt and Syria amounted to 200,000. Similarly, Israel possessed 102 fighters and bombers compared with the 328 possessed by its adversaries.

The Kennedy administration became the first to grant Hawk ground-to-air missiles to a non-NATO country in order to counter this increase of Soviet missiles in Egypt. The White House regarded this as 'a one-off' and, given the close call of the Cuban missile crisis, was only too aware of how misinterpretations and accidents could lead to a world war. The USA wanted to resolve the Arab refugee crisis and to link the return of some – possibly 10 per cent – to the delivery of the missiles to Israel.

In November, the Supreme Court heard the case of Oswald Refeisen, aka Brother Daniel, who had converted to Christianity in 1942 in Europe. He argued that his Jewish nationality had not been compromised and insisted that citizenship be awarded to him under the Law of Return.

President Ben-Zvi turned down a plea of clemency for Eichmann to escape the hangman's noose. His wife, Vera, was permitted to visit him and he was hanged at Ramla prison, cremated and his ashes deposited at sea.

123

1963

Foreign minister Golda Meir had strongly condemned apartheid in South Africa at the United Nations and developed Israeli aid to newly emergent African countries. She proposed a six-point plan to the UN General Assembly 'to allay the fears of armed conflict' and 'to achieve complete disarmament with mutual inspection, covering all types of weapons'.

Golda Meir is attempting to construct a *Sukkat Shalom* – 'a canopy of peace' – before the onset of the Jewish festival of Succot (Tabernacles). The UN delegates seem bemused and bewildered at her approach.

Arie Navon (*Davar* 2 October 1963)

7 Jan Yossele Schumacher's uncle sentenced to three years for kidnapping and perjury

21 Jan Begin asks the Liberals to reconsider forming a Knesset bloc with Herut

23 Jan Herut conference votes to establish a faction in the Histadrut 546–320

3 Feb Bus fares increased by an average of 10 per cent due to devaluation

5 Feb Herbert Samuel, first Palestine High Commissioner, dies in London aged 92

8 Feb Iraqi Ba'athists overthrow Abd al-Karim Qasim's regime in Iraq

6 Mar El Al aircraft grounded after dispute about working procedures

7 Mar Knesset endorses plans for an experimental educational television system

8 Mar Syrian Ba'athists and Nasserists stage successful military coup

20 Mar Knesset calls upon West Germans to stop their scientists working in Egypt

25 Mar Mossad head, Isser Harel, resigns over Ben-Gurion's tactics in Operation Damocles

2 Apr Remains of Ber Borokhov, Marxist–Zionist ideologist, brought to Israel

16 Apr Chief Rabbi Nissim endorses Pope's call for ban on nuclear weapons

23 Apr President Yitzhak Ben-Zvi dies in Jerusalem aged 78

1 May Ahdut Ha'Avoda proposes left-wing alignment with Mapai and Mapam

9 May Nine yeshiva students fined for damage to Finnish Christian mission

21 May Shneur Zalman Shazar elected third president of Israel

23 May Shazar pardons killers of Kasztner and kidnapper of Yossele Schumacher

26 May Arrival of former West German defence minister, Franz Josef Strauss

16 June Ben-Gurion resigns as prime minister

19 June Levi Eshkol appointed prime minister

28 June USA announces decision to transfer Hawk missiles to equip Israeli battalion

18 July Nasserists fail to take power in attempted military coup in Damascus

23 July Israeli fighters intercept two Egyptian MiG-17s in southern Israel

5 Aug Israel signs nuclear weapons ban treaty agreed by USA, USSR and UK

9 Sept King Mahendra of Nepal arrives in Israel

24 Sept Israeli given ten years in Ukraine for desertion from the Red Army in 1945

24 Sept Israel recalls minister from South Africa in protest at apartheid policies

10 Nov Haifa Orchestra cancels Wagner concert owing to Kristallnacht anniversary

25 Nov Israel observes three days of mourning after assassination of President Kennedy

26 Nov Yigael Yadin announces Dead Sea scroll of Psalms 81–85 located at Masada

28 Nov Abba Hillel Silver dies in Cleveland, Ohio, aged 70

14 Dec Yitzhak Rabin appointed next IDF Chief of Staff

Shabbat breaking and the presence of Christian pilgrims in Jerusalem catalysed demonstrations by young haredim during the summer. The Mandelbaum Gate in Jerusalem, the crossing point between Jordan and Israel, was the site of protests against Baptists who were embarking on a tour of the holy places on the Shabbat. Anger was first directed against the bus drivers who were thought to be Jewish, but were not – and then against the owners of the buses, the Hamkasher cooperative. Amidst fighting between the protesters and the police, vehicles were damaged. Hamkasher responded by suspending all services for three days to the ultra-orthodox Mea Shearim district of Jerusalem.

The protests were led by the Neturei Karta sect of the Satmar Hasidim, accompanied by youths, often under seventeen years of age, from the Satmar yeshiva. They attacked a disabled man in his car who had driven through their neighbourhood on the Shabbat and threw stones at Christian tourists and UN personnel at the Mandelbaum Gate. While many of the youths were subsequently fined, a succession of incidents led to a cabinet discussion to find a solution to the problem. Opinion was divided between the religious ministers who argued for greater sensitivity and secular ones who opposed religious coercion.

At the beginning of the year, President Ben-Zvi and Zerach Warhaftig, minister of religious affairs, refused to attend the opening ceremony of the Hebrew Union College in Jerusalem under the auspices of Reform Judaism. Ben-Gurion did attend and said that he believed in 'the tenet of Jewish solidarity which demands mutual respect on the part of all Jews'.

In September, a hundred haredi youths invaded the Scottish and French mission schools in Jerusalem. At the end of the year, cars containing Kol Yisrael radio workers and Israeli soldiers were stoned and damaged by haredim.

In February, the abolition of military government was narrowly averted by a Knesset vote of 57 to 56. Former military commanders such as Moshe Carmel and Yigal Allon considered military rule over Arabs as redundant. Ben-Gurion, however, supported military rule and argued that it was important for reasons of security, uncovering espionage and countering infiltration. He remarked that only two thousand people were actually restricted in terms of their movement.

Golda Meir's statement to the Knesset in March signified the increasing alarm with which the cabinet viewed the presence in Egypt of several hundred German scientists who were working on missile programmes for Nasser. There were rumours that Egypt was in possession of radioactive isotopes cobalt-60 and strontium-90. Golda Meir commented that 'the West German government cannot remain indifferent to the fact that eighteen years after the fall of the Hitlerite regime, we again find members of that people responsible for acts designed to destroy Israel within which survivors of the Nazi Holocaust have been gathered'.

It followed the arrest in Basel of an Israeli, Yosef Ben-Gal, and an Austrian, Otto Jukelik, who had threatened the daughter of a German electronics expert in order to influence her father to cease working for the Egyptians. This followed Operation Damocles – attempts by the Mossad under the direction of Yitzhak Shamir to assassinate and abduct other scientists.

Nasser had revealed the existence of al-Zahir and al-Qahira missiles and there was concern that they would be able to carry biological and chemical warheads. Although Israel had protested privately to the Bonn government, an open campaign had been initiated in the hope that public opinion would halt the involvement of well-paid German scientists in Egypt. Animosity in Israel deepened, such that the visit of former defence minister Franz Josef Strauss took place away from public gaze.

The Basel affair and a disagreement about the tactics used by Ben-Gurion in Operation Damocles led to the resignation of the head of the Mossad, Isser Harel, and his replacement by Meir Amit. This reflected the sensitivity towards West Germany within official circles in Israel, despite Ben-Gurion's repeated defence of the Adenauer government.

Ben-Gurion attacked critics of a plan to reconstruct the Mashiyah district of Tel Aviv simply because the architects were West German. In November, the Haifa Symphony Orchestra abruptly cancelled plans to perform Wagner. The attitude towards West Germany also created differences between Ben-Gurion and Golda Meir. Mapam, the Liberals and Herut wanted a debate during Passover week about the resignation of Harel. It was lost by a vote of 67–47.

While Peres was lauding the development of nuclear energy – for peaceful purposes – at Dimona, Khrushchev proposed a nuclear-free zone in the Mediterranean area. Ben-Gurion welcomed the initiative but called for a general disarmament in the Middle East. He condemned the arms race due to the influx of Soviet war materiel.

This arose after Ba'athist *coups d'état* within weeks of each other in both Syria and Iraq. Syrian gunners repeatedly fired on Israeli farmers from across the border. Ben-Gurion was worried that a federation would be agreed with Egypt which would threaten Jordan and thereby encircle Israel. The Egyptians acquired Soviet Komar class naval vessels which were capable of firing ship-to-shore missiles. These weapons had already been supplied to Cuba and were particularly effective in attacks against coastal cities. President Kennedy reiterated his determination to prevent any aggression in the Middle East.

By July, the USA for the first time agreed to provide heavy water for a research project at the Technion. Israel also agreed to sign the partial nuclear test ban treaty, initialled by Washington and Moscow.

Ben-Gurion unexpectedly resigned in mid-June for 'personal reasons' and was succeeded by Levi Eshkol, who formed a government based on the same four-party coalition. Abba Eban was appointed to the new role of deputy prime minister. By August, Ben-Gurion returned to making public pronouncements – in particular, countering anti-German animosity in Israel and stressing his friendship with Adenauer.

127

Israel took a firm stand against the apartheid regime in South Africa in the International Labour Organisation. It placed an embargo on arms shipments – in particular, the sale of Uzi machine guns. It recalled its minister in South Africa, Simcha Pratt, and replaced him with a chargé d'affaires. The South African prime minister, Hendrik Verwoerd, condemned this but stated that South African Jews should not be held responsible for the Israeli government's policy. There was also consideration to halt El Al flights to South Africa.

The assassination of President Kennedy in November profoundly shocked Israel. Many Jews had identified with him and an overwhelming majority had voted for him rather than for Richard Nixon. During the election period in 1960, he had commented, 'Are we going to admit to the world that a Jew can be elected Mayor of Dublin, a Protestant can be chosen Foreign Minister of France, a Moslem can serve in the Israeli Parliament – but a Catholic cannot be President of the United States?'

President Kennedy had also raised the question of the ban on Jewish Americans serving in Saudi Arabia when King Saud visited the White House during the spring of 1962.

A special session of the Knesset was held in which the late president was eulogised. At the Yeshurun synagogue in Jerusalem, services were conducted by Chief Rabbi Yitzhak Nissim, and the eulogy given by Zerach Warhaftig, the minister for religious affairs. The memorial prayer, *El Mole Rahamim*, was recited. A three-day period of national mourning was declared and flags were flown at half-mast.

New president Zalman Shazar and foreign minister Golda Meir attended the requiem services for President Kennedy at St Matthew's cathedral in Washington.

1964

ב.ג. חוזר לפעילות.(מן העתונות)

Levi Eshkol began to follow different policies as prime minister, distinct from those of his predecessor, David Ben-Gurion. While the members of Mapai look on, Ben-Gurion walks by the broken tablets of his views: 'You shall not reconcile over the Lavon affair'; 'You shall not bring back the remains of Jabotinsky to Israel'. Ben-Gurion is depicted as returning to action and about to carve new commandments on the tablets of stone.

Ze'ev (*Ha'aretz* 15 May 1964)

1 Jan First desalination plant in Eilat begins operation

5 Jan Pope Paul VI visits Israel and meets President Shazar at Megiddo

13 Jan Arab summit meets to discuss Israel taking River Jordan's water

16 Jan Aharon Zisling, Israel's first minister of agriculture, dies at Kibbutz Ein Harod

26 Jan Israel recognises new revolutionary regime in Zanzibar

5 Feb Hirsh Barenblatt, State Opera conductor, given five years as Nazi collaborator

18 Feb Moshe Dayan challenges official version of Lavon affair

22 Feb Mapai backs Eshkol in not reopening Lavon affair

15 Mar Cabinet agrees to transfer Jabotinsky's remains for reburial in Israel

22 Mar Strike by 6,000 hospital employees in non-medical capacities

24 Mar Israel admitted to Afro-Asian bloc at UN, now under African leadership

31 Mar Protestant preacher and two Syrians hanged as Israeli spies in Damascus

12 Apr Isser Yehuda Unterman installed as the new Ashkenazi Chief Rabbi

19 Apr Two Israeli Jews sentenced as spies for Egypt

27 Apr Agreement with the European Common Market to reduce tariff on exports

13 May Two Swiss citizens sentenced in Zurich for spying for Israel

28 May First Palestine National Council held in East Jerusalem

2 June Palestine Liberation Organisation founded in Jerusalem

10 June National Water Carrier which transports water to the Negev starts operation

15 June Ben-Gurion proposes constituency-based electoral system for Israel

18 June Habima stages Hochhuth's controversial play about Pius XII in Tel Aviv

9 July Vladimir Jabotinsky laid to rest on Mount Herzl

12 July Supreme Court recognises that civil marriages abroad cannot be revoked

27 July Indian Bnei Israel sit-down protest at rabbinate's refusal to recognise status

19 Aug Strike by 800 rubbish collectors in Tel Aviv

7 Oct USSR agrees purchase of Soviet properties in Israel by Israeli government

20 Oct Syria stations tanks near the demilitarised zone, north of the Israeli border

22 Oct Ben-Gurion revives claim that Lavon issued the order in 1954 mishap case

26 Oct Mapai votes for Ahdut Ha'Avoda alignment

4 Nov Moshe Dayan resigns as agriculture minister over differences with Eshkol

11 Nov Ben-Gurion calls for new investigation into the Lavon affair

13 Nov Three Israelis killed and 11 injured by Syrian machine guns and mortars

15 Nov Ben-Gurion resigns from Mapai central committee over alignment plans

14 Dec Eshkol resigns over new Lavon probe and alignment dispute

22 Dec Eshkol establishes new cabinet despite Ben-Gurion's opposition

27 Dec Cabinet rejects proposal to reopen the Lavon affair

129

In mid-January, a conference of thirteen Arab states in Cairo discussed measures to counter Israel's water development project of pumping water from the River Jordan and the Sea of Galilee to the Negev in the south of Israel. Mekorot, the company in charge, began to test pump and pipe pressures along the 70-mile carrier to the central distribution station near Petah Tiqvah. More than 30 billion gallons per annum would be taken from the Sea of Galilee initially and then increased to 75 billion within a few years.

Eric Johnston, a special US ambassador, negotiated a regional division of the water between Israel and the Arab states in 1955. Jordan had already embarked on its own plan to divert the Yarmuk to irrigate the east bank of the Jordan. At a five-day summit, while there was no unanimity between the thirteen Arab states present owing to political differences, decisions were taken to divert the headwaters of the River Jordan and its major tributaries in Syria, Lebanon and Jordan. However, the huge expense would have to be funded by the oil-rich Arab states, which were reticent to make such an outlay to facilitate the plan.

The Syrian coup during the previous year, led by Muhammad Umran, Salah Jadid and Hafez Assad for the Ba'athists and Rashid al-Qutayni and Muhammad al-Sufi for the Nasserists, did not coalesce into a working coalition. Although there had been an agreement between Egypt and the new regimes in Syria and Iraq to form a federal union, it lasted only a few weeks. In Syria there were open clashes between Ba'athists and Nasserists – and a failed Nasserist coup during the previous summer. Such upheavals manifested themselves in a build-up of Syrian forces on Israel's border, incursions into Israeli territory and repeated gun attacks on civilians and army patrols.

In mid-November, Syrian tank and mortar fire opened up on Kibbutz Dan and the village of She'ar Yashuv, close to the border, in which three Israelis were killed and another eleven injured. Israeli jets were engaged to attack the Syrian tanks and to drive off an incursion by Syrian MiG-21s.

In the maelstrom of such difficult relations between Arab states, Nasser returned to the question of Palestine, in part as a diversionary measure, in part to reassert his authority within the Arab world. While he had no desire to go to war with Israel over Palestine, the proposal to establish the Palestine Liberation Organisation (PLO), representing Palestinians, under the aegis of Egypt, was a significant initiative.

In May, four hundred members, representing Palestinian communities in several Arab countries, constituted the newly formed Palestine National Council and met in East Jerusalem. Ahmed el-Shuqeiri, its chairman, stated that missions and information offices would be opened abroad. A news agency and a broadcasting channel would also be launched.

In mid-September, a second gathering of Arab states in Alexandria supported the formation of a Palestine Liberation Army among Palestinian refugees. Three brigades would initially be stationed in Egyptian-controlled Gaza, Syria and Iraq. Arms would be sought from Moscow and Beijing.

Although no longer prime minister, Ben-Gurion never shied away from giving his opinion. It was marked by two intertwined questions, the possibility of an alignment between Mapai and Ahdut Ha'Avoda and a renewed investigation into the Lavon affair. Moshe Carmel, who had commanded the northern front in 1948, said in the Knesset that mistakes had been made which prevented 'the total liberation of Palestine'. Carmel, who belonged to the maximalist Ahdut Ha'Avoda of Yitzhak Tabenkin, laid the blame at the feet of Ben-Gurion and the politicians.

In March, in an interview with the daily *HaBoqer*, Ben-Gurion remarked that if Moshe Dayan had been Chief of Staff in 1948, then Israel's borders would have been 'different' and its military achievements 'greater'. All this inevitably sparked a storm of protest from those who led Israel's forces – Dori, Allon, Yadin, Carmel, Laskov, Makleff, Galili. Menahem Begin called for a public inquiry into Ben-Gurion's decisions in 1948.

In June, Ben-Gurion advised a meeting of Mapai leaders to adopt the British constituency electoral model rather than the proportional representation system in use at present. This, he argued, was the way forward and not an alignment with Ahdut Ha'Avoda.

Pinhas Lavon, as minister of defence, had been held responsible for Operation Susannah – the attempt to carry out attacks on US and UK targets in Cairo and Alexandria by an espionage ring of Israelis and Egyptian Jews in 1954 and to blame instead Egyptian Communists and the Muslim Brotherhood. Lavon was exonerated for having given the order to activate the network for Operation Susannah by a further judicial inquiry. Mapai was thrown into turmoil by having to choose between Ben-Gurion and Lavon. Lavon was consequently removed from his post as Histadrut secretary-general in 1961.

Ben-Gurion submitted a 'white book' which once more addressed the Lavon affair of 1954. It revealed new facts, alleging that the Israeli agent Avri Elad, operating as 'Paul Frank', had been turned to work for Egyptian intelligence. The Attorney-General, Moshe Ben-Zeev, published his legal opinion in which he accepted Ben-Gurion's contention that there was sufficient evidence to doubt the finding of a 1960 Ministerial Committee which absolved Lavon of responsibility of having given the order. This was endorsed by Dov Joseph, the minister of justice.

This reinforced Ben-Gurion's opposition to Eshkol who wished to follow his own path such as bringing back the remains of Jabotinsky from the USA and interring him on Mount Herzl in Jerusalem. Unlike Sharett previously, Eshkol was not going to give in to Ben-Gurion. Dayan resigned as agriculture minister and Teddy Kollek stepped down as head of the Prime Minister's Office. Such political interventions by Ben-Gurion were symbolic of his desire to disparage the old guard and promote his own followers – Dayan, Peres, Kollek and others. Both Dayan and Peres, who had been involved in defence matters, had originally testified against Lavon.

While Golda Meir, Eban, Sapir and Sharett supported Eshkol, he was not prepared to bring Lavon back into Mapai and to place him on the candidates' list for the next election. Lavon broke away to form a new party, Min Hayesod.

In mid-November, Mapai's central committee voted 182–8 with 25 abstentions for the alignment with Ahdut Ha'Avoda – which had always supported Lavon's position. The agreement between the two parties allowed Ahdut Ha'Avoda to establish an independent section within the Histadrut. Ben-Gurion immediately resigned from the central committee. A resolution to hold a party conference to discuss a change in the election system was defeated 109–51. Ben-Gurion's refusal to seek a compromise with his opponents and abstentions in the Knesset led to Eshkol's resignation. Yet Mapai closed ranks against Ben-Gurion such that Eshkol was quickly able to form a new government with a similar composition – and the new cabinet decided not to reopen the Lavon affair.

At the United Nations, Israel was finally given full membership of the Afro-Asian bloc which constituted sixty-two countries. Muslim countries such as Indonesia, Pakistan and Mauritania vociferously attempted to reverse the decision and allied themselves with the Arab world. Israel's condemnation of the apartheid regime in South Africa and Salazar's Portugal, however, gained the support of newly emergent African nations.

131

1965

Amram Blau, the head of the Neturei Karta sect of the Satmar Hasidim, aged seventy, married a Catholic convert, Ruth Ben-David, aged forty-four, after his wife had passed away. This caused scandal and controversy in the haredi community, and Blau is seen in the background being admonished for his behaviour.

In the foreground, Ben-Gurion, dressed as a hasid, is bringing his 'bride', the new Rafi faction, to effectively challenge Eshkol and the 'Mapai community'. He too is admonished for his action in a cartoon entitled 'Divorce: Israeli-Style'.

Ze'ev (*Ha'aretz* 20 August 1965)

5 Jan	Arab League threatens to blacklist Chase Manhattan Bank over Israel Bonds
7 Jan	Knesset agrees to exclude 60,000 low-paid workers from paying income tax
19 Jan	Eshkol confirms the presence of Israeli instructors in the Congo
25 Jan	Eshkol eulogises Churchill in an address to the Knesset
25 Jan	Lavon removed from Histadrut central committee due to leaving Mapai
2 Feb	Omar Mahmud Ariffi, Lebanese spy, sentenced to 15 years by Haifa court
7 Feb	Liberals agree to establish committee to find way to cooperate with Herut
15 Feb	Knesset condemns West Germany's arms halt due to Egyptian pressure
16 Feb	Tenth Mapai annual conference opens, facing factional splits
4 Mar	Shimon Agranat nominated as next Supreme Court president
7 Mar	Independent Liberal party formed from opposition to Liberal–Herut bloc
9 Mar	Ahdut Ha'Avoda conference agrees to alignment with Mapai
16 Mar	Knesset votes to accept West German proposal for full diplomatic relations
21 Apr	Shrine of the Book, housing Dead Sea Scrolls, formally opened in Jerusalem
21 Apr	Tunisian President Bourguiba suggests Israeli–Palestinian peace talks
26 Apr	Herut and Liberals agree electoral pact as Gahal
11 May	Israel Museum opens in Givat Ram, Jerusalem
12 May	Diplomatic relations between Israel and West Germany established
18 May	Eli Cohen hanged in Marjeh Square, Damascus for spying for Israel
7 June	Eshkol defeats Ben-Gurion in Mapai central committee vote for next PM
13 June	Martin Buber dies in Jerusalem aged 87
29 June	Ben-Gurion announces split from Mapai to form a new electoral list
7 July	Moshe Sharett dies in Jerusalem aged 70
19 July	Cabinet approves the establishment of a non-commercial television service
16 Aug	Israel's population stands at 2,525,600, 16 per cent of world Jewry
21 Aug	Wolfgang Lotz sentenced to life imprisonment in Cairo for spying for Israel
1 Sept	Maki and Rakah established after formal split in the Communist party
20 Sept	Mapai–Ahdut Ha'Avoda alignment achieves only 50.8 per cent in Histadrut vote
20 Sept	Herut–Liberals list wins 17.5 per cent in Histadrut vote at first attempt
2 Nov	Ben-Gurion's Rafi receives only ten seats in parliamentary election
14 Nov	Teddy Kollek becomes new mayor of Jerusalem
17 Nov	Israel votes against the admission of Mao's China to the UN
21 Nov	The Swedish vessel *Vingeland* becomes the first ship to dock at Ashdod
2 Dec	Israel opposes Rhodesian Unilateral Declaration of Independence at the UN
6 Dec	Ritual slaughterers go on strike in Jerusalem for higher pay
21 Dec	El Salam mosque dedicated in Nazareth
28 Dec	Golda Meir announces her retirement as foreign minister

Members of Fatah commenced military operations against Israeli settlements from bases in Jordan. On 1 January, it directed an attack on the National Water Carrier, following the Arab League's plan to divert water from the Hasbani and the Banias. This would have reduced Israel's water supply by a tenth. It marked the onset of planned and regular military incursions and the emergence of a solely Palestinian fighting force.

On 7 January, Fatah attempted to sabotage a water tank at a religious Zionist moshav, Nehusha, at Lachish. Other attacks throughout the year occurred at Rosh Ha'ayin, kibbutzim Beit Nir, Eyal and Metzer, and moshavim Aderet, Zanoah, Givat Yeshayahu and Amatzia. Most attacks were on irrigation and water pumping stations, close to the Jordanian border. This provoked Israeli retaliatory raids at locations in Jordan and an incursion across the Lebanese border – the first since the armistice agreement between the two countries in 1949. Raids such as that against Mis el Jamal in Lebanon were similarly directed at water reserves. This eventually provoked Jordanian suppression of Fatah operations and the closure of its bases – although Syria maintained its support.

In contrast, the Tunisian president, Habib Bourguiba, gave a speech in Jericho which suggested a political solution to the Israel–Palestine problem. This was followed by more concrete proposals and condemnation from Nasser.

The year also marked the beginning of the disintegration of the Israeli Left and the coalescence of the Israeli Right. In January, Levi Eshkol appealed 'to all parties concerned' to 'leave the Lavon affair alone'. Ben-Gurion took no notice. He also continued to be concerned by the prospect of an alignment between Mapai and Ahdut Ha'Avoda and frustrated by his inability to move against Eshkol as he did against Sharett a decade before. Yitzhak Tabenkin, the ideological mentor of Ahdut Ha'Avoda, also opposed a limited alignment of the two parties.

Ben-Gurion had already published a 'white book' detailing the Lavon affair, written for him by Haggai Eshed, which also laid out his vision of the future including electoral reform.

At the annual conference of Mapai, which then boasted a membership of 200,000, there were more than two thousand delegates, but a bitter clash took place between the supporters of Eshkol and those of Ben-Gurion, who wanted to establish another judicial review of the Lavon affair despite numerous previous investigations. Rachel Yanait Ben-Zvi, the widow of Yitzhak Ben-Zvi, called for party unity, but asked Ben-Gurion, 'What is it you want from us?' while a dying Moshe Sharett was brought in a wheelchair and denounced his former leader in vociferous terms. The foreign minister, Golda Meir, and deputy prime minister, Abba Eban, both criticised Ben-Gurion, while Shimon Peres and Moshe Dayan spoke in his support. Golda Meir pointed to Ben-Gurion's inconsistency in his dealing with the investigations into the Lavon affair. Ben-Gurion, stung by Golda Meir's attack, walked out of the conference. A majority of Mapai delegates, however, supported Eshkol in a vote.

In May, at a meeting of the party secretariat, Ben-Gurion raised the possibility of a split in Mapai and publicly stated that Eshkol was not fit to lead the country. This suggestion resulted in the secretariat expressing full confidence in Eshkol. The Tel Aviv branch of Mapai then argued that Ben-Gurion should head the party's candidates list for the national elections. The Mapai majority responded in the affirmative, with the proviso that Eshkol would remain as prime minister. Eshkol was duly confirmed as the next prime minister by the Mapai central committee and Knesset members by 179 votes to Ben-Gurion's 103.

Ben-Gurion then asked that his supporters in the cabinet resign from their posts and Shimon Peres and Yosef Almogi subsequently did so. In June, Ben-Gurion threatened to set up his own list for the forthcoming elections. He predicted that any split would bring Menahem Begin's Herut to power.

Despite frantic efforts over the summer to prevent a split, Rafi (the Israel Workers' List) came into existence in July, consisting of seven former MKs. Ben-Gurion and his supporters were suspended from Mapai. The party's court of honour heard Rafi derided as 'a neo-fascist group based on the leader principle'. The split reduced the government coalition majority to a bare minimum of sixty mandates. Rafi published its own weekly journal, *Mabat Hadash*.

The Histadrut elections in September indicated a dramatic drop in support for the Mapai–Ahdut Ha'Avoda alignment with just half the vote, but Rafi, which projected itself as 'the real Mapai', attained only 12.1 per cent. In contrast the Right, running as Gahal (Herut–Liberals), emerged as the second largest party. Menahem Begin had already reversed Jabotinsky's policy of not running in Histadrut elections and he remarked that this election result represented a turning point for the Right.

The Knesset election in November resulted in a remarkable victory for Eshkol – some 36 per cent of the vote – while Ben-Gurion's Rafi attained only 8.2 per cent and a desultory ten seats. Rafi's sole success was the election of Teddy Kollek as mayor of Jerusalem. Eshkol called upon all members of Rafi to return to Mapai.

The Mapai–Ahdut Ha'Avoda alignment, Rafi and Mapam accounted for sixty-four seats; the Liberals, Herut and the Independent Liberals for thirty-four and the religious parties for seventeen. The possible scenario of a movement from Left to Right by part of the labour movement as well as by the religious parties now became a distinct possibility.

The election also indicated that mergers did not always increase the number of seats. The Labour alignment actually lost five seats – some of which switched to Ben-Gurion's Rafi. The pact of Herut with the Liberals meant the total loss of eight seats and the emergence of the Independent Liberal party (ILP), which gained five. The ILP was a breakaway from the Liberals because they refused to ally themselves with Herut's right-wing position.

Despite an attempt by the Kremlin to avert a split, the Communists divided into Maki and Rakah. Maki, under Moshe Sneh and Shmuel Mikunis, effectively repeated the past in that Jewish Communists had been unable to work with Arab Communists regarding the question of Palestine. Rakah was led by Meir Vilner and Tawfik Toubi. The two factions held separate conferences. Maki sang both the *Hatikvah* and the *Internationale* at their conference.

The split reflected the growing division within the international Communist movement into the uncritical Kremlin supporters and Eurocommunists. There were also different opinions on the Sino-Soviet clash. Maki was reduced to one seat with Rakah securing three. Uri Avnery's left-wing party, Meri, picked up a seat from the schism in the Communist party.

The Right also vehemently opposed the establishment of diplomatic relations with West Germany. Angered by Nasser's invitation to East Germany's Walter Ulbricht to visit Cairo, West Germany resumed arms supplies to Israel. Although Nasser did not recognise East Germany, the visit prompted West Germany to initiate the establishment of diplomatic relations with Israel. In the Knesset, Herut voted with the Left – Mapam and the Communists – in opposing links with Ludwig Erhard's West Germany.

The nomination of Rolf Pauls, a former Wehrmacht officer, as ambassador caused protests and repeated arrests of demonstrators in Israel. Alexander Toeroek, the new counsellor at the embassy, had been a Hungarian diplomat in Berlin while deportations and death marches of Jews had taken place in Hungary. When Pauls presented his credentials, the Israeli press reported that President Shazar was 'agitated' during the ceremony, while Golda Meir looked down at the floor during the formal speeches.

1966

Shmuel Yosef Agnon – Shai Agnon – the noted Hebrew poet and writer, won the Nobel Prize for Literature, together with the German Jewish poet, Nelly Sachs. Agnon spoke in Hebrew at the ceremony in Stockholm and told the audience:

'As a result of the historic catastrophe in which Titus of Rome destroyed Jerusalem and Israel was exiled from its land, I was born in one of the cities of the Exile. But always I regarded myself as one who was born in Jerusalem.'

The award was a recognition of Hebrew as a living and literary language. He is depicted here as working at home in Jerusalem while the population outside is celebrating his achievement. They are being told: 'Quiet everyone! Agnon wants to work!'

Ze'ev (*Ha'aretz* 21 October 1966)

2 Jan   Avri Elad, 'the third man' in the Lavon affair, stages hunger strike in prison

12 Jan   Eshkol's new coalition government approved in Knesset vote 71–41

11 Feb   USA agrees to sell 24 A-4E Skyhawk bombers to Israel

13 Feb   Income taxes to be raised from 1 to 2.5 per cent on monthly incomes

21 Feb   Eshkol announces government cuts of $33 million in austerity policy

22 Feb   Agriculture ministry announces drought damages for field crops

28 Feb   Abie Nathan flies to Egypt on peace mission, crash lands near Port Said

24 Mar   Educational television begins its service

5 Apr   Coca-Cola confirms its refusal to sell the drink in Israel

28 Apr   Mordechai Hod becomes head of air force, succeeding Ezer Weizman

1 May   Convicted spy Israel Beer dies of a heart attack in prison

2 May   Konrad Adenauer arrives in Israel for an eight-day visit

16 May   Two Israelis killed by Syrian mine near Moshav Almagor

18 May   Eshkol reiterates that Israel will not be the first to introduce nuclear weapons into the region

21 May   PLO's Shuqeiri states that Palestinians are receiving military training in China

22 May   Founding Rafi convention calls for electoral reform on British model

23 May   Knesset approves $40 million loan from West Germany

31 May   Labour ministry reports sharp increase in the number of unemployed

1 June   Religious affairs minister denounces establishment of birth control clinic

13 June   Haifa dockers return to work after seven-week work-to-rule slowdown

15 June   Syrian anti-aircraft fire sets 500 acres ablaze near Kfar Hanassi

19 June   Israel Philharmonic announces that it will perform works by Wagner

28 June   Menahem Begin offers to resign as chairman at eighth Herut conference in Ramat Gan

29 June   Intellectuals demand initiative to prevent spread of nuclear weapons

16 July   Syrian troop concentrations build up on Israeli border

17 July   Agudat Yisrael launches campaign against post-mortems in hospitals

18 July   Government introduces Shabbat observance bill to fine employers

8 Aug   Yosef Shemesh, held in Syria for 12 years, returns to Israel with five others

15 Aug   Syrian MiG-17 and MiG-21 shot down after shelling of Israeli fishing boats

30 Aug   New Knesset building inaugurated in Jerusalem

11 Sept   Cabinet approves new austerity programme after nine-hour session

18 Sept   Cabinet approves Israeli non-involvement in Vietnam War

24 Sept   Vera Weizmann dies aged 87

20 Oct   Shai Agnon awarded Nobel Prize for Literature

8 Nov   Compulsory military service for men extended from 26 to 30 months

13 Nov   Large-scale military assault on Jordanians at village of Samu after Fatah attacks

28 Nov   Strike by 28,000 university students over increase in tuition fees

1 Dec   Israel abolishes military government over border areas

Several raids across the Jordanian, Syrian and Lebanese borders by members of Fatah marked an escalation in its activities. Mines were planted on Israeli territory near the Syrian border and acts of sabotage carried out on Israeli territory. Syria was blamed by the Israeli government for sponsoring and assisting in Fatah raids.

In June, King Hussein stated that he would ban the PLO from Jordan and stop its recruiting activities. The Jordanians initiated passport control instead of requesting identity cards at their border with Syria. Ahmed el-Shuqeiri subsequently called for the dismissal of the Jordanian cabinet and then for the overthrow of the Jordanian monarchy.

While President Bourguiba of Tunisia had said that war with Israel was futile, the PLO received arms and training from Mao's China. The Viet Cong supported its armed struggle against 'Israel, the aggressive tool of imperialism, and [for] the realization of their hope of returning to Palestine'.

The IDF responded by conducting reprisal raids on locations such as Kalayet and Hirbeit and often blowing up the homes of targeted Palestinian militants. Such villages were often located just inside Jordan. All this created friction with King Hussein's armed forces. The head of the IDF, Yitzhak Rabin, argued that Fatah's operations out of Jordan allowed the Syrians to evade responsibility and Israeli retaliation.

Eli Cohen had been executed by the Syrians in the previous May. Cohen had provided information about Syria's military intentions. In February and March, Syrian gunners fired on Israeli tractor drivers in fields close to the border. In May, a dogfight took place between Syrian fighters and Israeli Mirage-3 jets in which a Syrian MiG-21 was shot down. Military exchanges between Israel and Syria often set fire to fields on both sides of the border. In October, four Israeli border policemen, rushing towards previous explosions, were killed at Sha'ar Hagolan when their jeep hit a buried mine.

The USSR strongly supported the Syrians – and this drew rare criticism from both Mapam and the Israel Communist party. Prime Minister Eshkol extended the period of compulsory military service for Israeli men by an extra four months in November to cope with the increase in infiltration.

In November, three Israeli soldiers were killed and ten were injured when their patrol car went over a mine. This provoked a retaliatory raid on the village of Samu near the Jordanian border.

The economic situation in Israel continued to deteriorate with a steep rise in consumer prices. The price of cigarettes increased by 25 per cent and the change in the cost of petrol forced an increase of 5 per cent in travel costs. A tax of 150 per cent on diesel was introduced. Company income taxes were raised from 28 to 30 per cent. Postal services charges and all licence fees were increased.

Eshkol's government raised income tax to secure funds for the next budget in order to pay for the expansion of health and education services. Pinhas Sapir argued in a Knesset debate that 'the economy has reached a point where the transition from a rapidly developing economy to one of modern production can be made without undue hardships'. Eshkol gave three 'fireside talks' by radio to explain the government's policy.

The situation produced a call for wage restraint, endorsed by the Histadrut, to prevent hyperinflation. Jerusalem's mayor, Teddy Kollek, and his four deputies announced that they would renounce 10 per cent of their salaries to help the anti-inflation movement. University lecturers, journalists and executives followed and took voluntary pay cuts. The Histadrut instructed its members to work during tea breaks.

Eshkol further announced that government expenditure would be cut by $33 million. A cutback in the development budget and reduced subsidies to agriculture and industry were initiated. This came on top of an announcement by the Ministry of Agriculture that two-thirds of all crops had been damaged by a severe drought. Wheat losses amounted to 70 per cent of cultivated areas, barley to 61 per cent and hay to 56 per cent. This meant importing such basic foodstuffs at a cost of $15 million.

The new port of Ashdod had experienced several slowdowns and strikes at the beginning of the year such that the Citrus Marketing Board ordered a halt to the shipment of fruits which were ready for loading. Ashdod was eventually closed down and ships diverted to Haifa until the disputes could be resolved. There were further strikes when management at Ashdod handed out dismissal notices to the workforce at the Leyland truck assembly plant. There were clashes with the police and attacks on Mapai-sponsored buildings in Ashdod. At Dimona, a protest led to the arrest of six demonstrators. In Haifa, port workers went on a go-slow over a seven-week period as negotiations proceeded, costing shipowners an estimated $6 million. It was resolved when stevedores and dockers were awarded a 10 per cent wage increase. In April, 35,000 unemployed had registered with the authorities. Even employees of the Jerusalem Religious Council went on strike to protest at non-payment of their June salaries and arrears they were owed.

Pinhas Sapir put forward a three-year plan of economic liberalism to solve the crisis. It involved an eighteen-month wage freeze, higher taxes and the cancelling of cost-of-living increases for the following year. All the major parties protested and Sapir made amendments to his approach. Mapai, Ahdut Ha'Avoda and the NRP all eventually endorsed Sapir's plan, but Mapam threatened to leave the coalition unless there was some amelioration of the workers' plight. The Independent Liberals demanded a reduction in income tax. Eventually the Mapam central committee decided by a vote of 52–20 to remain in government and 'fight from within'.

Herut deemed it 'the worst of all inflationary budgets presented to the Knesset'. Herut, however, had its own problems. Its electoral alliance with the Liberals, Gahal, had not provided any real advance. Before the election, Herut and the Liberals had seventeen seats each. In the election, Gahal attained only twenty-six. In the Knesset, however, there was increasing cooperation with Ben-Gurion's Rafi. At the end of June, the Herut conference took place in Ramat Gan. The opposition to its long-time leader, Menahem Begin, who had led them to defeat in six elections, found itself in a majority. Begin announced his resignation as party chairman and intimated that he would step down from the Knesset as well. Yet by the end of the conference Begin was able to defeat his opponents by a vote of 252–249. Yohanan Bader was deputed to be Begin's successor as moves were instigated to bring him back as chairman.

Herut now began to explore ways in which, together with the Liberals and Rafi, a new party of the Right could be formed to oppose a Mapai-dominated alliance of socialist parties.

In May, President Nasser told the BBC that Israel possessed a 24-megawatt nuclear reactor that could produce plutonium and that the Arab world should start its own nuclear programme. Prime Minister Eshkol responded that Israel would not be the first to introduce nuclear weapons into the Middle East.

Even so, there was concern in the US Senate about nuclear proliferation in the region. Fifty-five Israeli academics called upon the Eshkol government to take the initiative to prevent the spread of nuclear weapons. Ernst Bergmann, head of the Atomic Energy Commission who had been appointed by Ben-Gurion, tendered his resignation.

139

1967

The victory of the Six Day War over the forces of Egypt, Syria and Jordan brought with it the enmity of the Soviet Union which broke off diplomatic relations with Israel.

At the UN Security Council, the USSR demanded an immediate Israeli withdrawal from 'the occupied Arab territories'.

'Srulik', the archetypal Israeli, gun in hand, has just reached the sunny uplands of the cliff of 'peace and security' and has little intention of returning to the shark-infested waters of the situation before the war.

Dosh (*Ma'ariv* 14 June 1967)

3 Jan	Syrian troops enter Israeli territory in the Korazin area
12 Jan	USSR deports 12 Israelis for contact with Soviet Jews
24 Jan	Freighter *HaShlosha* lost off Sardinia at a cost of 23 lives
12 Feb	Wives blockade Ashdod port after their husbands are laid off
12 Feb	*Bul* magazine editors sentenced to one year for security disclosure
28 Feb	Yigal Allon states that unemployment tripled in 1966
28 Feb	Franz Stangl, Treblinka commandant, arrested in Brazil
9 Mar	Unemployed sit-down strike at Tel Aviv labour exchange
15 Mar	Haredim protest against autopsies in Israeli hospitals in Jerusalem
21 Mar	Shmuel Tamir announces Free Centre breakaway from Gahal
23 Mar	Free Centre forms Knesset faction of four MKs
7 Apr	Syrian MiG-21s shot down in air clash over the Golan Heights
14 May	Egyptians cross the Suez Canal in increasing numbers and enter Sinai
16 May	Nasser demands departure of United Nations Emergency Force (UNEF) from Sinai
20 May	UNEF evacuates Sinai and Gaza outposts
22 May	Nasser declares that the Straits of Tiran are closed to Israeli vessels
30 May	Egyptians and Jordanians form joint command
1 June	Menahem Begin enters national unity government
4 June	Israeli cabinet votes to go to war
5 June	Israel destroys Egyptian aircraft in airfields in Sinai and Gaza
5 June	Arab states agree to suspend oil supplies to all those who support Israel
6 June	Ammunition Hill captured in assault on Jordanian position
6 June	Israel occupies Gaza
7 June	Israel takes Old City of Jerusalem and begins conquest of the West Bank
8 June	Israel torpedoes sink USS *Liberty* in international waters, killing 34 crew
10 June	Soviet bloc breaks off diplomatic relations with Israel
19 June	Government votes unanimously to return Sinai and Golan
27 Aug	Israelis return to Kfar Etzion, evacuated in 1948
28 June	Israeli law extended to East Jerusalem which is unified with West Jerusalem
27 Aug	Mapai agrees to merger talks with Ahdut Ha'Avoda and Rafi
1 Sept	Arab world proclaims no peace, no recognition, no negotiations
4 Sept	Bomb in Tel Aviv central bus station kills one and injures 72
21 Oct	Three Egyptian missiles sink Israeli destroyer *Eilat* near Port Said
19 Nov	Israeli pound devalued by 14.3 per cent
22 Nov	Israel and Arab world vote for UNR 242
27 Nov	De Gaulle defines Israeli Jews as 'an elitist, domineering people'
1 Dec	Avshalom Feinberg of Nili reburied in Israel

The central event of the year was the Six Day War in June, during which the territory controlled by Israel expanded almost fourfold. It proved to be a watershed in the history of Israel and broadly indicated a breaking with the political philosophy and ideology that had characterised the first two decades of the state's existence.

There had been escalating skirmishes with the armed forces of Egypt, Syria and Jordan during the first few months of the year. In early January, Syrian forces had entered Israeli territory in the Korazim area, followed by tank fire at Israeli farmers in the Tel Katzir region a week later. Syrian mines killed a spectator at a local football game at Dishon. In April, several Syrian MiG-21s were shot down in a dogfight over the Golan Heights. Incidents along the Jordanian and Lebanese borders added to the rising tension. The Kremlin had further alarmed the Egyptians by suggesting falsely that the IDF was massing on their border.

All this was augmented by the Egyptian closure of the Straits of Tiran to Israeli and Israel-bound shipping in May and Nasser's demand that UNEF – the United Nations Emergency Force established after the Suez war – evacuate Sinai, thereby dissolving the peacekeeping force that separated Israelis and Egyptians.

Following Israel's remarkable victory, the Egyptians did not fade away, despite the decimation of their air force and the capture of large numbers of troops and weapons. This was because the public were unaware of the real situation, owing, in part, to the false information propagated by both the political leadership and the military, including the issuing of a victory stamp. When the reality of the overwhelming defeat finally dawned, Nasser publicly resigned – and then rescinded his resignation. Instead Field Marshal Mohammed Abdul Hakim Amer was held responsible and arrested. He committed suicide two weeks later.

Jews in Arab countries were not protected by their governments. In Egypt, religious and lay leaders were arrested. Seventy-five Jews of foreign nationality were placed on ships in Alexandria and deported. A UN envoy who was sent to Cairo to investigate the situation of Egyptian Jewry was ignored by the Nasser regime. In Iraq, Jews were arrested during the Jewish New Year and often only released on payment of a heavy fine. In Aden, the last Jew left the city.

Fatah was increasingly involved in military actions, often in the West Bank, leading to an Israeli response. In December, Ahmed el-Shuqeiri, the head of the PLO, resigned.

At the beginning of July, 120 Egyptians attempted to create a bridgehead by crossing the Suez Canal near Ras el Eish, ten miles south of Port Said. At the end of August, a Sukhoi SU-7 bomber was shot down at Bir Gifgafa. On the political front, the Arab world pronounced the three 'noes' at a conference in Khartoum. No peace, no recognition, no negotiations with Israel.

The Israeli cabinet unanimously offered to return Sinai to the Egyptians and the Golan Heights to the Syrians. The unanimity was achieved by omitting any mention of the future of the West Bank. A wall-to-wall coalition of political parties had been formed on the eve of the war. Herut's Menahem Begin had been brought in as a minister without portfolio – and this was the first time that the Zionist Right had entered an Israeli government. Begin regarded the West Bank as part of the Land of Israel – as Judaea and Samaria – and that it should never be handed back. He based his approach on the two partitions of the land in 1922 and in 1947, which nationalists had always opposed. In this he was supported by many religious Zionists who related to the biblical splendour of such locations as Hebron, Jericho and Nablus.

In addition, within weeks of the victory, maximalists from both Left and Right, founding fathers and cultural icons such as Uri Zvi Greenberg, Yitzhak Tabenkin and Natan Alterman were coalescing to a establish a movement for 'an undivided Israel'. There was also a desire to return to Hebron which Jews had left in 1929 and to Kfar Etzion which had been lost in 1948. The Zionist Left was split, with Mapai figures such as Abba Eban arguing for a return of territory whereas

Ahdut Ha'Avoda was more interested in establishing new kibbutzim on the West Bank. At a Rafi rally, Moshe Dayan called upon Israelis not to miss this opportunity to retain Hebron, Jericho, Shilo and Bethlehem.

In mid-June, the cabinet voted 11–10 to return Sinai and the Golan Heights, with a special arrangement for Sharm el-Sheikh. Gaza was to be retained as a security asset to prevent a future Egyptian invasion, while the future of the West Bank was left in abeyance. Dayan opposed this, while Eshkol challenged Allon's proposal to start a settlement programme in the territories.

In addition, the Allon plan proposed effectively a partition of the West Bank between Israel and Jordan. The eastern part of the West Bank, the Jordan Valley and the Judaean Desert, along the Jordan River and the Dead Sea, would be controlled by Israel as its defence border. Territory in the Jerusalem corridor would be annexed. Jordan would control the major Palestinian population centres in two enclaves which would be connected through a land corridor via Jericho. The Israeli and Palestinian areas would require link roads to connect them.

At the Khartoum summit in August, the Arab states agreed to neither negotiate with Israel nor recognize it. This undermined the leading doves in the cabinet, Eban and Sapir. Both Israel and the Arab states agreed to UN Resolution 242. This called for the withdrawal of Israeli armed forces from the conquered territories. The English version of the resolution referred to 'territories' whereas the French version spoke of 'the territories'. The combatants signed up because of the ambiguity of wording.

The negotiations between the different parties on the Left to unify as a Labour party proved successful and it was agreed by Mapai and by Ahdut Ha'Avoda. In mid-December, Rafi finally voted for this merger, but significantly Ben-Gurion abstained and decided to stay with the minority.

143

The conquest of East Jerusalem brought access to the Western Wall and to the Old City which resonated with many, regardless of whether they were religious or nationalist, or those who understood the significance of this in historical terms. For many Christian evangelicals, particularly in the United States, it heralded the second coming of Jesus and the genesis of political support for Israel.

Although the USSR immediately began to rearm Egypt, the price of the Kremlin's internal compromise, not to intervene directly, was the breaking off of diplomatic relations with Israel by the Soviet bloc and Yugoslavia – with the exception of Romania. Poland refused to issue visas to five deaf Israelis who had been invited to a conference on deafness in Warsaw. A meeting of the Interparliamentary Union in Moscow was cancelled because the USSR refused to issue visas to the Israeli delegation. More than two thousand Israelis who had fought in the forces of the Soviet bloc countries during World War II returned their medals at the Finnish Embassy.

The war inspired a growth of the nascent emigration movement of Soviet Jews. It galvanised the intelligentsia in many Communist countries. The non-Jewish Czech dissident Ladislav Mnachko announced his intention to depart for Israel.

In February, Yigal Allon reported a huge increase of the unemployed from 91,000 in 1965 to 857,000 in 1966.

1968

The USSR broke off diplomatic relations with Israel because of the defeat in 1967 of the Arab states which it had supported and armed. Soviet leaders Kosygin, Brezhnev and Podgorny are depicted as the three wise monkeys: 'See no evil, hear no evil, speak no evil.'

They ignore a hijacking by the PFLP to Algiers of an El Al flight the week before, but continue to exhort the Israelis to leave the territories conquered during the Six Day War and demand 'no further aggression'.

Ze'ev (*Ha'aretz* 29 July 1968)

1 Jan	Mortar attack on Kfar Ruppin amidst exchange of gunfire with Jordanians
1 Jan	Repatriation of 500 Egyptian prisoners of war under Red Cross supervision
9 Jan	Eilat–Ashdod oil pipeline attacked
15 Jan	USA condemns plans to build housing in Sheikh Jarrah and on Mount Scopus
27 Jan	Air and sea search for lost Israeli submarine *Dakar*
29 Jan	Paula Ben-Gurion dies at Sde Boqer aged 76
31 Jan	Ultra-orthodox demonstrate in Jerusalem against carrying out of autopsies
14 Feb	Eshkol says that he considers the River Jordan to be Israel's natural frontier
17 Feb	Yitzhak Rabin arrives in Washington, DC as Israeli ambassador to the USA
25 Feb	Employers and employees to give 15 days' advance notice on strikes
3 Mar	Interior minister explains ruling that West Bank is no longer 'enemy territory'
7 Mar	Rouhi el Khatib, former East Jerusalem mayor, is deported to Jordan
10 Mar	Chief Rabbi Nissim requests halt to archaeological work at Western Wall
18 Mar	School bus carrying teachers and children blown up by mine north of Eilat
21 Mar	Army launches incursion into Jordan to destroy Fatah camp at Karameh
7 Apr	President Shazar sends condolences following Martin Luther King's killing
15 Apr	Moshe Levinger and his followers celebrate Passover at Hebron's Park Hotel
17 Apr	Yigal Allon welcomes return of religious Jews to Hebron
2 May	First broadcast of Israeli television
8 May	Defence Ministry states that Fatah members are not prisoners of war
22 May	Israelis and Egyptians exchange fire across the Suez Canal
4 June	Jordanian long-range guns attacked by Israeli jets after artillery barrage
5 June	Sirhan Sirhan, born in Jerusalem, shoots Robert Kennedy in Los Angeles
17 July	Religious affairs minister announces construction of religious quarter in Hebron
18 July	West Bank curfew lifted after thirteen months
23 July	El Al flight 426 hijacked to Algiers by PFLP
11 Aug	Two Syrian air force MiG-17 interceptor jets defect to Israel
21 Aug	Both Maki and Mapam denounce the Soviet invasion of Czechoslovakia
9 Oct	Bomb thrown at the Cave of Makhpela in Hebron injures 47 civilians
23 Oct	Labour party secretariat votes 242–136 for alignment with Mapam
4 Nov	Stoke Mandeville games opened by President Shazar in Ramat Gan
5 Nov	Richard Nixon elected 37th president of the USA
6 Nov	Dayan proposes single economic unit stretching from Gaza to Jerusalem
22 Nov	Bomb in Jerusalem's Mahane Yehuda market kills 11
19 Dec	Yitzhak Sullam, recipient of Israel's first heart transplant, dies in hospital
20 Dec	Max Brod, writer and keeper of Kafka's works, dies in Tel Aviv aged 84
28 Dec	Israeli raid on Beirut airport destroys 12 Lebanese passenger planes

145

The aftermath of the Six Day War was marked by the commencement of a war of attrition. The Beit She'an (Beisan) Valley, close to the Jordanian border, was often targeted by Jordanian gunners. On 1 January, a mortar attack from across the River Jordan was aimed at Kfar Ruppin in the Beisan Valley, followed by a two-hour exchange of fire between the Jordanians and Israeli forces on the West Bank, about ten miles north of Damiyah Bridge. The New Year weekend also saw grenades thrown near a cinema in Gaza, a mine exploding under an Israeli half-track in Khan Yunis, a car driver wounded by sniper fire on the Golan Heights and a firing on workers in the fields of Ein Yanav in the northern Arava near the Dead Sea. A Chinese-manufactured mine killed one soldier and injured four border policemen in their jeep near Kibbutz Gesher in the Beisan Valley.

Fatah, which had established bases in Jordan, often crossed the border to plant mines to damage water pumping stations or electrical power units and thereby disrupt services to kibbutzim and moshavim in the region. The Eilat–Ashdod pipeline was also damaged near Mitzpe Ramon. Israeli naval vessels turned back Jordanian speedboats which had left Aqaba in the direction of Eilat.

An exchange of gunfire regularly took place across the Suez Canal which had been closed to shipping since June 1967, leaving fifteen vessels stranded. In late January, the Egyptians opened fire on Israeli units at Qantara and in the Canal region. The Israelis destroyed two Egyptian tanks in response and five Israeli soldiers were wounded in the clash.

Jerusalem and its environs were another front between Israeli troops and members of Fatah. In March, a fuel tank, tractors and machinery belong to Mekorot, the national water works company, were destroyed and a Druze night watchman was killed near Abu Ghosh.

In May, there was a mortar attack on Kibbutz Manara near the Lebanese border, a region which had been quiet during the previous year.

In the south, a school bus on an awayday excursion from Herzliya drove over a landmine planted in the road near Beer Ora in the Negev, killing teachers and injuring many children.

Following the conquest of East Jerusalem and its reunification, there had been periodic closures of merchants' shops and teachers' strikes in protest. In March, Israel deported Rouhi el Khatib, the deposed mayor of Jerusalem, to Jordan on the basis that he had served as a conduit for funds which financed such protests. The sympathies of the population of the West Bank became an issue for the Israeli military. In a meeting with Sheikh Mohammed Ali Jabari, the pro-Jordanian mayor of Hebron, and other Arab officials, Moshe Dayan asked them not to give shelter to Fatah infiltrators.

In mid-February, King Hussein pledged to take action against Fatah militants who were operating from Jordan. The Jordanian parliament, however, was split on whether or not to curtail Fatah activities and thus close down bases on their territory. In March, Israel mounted a large-scale operation into Jordan, targeting the locations of Karameh and Safi, in which as many as 150 Fatah militants and 84 Jordanian soldiers were killed. More than thirty Israeli troops were killed in the heavy fighting.

In June, Eshkol reported that 184 Israelis had been killed and 617 wounded, including the crew of the *Eilat*, since the end of the Six Day War. Most of the Israeli casualties had occurred within a twenty-mile stretch between Kinneret and Tirat Zvi.

In July, an El Al Israel flight from Rome to Israel was hijacked by members of the Popular Front for the Liberation of Palestine (PFLP) and forced to proceed to Algiers. The non-Jewish passengers were allowed to depart for Paris. Israeli women and children were then released while the men remained. Following five weeks of quiet negotiations, Israel agreed to release sixteen Palestinian prisoners for the release of both captives and aircraft.

146

At the very end of the year, the PFLP attacked another El Al aircraft at Athens airport, in which a passenger was killed and a female flight attendant injured. Two days later, the Israelis responded by sending in a Sayeret Matkal squad to destroy twelve passenger aircraft and two cargo planes belonging to Lebanese and Arab airlines at Beirut airport.

The settlement of the conquered territories brought criticism from the US State Department when plans for building in Jerusalem were revealed. Eshkol announced the establishment of a Nahal outpost near the ruins of Kibbutz Beit Ha'Arava which had been abandoned to Jordanian forces during the war of 1948.

Maximalists from both Left and Right supported settlement on the West Bank. In April, Yigal Allon greeted about seventy Jews who were arriving to re-establish a Jewish community in Hebron since the killings and departure in 1929. He also met leaders of the Greater Israel movement. In July, plans were announced to build housing for families, dormitories for yeshiva students, a dining hall and medical clinics in Hebron. Four hundred Arab notables protested about the government's refusal to remove the settlers. On Yom Kippur, Jews worshipped near the Cave of Makhpela in Hebron. A few days later, a hand grenade exploded on its steps.

A similar attempt was made to re-establish a Jewish quarter in the Old City of Jerusalem and to resurrect destroyed or damaged buildings. Sixteen acres were appropriated. In May, Eshkol stated that Jerusalem would remain a united city amidst plans to relocate government departments to East Jerusalem. Neve Ya'akov, which had been occupied by the Jordanians in 1948, was now incorporated into Jerusalem. Bnei Akiva of North America was given permission to establish a study institute at Kfar Etzion, overrun in 1948.

Moshe Dayan argued that the Golan Heights would have to be settled. He also suggested that Sharm el-Sheikh should be a permanent Israeli base. The first civilian settlement in northern Sinai was established.

147

Allon argued that the Jordan Valley, with a population of 18,000, should be further settled by Jews, with a corridor connecting the Judaean and Samarian mountains with the East Bank of the River Jordan. The Allon plan was designed to partition the West Bank between Israel and Jordan rather than annex it in its entirety. This brought condemnation from adherents of the Greater Israel movement such as the poet Natan Alterman.

Despite the formation of a united Labour party, there were profound ideological differences. When Rafi's Dayan proposed a single economic unit from Gaza to Jerusalem encompassing Beersheba and Hebron, he was strongly opposed by Mapai's Pinhas Sapir, who argued that it would lead to a binational state.

King Hussein proposed the establishment of a separate Palestinian state in 'a special relationship with Jordan', the capital of which would be situated in East Jerusalem.

There was continuing unrest in the West Bank amidst demonstrations, strikes by businesspeople and the closure of schools. Curfews were imposed. Palestinian Arab activists – Nasserists and Communists – were expelled to Jordan.

In January, the founding conference of the Labour party took place, integrating Mapai, Ahdut Ha'Avoda and Rafi – with the exception of Ben-Gurion who remained outside. The Labour secretariat voted 242–146 to form an alignment with Mapam. This alignment possessed more than sixty-one seats and therefore, in theory, could govern without forming a coalition with non-socialist partners.

1969

Charles de Gaulle is depicted as Cato the Elder, preaching to the Roman Senate. De Gaulle had strongly condemned Israel's attack on aircraft at Beirut airport in December 1968 and instituted an embargo on all military equipment to Israel.

When nine Iraqi Jews were publicly hanged as 'spies' in Baghdad in a holiday atmosphere a few weeks later, France did not make 'a moral protest'. De Gaulle argued that the executions could not be separated from the wider Arab–Israel conflict.

De Gaulle is depicted as saying: 'Outside of this, I do believe that Israel must be pressured.'

Ze'ev (*Ha'aretz* 31 January 1969)

6 Jan	Military announces Israel suffered 281 killed, 1,115 injured since June 1967
13 Jan	Jewish Agency states that it will establish 22 settlements on the Golan Heights
19 Jan	Agreement between Labour and Mapam to form alignment of four parties
27 Jan	Nine Jews hanged publicly as Israeli spies in Baghdad's Liberation Square
4 Feb	Yasser Arafat elected chairman of the PLO
5 Feb	Foreign Minister Eban rejects West Bank Palestinian entity as 'unrealistic'
14 Feb	First Katyusha attack on Israel itself targets Mitzpe Ramon in the Negev
18 Feb	PFLP attack on El Al aircraft at Zurich airport prevented by security guard
21 Feb	Itzik Manger, Yiddish poet and essayist, dies in Tel Aviv aged 67
21 Feb	Two killed, nine injured in Jerusalem Supersol supermarket bombing
26 Feb	Prime Minister Levi Eshkol dies of heart attack aged 73
5 Mar	Dayan calls for economic and legal integration of the territories into Israel
6 Mar	Hebrew university cafeteria bombed by a PFLP cell, injuring 28
9 Mar	Abdel Munim Riad, head of Egyptian armed forces, killed in Israeli mortar attack
11 Mar	Golda Meir named as Israel's fourth prime minister
24 Mar	Abba Khoushi, mayor of Haifa (1951–69), dies
16 Apr	Jewish Agency announces development projects at Kfar Etzion, evacuated in 1948
19 Apr	Egyptian commando raid across Suez Canal at Ismailiya
28 Apr	Justice Ministry authorises registration of businesspeople in East Jerusalem
14 May	Ramat Eshkol building project inaugurated in Jerusalem
19 May	Agudat Yisrael proposes Knesset no-confidence motion about seven-day television
31 May	PFLP attacks Saudi Arabia–Lebanon oil pipeline on Golan Heights
9 June	Knesset approves change of name of unit of currency from pound to shekel
24 June	Fatah destroys oil pipeline section in the port of Haifa
21 Aug	Australian sheep herder sets fire to al-Aqsa mosque in Jerusalem
29 Aug	TWA aircraft containing Israeli passengers hijacked to Damascus
2 Sept	Labour Alignment loses support, a decrease of 17 per cent, in eleventh Histadrut election
8 Sept	Two hand grenades thrown into the El Al Brussels office
26 Sept	Swiss police charge Alfred Frauenknecht with selling Mirage secrets to Israel
15 Oct	Opening of magistrates' court at Quneitra on the Golan Heights
28 Oct	Labour Alignment loses seven seats at general election
10 Nov	Meir reveals letter of 18 Georgian family heads wishing to emigrate to Israel
16 Nov	Two Israeli merchant vessels damaged by explosives in Eilat harbour
27 Nov	Hand grenade thrown into El Al Athens office
9 Dec	US secretary of state, William Rogers, proposes new peace plan
15 Dec	Ezer Weizman enters new cabinet as Gahal transport minister
25 Dec	Five embargoed gunboats, purchased by Israel, slip out of Cherbourg

149

The raid on Beirut airport in response to the attack on an El Al airliner at Athens was met by widespread international condemnation. In February, an El Al Boeing 720B airliner was machine-gunned by PFLP members as it taxied on the runway at Kloten International Airport, Zurich. At the end of August, the PFLP hijacked a TWA airliner carrying several Israeli passengers and diverted it to Damascus. In the following months, hand grenades were thrown into El Al's Brussels and Athens offices.

President de Gaulle intensified the embargo on arms and spare parts which France had implemented after Israel's victory in the Six Day War. French helicopters were used by the Israelis in the attack on Beirut airport and France had a large investment in the commercial airliners that were destroyed. France refused to deliver the fifty Mirage V jet fighters ordered in 1966 and already paid for.

In September, Swiss police arrested Alfred Frauenknecht, who sold huge quantities of Mirage documentation to the Israelis in an attempt to circumvent the French embargo.

Georges Pompidou continued this policy on succeeding to the presidency in June and refused to deliver five remaining gunboats, also ordered by Israel in 1966 and paid for. The boats slipped out of Cherbourg on Christmas Day after they were sold to an Oslo front company, ostensibly conducting North Sea oil exploration. Flying the Norwegian flag, the gunboats entered Haifa harbour on 31 December.

At the beginning of the year, Israeli military authorities announced that since the end of the Six Day War, 600 Arab militants had been killed and 1,500 captured, plus many from conventional Arab armed forces. There were 1,280 reported border incidents, of which 920 were on the Jordanian front.

In February, Yasser Arafat announced that several European volunteers were fighting with Fatah. Moshe Dayan reported to the Knesset that Mao's China was providing both arms and training to the PLO.

Attacks by mainly Fatah militants increased in a wide variety of civilian locations. A trial in January revealed attempts to blow up a Tel Aviv cinema and the offices of the daily *Yediot Aharanot*. Two people were killed by a bomb placed in Jerusalem's Supersol supermarket. An East Jerusalem television shop jointly owned by Jews and Arabs was also bombed. A car bomb was detonated in Tel Aviv's Dizengoff Street.

In June, three bombs were set off in Bab el Wad Street in Jerusalem in order to target visitors to the Western Wall. In late October, several bombs exploded in the Kiriat Sprinzak and Neve Sha'anan quarters in Haifa. In Eilat, underwater explosives, planted by frogmen, damaged two Israeli merchant vessels.

More powerful Katyusha rockets now featured in attacks on Mitzpe Ramon and the Timna copper mines. The PFLP blew a hole in the Aramco pipeline in the Golan Heights which carried crude oil from Saudi Arabia to Lebanon. A similar attack took place in June when a pipeline in Haifa harbour was destroyed. Pylons were demolished in the eastern Negev, cutting off the delivery of electricity.

Attacks from Fatah and the PFLP clearly impressed Palestinian youth in the West Bank and Gaza. In February, there were demonstrations and strikes by high school students in many West Bank locations as well as business closures. Posters of Yasser Arafat were displayed. Several leaders of the protests were deported to Jordan.

In mid-February, King Hussein and Yasser Arafat met for the first time in Amman to discuss the movement of several thousand PLO fighters from Egypt to Jordan. There were subsequent press leaks that Hussein had clandestinely met both Abba Eban and Yigal Allon in London.

At the same time, there were military exchanges between Jordanian and Israeli forces as well as retaliation against Palestinian positions on Jordanian soil. Abba Eban dismissed the notion of a

Palestinian entity on the West Bank and generally supported the Allon plan which returned demilitarised territory to Jordan. In April, Hussein presented a peace plan based on UN Resolution 242, which was quickly rejected by the Israeli government. Presented with Nasser's approval, it was also rejected by Syria, the PLO and many other Arab states. Hussein then moved to attain greater political and military control in Jordan and to rally pro-Jordanian Palestinians on the West Bank.

The Ba'athist government of Ahmed Hassan al-Bakr sent Iraqi troops to Jordan to take part in military exchanges with Israel. In early December, Israeli aircraft attacked Iraqi positions in northern Jordan in retaliation for the shelling of settlements in the Galilee region. This laid the basis for the arrests of Jews accused of being part of a CIA–Zionist conspiracy to overthrow the Baghdad government. It was claimed that they trained in sabotage in Abadan, Iran. This government had come to power in a coup in July 1968, but feared that it would be quickly supplanted. Al-Bakr thereby attacked 'fifth columnists' at a rally. This laid the basis for the public execution of nine Iraqi Jews – mainly from Basra – in Baghdad's Liberation Square at the end of January. It was promoted by the regime as a festival of celebration and tens of thousands were bussed in. This created great anger within Israel, but was also criticised within the Arab world. More Iraqi Jews were executed in August. Both Yasser Arafat and Radio Moscow justified the executions. Golda Meir told the Knesset at the end of the year that fifty-three people including eleven Jews had been hanged and many imprisoned.

There were ongoing military exchanges across the Suez Canal. This was accompanied by raiding parties on the opposite bank by both sides. Israeli incursions went further into Egyptian territory. In December, the US secretary of state, William Rogers, proposed a plan to end the war of attrition between Israel and Egypt.

In November, Golda Meir's government openly publicised the activities of the Jewish emigration movement in the USSR. The pressure of Soviet immigrants in Israel, the growing involvement of Diaspora Jewry and attacks from the Israeli Right promoted the publication of a letter from the heads of eighteen Georgian Jewish families. Israeli policy moved from promoting civil rights for Soviet Jews to one of free emigration.

The formal establishment of the Labour Alignment at the end of January did not mean an end to ideological disputes and the threat of breakaways. Indeed Shimon Peres thought that Rafi could win more seats outside Labour. Rafi and Ahdut Ha'Avoda favoured more settlement in the West Bank, while Mapam and parts of Mapai did not. When Golda Meir came out of retirement to become prime minister after the sudden death of Levi Eshkol, there were party abstentions by supporters of Dayan who believed that he should have stood for the post. In the Knesset, Ben-Gurion abstained in the vote of confidence in Golda Meir and proceeded instead to establish the State List with the remnant of Rafi.

Dayan wanted to annex the Golan Heights, Gaza and a section of the Sinai peninsula which would link to Sharm el-Sheikh. Ahdut Ha'Avoda's Yigal Allon wanted the River Jordan to be 'Israel's security frontier'.

The election produced a loss of seven seats for the Labour Alignment which went mainly to Ben-Gurion's new State List. Gahal remained static at twenty-six seats, but the breakaway Free Centre under Shmuel Tamir gained two mandates. Gahal had not advanced despite the very open divisions within Labour. While most parties remained static electorally, this marked the beginning of the fragmentation of the Labour consensus and a gradual movement to the Right.

151

The 1970s

The 1970s was the decade when the Israeli Left stopped being the natural party of government. In 1977, Labour fragmented with the establishment of the Democratic Movement for Change under Yigael Yadin. This allowed Menahem Begin's Likud to come through the middle and establish the ascendancy of the Israeli Right. Under Begin, the dismantling of state enterprises, the primacy of private enterprise and privatisation proceeded apace. The decade also saw the expansion of the settlement drive on the West Bank – ideological settlements often in the heart of Palestinian population centres rather than security settlements in strategic locations. It also saw a rapprochement with Egypt when Begin and Anwar Sadat agreed the Camp David Accords in 1979.

Here a perplexed Golda Meir, the prime minister, holding a map, is seeking to lead the labour movement forward. Following her into the wilderness are the leaders of the antagonistic factions of the Labour Alignment who hold profoundly different views about peace and the Palestinians. Nixon, Sadat and King Hussein look on in bewilderment.

Dosh (*Ma'ariv* 5 April 1971)

1970

Five passenger aircraft were hijacked by the PFLP to Dawson's Field, a remote airstrip near Zarqa in Jordan, where they were eventually blown up. The Jewish passengers were separated from the non-Jewish ones who were released. This incident was a central factor in King Hussein's decision to militarily confront the Palestinians during 'Black September'.

The inaction of the United Nations is depicted by the crumbling UN building in New York since four of the aircraft were bound for New York. The skull and crossbones, the insignia of piracy, is emblazoned on the tail fin of one aircraft.

Mike (*Yediot Aharanot* 10 September 1970)

1 Jan	Shmuel Rosenwasser kidnapped from Metula while on guard duty
7 Jan	Israeli aircraft bomb military installations 30 km from Cairo in Operation Priha
10 Jan	Two Sukhoi SU-7 fighters shot down by Hawk ground-to-air missiles over Suez
15 Jan	Leah Goldberg, Hebrew poet, writer and translator, dies aged 58
23 Jan	Supreme Court decides the nationality of Shalit's children
24 Jan	Huge ammunitions explosion in Eilat kills 21
27 Jan	Letter from 25 Moscow Jews asking to go to Israel submitted to UN
6 Feb	Naval auxiliary vessel in Eilat sunk by Egyptian frogmen
6 Feb	Soviet-built 700-ton Egyptian minelayer sunk by Israeli forces in Gulf of Suez
8 Feb	Egyptians cross Suez Canal and penetrate into Sinai as far as the Mitla Pass
9 Feb	New sales tax increases price of imported cars as much as fourfold
10 Feb	DFLP attack passenger bus at Munich airport
17 Feb	Nobel Prize winner and Hebrew writer Shmuel Yosef Agnon dies aged 82
21 Feb	PFLP-GC bomb on board Tel Aviv Swissair flight kills all crew and passengers
4 Mar	Pro-Kremlin Soviet Jews appear at press conference to condemn Israel
9 Mar	Yigal Allon reveals plans to build a Jewish suburb of Hebron
10 Mar	Knesset agrees Jewish status is based on Halakha after Shalit case
23 Mar	US Secretary of State Rogers rejects request for more Skyhawk and Phantom jets
28 Mar	Poet Natan Alterman dies in Tel Aviv aged 59
8 Apr	Knesset rejects possibility of Nahum Goldmann meeting Nasser in Cairo
29 Apr	Government confirms Soviet pilots are flying defence missions over Egypt.
4 May	Dayan announces that Israel has halted deep penetration raids into Egypt
18 May	David Ben-Gurion resigns from the Knesset
22 May	Eight children on Avivim bus killed in a PFLP attack near the Lebanese border
10 June	PFLP kill Robert Perry, assistant military attaché at US Embassy in Amman
12 June	King Hussein dismisses army head following clashes with Palestinian forces
15 June	Foiled attempt by refuseniks to take aircraft at Smolny airport, Leningrad
25 June	Rogers proposes revamped peace plan including 90-day ceasefire
16 July	Haim Moshe Shapira, NRP leader and government minister, dies aged 68
4 Aug	Gahal votes 117–112 to leave government over acceptance of Rogers plan
7 Aug	Israel and Egypt agree to 90-day ceasefire
7 Sept	Yitzhak Gruenbaum, Polish Zionist leader and government minister, dies aged 90
12 Sept	PFLP blow up five hijacked passenger aircraft in Dawson's Field in Jordan
16 Sept	Armed conflict breaks out between Palestinian forces and Jordanian army
28 Sept	President Nasser dies of a heart attack in Cairo aged 52
5 Oct	Anwar Sadat nominated to serve full five-year term as Nasser's successor
24 Dec	Kuznetsov and Dymshits sentenced to death in Leningrad aircraft affair trial

The war of attrition continued with great ferocity with raids on the opposite bank of the Suez Canal by commandos of both sides The Soviet Union continued to replace Egyptian air defence equipment such as radar installations and SAM ground-to-air missiles which had been destroyed by Israeli warplane attacks. These attacks on SAM-2 missile sites penetrated even deeper into Egyptian territory and closer to Cairo. In March, large numbers of Soviet personnel arrived to operate the newly arrived and more effective SAM-3 missiles. This led to a delay in the official US decision to reject Israeli requests to deliver additional Skyhawk and Phantom jets for fear of igniting a full-scale war. At the end of April, Israel Radio told its listeners that Soviet pilots were flying operational missions from military installations under their control in central Egypt. While Soviet-piloted aircraft did not interfere with Israeli air-strikes on Egyptian positions in the Canal Zone, the Soviet defence of Cairo, Alexandria, the Aswan Dam and their environs allowed Egyptian pilots to concentrate their attacks in other locations. In May, Dayan announced the cessation of Israeli attacks deep into Egyptian territory to avoid any clash with the Soviets. US Secretary of State Rogers proposed a revised peace plan in June which included a ceasefire between Israel and Egypt. The Egyptians gradually moved their SAM-3 missiles towards the Canal Zone and these were fired at Israeli aircraft by Soviet personnel in early July. A ninety-day ceasefire was agreed and came into effect in early August. Although the status quo was to extend to 50 km on both sides of the Canal without further military build-up, Egypt immediately moved missiles into their zone. Between forty and fifty new missile bases were established in the central sector of the Canal between the Cairo–Ismailia and Cairo–Suez roads.

Nahum Goldmann, president of the World Jewish Congress, wrote an article in *Foreign Affairs Quarterly* which bemoaned the admiration of and support for Israel by 'reactionary, nationalistic groups' as a result of 'this permanent state of war'. It was then disclosed that Goldmann might be invited to visit Egypt to meet Nasser, but only if there was official Israeli authorisation and that any such visit should be made public. The initiative had come about following Goldmann's contact with Marshall Tito of Yugoslavia.

This brought criticism from Abba Eban, Moshe Dayan, Golda Meir and most vociferously, Herut's Menahem Begin. Goldmann's initiative was condemned in a Knesset vote on the grounds that he was unelected. This brusque rejection led to student demonstrations and a meeting between Golda Meir and high school seniors. Only President Shazar defended Goldmann, arguing that he should not be turned into a second Uriel Da Costa, the seventeenth-century philosopher who challenged orthodoxy and was excommunicated by the Jewish community of Amsterdam.

King Hussein's attempt to assist Palestinian militants from his side of the border while simultaneously trying to make them desist became more difficult. While Palestinians came to Jordan from Lebanon and Syria to participate in the armed struggle, others felt committed to the state of Jordan. In addition Arafat was unable to control the more revolutionary elements of the Palestinian national movement. The Popular Front for the Liberation of Palestine (PFLP) and the Democratic Front for the Liberation of Palestine (DFLP) began to advocate the overthrow of the Jordanian regime, which undermined Arafat's relationship with King Hussein. In early June, gunmen fired on Hussein's motorcade which ignited a shelling of Palestinian refugee camps by the Jordanian military. The PFLP responded by taking more than fifty hostages from two Amman hotels.

In early September, the PFLP hijacked two passenger planes from Frankfurt and Zurich to Dawson's Field at Zarqa in Jordan, while an attempted hijack of an El Al flight from Amsterdam was foiled. Leila Khaled was arrested by British police after an emergency stop-off in London. The other hijacker, Patrick Argüello, a member of the Nicaraguan Sandinistas, was killed in a gunfight on board the aircraft. He had been trained by the DFLP. A Pan Am flight was hijacked to Cairo and a couple of days later, a BOAC flight from Bahrain was taken to Dawson's Field in the hope of freeing Khaled. All the aircraft were blown up.

Several of the flights had originated in Tel Aviv and a majority of their passengers were Israeli. The Jewish passengers were separated from the non-Jewish ones. Many were detained in a hotel in Amman before release.

While Arafat meandered between approval and disapproval, Hussein took military action as parts of his kingdom had been taken over by Palestinian militants. The Jordanian air force stopped a Syrian incursion in support of the Palestinians. As a result of Hussein's assault against Palestinian militants in Jordan during 'Black September', Arafat was eventually forced to recognise the authority of the king, while the leaders of the PFLP and the DFLP fled to Damascus. This marked the genesis of the Black September group, based on Fatah members.

Gahal, while part of the government coalition, suffered internal dissension between its Herut and Liberal components. Following the Supreme Court's decision to rule that the nationality of Binyamin Shalit's wife and children should be considered to be 'Jewish', Herut aligned itself with the religious parties in a vote in the Knesset in March on the question of definition of Jewishness. It also took exception to the government's interpretation of UN Resolution 242 which could be understood as withdrawal from the West Bank. Gahal became supportive of the Rafi wing of the Labour party and Dayan's statements on the territories. Golda Meir was concerned that ideological differences between Rafi and other wings of the party would result in a defection to Gahal.

The Rogers peace plan exacerbated the factional division within Gahal, with Herut vociferously opposed to any withdrawal from conquered territory. While the Liberals disagreed and rejected any departure from government, they were also not prepared to break up their alliance with Herut. In August, the Knesset voted 66–28, with 9 abstentions, to accept the Rogers plan. All six Gahal ministers then resigned from Golda Meir's government. In a subsequent debate, Begin termed the initiative 'a Munich diktat'. Dayan, however, did not resign. Yet within a few weeks of the vote, construction work began on Kiriat Arba, a settlement abutting Hebron. Begin further argued that the Israeli presence in the Suez Canal region was a service to the free world, delaying the delivery of Soviet arms to North Vietnam by another sixteen days. In December, Gahal opposed the resumption of peace talks under the auspices of the UN's Special Representative for the Middle East, Gunnar Jarring, calling instead for direct talks with the Arabs.

In June, several refuseniks, mainly from Riga, were arrested on the tarmac of Smolny airport, Leningrad. Their plan was to seize a twelve-seater small aircraft, fly it to Priozersk near the Finnish border, pick up another four passengers and hop over the border to Sweden. The KGB knew of their plans all along and intended to utilise this futile attempt to entrap the mainstream refuseniks and thereby extinguish the growing emigration movement in the USSR.

Their trial opened in mid-December in Leningrad. Two defendants, Mark Dymshits and Eduard Kuznetsov, were sentenced to death on Christmas Eve on a charge of treason. This led to international protests, especially among figures on the Left including Salvador Allende and many leading Eurocommunists. A private appeal by the Israelis to General Franco in Spain had led to the commuting of the death sentences on several Basque prisoners. The Kremlin felt that it could not fall below the standards of Francisco Franco and the sentences on Dymshits and Kuznetsov were commuted to fifteen years' imprisonment.

157

1971

The Kremlin cracked down on Jewish activists in a series of show trials in an attempt to suppress the emigration movement. The Second Leningrad trial occurred in May.

Leonid Brezhnev and Alexei Kosygin are seen here processing Soviet Jews on a conveyor belt leading to Soviet courtrooms. The cartoon is titled 'Stakhanovich' or son of Stakhanov. This alludes to Alexei Stakhanov who outperformed all other workers in a robotic, superhuman fashion – and was promoted as the ideal Soviet worker during Stalin's regime. The all-out attack on those Soviet Jews who wished to leave for Israel is seen in Stakhanovite terms.

Ze'ev (*Ha'aretz* 14 May 1971)

11 Jan   Soviet immigrant Natan Tsirulnikov becomes three millionth Israeli citizen

26 Jan   Dayan states in Knesset that SAM-2 missiles now deployed in Syria

31 Jan   Government withholds approval for advertising on television

8 Feb   Jarring peace plan sent to Israel and Egypt

15 Feb   Israeli military governor takes over administration of Gaza

21 Feb   Jerusalem municipal council approves plan to build three dormitory cities

23 Feb   World Conference on Soviet Jewry opens in Brussels

28 Feb   Shmuel Rosenwasser exchanged for Mahmoud Hidjazi after 424 days

1 Mar   Jordanian army begins offensive to drive out Palestinian militants

10 Mar   Soviet Jews stage sit-in at Presidium of Supreme Soviet reception room

15 Mar   Jewish Agency head states a quarter of a million Israelis below poverty line

12 Apr   Land of Israel members prevented from marching to Hebron

18 Apr   Israeli Black Panthers battle police during Mimouna festival

11 May   Second Leningrad trial of Soviet refuseniks opens

13 May   World Bank offers $15 million loan to build the Ayalon motorway in Tel Aviv

17 May   Knesset amendment granting citizenship in absentia to any Jew abroad

22 May   Istanbul consul's body discovered after kidnapping by Turkish People's Liberation Front

25 May   Mapam MK Abdel Aziz-Zuabi appointed deputy minister of health

27 May   USSR and Egypt sign 15-year friendship and cooperation treaty

30 May   Health minister, Victor Shemtov, estimates 12,000 drug addicts in Israel

2 June   First El Al jumbo jet goes into service

5 June   South Africa criticises Israeli medicines donation to the Organisation of African Unity

14 June   Supreme Court appoints commission to investigate bribes in football

15 June   Strike by 4,000 management and service personnel at 29 government hospitals

27 June   Cabinet approves five-year national slum clearance programme

6 July   Yitzhak Tabenkin, socialist Zionist ideologist, dies in Ein Harod aged 83

7 July   Katyusha attack kills four in Petah Tiqva

17 July   Dozens of Palestinian militants flee to Israel, escaping Jordanian army

6 Aug   Yitzhak Meir Levin, veteran Agudat Yisrael politician, dies aged 77

9 Aug   Golda Meir signs emergency regulations ordering doctors to return to work

10 Aug   Four high school students refuse military service in West Bank and Gaza

20 Aug   Israel's pound devalued by 20 per cent

1 Sept   U Thant presented with a letter signed by 531 Georgian refuseniks

3 Oct   Health Ministry reports 25 per cent of school students smoke regularly

11 Oct   Newly arrived MiG-23s invade Israeli airspace from Egypt

10 Nov   Advocates of civil marriage hold 'Mamzer Day'

28 Nov   Assassination of Wasfi el Tal, Jordanian prime minister, by Black September

An international conference on Soviet Jewry took place in Brussels in February. It brought together Diaspora communities from fifty countries and was addressed by Ben-Gurion. It symbolised the desire of Golda Meir's government to act openly and to rally support for the emigration movement that was growing in the USSR. It also marked the formal intervention of the leadership of Jewish communities since previous protests about the fate of Soviet Jewry had been left to young people and individual groups of activists. The conference was also an open display of opposition to the ongoing series of trials against Jews who wished to leave the USSR for Israel. The Kremlin also sent its own delegation of 'loyal' Soviet Jews, headed by General David Dragunsky, which held its own parallel meeting in Brussels.

While Kuznetsov and Dymshits had been reprieved at the end of 1970, collective trials of refuseniks took place in Leningrad, Riga and Kishinev. In addition there were numerous trials of individuals – Valery Kukui (Sverdlovsk), Raisa Palatnik (Odessa), Emelia Trakhtenberg (Samarkand), Boris Azernikov (Leningrad) – in a widespread crackdown to suppress the emigration movement. Actions by Soviet Jews moved beyond the publication of collective letters. In March, more than a hundred Soviet Jews staged a sit-in in the reception room of the Presidium of the Supreme Soviet in Moscow. This came several weeks before the Soviet Communist party was due to open its own conference in Moscow.

Further occupations of official premises took place in several Soviet cities. In Riga, Jews occupied the emigration office. In Vilnius there was a sit-in at the Communist party headquarters. In Tbilisi, three hundred demonstrated outside the Georgian party building. While such demonstrations had not happened since the 1920s, some thirteen thousand Jews were allowed to leave in 1971 – the largest number for many decades. Hunger strikes now took place and 531 Georgian Jews signed an appeal, entitled 'Israel or Death', which was presented to Secretary-General U Thant at the United Nations. The actions of Soviet Jews also attracted the support of figures in the intellectual and artistic worlds such as Laurence Olivier, Charlie Chaplin, Arthur Miller, Benjamin Britten, W. H. Auden, Stephen Spender, Henry Moore, Artur Rubinstein and Ingmar Bergman. In the Knesset, its members pressed for a citizenship act which would allow Soviet Jews who intended to emigrate, but were prevented, to be granted Israeli citizenship

In a speech in the village of Tanta in the Nile delta, President Sadat disclosed that Soviet troops were manning missile sites near the Suez Canal and that some had been killed in a strike against a missile base at Dashur near Cairo. Moshe Dayan told the Knesset that there were ten thousand Soviet military personnel in Egypt plus several squadrons of MiG-21s, flown by Soviet pilots, as well as SAM missiles installed in Syria. Several MiG-23 interceptor jets, Sukhoi-11 fighter bombers and TU-16 Badger reconnaissance-bombers were now stationed in Egypt, which reinforced further Israeli pleas to the Nixon administration to lift the embargo on the sale of Phantom jets to Israel. In May, a fifteen-year treaty of friendship and cooperation was signed between the USSR and Egypt.

Sadat announced to the Egyptian National Assembly an initiative to reopen the Suez Canal and hinted at an acceptance of the existence of Israel. He was also ready to accept an international force at Sharm el-Sheikh, but not the demilitarisation of Sinai. Golda Meir rejected Sadat's proposals and wished to separate the question of withdrawal from the Canal Zone from other issues. Israel later rejected a six-point plan from US Secretary of State Rogers for an interim settlement over Suez. Both Israel and Egypt reacted positively to the peace plan of Gunnar Jarring in early February.

In September, the ceasefire with Egypt was broken with exchanges across the Suez Canal for the first time in more than a year. Egyptian missile sites were attacked in retaliation for a missile strike on an unarmed Israeli transport plane over Sinai.

A government plan to build an arc of suburbs in East Jerusalem for 200,000 residents was criticised by the Muslim Council, Israeli Jews who argued that the city's 'unique beauty' would be disfigured and a panel of international consultants. Some argued that there had been no public consultation and display of the plans, while others said that it would inhibit any negotiations. In March, the housing minister, Ze'ev Sharef, stated that 750 units would be built in the Neve Ya'acov area, 550 in Ramot, 600 in East Talpiot and 700 in Gilo. The cabinet rejected a 14–0 vote in the UN Security Council condemning the construction of new suburbs. Sharef later commented that a new settlement, Hitnahalut, would also be built across the Eilat–Sharm el-Sheikh road some fifty miles south of Eilat. In October, it was announced that another four settlements would be built in Gaza in addition to Bnei Darom.

In a State Department report on foreign policy, US Secretary of State Rogers noted that 'Jerusalem should be a unified city' and 'Israel and Jordan should both have roles in its civic, economic and religious life.'

In an interview, Golda Meir stated that Israel would be prepared to return most of the West Bank while retaining East Jerusalem, the Golan Heights, the Gaza Strip and Sharm el-Sheikh in southern Sinai. This led to condemnation by Gahal's Menahem Begin, who argued that territories conquered in 1967 should be retained either because they were part of the national heritage or through right of conquest. In a Knesset debate, Golda Meir opposed the establishment of an independent Palestinian state on the West Bank and emphasised the need for secure, recognised frontiers, determined by negotiations and not by international guarantees. In contrast, in August, Moshe Dayan declared that Israel should regard itself as the permanent regime in the occupied territories.

Despite Arafat's agreement with King Hussein during the previous October, the PFLP and the DFLP continued to attack Jordanian forces. Hussein was determined to bring Jordan once again under his sole control. The conflict between Palestinian nationalists and the Jordanian army therefore continued in the north of the country despite the withdrawal of funding to Jordan by both Kuwait and Libya, criticism from Cairo and the severing of diplomatic relations by Iraq. Jordanian forces confronted Palestinian militia in Jarash, Ajloun and Irbid such that by July Palestinian militants were fleeing to Israel to escape this heavy military crackdown. Large numbers of Palestinians surrendered to Jordanian forces, but were allowed to leave for Lebanon via Syria. By September, King Hussein stated that he was ready to conclude a separate peace with Israel.

Young women, one from Holland, the other from Peru, were persuaded by their lovers to take suitcases on El Al flights. The luggage was packed with explosives which did not detonate.

The 'Black September' group was established to carry out reprisals. Wasfi el-Tal, the Jordanian prime minister who was also minister of defence, was held responsible for the military confrontation and the eventual rout of the Palestinians in Jordan. He was assassinated by Black September outside the Sheraton Hotel in Cairo in November.

This division was reflected amongst the inhabitants of the West Bank – between pro-Jordanian Palestinians and those who supported Fatah and other groups. The PFLP and DFLP had stated their intention to overthrow King Hussein. In Gaza, the Israelis dismissed the mayor for lack of cooperation and replaced him with a military governor.

161

1972

The killing of Israeli athletes at the Munich Olympics by members of Black September reflected badly on both the Olympic Committee and the city's police force.

The member of Black September, carrying a machine gun and laden with hand grenades, is accorded the gold medal. The dismayed member of the Olympic Committee in second place on the podium is concerned that 'the Games must go on', while the hapless representative of the Munich police, responsible for the incompetent, botched attempt to rescue the athletes at the airport, stands on the lowest position on the podium.

Mike (*Yediot Aharanot* September 1972)

1 Jan David (Dado) Elazar becomes IDF Chief of Staff, succeeding Haim Bar-Lev

18 Jan The largest group of Soviet Jews so far, 300, arrive in Israel on an El Al 747

18 Jan Police attack Black Panther protesters outside WZO Jerusalem conference

26 Jan Bnei Brak to receive first public library despite haredi objections

27 Jan Income tax to be levied on Israeli inhabitants of Golan Heights

4 Feb Israel recognises Bangladesh

1 Mar Moshe Sneh, Hagana commander and leader of the Communist party Maki, dies aged 63

30 Mar Idi Amin's Uganda breaks off diplomatic relations with Israel

1 Apr Protest near Kerem Shalom about the evacuation of Bedouin

2 Apr King Hussein calls for Jerusalem to be declared an 'open city'

4 May Golda Meir meets Nicolae Ceauşescu on an official visit to Romania

7 May Cabinet ratifies Montreal Convention on hijacking of aircraft

9 May Hijacked Sabena 707 aircraft at Lod airport stormed by Sayeret Matkal

15 May University students strike over the doubling of tuition fees

25 May Soviet Jews stage hunger strike at Western Wall before Nixon's USSR visit

30 May Cabinet confirms plans to build 200 new apartments in Kiriat Arba

30 May Japanese Red Army kill 26 civilians in assault at Lod airport

13 June Two Egyptian MiG-21 interceptors shot down over Mediterranean

23 June Cabinet rules that former inhabitants cannot return to Baram and Iqrit

18 June Sadat expels 20,000 Soviet advisers from Egypt

3 Aug Soviets introduce diploma tax for potential emigrants from USSR

16 Aug Two British women unknowingly take a record-player bomb on board an El Al flight

5 Sept Israeli athletes held hostage by Black September at Munich Olympics

6 Sept Israeli athletes and Palestinian captors die at airport in botched rescue attempt

11 Sept Supreme Court votes to expel gangster Meyer Lansky

19 Sept Letter bomb kills attaché Ami Shechori at Israel's London Embassy

4 Oct Jackson–Vanik amendment introduced in US Congress

11 Oct Tel Aviv court bars Meir Kahane from leaving Israel for USA

15 Oct Shlomo Goren and Ovadia Yosef elected Ashkenazi and Sephardi chief rabbis

29 Oct Three Munich gunmen exchanged for passengers of hijacked Lufthansa 727

6 Nov Netzarim established as a settlement in Gaza

8 Nov Richard Nixon re-elected US president

15 Nov Israel votes for anti-apartheid motions at the UN

7 Dec Police announce arrest of 'Red Front' members, directed by Syrian intelligence

7 Dec Israel and South Vietnam sign a mutual recognition agreement

21 Dec Ezer Weizman resigns as Herut chairman after clash with Begin

28 Dec Black September seizes Israeli Embassy in Bangkok

163

Black September, which had been initiated by Fatah members in 1971, was responsible for the hijacking of the Sabena flight from Vienna in May and the killing of an attaché by a letter bomb at the Israeli Embassy in London in September. Letter bombs were also posted to Israeli diplomats in various countries and to government functionaries in Jerusalem.

Black September was also responsible for the kidnapping and torturing of Israeli athletes in the Olympic village in Munich and the eventual deaths of eleven athletes during a botched rescue attempt by untrained German police at Fürstenfeldbruck airport. Black September had demanded the release of several hundred Palestinian prisoners in Israel and the freeing of members of the Baader–Meinhof Gang in West Germany. King Hussein, the Soviet Union and China all condemned the attacks.

The bodies of five Palestinians who had also been killed were flown to Libya and buried with full military honours. The three surviving gunmen were exchanged for thirteen passengers and seven crew members of a Lufthansa 727 jet which had been hijacked for this purpose on a flight from Beirut to Ankara. The West German foreign minister, Walter Scheel, allegedly met a Black September operative several months later. The PLO would cease attacks on German soil in exchange for an 'upgrade' in political relations. Protesters demonstrated outside the West German Embassy in Tel Aviv. Four Israeli security personnel were asked by Golda Meir to resign following the recommendations of the Koppel inquiry into the Munich killings.

In May, Sayeret Matkal commandos released passengers from a Sabena flight held at Lod airport by supporters of Black September. A few weeks later, members of the Japanese Red Army attacked visitors and staff at the airport. This PFLP operation resulted in the deaths of a large number of visiting Christian pilgrims. In August, a record-player bomb, unwittingly carried on board by two passengers, forced an El Al flight to return to Rome airport.

Israel continued to attack Fatah military encampments in both Syria and Lebanon. Settlements such as Ein Zivan, Nahal Golan and Ramat Magshimim and army positions on the Golan Heights were fired upon from Syria. Attacks from Fatahland in southern Lebanon, where an estimated five thousand Palestinian fighters were located, targeted major Israeli locations such as Nahariya, Acre, Kiriat Shemona and Safed. In February, Albert and Florence Malka were returning from a barmitzvah celebration in Nahariya when their vehicle was hit by a bazooka shell three miles from the border. Such incidents provoked air and ground attacks on concentrations of Palestinian fighters stationed in villages such as Yanta, Ainata and Hebbariye. Other locations such as Rasheiya Fakhar on the slopes of Mount Hermon were hit.

In the first half of the year, periodic clashes between Israeli and Egyptian aircraft took place, often with Soviet back-up for Sadat's forces. Despite the visit of the Soviet defence minister, Marshal Grechko, Sadat announced the departure of twenty thousand Soviet personnel a few weeks later. The firing of SAM missiles by the Egyptian military in the Suez Canal area then ceased for several months, but resumed once more in October. Soviet support continued for Syria, where a thousand personnel were stationed. In October, a Soviet airlift of arms for the Assad regime took place over several days.

The Labour Alignment, consisting of Mapai, Rafi, Ahdut Ha'Avoda and Mapam, demonstrated public infighting over the future of the territories conquered in 1967. As there was virtually no movement towards peace negotiations with the Arab states five years after the Six Day War, more people advocated the settlement of the West Bank. In an interview with CBS, Moshe Dayan stated that even if a peace treaty was signed with Jordan, Israel should have the right to build Jewish settlements on the West Bank. If peace was reached with Egypt, then much of Sinai would be returned, with Israel retaining Sharm el-Sheikh and a coastal strip connecting that strong-point with Israel proper. In February, the Jewish National Fund announced plans to build four new settlements on the West Bank and a 55-mile road which would link Jerusalem with the Beisan Valley.

The plans to move Bedouin with compensation in order to build a settlement adjacent to Rafah in southern Gaza was strongly opposed by Meir Ya'ari and Yaakov Hazan of Mapam. This pitted them against the leadership of Rafi, which advocated pushing the party out of the coalition. In November, Netzarim was established on the outskirts of Gaza.

Israel Galili of Ahdut Ha'Avoda argued that the River Jordan was Israel's natural frontier. His party colleague Yigal Allon, the deputy prime minister, argued that Jewish settlements should be constructed along the ceasefire lines as this would advance the expansion of the nation's economic infrastructure and 'will serve as a lever in our struggle over the future map of Israel in the political arena'.

In May, the cabinet voted to expand Kiriat Arba, next to Hebron, by adding another two hundred apartments. Mapai ministers Abba Eban, Pinhas Sapir, Zev Sharef and Yaacov Shapiro, together with Mapam's Natan Peled, all abstained. Sapir, however, supported the establishment of settlements on the Golan Heights and presided over the opening of an industrial plant at Bnei Yehuda at the southern end of the Heights. Sapir also opposed the influx of cheap Arab labour to do menial tasks in Israel.

Golda Meir had to balance all these opposing viewpoints in order to keep her coalition together. She too opposed outright annexation of the West Bank and was prepared to return the populated part of the conquered territories. She rejected any suggestion of allowing the inhabitants of the villages of Birim and Iqrit near the Lebanese border, evacuated in 1948, to return.

Most politicians were opposed to returning to the 1967 borders and thereby dividing Jerusalem. King Hussein's public offer of ruling over both the East and West Banks, a federal kingdom, and the suggestion that Jerusalem could become an 'open city' jointly administered by Arabs and Israelis, was rejected by Meir.

Disputes occurred also in Herut such that the party's convention was delayed. Ezer Weizman challenged Menahem Begin and his supporters from the days of the Irgun without success. He resigned from Gahal.

The number of Soviet Jews allowed to leave the USSR in 1972 increased from 13,000 to 32,000 and the number of applications to leave for Israel also increased. There were further trials, such as those of Yuli Brind and Vladimir Markman, alongside general harassment and temporary imprisonment – especially before the visit of President Nixon to Moscow and against the imposition of a diploma tax to deter professionals from leaving. In the US Congress in October, Senator Henry Jackson's amendment linked 'most favoured nation' trade status with Jewish emigration. This was initially opposed by Nixon and the US secretary of state, Henry Kissinger, who feared that it would damage their efforts to secure detente with the Soviet Union.

In 1971, the Black Panther party had been formed to protest against the economic and social injustice which affected the Mizrahim in Israel. The availability of funds for the emigration of Soviet Jews but not to tackle social deprivation in Israel became a burning issue. On May Day, police used tear gas for the first time against Black Panther demonstrators in Jerusalem.

There was also a demonstration outside the Knesset by former Soviet Jews protesting against the suspension of government business to celebrate May Day. They were received by members of Gahal and the NRP. There was another protest against the Vietnam War by American students outside the US Consulate. There was also a women's demonstration for free abortion, civil marriage and equal pay.

165

1973

The Geneva Conference opened in the aftermath of the Yom Kippur War – a conflict in which Israel was caught unprepared and consequently suffered heavy casualties. The Arab world is lined up on one side of the court with a solitary Israel on the other side. The referees, a military commissar from the USSR, the USA's Uncle Sam and the UN's secretary-general, Kurt Waldheim, appear determined to control 'the game' according to their own interests.

Shmuel Katz (*Nebelspalter* 9 January 1974)

3 Jan	Engineers, technicians, hospital workers go on strike
15 Jan	First meeting between a pope and an Israeli PM as Golda Meir meets Paul VI
22 Jan	Yaakov Dori, first IDF head, dies in Haifa aged 73
26 Jan	Mossad agent Baruch Cohen is gunned down in Madrid
11 Feb	Syrian spy ring trial of Udi Adiv and Dan Vered begins in Haifa
21 Feb	Libyan aircraft enters Israeli airspace and is shot down over Sinai
12 Mar	Businessman Simha Glitzer shot dead in Nicosia, Cyprus
4 Apr	Bader–Ofer amendment, dealing with surplus votes, passed in Knesset
9 Apr	Attacks on Israeli ambassador's home and at El Al terminal in Nicosia
10 Apr	Special forces kill senior Fatah and DFLP commanders in Beirut and Sidon
10 Apr	Ephraim Katzir defeats Ephraim Orbach to become president
11 May	Trial of Meir Kahane and Amihai Paglin begins, charged with arms smuggling
18 May	Avraham Shlonsky, writer and poet, dies in Tel Aviv aged 73
23 May	Attempted bombing of El Al freight terminal at Kennedy airport
1 July	Military attaché Col. Yosef Alon shot in Maryland, probably by Black September
20 July	JAL flight from Amsterdam to Tokyo hijacked by PFLP
21 July	Mossad mistakenly kills Moroccan waiter in Lillehammer
3 Aug	Seamen go on strike, preventing ships from unloading and sailing
5 Aug	Black September attacks Athens airport, killing 3 and injuring 55
10 Aug	MEA flight from Beirut forced to land at army base in Israel
20 Aug	Cabinet approves establishment of Open University
9 Sept	Castro severs diplomatic ties between Cuba and Israel
13 Sept	Thirteen Syrian MiG-21s shot down in dogfight
13 Sept	Formation of right-wing bloc, Likud, led by Menahem Begin
16 Sept	Labour condemns Pinochet coup in Chile
28 Sept	Soviet Jews taken hostage on train at Austrian–Czech border
6 Oct	Yom Kippur War begins
12 Oct	Nixon sends weapons and supplies to Israel
17 Oct	OPEC raise oil prices by 70 per cent
19 Oct	Oil embargo declared by Arab states against the United States
11 Nov	Israel and Egypt sign ceasefire agreement at Kilometer 101
1 Dec	David Ben-Gurion, 'first citizen of Israel', dies in Ramat Gan aged 87
10 Dec	Austria closes transit camp for Soviet Jews at Schoenau
17 Dec	El Al lounge, Pam Am Boeing, attacked at Rome airport, 30 killed
21 Dec	Middle East peace conference opens in Geneva
31 Dec	Labour wins election, but Likud now comes within striking distance

The Yom Kippur War was, at its end, more a draw than a victory or defeat. After weeks of fighting, an unprepared Israel had recovered militarily and advanced into Egypt and Syria. The change in fortunes was such that both Cairo and Damascus were threatened. This march on these major cities brought about a ceasefire.

Israel had not expected an Egyptian crossing of the Suez Canal as there had been few clashes between them. However, suspicions were aroused at this appearance of normality when the families of Soviet personnel in Egypt began to leave a couple of days before the outbreak of war. The Soviet Union had rearmed and trained Egyptian forces after the Six Day War and supplied them with SAM missiles. These initially formed a protective umbrella to prevent a repetition of the 1967 decimation of Egyptian aircraft. Prime Minister Meir did not order a pre-emptive strike, but instead ordered a mass mobilisation.

By the evening of the first day, five bridgeheads had allowed a hundred thousand Egyptian troops to cross the Canal and engage a much smaller number of Israeli forces. An initial Israeli counter-offensive failed, but when Egyptian forces moved forward into Sinai, Pattons and Centurions, plus Israeli expertise, proved far superior to Soviet tanks. Eventually the Israelis reversed the military situation, broke out and crossed into Egypt, north of the Great Bitter Lake. The war was also a confrontation between the superpowers, and the conflict only came to an end when Brezhnev and Kissinger effectively reached an agreement. Its terms were presented as UN Resolution 338.

If the Israelis were unprepared for an Egyptian military initiative, this was not the case with Syria as there had been ongoing clashes and dogfights throughout the year. At the end of September, King Hussein warned Golda Meir that Syria appeared to be redeploying its forces for an offensive war. There was also intelligence from Mossad agents.

The Syrian offensive was also protected from air attack by Soviet SAM missiles. The Israeli forces that stood in its path were very few in number with few armaments. A major tank battle north of Quneitra prevented a Syrian advance into Israel itself. The offensive was halted when fresh forces arrived to reinforce the outnumbered Israelis.

Israeli Phantom F-4s then bombed the Syrian General Staff headquarters in the centre of Damascus and attacked storage facilities in Homs and Aleppo. Israeli naval forces shelled storage facilities in Latakia and Tartus. Israeli forces then advanced to within twenty miles of Damascus.

While the superpowers organised a peace conference amongst the warring parties in Geneva, there was deepening criticism of Golda Meir's handling of the war and calls for the resignation of the minister of defence, Moshe Dayan.

As a result of the war, the national election was put back until the end of the year. However, a right-wing coalition was being forged when the Gahal executive sent out proposals to the Free Centre, the State List, Rafi and the Independent Liberals in early August. This was given further urgency by the departure of Ariel Sharon from the army and his immediate involvement in right-wing politics. Meir Kahane's movement was barred and both Rafi and the Independent Liberals decided not to join. This new alignment of the Right, the Likud, was formed in September, but early opinion polls indicated that it would not fare better than its constituent parts. The failure of the Labour government to predict the war and the huge number of Israeli casualties – more than 2,500 killed – was a major factor in persuading voters to move to the Likud.

A new generation viewed Menahem Begin as a founding father of Israel and the Likud appealed strongly to the young, the Mizrahim, the undereducated and the working class. It coincided with the decline of socialist Zionism. In the election at the end of December, 39.6 per cent voted Labour while 30.2 per cent voted for the Likud, now only some twelve seats behind. It marked a political breakthrough for the Israeli Right. It also marked the breakaway of Shulamit

Aloni's civil rights movement, Ratz, from the old guard of Labour. Ratz promoted peace, secularism and women's rights.

There were several attacks on European airports by Palestinian militants in attempts to secure the release of prisoners in Israel. In August, Black September operatives killed three people and took thirty-five as hostages at Athens airport. In December, Rome airport was attacked by Palestinians and a Pan Am airliner set on fire, resulting in the deaths of more than thirty passengers. A Lufthansa flight was hijacked to Kuwait by the remaining gunmen.

In the aftermath of the killing of Israeli athletes at the Munich Olympics, Operation Wrath of God was initiated to kill all those involved. At the end of 1972, the PLO representatives in Paris and Rome had been killed. This was followed by the Fatah representative in Cyprus. Israeli intelligence carried out an ongoing assault on those behind Black September.

The Lillehammer affair represented a botched Mossad attempt in July to kill Ali Hassan Salameh, an architect of the Munich killings, but which mistakenly took the life instead of Ahmed Bouchiki, a Moroccan waiter. This led to the arrest of members of the Mossad's Kidon team and a diplomatic fallout with the Norwegians.

A Libyan airliner which had strayed into Israeli airspace was shot down because it was feared that it had been hijacked by Black September and was about to be crashed into an Israeli city. The pilot had feared retribution from Gaddafi if he landed, as ordered, in Israel.

Aircraft hijackings were mainly carried out by the Popular Front for the Liberation of Palestine. In August, a Middle East Airlines (MEA) flight from Beirut was forced to land at an army base in Israel because it was believed that the PFLP's head, George Habash, was one of eighty-one passengers on board. This flight had replaced an Iraqi Airlines flight – and Habash had decided not to take it at the last moment. The interception was condemned by the Israeli Pilots Association.

Diaspora Jews were also targets. In April, the Kashkosh family of five was preparing to leave Iraq, but they were all killed at home. This came two days after the Sayeret Matkal operation, led by Ehud Barak, against PLO commanders in Beirut, which led to the killing of the Black September operative Mohammed Yusuf al-Najjar and his wife. This operation also demolished the headquarters of the PFLP in Beirut.

At the end of the year, Teddy Sieff, a well-known British Jewish businessman and prominent Zionist, was shot in London in a failed assassination attempt by Carlos the Jackal on behalf of the PFLP. This followed the targeting of Israeli intelligence operatives abroad. In Madrid, Baruch Cohen was killed.

Financial pressure from the Arab world, culminating in the oil embargo as a result of the Yom Kippur War, forced twenty-five African nations to sever diplomatic ties with Israel. The Organisation of African Unity (OAU) conference in Ethiopia and a gathering of non-aligned states in Algeria forced friendly nations such as Nigeria and Zaire to break off ties. Fidel Castro's Cuba, which unlike other Communist states, had maintained relations, now also cut ties.

At the end of 1972, Udi Adiv and several members of the Red Front – a breakaway from the far Left group Matzpen – were arrested. Adiv had travelled to Damascus under an assumed name and passed on information to Syrian intelligence. He was sentenced to seventeen years' imprisonment at a trial in March.

1974

More than 2,500 Israelis were killed during the Yom Kippur War and thousands more injured. The interim report of the Agranat Inquiry into the conduct of the war, published in April, called for the resignation of many senior commanders. Motti Ashkenazi, the commander of the solitary post at Suez that did not fall to the Egyptians, staged a one-man protest outside Prime Minister Golda Meir's office. The responsibility of Moshe Dayan, the minister of defence, was regarded as beyond the remit of the inquiry. Yet, like Meir, he came under much public scrutiny, and by June both had resigned.

Dayan is seen as Goliath, hiding behind the shield of the Agranat Commission, while Motti Ashkenazi has aimed his slingshot at the embattled minister.

Mike (*Yediot Aharanot* 4 May 1974)

1 Jan Police warn British Jews after attempted assassination of J. Edward Sieff

7 Jan Trial opens in Lillehammer of Mossad unit for the murder of a waiter

18 Jan Nixon announces Israeli–Egyptian military disengagement agreement

22 Jan Sharon and Begin lose Knesset vote on agreement 76–35

27 Jan Government abolishes subsidies on basic food commodities

28 Jan Israeli forces complete first phase of withdrawal from Suez Canal

3 Feb Teddy Kollek elected for third term as mayor of Jerusalem

7 Feb Founding conference of Gush Emunim to establish settlements in the West Bank

11 Feb Motti Ashkenazi's protest about war leadership gathers momentum

27 Feb Kissinger brings list from Damascus of 65 POWs

1 Apr Agranat Commission interim report recommends dismissal of IDF head David Elazar

11 Apr Golda Meir announces her resignation as prime minister

11 Apr PFLP-GC attack on Kiriat Shemona school kills 18 Israelis

22 Apr Labour's central committee elect Yitzhak Rabin as next premier 298–254

13 May Deserted town of Quneitra on Golan Heights taken over by settlers

15 May DFLP takes 115 hostages at Ma'alot, killing 22 children and 3 adults

31 May Israel and Syria sign disengagement agreement in Geneva

3 June Rabin government wins Knesset vote of confidence 61–51

171

5 June Zvi Yehuda Kook and Ariel Sharon visit new settler site next to Nablus

13 June Three killed in attack on Kibbutz Shamir by PFLP-GC

16 June Richard Nixon is first American president to visit Israel

24 June Israel Philharmonic agrees not to play Wagner at forthcoming concert

24 June Seaborne Fatah attack in Nahariyah kills mother and two children

28 July Gush Emunim leave Sebastia encampment as army arrives

9 Aug Gerald Ford becomes US president after Nixon's resignation

11 Aug Cabinet agrees austerity cuts in ministry budgets

18 Aug Hillarion Capucci, Melikite Greek Catholic archbishop, arrested

22 Aug Sylvia Zalmanson released from Soviet camp in prisoner exchange

3 Sept Mitzpe Ramon citizens protest against government neglect with mass hunger strike

5 Oct Former president Zalman Shazar dies in Jerusalem aged 84

9 Oct Gush Emunim begins mass attempt to establish West Bank settlements

24 Oct NRP central committee votes 60 to 40 per cent to join government coalition

30 Oct PLO recognised as sole legitimate representative of Palestinians at Rabat summit

9 Nov Israeli pound devalued by 43 per cent

13 Nov Yasser Arafat addresses UN General Assembly, sporting gun and olive branch

19 Nov DFLP attacks Beit Sh'ean, killing four civilians

11 Dec Grenade thrown into Chen cinema in Tel Aviv, killing three

The general election held on the last day of 1973 indicated a breakthrough for the Likud which attained approximately 30 per cent of the vote compared with Labour's 40 per cent. Together with the NRP, Menahem Begin could count on forty-nine seats compared with Labour's fifty-one. Although Golda Meir could expect support from the Left and the liberals, Labour did not have a blocking majority of sixty-one without relying on the Communist, haredi and Arab parties. The central committee of the NRP, which was mired in bitter dispute between its factions, voted narrowly to remain within the Labour-led coalition, but this eventually took months to implement.

Following the publication of an interim report by the Agranat Commission on the Yom Kippur War, Golda Meir resigned as prime minister. The report called for the dismissal of several senior military intelligence officers. The Chief of Staff, David Elazar, resigned and although there was no criticism of the minister of defence, Moshe Dayan, there were numerous calls for him to go.

Pinhas Sapir declined to succeed Golda Meir. Instead Yitzhak Rabin, a member of the succeeding generation, became prime minister and appointed Yigal Allon as foreign minister, ousting Abba Eban. Rabin was a member of Ahdut Ha'Avoda – this was the first time that a non-member of Mapai had led the Labour Alignment. Yitzhak Rabin's coalition survived a Knesset vote of no confidence when the religious parties, the NRP and Aguda, aligned themselves with the Likud.

In the municipal elections, Shlomo Lahat won the Tel Aviv mayoralty on behalf of the Likud while Teddy Kollek lost support for Labour in Jerusalem.

Ariel Sharon, who had resigned from the Liberals, emerged as a prominent standard bearer for the Right. He condemned the IDF's handling of the Yom Kippur War, blamed Labour for the killings of Israeli civilians by Palestinian militants and called for a national referendum on the future of the West Bank. Menahem Begin had strongly criticised the disengagement agreement with Egypt which had been facilitated by US secretary of state, Henry Kissinger. Sharon advocated a pullback from a demilitarised Sinai while retaining Sharm el-Sheikh and the Abu Rodeis oil fields. The Knesset voted in favour of the disengagement 76–35.

Prior to his appointment as prime minister, Rabin had called for the return of the populated areas of the West Bank to Jordanian sovereignty but with an Israeli military presence for a fifteen- to twenty-year period. Israel would retain sovereignty over some parts of the West Bank. In August, the Knesset voted to remove settlers from Sebastia. Rabin was supported by Dayan and opposed by the Likud and the NRP.

Both the Likud and Ahdut Ha'Avoda opposed any return of territory on the Golan Heights in the event of a disengagement agreement with Syria. Mapam voted to establish a kibbutz on the Golan Heights so that it would form a defence line to safeguard the Hulah and Galilee settlements within Israel itself.

The Soviet Union had provided the Syrians with $2 billion in arms since the end of the Yom Kippur War. In February, Israel announced the construction of a new town on the Golan Heights, located on the Quneitra road about 16 km from the 1967 ceasefire lines. The Syrians responded by shelling Ramat Magshimim, and an American immigrant and a Druze policeman were killed. Nahal Geshor and Ein Zivan on the Golan were also shelled as was Metulla on the Lebanese border. In May, settlers from the West Bank moved into the deserted Syrian town of Quneitra. A Cuban armoured brigade and North Korean pilots were stationed in Syria.

In April, Israel shot down four Syrian MiGs. At the end of May, a disengagement accord was agreed with Syria in which Israel agreed to withdraw from Quneitra.

A few weeks later, Sharon joined Zvi Yehuda Kook and several NRP MKs in an attempt to establish without government approval a settlement at Sebastia, adjacent to Nablus. A cabinet decision to use the army to evict the settlers brought about a voluntary exodus as the government deadline approached. The proposed settlement proved to be a rallying call for the Right whose leadership visited the settler encampment. Further attempts by Gush Emunim to enter the West Bank against both IDF and government wishes resulted in some officers and men refusing to obey orders and being sentenced to twenty-one days' imprisonment.

The emergence of the Right as a political force also reflected Israeli bitterness at repeated Palestinian attacks on civilians. In April, the PFLP-GC attacked Kiriat Shemona, killing eighteen civilians. A few weeks later a DFLP attack on Ma'alot resulted in the killing of thirty-one, the majority of them children. Kibbutz Shamir was similarly attacked by members of the PFLP-GC, disguised as 'hippies'. A Fatah group then attacked Nahariyah, causing the deaths of a family of three.

All these attacks had been carried out from Lebanon. DFLP members had also come across the Jordanian border and attacked Beit Sha'an in November, killing three people. An attack on the Chen cinema in Tel Aviv in December injured scores and killed three. The assailant carried a forged British passport.

A Mossad unit searching for Ali Hassan Salameh, 'the Red Prince', head of operations for Black September, thought they had located him in Norway. However, they selected the wrong target for assassination, namely a Moroccan waiter in Lillehammer. Fifteen members of the squad suddenly appeared in this small Norwegian town. Six members of the cell were apprehended, one being a former diplomat at the Paris Embassy. Two were found in the Oslo apartment of an Israeli diplomat, Yigal Eyal, who was declared *persona non grata*. Incriminating documentation was discovered about Mossad personnel, locations and operations throughout Europe.

Their trial began in January and finished in March. The convicted defendants were given differing terms of imprisonment.

In September, Egypt and Syria recognised the PLO as 'the sole legitimate representative of the Palestinians' in an effective challenge to King Hussein over who should exert authority in the West Bank. This was ratified at a conference in Rabat the following month. Yasser Arafat, PLO chairman, was permitted to address the UN General Assembly and promised a future Palestine, inhabited by Muslims, Christians and Jews. Arafat told his audience that he carried both a revolver and an olive branch. Zionism was portrayed as racist and neo-colonialist. The struggle of the PLO was placed in the context of other liberation struggles such as those in South Africa and Rhodesia. Theodor Herzl was compared to Cecil Rhodes. Arafat paid tribute to Udi Adiv, a member of the Red Front who was serving a seventeen-year sentence as an agent of Syrian intelligence. The PLO was accorded observer status at the UN.

Many African countries had broken off diplomatic relations due to Arab economic pressure after the Yom Kippur War. Opposed by the Arab world, Muslim states, the Soviet bloc and now the developing world, Israel established quiet contacts with apartheid South Africa. In November, Shimon Peres clandestinely visited Pretoria in an effort to sell Chalet missiles to the regime.

The Jackson–Vanik Amendment to the US Trade Reform Act tied the liberalisation of trade with the USSR to freedom of emigration of Soviet Jews. It was opposed by both Nixon and Kissinger who feared that it would undermine détente between the superpowers. The Kremlin lifted the education tax on emigrants just before President Ford signed the amendment into law.

173

1975

This was a time of great economic crisis and financial hardship for many Israeli families.

Theodor Herzl, the founder of the modern Zionist movement, is depicted as a rather frightened Lion of Judah. He is apprehensive about jumping through a fiery hoop whose flames spell out 'Inflation' and 'Unemployment'.

The holder of the hoop and whip is Moshe Zanbar, the governor of the Bank of Israel. A basket of foreign currencies occupies the other corner.

Ze'ev (*Ha'aretz* 2 June 1975)

3 Jan   Jackson–Vanik Amendment signed into law as part of the US Trade Reform Act

12 Jan   Herut national convention opens in Kiriat Arba

13 Jan   Failed bazooka attack by Carlos the Jackal on departing El Al flight at Orly airport

15 Jan   Two abortion bills approved by Knesset on first reading

19 Jan   Second failed attack by Carlos on El Al aircraft at Orly airport

29 Jan   Aharon Yariv resigns as minister for information

24 Feb   Finance minister introduces 20 per cent increase in telephone and postal charges

2 Mar   Army removes Gush Emunim members from Ma'ale Adumim site

4 Mar   PLO sea attack on Tel Aviv's Savoy Hotel kills eight civilians

11 Mar   Three directors of Habima theatre sentenced to prison terms for embezzlement

24 Apr   Parcel bomb in Herzliya post office kills youth

28 Apr   Security head at Johannesburg Consulate killed by deranged employee

3 May   Katyusha shells fired into West Jerusalem

23 May   World Bank approves $35 million loan to finance private industrial project

23 May   Michael Tzur, former Zim head, sentenced to 15 years for bribery, fraud, larceny

17 June   Israeli pound devalued by 2 per cent

24 June   Shopkeepers stage one-day strike to protest against rising taxes

25 June   Bodies of Eliahu Hakim and Eliahu Beit Tzuri, hanged in 1945, returned by Egyptians

4 July   Booby-trapped fridge kills 15 and injures 77 in Zion Square, Jerusalem

16 July   Forty Islamic nations demand Israel's expulsion from UN

12 Aug   Pinhas Sapir dies suddenly of a heart attack aged 68

4 Sept   Israel and Egypt sign second disengagement agreement in Geneva

8 Sept   Population of Israel, 3,451,000: 2,921,000 Jews and 530,000 non-Jews

9 Sept   Israeli pound devalued for a second time by 1.9 per cent

21 Sept   First settlers move into Ma'ale Adumim

27 Sept   Israeli pound devalued for a third time by 10 per cent

29 Sept   Greek cruise ship is first vessel to sail directly from Egyptian to Israeli port

10 Nov   UN passes 'Zionism is racism' motion 72–35 with 32 abstentions

13 Nov   Bomb in Jerusalem's Jaffa Road kills 7 and injures 45

25 Nov   Gush Emunim members removed by army from Sebastia site

8 Dec   Israel air force attacks Palestinian bases in Lebanon

8 Dec   Israeli ambassador in Stockholm recalled because of Swedish support for PLO at UN

8 Dec   Shimon Peres agrees to settler presence at Sebastia in exchange for voluntary evacuation

17 Dec   Tewfik Ziad elected mayor of Nazareth with Communists' help

17 Dec   Leftist Ya'ad splits over whether or not to negotiate with PLO

22 Dec   Austerity budget of IL 84.2 billion cut, approved by cabinet

The PLO continued its diplomatic assault at the United Nations and within international bodies, while it left attacks in urban centres in Israel and hijackings to other Palestinian groups. Two attempts to attack El Al passenger flights at Orly airport in Paris took place within days of each other in mid-January. In the second, hostages were taken, and in exchange for their release, the assailants were allowed to fly out.

A few weeks later, a seaborne attack by Palestinians from southern Lebanon similarly failed to achieve its objectives. Its practitioners found themselves instead holed up in the Savoy Hotel in a run-down section of Tel Aviv's seafront.

This was followed by bus bombs and parcel bombs. In Jerusalem, the Popular Struggle Front planted bombs in apartment blocks. In July, a refrigerator, packed with explosives, blew up in Jerusalem's Zion Square, killing many shoppers who were preparing for Shabbat. This provoked attacks by Jews on Arabs in Jerusalem.

In October, a car bomb was detonated outside the Hotel Eyal in Jerusalem and a few days later a handcart exploded near the Café Neva on the Jaffa Road, killing seven people.

Attacks were also averted by arrests at Ben-Gurion airport and the discovery of 'suspicious packages' in Mahane Yehuda market and in apartment blocks.

Katyusha rockets were often fired across common borders at urban areas. Safed, Moshav Avivim and Nahariya were all hit at the end of May. An empty kindergarten in Kiriat Shemona was hit on the eighth anniversary of the start of the Six Day War. This was met by repeated IDF forays into southern Lebanon – 'Fatahland'.

Three yeshiva students were killed in the settlement of Ramat Magshimim on the Golan Heights by infiltrators from Syria.

The decision in 1972 not to allow the residents of Iqrit and Birim to return to their villages on the Lebanese border had been the subject of many peaceful demonstrations when Golda Meir was prime minister. The Greek Catholic villagers of Iqrit had welcomed the Oded Brigade as 'liberators', but had been moved out in November 1948. The military imperative in 1948 had been to establish a security belt south of the Lebanese border. Despite a ruling by the Supreme Court in 1951 that the villagers of Iqrit could return 'as long as there is no emergency decree', there was a great reluctance to establish such a return for fear that it could set a precedent for other destroyed villages. Under a different leadership, the new foreign minister, Yigal Allon, submitted a motion to the cabinet that the villagers should now return to Iqrit and Birim.

At the UN, Arafat's 'gun and olive branch' address in 1974 was followed by UNR 3379 'Zionism is a form of racism' which was passed in November. This signified the dominance of the Warsaw bloc, the Arab and Muslim worlds and the developing world in securing a majority vote on any issue regarding Israel. Regarding the 'Zionism is racism' resolution, the vote was 72 in favour with 35 against, and 32 abstentions. A similar political line invoking racism and apartheid was taken by UNESCO and at international conferences. The United States and most European nations retaliated by walkouts and non-participation.

The question of which territory conquered in 1967 should be returned continued to divide the Labour party. Shimon Peres had advocated the idea of administrative autonomy for the West Bank Palestinians. However, Naftali Feder, Mapam's political secretary, met a PLO representative in Prague and was threatened with prosecution by members of the Likud as well as facing severe criticism from Labour MKs.

Earlier in the year, Ratz, the civil rights movement, had formed an alliance with Arieh Eliav, the former secretary-general of the Labour party, to form Ya'ad. By the end of the year, it fragmented, mainly owing to the question of how to approach the PLO.

There was considerable opposition from the Left to cabinet endorsement of an industrial development at Ma'ale Adumim on Jerusalem's outskirts. The site was occupied by members of Gush Emunim including women and children. A few days later Gush Emunim occupied a site near Ramallah at the location of biblical Shilo. The 'Young Guard' of the NRP strongly supported these actions.

In June, government plans were disclosed to build a third deep-water harbour, in addition to Haifa and Ashkelon, at Yamit in the Pithat Rafiah region between the Gaza Strip and northern Sinai. It was estimated that it would be completed by the mid-1980s.

At the end of the year, Gush Emunim made another attempt to settle Sebastia. Following a statement by Shimon Peres to the Knesset that settling the West Bank was more a question of timing and law, a token number of settlers were allowed to remain while the majority were evacuated by the IDF. This compromise angered doves such as Yigal Allon, but the hawks within Labour welcomed it in the aftermath of the UN resolution. The settlers were allowed to remain at the nearby Kadum army base.

On the Golan Heights, four new settlements were planned. Herut's national conference took place significantly at Kiriat Arba, next to Hebron. Resolutions called for the imposition of Israeli sovereignty on the 'liberated areas of the motherland'. In the wake of the American evacuation of Saigon, Menahem Begin commented that international guarantees on territorial concessions were not worth the paper they were written on.

The possibility of Israeli concessions to bring about a second disengagement agreement with Egypt was opposed by Herut. A Knesset motion to decrease the military presence in Sinai as a unilateral gesture was supported by neither the Liberals nor the Free Centre, Herut's partners in the Likud. By August, the leadership of the Likud was calling for a referendum before any territorial concessions in Sinai. Following the second disengagement agreement, the Likud objected to an American presence in Sinai, even though US personnel had been members of a supervisory force charged with guaranteeing the truce since 1948.

The Jackson–Vanik amendment to the 1972 US Trade Reform Act was finally signed into law by President Ford. It effectively placed restrictions on granting most favoured nation status to the USSR because of its harassment of Soviet Jews and refusal to allow them to emigrate. It came as a response to the education tax placed on emigrants who were expected to compensate the Soviet Union for the cost of their education. The introduction of this tax symbolised Soviet fears that a mass emigration movement was developing.

A discussion had taken place in the Soviet politbu002ro in March 1973 which resulted in the education tax not being implemented while remaining on the books. A KGB report had indicated that Soviet emigration came essentially from areas where religious and cultural traditions remained strong and that the urban intelligentsia was hardly tempted by the prospect of leaving the USSR.

Nixon's resignation in 1974 finally overcame the impasse because the amendment had been perceived by the president as a challenge to détente between the superpowers. Export–Import Bank legislation, however, also prohibited the US government from lending the Soviet government more than $300 million over the next four years without congressional consent. A week later the Kremlin refused to give assurances on the question of emigration. Secretary of State Kissinger concluded that the 1972 Act could not be implemented.

177

1976

The rescue of one hundred Israeli and Jewish passengers from Entebbe airport by commandos took place at the beginning of July. The commander of the operation, Yonatan Netanyahu, was killed during the gunfight. The Air France Airbus had been hijacked by a breakaway faction of the PFLP and members of the far Left German Revolutionary Cells in connivance with Idi Amin, the president of Uganda. A bemedalled and bewildered Amin is seen here standing on a deflating pedestal and literally about to be brought down to earth. Titled here 'Operation Uganda', it became popularly known as 'Operation Yonatan' after the slain Netanyahu.

Moshik Lin (*Ma'ariv* 8 July 1976)

4 Jan Israeli pound devalued again to 7.24 to the dollar

5 Jan Government closure of Timna copper mine provokes strike in Eilat

13 Jan City council agrees development of no-man's-land in Mamilla, Jerusalem

14 Jan Israel's population estimated at 3.49 million

24 Jan Pinhas Lavon dies in Tel Aviv aged 71

26 Jan Israel opens border to Lebanese Christians fleeing civil war

29 Jan Knesset amendment to legalise abortion opposed by haredi MKs

2 Feb First ever evening-long television discussion about homosexuality

10 Feb First reading on legalising abortion passed 46–27 in Knesset free vote

14 Mar Anwar Sadat abrogates Soviet–Egyptian friendship treaty of 1971

21 Mar Ariel Sharon resigns as Rabin's aide in return to political arena

30 Mar Eight Arabs killed and 35 Israeli soldiers injured in Land Day clashes

8 Apr South African prime minister Vorster visits Israel

12 Apr PLO and Communists triumph in West Bank municipal elections

12 June Mapam conference decides to remain within the Labour Alignment

23 June Knesset defeat for civil marriage bill 51–18

23 June Israeli pound devalued by 2 per cent

27 June Air France Airbus flight to Tel Aviv hijacked to Entebbe by PFLP faction

4 July Israeli commandos rescue 102 hostages in Operation Thunderbolt (Yonatan)

18 July Cabinet authorises construction of two nuclear power plants for civilian use

2 Aug Army prevents Gush Emunim group from reaching Jericho to establish settlement

8 Aug South African navy personnel training in Israel to operate missile boats

11 Aug PFLP attack on El Al passengers at Istanbul airport

16 Aug Grocers go on strike to protest against imposition of VAT

22 Aug Israel ousted from Asian Football Confederation at Malaysia meeting

31 Aug Registration begins for homes in Katzrin on the Golan Heights

15 Sept Strike by 12,000 nurses, with a go-slow by hospital doctors

9 Oct Arabs and Jews clash in Hebron on the eve of Yom Kippur

17 Oct Egypt dismantles final missile site on the east bank of the Suez Canal

18 Oct Asher Yadlin, designated Bank of Israel governor, arrested for bribery

2 Nov Jimmy Carter wins US election for the Democrats

11 Nov USA supports UN Security Council condemning West Bank settlements

16 Nov Ariel Sharon announces intention to form Shlomzion party

22 Nov Yigael Yadin announces formation of Democratic Movement for Change

26 Nov Israel denounces UN call for Palestinian state in West Bank and Gaza

12 Dec Government declares all of Israel to be a rabies danger zone

20 Dec Yitzhak Rabin resigns as prime minister after NRP ministers leave coalition

The remarkable rescue of mainly Israeli passengers at Entebbe airport in July was applauded both in Israel and internationally. The Air France Airbus had been hijacked by a breakaway faction of the PFLP and two members of the German Revolutionary Cells. Identifiable Jews and Israelis were separated from the other passengers. Lt. Col. Yonatan Netanyahu who led the operation was killed as were the hijackers and forty-five Ugandan soldiers.

At the beginning of the year, Yitzhak Rabin commented that any consideration of dropping the boycott of the PLO would be predicated on its recognition of Israel and its renunciation of the Palestinian Covenant. Israeli doves, however, quietly met PLO representatives in Paris to discuss the conflict. The details of the discussion were later conveyed to Rabin. In November, Moshe Dayan suggested that Israel should talk to the PLO and assist in the establishment of a Palestinian home within Jordan. In New York, PLO representatives Sabri Jiryis and Issam Satawi met with small groups of US Jews under Quaker auspices and a two-state solution was discussed. A poll in *Ha'aretz* suggested that 39 per cent of Israelis would accept participation by the PLO in a reconvened Geneva peace conference if it recognised Israel's right to exist.

At the UN, Palestinian representatives pressed for the return of all refugees who had left since 1948 and the restoration of their property. At the end of the year, the UN General Assembly called for the establishment of a Palestinian state in the West Bank and Gaza. Resolutions at UNESCO and the WHO condemning Israel and supporting Palestinian rights were supported by states of the Warsaw bloc, the Islamic and the developing worlds. Israel was ousted from the Asian Football Confederation which it had helped to establish in 1954.

The Yarmouk, Kedessiyeh and Hittin brigades of the Palestine Liberation Army entered the Lebanese civil war under Syrian auspices and positioned themselves partly in Fatahland in southern Lebanon. Israel's northern border was opened to allow any fleeing Lebanese Christians to enter. Anwar Sadat also commented that Egypt would not be drawn into a new war between Syria and Israel. This came after Henry Kissinger confirmed US plans to sell six Hercules C-130 military transports to Egypt after the end of the alignment with the USSR and despite Rabin's protest. In March, Sadat abrogated the 1971 friendship treaty with the Soviet Union.

In April, the South African prime minister, John Vorster, visited Israel. While the Rabin government condemned apartheid, he was given a state banquet and duly signed an economic agreement. The visit was criticised by American Jewish organisations, but in reality it reflected Israel's global isolation.

In May, the cabinet held a nine-hour meeting on unauthorised settlements which resolved little and ended with the publication of an ambiguous statement. A majority of cabinet members agreed to the evacuation of the Kadum settlers and their transfer to another site – one which would be authorised by the government. By the end of the year, the Kadum settlers still had not moved and they celebrated the first anniversary of the settlement in the presence of Menahem Begin, Ariel Sharon and Ashkenazi Chief Rabbi Shlomo Goren.

An attempt to establish a settlement at Jericho by a small group of Gush Emunim members was prevented by the army, while the government refused to grant permission to the organisation to take over the former Hadassah hospital in Hebron and convert it into a synagogue. Yet the military authorities took no action against a Gush Emunim leader, Moshe Levinger, when he entered Hebron, contravening the military government's ruling.

Events on the eve of Yom Kippur led to heightened tensions in Hebron. There was a tearing of Torah scrolls and prayer books amidst Arab claims of a trampling on the Quran. Clashes ensued between Arabs and Jews while Israeli soldiers attempted to limit the violence by preventing Jews from nearby Kiriat Arba conducting Shabbat services at the old Ohel Avraham synagogue a few yards from the Cave of Makhpela.

At the end of March, there were serious disturbances both on the West Bank and within Arab towns and villages in Israel. The pro-Kremlin Rakah party organised a general strike against land expropriation. Municipal elections held on the West Bank returned PLO supporters rather than pro-Jordanian figures. This represented the emergence of a younger generation which regarded themselves as first and foremost Palestinians. This led Yigal Allon, who favoured the Jordanian option, to criticise Shimon Peres, who had advocated elections. In December, the Arab municipalities organised a one-day strike in protest against the imposition of VAT, which shut down both the West Bank and East Jerusalem.

In addition, there were attacks on civilians within Israel. A bomb was left on board a bus south of Tel Aviv, while a Katyusha rocket landed in the Abu-Tor district of Jerusalem. Two bomb disposal experts were killed in central Jerusalem when they attempted to defuse an explosive hidden in a paint pot, while a pipe bomb was activated by remote control in a Tel Aviv cinema.

Within weeks of the success of the rescue at Entebbe airport, passengers waiting to board an Israel-bound El Al flight at Istanbul airport were injured when grenades were thrown at them by PFLP members as they were going through the final security checkpoint .

The government began to provide mobile homes for the remnant of the Gush Emunim group from the unauthorised settlement of Sebastia who had been permitted to live at the army base at Kadum. This provoked a demonstration outside Kadum by Mapam and the left-wing party Moked against Gush Emunin. The NRP reacted to this by threatening to bring down the government coalition if the settlers at Kadum were evacuated. The settlers then formally established a settlement adjacent to the army base and twenty thousand supporters of Gush Emunim participated in a two-day march from Beit El to Jericho. This was opposed by counter-marches of Arabs from Nablus and El Bireh.

The Kadum controversy nourished a growing split within the governing Labour party, with Shimon Peres, Shlomo Hillel and Gad Yaacobi aligning themselves with the Gush Emunim settlers amidst deepening criticism of Yitzhak Rabin's leadership and policies. Yigael Yadin formed a new party to attract Labour voters, while Dayan hinted that he might leave the party. Likud (39), NRP (10) and Agudat Yisrael (5), parties which supported the settlers, accounted for 54 mandates. The Likud believed that there would be up to eight defectors from Labour which could provide them with a majority in the Knesset.

Rabin's authority was also undermined by the worsening economic crisis. Israel's export earnings had dropped from 18 to 4 per cent since 1969. By the beginning of the year, the Israeli pound had been devalued by 66 per cent since November 1974. By June, there had been ten devaluations since the same period in 1975. The government considered a policy of 'creeping devaluation' such that the pound would be devalued by up to 2 per cent each month.

This was followed by *Haolam Hazeh*'s revelations of corruption within Labour's elite. Asher Yadlin was due to be appointed governor of the Bank of Israel in November. Instead he was charged with bribery. The minister of housing, Avraham Ofer, was accused of embezzling funds in favour of the Labour party – a charge he denied. Shimon Peres, Rabin's rival, utilised such developments to further undermine the prime minister.

The Rabin government collapsed in December when the NRP left the coalition owing to its objections to the arrival of F-15s in Israel from the USA close to the onset of the Shabbat.

181

1977

The coming to power of Menahem Begin's Likud spelled the end of Labour's hegemony as the natural party of government. Through a shrewd building of coalitions with other parties, Begin's party, Herut, had achieved the ascendancy of the Israeli Right.

The car of a joyous Begin is being filled up with petrol by a kipa-wearing attendant, signifying the Likud's reliance on the National Religious party – a party which had moved to the Right and strongly supported the settlement drive on the West Bank. The number '61' seen on the pump is the number of seats required to achieve a blocking majority in a Knesset of 120 seats. In the background is the pipe-smoking Yigael Yadin, the leader of the new Democratic Movement for Change, who expects to join the new government.

Mike (*Yediot Aharanot* 20 May 1977)

3 Jan Minister Avraham Ofer commits suicide over corruption allegations

6 Jan Herut conference offers territorial concessions on Sinai and Golan

30 Jan Meir Kahane's bid for Knesset seat endorsed by Zvi Yehuda Kook

31 Jan Knesset passes abortion bill on third reading

13 Feb Government and Histadrut agree a three-month wage freeze

22 Feb Asher Yadlin, Bank of Israel governor-designate, given five years for bribery

23 Feb Rabin defeats Peres for Labour leadership by 1,445 to 1,405 votes

16 Mar US President Carter states that a Palestinian homeland is a requisite for peace

18 Mar Sheli, led by Arieh Eliav and Uri Avner, formed by different left-wing groups

22 Mar Israel's three seaports paralysed by a general strike of 4,500 workers

6 Apr Sadat comments that he 'accepts' Israel and a normalization of relations

7 Apr Rabin resigns as prime minister owing to illegal Washington bank account

10 Apr Peres elected Labour party leader

24 Apr Egyptian Jews, Marzouk and Azar, hanged as spies, reburied on Mount Herzl

10 May Helicopter crashes killing all 54 officers and soldiers on board

12 May Israel and Portugal announce the establishment of full diplomatic ties

17 May Likud wins Israeli election, ending 29 years of Labour rule

23 May Begin states that Judaea and Samaria will never be given up

26 May Moshe Dayan accepts Begin's invitation to become foreign minister

18 June Israel to provide temporary haven for 66 Vietnamese boat people

21 June Likud-led government wins Knesset vote of confidence 63–53

21 June Labour retains control of Histadrut with 56 per cent against Likud's 28 per cent

19 July Egypt returns remains of 19 Israeli soldiers killed in the Yom Kippur War

25 July USA criticises legalisation of Ma'ale Adumim, Ofra, Elon Moreh settlements

31 Aug Sharon predicts two million settlers between 'the Golan and Ophira' in next 20 years

1 Sept Knesset votes 92–4, with 6 abstentions, not to negotiate with PLO

28 Sept Begin permits Gush Emunim to settle six unused army camps on West Bank

1 Oct USA and USSR call for Palestinian participation in Middle East peace talks

8 Nov Woman killed in Nahariya by katyusha fire from south Lebanon

9 Nov Sadat states that he is willing to go to Jerusalem to address Knesset

15 Nov Israeli Muslims leave to go on hajj to Mecca for first time

19 Nov Anwar Sadat pays a historic three-day visit to Israel

4 Dec UN General Assembly votes 100–12 for return of Palestinians to their homes

17 Dec Begin arrives in Cairo and visits synagogue

26 Dec Begin–Sadat summit ends in Ismailiya with little agreement

28 Dec Begin presents autonomy plan for Palestinians to Knesset

In May, the Right came to power in the *HaMahapakh* – 'the Earthquake' – that characterised the ninth Israeli election. For the first time since Herzl founded the modern Zionist movement in 1897, a coalition of the Right – astutely assembled by Menahem Begin – outstripped support for the Left and its liberal partners. The Labour party had been beset by scandal, corruption, defections and infighting between its dual leadership of Prime Minister Rabin and Defence Minister Peres. The Labour Alignment lost a third of its voters in the election – most of whom switched to Yigael Yadin's Democratic Movement for Change (Dash) which garnered fifteen seats. The NRP, influenced by its Young Guard and Gush Emunim, moved to the Right and also gained seats. Ariel Sharon's Shlomzion and the party of Shmuel Flatto-Sharon, who was standing to escape extradition to France, both attained a couple of mandates. While Sheli entered the Knesset, both the Civil Rights Movement and the ILP lost a majority of their seats. The Right coalesced as the Left fragmented.

Labour was plagued by scandal. Avraham Ofer, the minister of housing, committed suicide after unfounded accusations while Asher Yadlin was sentenced to five years' imprisonment. Rabin was increasingly perceived as both indecisive and unlucky. In a vote for the Labour party leadership, he defeated Peres by a mere 41 votes out of a total of 2,780 ballots cast. He was finally brought down when Dan Margalit, a *Ha'aretz* reporter, discovered an unauthorised joint bank account in Washington, still used by Leah Rabin as 'pocket money' for her visits to the USA, but crucially in use after the Rabins had returned to Israel.

With Peres as the new leader, Yigal Allon and Abba Eban were given second and third places on the list of Labour candidates, Moshe Dayan sixth and Yitzhak Rabin down at number seventeen. Opinion polls predicted that both parties would lose seats, Labour down to forty, Likud down to thirty-five. The result turned out to be a far greater loss for Labour (thirty-two) and a gain for the Likud (forty-three). Sharon's Shlomzion merged with the Likud shortly afterwards, which provided another two seats.

Begin built on his coalition of the Right by attracting a disillusioned Moshe Dayan as the new foreign minister. An empowered NRP was given three ministries – Education, Religion and Internal Affairs. Agudat Yisrael, while not serving in the cabinet, was given the chair of the important Knesset Finance and Welfare Committee. Dash joined the government in October with Yadin becoming deputy prime minister. Stalwarts of the Irgun and Lehi such as Shmuel Katz and Geula Cohen were also given positions. The Labour Alignment rejected repeated offers to join the Begin government.

The Liberal party component of the Likud embarked on changing Israel's command economy to one based on free enterprise, entrepreneurship and privatisation.

Begin's position and that of his Herut movement was that the West Bank – referred to as Judaea and Samaria by the religious and the Right – was non-negotiable, but other territories conquered in 1967 were a subject for discussion. Despite President Jimmy Carter's repeated comments about the Palestinians and his opposition to new settlements, the idea of a Palestinian state was opposed by Begin and the Right. Palestinians in the West Bank could apply for Israeli citizenship or keep their previous citizenship. Begin argued for autonomy in specific areas for the inhabitants of the West Bank. The Labour party, however, was severely split on the nature of territorial concessions.

At its conference in February, Labour agreed a platform which expressed Israel's readiness for territorial concessions in 'all sectors' in exchange for peace. This was passed by a vote of 659–606 – with Dayan leading the opposition to a resolution designed to keep the left-wing Mapam within the Alignment. Dayan further argued that the entire West Bank should be open to Jewish settlement and that the Jordan Valley and the Jerusalem region be exempted from any restrictions on settlement.

Meetings were already taking place outside the Middle East between PLO representatives such as Issam Sartawi and left-wing Israelis such as Matti Peled. In the United States, the Quakers facilitated such contacts between US Jews and Palestinians. Most Jewish organisations in the USA strongly condemned such discussions – as did Farouk Kaddoumi who was in charge of foreign policy for the PLO. A Palestinian National Council meeting in March produced a hardline approach, but also indicated clear divisions within Palestinian ranks. President Carter was now speaking about 'a Palestinian homeland'.

Civilians were targeted as bombs went off in marketplaces in Petah Tiqva, Beersheba and Tel Aviv, in a supermarket in Nahariya, a rubbish bin in Netanya, a bus in Rehovot and a zoo in Jerusalem. A bomb on a bus from Kiriat Shemona blew up as it entered the Afula bus station. The civil war in Lebanon pitched Palestinian forces against Christian Lebanese. The breakdown of a ceasefire in southern Lebanon resulted in katyusha rockets being repeatedly fired at Kiriat Shemona, Safed and Nahariya. Christian military officers from southern Lebanon openly visited Israel and conferred with their opposite numbers.

Anwar Sadat repeatedly commented on the possibility of peace during the first half of the year, gradually impressing Labour government ministers. Sadat had made several comments at the beginning of the year about peace with Israel and stating that any Palestinian state should be linked to Jordan. In April, he visited West Germany, France and the White House after several years of distancing himself from the USSR. During a press conference, he said that he 'accepted' Israel and desired a normalisation of relations. He told an Israeli journalist that Egypt accepted UN Resolution 242 and that he was ready for a peace agreement with Israel. Egypt returned the bodies of Israeli soldiers killed in the Yom Kippur War, as well as two Egyptian Jews hanged as spies during the Lavon affair.

President Carter's call to 'recognise the legitimate rights of the Palestinians' was supported by nine European countries.

185

Sadat arrived in Israel in November and prayed at the al-Aqsa mosque in Jerusalem. In his address to the Knesset, he listed five points as the basis for a peace treaty. One was 'the achievement of the fundamental rights of the Palestinian people and their right to self-determination, including their right to establish their own state'. In response Begin recalled the history of the Jews – from Abraham to the establishment of the state in 1948 – and commented that 'there are no eternal enemies'. He invited the leaders of Syria and Jordan to also engage in a dialogue with Israel. The Palestinians, however, were submerged in Begin's address. Even so, Begin invited 'genuine spokesmen of the Palestinian Arabs to come and hold talks with us on our common future'. A few days after Sadat's visit, there was a bomb attack on the Paris branch of Bank Leumi.

At the beginning of the year, the abortion bill passed its third reading and was strongly opposed by the haredi MKs. Three Aguda MKs immediately submitted private member bills to rescind the law. Even though doctors had rarely been prosecuted for carrying out abortions previously, the act was condemned by Ashkenazi Chief Rabbi Shlomo Goren and Mizrahi Chief Rabbi Ovadia Yosef.

1978

The peace negotiations with Egypt entertained the possibility of withdrawal from the territories conquered in 1967. This gave rise to the founding of 'Peace Now' – a movement which strove for peace with the Arab world and an end to the settlement drive.

This represents the struggle for Begin's mindset with the mainly secular Peace Now pulling the dove of peace behind them. The religious settlers' movement, 'Gush Emunim', is similarly pushing in the opposite direction against Begin's head and is being passionately egged on by a kipa-wearing advocate. The mass of ordinary Israeli voters look on.

Shmuel Katz (*al-Hamishmar* 30 April 1978)

1 Jan   La'am faction of Likud votes 54–16 to support Begin's peace moves

6 Jan   Shmuel Katz resigns as Begin's adviser on information

1 Feb   Jaffa oranges, spiked with mercury, poison children in Holland

19 Feb   Shimon Committee Report details growth of organised crime and its state connections

22 Feb   Mordechai Makleff, former IDF Chief of Staff, dies aged 58

6 Mar   348 reserve officers and soldiers write to Begin about peace and settlements

7 Mar   National Insurance Institute includes prostitution in its list of occupations

11 Mar   Fatah gunmen from Lebanon kill 38 civilians on coastal road

14 Mar   Operation Litani, invasion of southern Lebanon, commences

1 Apr   Peace Now demonstration in Tel Aviv

16 Apr   Raful Eitan becomes IDF Chief of Staff

19 Apr   Labour's Yitzhak Navon elected president

26 Apr   Bomb kills two Action Reconciliation Service Germans in Nablus

3 May   Pinhas Rosen, first minister of justice and founder of the Independent Liberals, dies aged 91

10 May   On 30th anniversary, Israel's population stands at 3,676,000

15 May   Museum of the Diaspora opens in Tel Aviv

20 May   El Al passengers attacked by Palestinian gunmen at Orly airport

2 June   Bomb kills six passengers on Jerusalem bus

29 June   Bomb explodes in Jerusalem's Mahane Yehuda market, killing two

12 July   Knesset legal committee rejects Aguda proposal to ban heart transplants

3 Aug   Bomb kills one and injures 50 shoppers in Tel Aviv's Carmel market

20 Aug   El Al crew in mini-bus attacked in London's Grosvenor Square

22 Aug   One hundred reservists send letter to Begin, refusing to guard settlements

23 Aug   DMC splits into Democratic Movement and Shinui

29 Aug   Shaul Avigur, founder of the Mossad and Nativ, dies aged 79

6 Sept   Camp David summit between Begin, Sadat and Carter begins

17 Sept   Begin and Sadat sign Camp David Accords at White House

24 Sept   Cabinet votes 11–2 to endorse Camp David Accords

28 Sept   Arens, Shamir, Allon do not vote for Accords in Knesset vote 84–19

25 Oct   Cabinet decides to expand Golan Heights settlements

27 Oct   Begin and Sadat awarded Nobel Peace Prize

1 Nov   Eretz Israel Loyalist Front formed in Tel Aviv

6 Nov   Israeli women and children evacuated from Iran amidst violence

19 Nov   Bomb in Tel Aviv-bound bus explodes near Ma'ale Adumim and kills four

8 Dec   Golda Meir dies in Jerusalem aged 80

17 Dec   Bomb explodes on bus in Jerusalem's Bayit VeGan neighbourhood

21 Dec   Katyusha rocket attack on Kiriat Shemona from southern Lebanon

Begin's autonomy plan for the West Bank called for the formation of an administrative council which would be responsible for education, transportation, housing, industry, commerce, tourism, agriculture, health, labour and the police. This proposal began to create schisms within the Likud coalition of Herut, La'am and Liberals. La'am split into its components of the State List and Greater Israel adherents. Even the DMC did not last a year with Shinui's secession.

Following Sadat's visit to Jerusalem, Palestinian groups, both inside and outside the PLO, made determined attempts to derail rapprochement at a time of impasse between Israel and Egypt through acts of terror directed at civilians. In March, a group of Fatah members from Lebanon landed by dinghy on a beach near Ma'agan Michael, further north than originally planned. Their intention had been to travel to Tel Aviv, take over a hotel and hold hostages. Their demands were for the release of Palestinian prisoners, including Kōzō Okamoto of the Japanese Red Army, and then to be flown to Damascus.

On landing, they shot an American photographer, Gail Rubin. First a large taxi, then a bus were hijacked and driven along the Haifa–Tel Aviv coastal road amidst a shooting spree. The bus caught fire at Herzliya, resulting in the deaths of thirty-eight civilians and injuries to more than seventy. The victims were mainly the families of Egged bus cooperative employees.

Three days later, Operation Litani, an incursion into southern Lebanon involving 25,000 Israeli troops, was launched in response to the killings to clear the region of Palestinian militants. In a week-long operation, large numbers of Lebanese villagers were displaced and civilians killed. Palestinian militants fled north of the Litani river. In June, United Nations Interim Force in Lebanon (UNIFIL) personnel began to patrol this area. In late December, katyusha rockets were fired from Lebanon at Kiriat Shemona, an Israeli town by the border, killing one and injuring nine. Israel attacked Palestinian positions at Nabatiyeh, north of the Litani river. The IDF withdrew from many positions in southern Lebanon later in the year.

Members of the Palestinian Abu Nidal group, opposed to any hint of compromise, began to assassinate PLO representatives in Europe. Said Hammami (London), Ali Yassin (Kuwait) and Izz-al-din al-Kalak (Paris) were all killed by Abu Nidal gunmen.

Outside Israel, there were attacks on El Al employees and passengers. In May, an attack by the PFLP took place at Orly airport. In August, the PFLP attacked El Al staff in a mini-bus en route to their hotel in London's Grosvenor Square after a transatlantic flight and a female flight attendant was killed.

Civilians in Jerusalem, in particular passengers on public transport, were also targeted. The no. 12 bus, which commenced in East Jerusalem, was a frequent target. Shoppers in Jerusalem's Mahane Yehuda and Tel Aviv's Carmel marketplaces were the victims of concealed bombs.

In April, two members of Aktion Sühnezeichen, a German volunteer programme which worked in countries that had been the victims of Nazism, were killed on a tour of Christian sites. On the first anniversary of Sadat's visit to Jerusalem, a bomb was thrown into a crowded bus at Mitzpe Yericho, a new West Bank settlement, en route from a Dead Sea spa to Jerusalem. In December, a device exploded outside an Arab butcher's shop near the Jaffa Gate in Jerusalem. It had been concealed in a case of soda drinks. Several more attempts were foiled before the explosives could go off.

At the beginning of the year, an official communiqué stated that the cabinet had decided to strengthen existing settlements in the Rafah approaches sector and along the Shlomo Gulf (Gulf of Aqaba) by 'expanding land for agricultural use and increasing the civilian population, both rural and urban'. Despite this, there was suspicion that there would be an evacuation of settlements in the Rafah salient and from northern Sinai – territory that would be returned to Egypt in the event of an agreement.

This catalysed divisions within the Likud coalition of parties and bitter opposition from within Begin's own Herut movement. In early January, Dayan hinted that the Israeli flag might not be raised in future at Ophira (Sharm el-Sheikh). Shmuel Katz, a hitherto strong supporter of Menahem Begin, resigned from his post as adviser on information because of his opposition to developments in the peace negotiations. Katz subsequently challenged Begin's personal nominee for a cabinet seat, Haim Landau, Begin's associate from his days in Poland, which was tantamount to a vote of no confidence in the Likud leader. Only 60 per cent of the Herut central committee voted for Landau, astounding Begin.

Opposition to Begin's approach to autonomy for the West Bank Palestinians was also voiced by the Ein Vered group of kibbutzniks and moshavniks in Labour, members of the NRP and the DMC, while Chief Rabbi Goren and Ariel Sharon hovered on the brink of open dissent. Clashes developed between the defence minister, Ezer Weizman, and Gush Emunim settlers. In March, Weizman instructed troops to stop a group of fifty Labour-oriented settlers from establishing a settlement at Kadesh Barnea in Sinai, 40 miles south-east of El Arish. Sharon in turn asked Begin to overrule Weizman's instruction. Weizman then threated to resign if his instructions to halt construction work by Gush Emunim settlers at Beit El and Nabi Saleh were not heeded. Simha Ehrlich, the finance minister and leading Liberal member of the Likud coalition, similarly threatened to leave, while the DMC's Yigael Yadin publicly declared that Weizman's orders would be carried out. Weizman and Ehrlich both wanted a cessation of settlement building while the peace process was in motion.

Following Begin's agreement at Camp David in September, Gush Emunim attempted to establish a new settlement on a hilltop at Elon Moreh near Nablus. It was subsequently declared a closed military area. In Hebron, settlers from Kiriat Arba were also removed from the Avraham Avinu synagogue. The agreement further split the far Right from the centre Right of the Likud. The initial vote in the Knesset to approve 'the framework for peace' indicated that twenty-three members of the seventy-strong government coalition did not support the agreement. Only nine of Herut's twenty-one members supported Begin. The Knesset vote for the draft agreement was 68–24, with 32 abstentions. In October, Geula Cohen, Yigal Hurwitz, Moshe Shamir and Haim Druckman – all from different party factions – formed the Eretz Israel Loyalist Front.

Begin was being pulled in several directions within the Likud, reflecting different views. Dayan argued that any freeze only applied to new settlements and therefore existing ones could be expanded. All this earned the ire of the Carter administration which condemned any settlement drive.

Yigal Allon for Labour attacked Begin's autonomy plan and argued once more for including Jordan in the deliberations. He also raised the demographic problem.

In contrast, the Peace Now movement, established in March by reservist officers and soldiers, spread widely and galvanised both the labour movement and the Left. Its slogan was 'Better Peace than a Greater Israel'. It staged demonstrations, strongly opposed settlement activity and, on the eve of Begin's departure for Camp David, challenged him not to miss a rare opportunity for peace with Israel's important neighbour, Egypt. It further attracted much support from Diaspora Jews, particularly in the USA, not only among the intelligentsia but also among communal leaders. Such protests also provoked others in support of Begin both in Israel and in the United States.

189

1979

The progress towards the peace agreement between Egypt and Israel in March was long and tortuous. President Carter had persuaded the two sides to sign the Camp David Accords, but there were outstanding issues which were always susceptible to different interpretations.

Begin and Sadat are depicted as snowmen around 'the negotiating table' and grimly debating without much apparent success. Their brooms are upright and not sweeping away the snow.

A convivial President Carter is asking them if they want something hot to drink to literally break the ice.

Moshik Lin (*Dvar Hashavua* 23 February 1979)

22 Jan Ali Hassan Salameh, Black September head of operations, killed in Beirut

1 Feb Ayatollah Khomeini returns to Iran from France

25 Feb Petrol price increases by 39 per cent

7 Mar Turkish TV refuses to take part in Eurovision Song Contest in Jerusalem

15 Mar One Israeli held prisoner by PFLP-GC exchanged for 76 Palestinians at Geneva

26 Mar Egypt and Israel sign peace treaty at the White House

30 Mar Far Right figures opposed to Camp David Accords form Tehiya

1 Apr Gali Atari wins Eurovision Song Contest for Israel with 'Halleluyah'

6 Apr Supreme Court orders halt to construction near Bedouin encampment

22 Apr PLF attack on civilians in Nahariya apartment block kills four

22 Apr Cabinet agrees to establish two new settlements at Elon Moreh and Shilo

1 May Eduard Kuznetsov and Mark Dymshits, Soviet prisoners, arrive in Israel

23 May Bus bomb kills three in Petah Tiqva

25 May Israeli–Egyptian opening of autonomy talks in Beersheba

26 May El Arish returned to Egypt

30 May First units of Israeli navy sail through Suez Canal

17 June Peace Now demonstrates against government settlement policy

25 June Soviet foreign minister Gromyko calls for Palestinian state

28 June Five MiG-21s shot down over southern Lebanon

7 July Bruno Kreisky officially meets Arafat in Vienna

10 July Begin and Sadat meet in Alexandria

31 July Bedouin protest against land seizure for construction of airbases

11 Aug Prices of basic foods – milk, bread, cheese, chicken – increased by 50 per cent

31 Aug Zim vessel rescues Vietnamese boat people in South China Sea

10 Sept Conference of Non-Aligned Nations condemns Israel–Egypt peace treaty

17 Sept Cabinet lifts ban on purchasing private land in West Bank and Gaza

26 Sept Third pull-out of Israeli troops returns 2,700 sq. miles of Sinai to Egypt

21 Oct Moshe Dayan resigns as foreign minister

22 Oct Supreme Court gives Elon Moreh settlers 30 days to leave

7 Nov Simcha Erlich resigns as minister of finance, replaced by Yigal Hurwitz

13 Nov Ambassador to Portugal, Ephraim Eldar, wounded in gun attack in Lisbon

14 Nov Since Khomeini's return, 15,000 Iranian Jews have arrived in Israel

20 Nov Bomb attacks on two Jerusalem buses

26 Nov Alma oil fields by the Gulf of Suez returned to Egypt

29 Nov Camp David Agreement declared invalid by UN General Assembly

16 Dec Consumer Price Index rises 102 per cent so far in 1979

27 Dec Tehiya Knesset motion to apply Israeli law on West Bank defeated

In mid-January, the Shah left Iran and Ayatollah Khomeini returned from exile in France a couple of weeks later. Following the toppling of Haile Selassie in Ethiopia in 1974, this further impaired Israel's doctrine of the periphery – supportive states outside the Arab world.

Khomeini's Islamic republic immediately ceased oil supplies to Israel. Iran had regularly shipped oil to Eilat, from where it travelled by pipeline to Ashdod and Haifa and from there to Western Europe. Israel therefore increased its oil supplies from Mexico and Venezuela.

The Israeli trade mission in Tehran was stormed and transfered to the PLO. Yasser Arafat became the first foreign visitor to Tehran. He stated that 'Under the Ayatollah Khomeini and with the help of Iranian freedom fighters, we shall free Palestine.' A 'security source' told MKs that if the regime stabilised, it could mean Iranian troops on Israel's borders within a couple of years.

Iran recalled its troops from the United Nations Interim Force in Lebanon (UNIFIL), these being replaced by Dutch forces. Even though Khomeini's representatives had stated that Jews, Christians and Muslims would enjoy equal rights, thousands of Jews left the country before the borders were closed. By the end of January, the Jewish Agency had brought three hundred children to Israel, leaving their parents behind in Iran. By mid-February, eight thousand Iranian Jews had arrived in Israel while another five thousand had left for other countries. El Al flights to Tehran were suspended and all Israelis were ordered to leave by 18 February. Some Israelis who had been in hiding with several Americans appeared and flew out to Frankfurt.

Both before and after the formal signing of the Israel–Egypt peace treaty at the end of March, there were deep divisions in the nationalist camp that Menahem Begin had painstakingly constructed during the previous thirty years. A freeze on settlement construction – for three months according to Begin, longer according to Carter – energised Gush Emunim and its supporters in the Knesset to stage protests. Within the Likud itself, Herut's Moshe Arens supported large-scale settlement, while the commerce and tourism minister, Yigal Hurwitz, of the La'am's faction of the Likud, resigned from the government. Long-term colleagues, such as the veteran minister without portfolio Haim Landau, increasingly criticised Begin. Returning territory to Egypt was viewed as the precursor to returning the West Bank and endangering the future of Jewish settlement there. Ezer Weizman, the minister of defence, on the other hand, advocated curtailing settlement on the West Bank. At the end of March, the noted theoretical physicist Yuval Ne'eman announced that he was establishing a breakaway party, Tehiya, which would oppose the evacuation of the Sinai settlements, Yamit and Ophira.

Seventy-six Palestinian prisoners were released in March in exchange for one Israeli. Simcha Erlich resigned as minister of finance due to protests about price increases on basic commodities. He was replaced by Yigal Hurwitz.

Within the broader government coalition, the Democratic Movement for Change began to fragment, with a separate faction, Shai, being formed. In the Labour party, differences about any agreement with the Egyptians were exacerbated by criticism of Shimon Peres's leadership by both Rabin and Allon.

President Carter's visits to Egypt and Israel to iron out differences took place during the context of vociferous debates in the Knesset. Carter's address to the Knesset was heard without enthusiasm and Begin was heckled. Shimon Peres's comment about continuing a dialogue with Palestinian leaders within the context of the Jordanian option mirrored Carter's repeated concerns. Peres had been forced by hawkish members of Labour to eliminate the phrase 'the legitimate rights of the Palestinians'. Like Begin, Peres publicly ruled out any contact with the PLO and indirectly criticised Soviet involvement in the Middle East.

Eduard Kuznetsov and Mark Dymshits were released from their strict regime labour camps in the USSR in a prisoner exchange and allowed to emigrate to Israel. Both had originally been sentenced to death in the first Leningrad trial in 1970 for attempting to take a small aircraft and fly to Sweden.

On the day of the treaty signing, flags flew on all public buildings and youth groups placed red carnations on the graves of those who had fallen in battle since 1948. Israel agreed to evacuate El Arish within two months and to withdraw from the oil fields in western Sinai and off-shore within seven months. Israeli troops would finally withdraw to a line from El Arish on the Mediterranean to Ras Mohammed on the Red Sea. Israel would give up its airbases at Refidim, Etzion and Eitam. One month after the exchange of the instruments of ratification, negotiations would commence for implementing the framework for Palestinian self-rule. The USA agreed to supervise the implementation of the agreement for the next three years.

The PLO and other Palestinian groups opposed the peace treaty because the fate of the Palestinians was being decided by others in their absence. When the autonomy negotiations opened at the end of May, Israeli, Egyptian and American diplomats avoided any mention of a Palestinian state. A conference of the non-aligned nations in Havana in September condemned the peace treaty. It instead endorsed the right of the PLO and Arab states to pursue 'the liberation of the occupied Arab territories … through all possible means, including force'. At the beginning of December, the UN General Assembly voted 75–33, with 37 abstentions, to declare that the Camp David Accords, signed in September 1978, 'have no validity'. Egypt was expelled from the Arab League, with Saddam Hussein's Iraq now attempting to fill the power vacuum in the Arab world.

The PLO indicated its discontent with the Accords by conducting attacks across the border from southern Lebanon. Within Israel itself, bombs exploded, killing and maiming civilians in Netanya, Tel Aviv and Jerusalem. Letter bombs en route to Israel were discovered in Frankfurt and the Israeli ambassador to Portugal was wounded in an assassination attempt in Lisbon. His Portuguese police detective was killed in a machine-gun attack.

Zuhair Mohsen, the head of al-Saiqa, a pro-Syrian faction of the Palestinian movement, was appointed by Assad. He was at odds with the PLO and was shot outside a casino in Cannes in July.

In April, Israeli aircraft attacked Palestinian artillery concentrations in Lebanon while Sidon and Tyre were shelled from the sea. There were also several attempts to attack coastal towns from boats that had originated in Lebanon. In June, a motorboat carrying katyusha rockets and heading for Haifa was intercepted by an Israeli patrol boat. There were attacks on Netanya and Nahariya and a naval patrol boat intercepted Palestinians at sea who had intended to land at Achziv.

A meeting of former German chancellor Willy Brandt and Austrian chancellor Bruno Kreisky with Arafat in Vienna was strongly condemned by the Begin government. The meeting was welcomed by Meir Pail and Uri Avnery of Sheli. Yet there were many who floated the idea of meeting the PLO if it gave up acts of terror. They included President Carter, the former head of the World Jewish Congress, Nahum Goldmann, and the Sephardi Chief Rabbi of Israel, Ovadia Yosef. Even the foreign minister, Moshe Dayan, met Haider Abdul-Shafi, known for his pro-PLO views, for an hour's discussion. In September, Begin rejected a Romanian proposal to meet PLO representatives.

Bassam Shaka, the mayor of Nablus, who had expressed pro-PLO views, was arrested and was about to be deported to Jordan. The mayors of the West Bank threatened a collective resignation and the deportation order was rescinded.

The 1980s

The 1980s was a decade of apparent confrontation between the West and the Islamic Republic of Iran. Israel was transformed from a subterranean friend of the Shah into the ayatollahs' 'Little Satan'. Yasser Arafat was welcomed in Tehran, and by the end of the decade the first tentative links with Hamas were established.

The Tehran hostage crisis led to a tremendous animosity between Iran and the United States under both Carter and Reagan. Yet contact was resumed, albeit beneath the surface. Here Reagan is depicted as looking the other way as Srulik feeds the voracious Ayatollah Khomeini.

Israel supplied Iran with arms in its war with Iraq, viewing Saddam Hussein as the greater danger and Iraq's army as having the potential to become the most powerful in the Arab world. Ariel Sharon, then minister of defence, sold hundreds of millions of dollars' worth of arms to Tehran, delivering them in unmarked aircraft. Iranian Jews were allowed to leave as part of the deal. In 1981, Israel bombed the Osirak nuclear reactor in Iraq.

The USA first wanted to use arms leverage to free the hostages in Tehran and then Hezbollah's American prisoners in Lebanon. The proceeds of this arms arrangement were further developed to fund the Contras in their struggle against the Sandinistas in Nicaragua. All this was revealed in the Iran–Contra controversy of the mid-1980s.

Dosh (*Ma'ariv* 21 November 1986)

1980

Several West Bank mayors were injured by car bombs planted by the Jewish Underground, composed of members of Gush Emunim. Bassam Shaka'a of Nablus lost both his legs and Karim Khalaf of Ramallah lost his foot, while the mayor of El Bireh escaped injury.

Inspired by Lehi and opposed to the Israel–Egypt peace treaty, the Underground hoped that such acts of terror would create a climate of fear within the Palestinian Arab population.

Here the Underground is depicted as a snake enveloping the dog's kennel – taking over the function of the security services in protecting the state of Israel. Its progeny are viewed as gnawing their way into the state and implicitly attacking the tenets of democracy.

Ze'ev (*Ha'aretz* 4 June 1980)

14 Jan Cabinet confirms Eliyahu Ben-Elissar as Israel's first ambassador to Egypt

17 Jan Petition calling for annexation of the Golan Heights signed by 750,000 Israelis

18 Feb Israeli Embassy in Cairo is formally opened

19 Feb Natan Yellin-Mor, leader of Lehi, dies aged 66

20 Feb Mordechai Rotem becomes the first Israeli Reform rabbi to be ordained in Israel

21 Feb Quintuplets born to Zippora Arzi, a 28-year-old teacher

24 Feb The shekel replaces the pound as unit of currency

29 Feb Yigal Allon, former deputy prime minister, dies in Afula aged 61

10 Mar Yitzhak Shamir becomes Israel's foreign minister

12 Mar Ministerial committee orders expropriation of 1,000 acres in Jerusalem

23 Mar Cabinet decision to establish religious institutions in Hebron

7 Apr Arab Liberation Front attacks children's quarters at Kibbutz Misgav Am

2 May Six yeshiva students killed in Hebron attack by members of Fatah

3 May Mayors of Hebron and Halhul and a kadi to be deported

8 May Sadat suspends autonomy talks with Israel

13 May Meir Kahane arrested and sentenced for planning attacks on Palestinians

15 May Knesset passes first reading of United Jerusalem Bill as Basic Law

22 May Israeli Olympic Committee votes 17–8 to boycott Moscow Olympics

25 May Ezer Weizman resigns as minister of defence

28 May Menahem Begin takes over as caretaker minister of defence

2 June Jewish Underground maims Nablus and Ramallah mayors with car bombs

13 June Venice declaration of Europeans supporting Palestinian right to self-determination

18 June Ya'akov Talmon, professor of modern history, dies in Jerusalem aged 64

22 June Peace Now rally demands Begin's resignation

1 July Body of eight-year-old Oron Yarden discovered in Netanya sand dunes

30 July Knesset passes Jerusalem, Capital of Israel, Bill 69–15 as Basic Law

20 Aug USA abstains as UN Security Council unanimously condemns Jerusalem Law

7 Sept Jerusalem devoid of foreign embassies as 13 countries move to Tel Aviv

22 Sept Iran–Iraq War breaks out

3 Oct Parcel bomb in Givatayim post office kills three

4 Nov Ronald Reagan wins US election for the Republicans

20 Nov Likud survives no-confidence motion on the economic situation, 57–54

24 Nov Ezer Weizmann leaves Herut

3 Dec Knesset votes 57–53 to restrict doctors' right to perform autopsies

12 Dec United Kibbutz Movement votes for annexation of the Golan Heights

18 Dec Shimon Peres confirmed as Labour leader at party convention, winning 70 per cent

25 Dec Knesset rejects recognition of non-orthodox Judaism by 42–26

While the first Israeli Embassy in the Arab world, headed by Eliyahu Ben-Elissar, opened to great political fanfare in Cairo in April, and the first Egyptian visa office in Israel opened in the lobby of the Tel Aviv Hilton Hotel, there were in parallel profound differences between the Israelis and Egyptians about the future of Palestinian autonomy. The ministerial team in the autonomy talks was now headed by the veteran NRP leader Yosef Burg. Egypt rejected Israel's twenty-six-point autonomy plan, which essentially divided the governance of the Palestinian territories into three categories – Palestinian, Israeli and joint supervision. Whereas the Egyptians wanted Palestinian autonomy to extend to full self-determination, the Israelis wished to restrict their powers to administrative functions such as police, transportation, agriculture, health services, religious affairs, local commerce and industry, labour and welfare, finance, education and culture. Israel would control imports and exports, security and general public works. Both Palestinians and Israelis would have joint responsibility for water distribution.

The Israeli government rejected Sadat's proposal for autonomy first in Gaza and wanted to control foreign affairs, defence, internal security, settlers and settlements in the territories, energy, the minting of currency, international communications, international mail and Israeli banking and insurance institutions in the territories.

Begin envisaged any future Palestinian state as being solely a PLO state and a Soviet satellite which, if militarised, would pose a security threat to Israel. The Israelis argued that they needed strategic depth and that there could be no return to the insecurity of the pre-1967 borders. Even so, Egypt had promised to sell two million tons of Sinai oil to Israeli companies, Sonol, Paz and Delek.

The Egyptian ambassador to Israel was invited by Moroccan Jews to celebrate Mimouna on the eighth day of Passover.

President Carter met both Sadat and Begin on separate occasions during their visits to Washington in April. However, informal talks about talks on autonomy in Herzliya between the protagonists stalled within days over the question of security. This prompted Sadat to suspend discussions about autonomy at both the ministerial and the working committee levels in early May. These talks were resumed, then suspended a second time, in part due to the passing of the Jerusalem Law by the Knesset at the end of July. This law stipulated that a united Jerusalem was the capital of Israel and the seat of its government and Supreme Court. This prompted criticism from King Hussein who called for 'a peaceful and free homeland' for the Palestinians. The USA abstained on UN Security Resolution 478 which declared the Jerusalem Law to be 'null and void'.

Such tension followed a petition by more than half the members of the Knesset and 700,000 Israelis, which called for the annexation of the Golan Heights. While El Al commenced a Tel Aviv–Cairo service, Sadat requested that any Egyptian should henceforth not conduct business in Jerusalem. The Egyptian foreign minister, Butros Butros-Ghali, cancelled a visit to Israel on the grounds that he would have to meet Yitzhak Shamir in Jerusalem.

In response to being left out of the Israeli–Egyptian deliberations, there were several Palestinian attacks both in Israel and abroad. In April, a group of the Iraqi-sponsored Arab Liberation Front infiltrated Kibbutz Misgav Am and held the children's sleeping quarters. A few weeks later, a Fatah group attacked yeshiva students on a Friday night after they had attended a Shabbat service at the Cave of Makhpela in Hebron. In June, the Israelis were successful in preventing a seaborne attack by a Palestinian group which was heading towards Nahariya.

There were also attacks on Jews abroad, by the Abu Nidal group and other Palestinian organisations opposed to the Camp David Accords. A bomb placed outside the Copernic Liberal Synagogue in Paris killed mainly bystanders shortly before many hundreds were due to attend a barmitzvah. The It-Tours travel agency, specialising in trips to Israel, was attacked in Paris.

The husband and wife proprietors, Edwin and Michelle Douek, were both shot dead and no valuables were taken.

At the beginning of the year, the head of the Palestinian library in Paris, Yusef Mubarak, was assassinated by the Abu Nidal group. In Antwerp, an international group of forty haredi children was attacked outside the Agudat Yisrael Centre as they waited to go to a summer school. A fifteen-year-old was killed and a score injured. In Brussels, the Israeli commercial attaché was killed. On New Year's Eve, the PFLP planted a bomb which killed sixteen people at the Jewish-owned Norfolk Hotel in Nairobi.

Begin was also under pressure from Gush Emunim activists in Kiriat Arba to permit settlement in Hebron itself and from the Carter administration to prevent it. In the USA, Christian evangelicals and religious Jews supported Begin's desire to settle the West Bank. Despite Ariel Sharon's demand for an activist settlement policy, the cabinet deferred taking a position after several discussions. Begin regarded such settlement as correcting a historic wrong following the expulsion of Jews from Hebron in 1929. In March, the UN Security Council voted to condemn Israeli settlement policy and was supported by the USA. Ezer Weizman, the minister of defence, argued in subsequent discussions that some settlements such as the dismantled Elon Moreh had no security value and criticised cabinet animosity towards the USA over the UN vote. In the Knesset, Moshe Dayan, now an independent MK, similarly attacked Begin's settlement approach. The Ministerial Expropriations Committee issued an instruction to expropriate a thousand acres of land in East Jerusalem between French Hill and Neve Ya'akov in order to provide territory for ten thousand new housing units. While Carter backtracked on US support for the UN vote, he regarded further settlement activity as an obstacle to progress on the autonomy talks with the Egyptians. The Americans further expressed concern at the cabinet decision to establish two religious institutions in Hebron.

199

Following the killing of six yeshiva students in Hebron in May, there were numerous demonstrations against Ezer Weizman's stand, such as the picket of his home in Ramat Hasharon. A few weeks later, the mayors of Nablus and Ramallah were injured by bombs planted by the Jewish Underground. Bassam Shaka'a of Nablus lost both his legs while Karim Khalaf of Ramallah lost his right foot. Israel deported the mayors of Hebron and Halhul and Kadi Tamimi of Hebron to Jordan.

Ezer Weizman followed in former Foreign Minister Dayan's footsteps a few months previously by resigning as minister of defence. Both opposed Begin's stand on the settlement drive and his inability to engage with the Palestinians. In a tilt to the Right, Yitzhak Shamir was appointed as foreign minister, but Begin was forced to take the defence portfolio himself – in part because Sharon was unacceptable to many members of the cabinet, but also because anyone who took this position would have to enact the dismantlement of settlements in Sinai in accordance with the Camp David Agreement.

Natan Yellin-Mor, a leader of Lehi, died of leukaemia. He had like Begin been an active member of Betar in pre-war Poland. He joined the Irgun and then broke away with Avraham Stern to form Lehi. He subsequently broke with both Begin and Shamir by moving to the Left after 1967 and advocating negotiations with the PLO. His funeral was attended by a remarkable ideological diversity of figures from both the Right and the Left.

1981

The bombing of the Osirak nuclear reactor, south of Baghdad, indicated Israel's fear of the growth of Saddam Hussein's military forces and especially the possibility to construct nuclear weapons. Israel thereby clandestinely supplied arms to Ayatollah Khomeini in the Iran–Iraq War.

This attack resulted in widespread condemnation in the Arab world.

Here Menahem Begin is pleading with President Reagan to open his umbrella to protect Israel through an American veto of any hostile motion at the United Nations. The storm clouds of the UN Security Council have gathered and it is just about to rain heavily.

Ze'ev (*Ha'aretz* 15 June 1981)

12 Jan Unemployment rate at 5.4 per cent with 72,000 out of work

12 Jan MK Hamad Abu Rabia, United Arab List, assassinated in Jerusalem

13 Jan Knesset votes to strip Aharon Abuhatzeira of his parliamentary immunity

20 Jan Yoram Aridor appointed minister of finance in place of Yigal Hurwitz

19 Feb Yosef Mendelevich arrives in Israel after 11 years in Soviet camps

7 Mar Palestine Liberation Front hang-gliders traverse northern border

25 Mar Poet, writer and Canaanite movement founder, Yonatan Ratosh, dies aged 72

22 Apr US administration decides to supply Saudi Arabia with AWACS

29 Apr Israel attacks Syrian SAM-6 missile sites in Lebanon

1 May President of Austrian–Israeli Friendship League gunned down in Vienna

8 May Poet and political ideologue Uri Zvi Greenberg dies in Ramat Gan aged 84

29 May Israel announces strike on Libyan missile sites in Lebanon

7 June Israel bombs nuclear facility Osirak near Baghdad with F-15s and F-16s

30 June Likud gains 48 seats as largest party in election

16 July Rocket barrage from Lebanon on Kiriat Shemona and Nahariya

17 July Heavy Israeli air raid on Beirut to destroy delivery of tanks and missiles

21 July Israeli mother of three killed by rocket fire on Kibbutz Misgav Am

24 July PLO and Israel agree ceasefire in Lebanon

5 Aug Begin appoints Ariel Sharon as defence minister

7 Aug Saudi Crown Prince Fahd proposes eight-point peace plan

11 Aug Traffic accident near Gaza kills 21, injures 45

18 Aug Reagan lifts embargo on delivery of military aircraft to Israel

29 Aug Palestinian attack during barmitzvah ceremony at Vienna synagogue

16 Sept Supreme Court says Rabbinate's rulings not binding on state officials

22 Sept Israel and Egypt agree to resume autonomy negotiations after 18-month interval

27 Sept International Atomic Energy Agency suspends technical aid to Israel

6 Oct Anwar Sadat assassinated at military parade in Nasser City

15 Oct Israel rejects Fahd peace plan

16 Oct Moshe Dayan dies of a heart attack in Tel Aviv aged 67

20 Oct Truck bomb explodes outside Antwerp synagogue, killing two

1 Nov Menahem Milson heads civilian administration on West Bank

5 Nov Military government closes Bir Zeit University after Balfour Day protests

12 Nov At the UN Israel calls for a nuclear-free zone in the Middle East

30 Nov Sharon and Caspar Weinberger sign memorandum of understanding

15 Dec Knesset votes 63–21 to annex Golan Heights

17 Dec Three-day strike by 14,000 Golan Heights Druze to protest against annexation

18 Dec Israel and Egypt agree ferry service between Ashdod and Port Said

18 Dec USA suspends memo of strategic cooperation due to Golan annexation

The spiralling inflation that had plagued the economy led to the resignation of the finance minister, Yigal Hurwitz, who wished to delay a rise in teachers' salaries until April 1982. Hurwitz, the leader of the eight-member La'am faction of the Likud, had followed a free market policy of cuts in government subsidies while promulgating a period of austerity. Within days of his resignation, El Al employees staged a national strike amidst widespread labour disputes. Moreover, three La'am members simultaneously left the government coalition and thereby the prospect of early elections loomed. While Begin's coalition appeared to be crumbling, the NRP opposed early elections because one of its representatives, the religious affairs minister Aharon Abuhatzeira, had been charged with taking bribes, while another, Yosef Burg, had been accused of blocking an investigation into financial irregularities in the Ministry of the Interior.

Begin unexpectedly appointed the chairman of the Herut Executive, Yoram Aridor, as minister of finance rather than a candidate from the Liberal faction of the Likud. Aridor proceeded to remove many of the restraints put in place by his predecessors. This coincided with the announcement that the election would take place in early July, later brought forward to late June. Despite such moves to alleviate the economic hardships, workers at power stations in Ashdod and Haifa went on strike in May. The Central Bureau of Statistics subsequently recorded a 12 per cent rise in living standards due to lower income tax. Spending on consumer goods was 25 per cent higher during the first half of 1981 compared with 1980.

The bombing of the Osirak nuclear reactor just outside Baghdad had been in the pipeline for a long time. It had been given urgency when the Camp David Agreement was signed and Iraq attempted to take Egypt's place as the pre-eminent military power in the political aftermath. The Iran–Iraq War had commenced and there was a good likelihood that Saddam Hussein's forces

would be victorious and emerge as the strongest military force in the Middle East. This persuaded Israel to clandestinely deliver arms to the ayatollahs in unmarked aircraft in exchange for the emigration of Iranian Jews.

There had been an attempt to sabotage the reactor while it was still in France, before delivery to Baghdad. An Egyptian nuclear scientist, Yahya el Mashad, who was deeply involved in the Iraqi programme, was killed in Paris. In July 1980, France delivered enriched uranium to Iraq. A few months later, the Israeli cabinet voted 10–6 to carry out an attack on the Osirak reactor.

Some were worried that such an attack would undermine relations with Egypt. Others believed expert advice that the reactor was unsuitable for manufacturing a bomb. The International Atomic Energy Agency (IAEA) conference subsequently voted to suspend all technical assistance to Israel.

The Reagan administration condemned the attack on the nuclear reactor, utilising US-made aircraft, as an obstacle to attaining peace in the region. While Washington joined Israel in opposing a resolution at the UN, it also moved to suspend the delivery of four F-16 aircraft to Israel.

The attack on the Osirak reactor occurred three weeks before the Israeli election. The improved economic situation and the attack provided a boost for the Likud which narrowly pipped the Labour Alignment by ten thousand votes to emerge as the largest party with forty-eight seats. Many smaller parties such as the Independent Liberals did not pass the electoral threshold into the Knesset and those that did only achieved single digit representation. The new party, Tehiya, represented the emergence of a far Right in the Knesset – those who dissented from the Camp David Agreement. The NRP lost half its seats due to the defection of Abuhatzeira, while Moshe Dayan's challenge never materialised as Telem only achieved two seats. Begin formed his second administration in August from mainly Likud and National Religious figures while he continued to cultivate Tehiya and Telem. His most controversial appointment was that of Ariel Sharon as minister of defence. A few weeks before his death, Moshe Dayan strongly advised Begin not to promote Sharon to this position.

The settlers continued to press government ministers to support unrestricted settlement throughout the West Bank and Gaza. Negotiations progressed to agree compensation terms for those who would have to leave their homes, such as in Ophira (Sharm el-Sheikh), in accordance with the Camp David Agreement. This often spilled over into a political dispute regarding any evacuation itself. In November, Begin agreed to meet settlers from Yamit, including one on a stretcher who had been on a liquid diet for forty days in protest against the evacuation plan. The meeting broke up in acrimony.

However, the formal annexation of the thirty settlements on the Golan Heights on a 63–21 vote in the Knesset was greeted with great approval. Begin's sudden initiative took Labour by surprise such that, while the leadership advocated a boycott of the vote, its Knesset representatives were split on the issue. Damascus stated that the annexation was 'a declaration of war' and two-thirds of the Golan's Druze population staged a three-day strike at the imposition of Israeli civil law. Although Begin believed that the Reagan administration's attention would probably be distracted by the imposition of martial law in Poland and the crackdown on the Solidarity trade union, the USA suspended a memorandum of strategic cooperation between the two countries, signed only two weeks before. This was not the first clash between the two governments.

There had been concerns when the Reagan administration announced its intention to sell to Saudi Arabia five AWACS surveillance aircraft and to provide upgrades on the combat capability of the F-15 fighters already in the possession of the Riyadh regime. While Washington argued that it would serve Saudi Arabia's ability to oppose Khomeini's Iran, Israel believed that it was a threat to its security.

This period was also peppered by the movement of Soviet missiles into strategic positions in Syria and Lebanon and the shelling of towns in northern Israel by Palestinian factions, as well as short hang-gliding flights to cross the border into Israel and take hostages in exchange for imprisoned militants. Israel's retaliatory military actions such as the shelling of the ports of Sidon and Tyre periodically brought acerbic comments from Washington, followed by bitter rebukes by Begin. The US Special Envoy to the Middle East, Philip Habib, shuttled between the parties and finally achieved a ceasefire. Begin stated that it was not only a question of national interest, but also one of moral duty to support beleaguered Lebanese Christians and to stop Syria from gaining control of the Sannine mountain range. In July, the Israeli air force destroyed bridges between the Litani and Zaharani rivers and bombed the regional headquarters of the DFLP. The build-up of arms supplies from the Syrians – tanks, anti-aircraft missiles, katyushas – worried the Israelis. While the ceasefire and Begin's visit to Washington in September certainly improved relations, he also strongly rejected the Fahd peace plan which called for a withdrawal from the 1967 borders and a Palestinian state with Jerusalem as its capital.

In October Anwar Sadat was assassinated by an Islamist gunman. In the weeks before his death, he had urged the Palestinians to establish a government and offered to host Israeli–Palestinian negotiations at El Arish in Sinai. Hosni Mubarak succeeded as president and continued Sadat's policies with regard to Israel. The Abu Nidal group attacked European Jewish institutions as well as killing PLO diplomats.

203

1982

שלושה בסירה אחת

'Three Men in a Boat' depicts the climax of the disastrous Lebanon war. Prime Minister Begin, IDF head Rafael Eitan and the minister of defence, Ariel Sharon, are in a boat shaped as the map of Israel, about to go over the rapids. The oars are the Cedars of Lebanon and all are blissfully unaware of the debâcle of this war. The attack dog is the foreign minister, Yitzhak Shamir, barking at Israelis who are warning about the latest episode, the evasive denial by government of both Israeli protest and the international outcry about the killing of Palestinians by Phalangist militia at the Sabra and Shatilla refugee camps. 'Three Men in a Boat' was published just after the massacre but before Begin finally agreed to set up a commission of inquiry – the Kahan Commission.

Ze'ev (*Ha'aretz* 22 September 1982)

3 Jan	Raful Eitan's tenure as Chief of Staff extended for another year
3 Jan	Cabinet appoints Moshe Mandelbaum as governor of the Bank of Israel
14 Jan	Yitzhak Tunik appointed State Comptroller and Ombudsman
15 Jan	Mifgash Israel restaurant in Berlin bombed, 25 injured
13 Feb	Arrest of Druze leaders accused of incitement leads to general strike
21 Feb	Gershom Scholem, philosopher and historian, dies in Jerusalem aged 84
9 Mar	Zvi Yehuda Kook, mentor of Gush Emunim, dies in Jerusalem aged 90
14 Mar	Begin establishes inquiry into Haim Arlosoroff's assassination in 1933
3 Apr	Israeli diplomat Yaakov Bar-Simantov shot dead by LARF in Paris
3 Apr	LARF machine-guns Israeli Embassy in Paris
11 Apr	Allan Goodman, sympathiser with Kach, kills two Arabs on Temple Mount
19 Apr	Last settlers leave Yamit in Sinai
19 Apr	Aharon Abuhatzeira is found guilty of breach of trust, fraud, larceny
25 Apr	Israeli withdrawal from Sinai is completed
2 May	Cabinet bans El Al flights on Shabbat and festivals
15 May	Diplomatic relations between Israel and Zaire restored
3 June	Attempted assassination of UK ambassador Shlomo Argov in London
6 June	Beginning of Operation Peace for Galilee, scheduled to last 48 hours
2 July	Yasser Arafat agrees to PLO evacuation from Beirut
31 July	Seven wounded by bomb at El Al terminal at Munich airport
9 Aug	Abu Nidal attack on the Jo Goldenberg restaurant in Paris kills 6, injures 22
21 Aug	Palestinian forces begin to leave Beirut for Tunis
29 Aug	Nahum Goldmann, long-time representative of World Jewry, dies in Germany aged 87
1 Sept	Reagan Plan sparks a hostile response from Begin
14 Sept	Bashir Gemayel assassinated in Beirut
15 Sept	IDF enters West Beirut
15 Sept	Yasser Arafat meets Pope John Paul II
18 Sept	Massacre of Palestinians by Phalangists at Sabra and Shatilla
21 Sept	Amin Gemayel elected president of Lebanon
25 Sept	Huge Peace Now war protest in Tel Aviv, after Sabra and Shatilla killings
26 Sept	IDF withdraws from Beirut
28 Sept	Kahan inquiry into Israeli conduct during Sabra and Shatilla killings
9 Oct	Abu Nidal attack on Rome synagogue, one killed, 37 injured
11 Nov	Attack kills 76 at IDF headquarters in Tyre
13 Nov	Aliza, wife of Menahem Begin, dies while he is visiting the USA
23 Dec	Bomb explodes in Israeli Consulate in Sydney, Australia

205

The Lebanon war of 1982 divided the country and the Jewish Diaspora. The conduct of both the political and military leadership led to the establishment of the Kahan Commission of Inquiry after the mass killings of Palestinians by Israel's Phalangist allies in the refugee camps of Sabra and Shatilla in September.

Arafat's presence in Beirut and repeated attacks on Israel by Palestinian forces in southern Lebanon became an increasingly urgent question for the Begin government. The existence of 'Fatahland' in Lebanon became another ingredient in the ongoing conflict between the different ethnic, political and religious groups in the country.

At the very beginning of the year, Labour's leaders, Peres and Rabin, warned about any binding commitment to the Christian militias in Lebanon. Yet Raful Eitan, whose term of office as IDF Chief of Staff had been extended, flew to brief Maronite leaders about Operation Peace for Galilee on the eve of the invasion.

The catalyst for the invasion was the attempted assassination of Shlomo Argov, the Israeli ambassador to the UK, at the Dorchester Hotel in central London. It was carried out by the anti-PLO Abu Nidal group, but supervised by Iraqi intelligence. One of the assassins was an Iraqi operative and the weapons had allegedly been brought in via the Iraqi Embassy diplomatic bag. At that time, Abu Nidal himself was operating out of Baghdad. The assassins were also planning to kill the PLO representative in London.

Menahem Begin and Ariel Sharon ignored this fundamental difference and viewed this episode as an opportunity to attack the PLO. They built on plans already in existence, but within the Israel cabinet the idea of an incursion into southern Lebanon was discussed, with often questioning ministers.

This incursion was supposed to last forty-eight hours, but it went far beyond the agreed demarcation of territory for this military operation under the guidance of Ariel Sharon, minister of defence. Its original intention was to clear an area which Palestinian forces had utilised for attacks on northern Israel. Yoram Aridor, the finance minister, told the Americans that Israel had moved into Lebanon to prevent another Pearl Harbor. Instead the IDF moved much further north and laid siege to Beirut as well as engaging with Syrian forces.

The Israeli cabinet, as well as the prime minister, Menahem Begin, were often kept in the dark about the latest military moves. Decisions agreed upon were often violated. Public perceptions of disarray in government were exacerbated by Begin's rhetoric, which often harked back to his experience in wartime Poland and in Stalin's camps.

Begin had long championed an alliance with the Lebanese Maronites. Bashir Gemayel's militia had been prominent in conflict with the PLO during the Lebanese civil war and his father had been a founder of the Christian Phalangists. Gemayel was elected president of Lebanon at the age of thirty-four and had been open about his contacts with Israel. However, he was reluctant to sign a formal peace agreement with Israel. His distancing from Israel did not prevent his assassination together with many other Phalangist leaders in a bombing of an apartment block. His death subsequently led to a Phalangist attack on the Palestinian camps at Sabra and Shatilla, resulting in a large number of civilians being killed. Israeli guards were stationed outside the camps.

While American Jewish celebrities such as Danny Kaye were imported to demonstrate solidarity, the Israeli leftist Uri Avnery met Arafat in Beirut for a two-hour conversation. Longshoremen at Piraeus refused to handle Israeli goods. There was a proliferation of anti-war demonstrations in Israel which were attended by a growing number of people. They were organised first by far-Left groups and then by Peace Now. Israelis in military uniform attended protests by 'Soldiers against Silence'. In July, Colonel Eli Geva asked to be relieved of his command. He argued with Begin and Sharon that his tank column would cause civilian casualties in Beirut.

Other soldiers refused to receive military decorations for the campaign. Begin called them 'rotten fruit'. No popular songs were written about Operation Peace for Galilee.

All this resulted in a huge demonstration in Tel Aviv after the Sabra and Shatilla killings, organised by Peace Now and attended by leading members of the Labour party. There were repeated calls for both Begin's and Sharon's resignations.

While the Knesset had voted 48–42 not to initiate an investigation, President Navon called for an independent judicial inquiry. In the Diaspora, however, even the most conservative Jewish organisations vocally supported President Navon. Menahem Begin attacked prominent Diaspora leaders such as Rabbi Arthur Hertzberg, an American opponent of the war.

The war also caused economic and political problems. In 1981, exports to the USA had increased by 28 per cent, but in June, the month of the invasion of Lebanon, the cost of living index rose by 6 per cent.

President Reagan's criticism of the war grew much more acerbic. In September, he put forward the Reagan Plan, after the evacuation of PLO forces from Beirut to Tunis. Using the Camp David Agreement as a basis, he called for Palestinian elections and self-government over a five-year period – during which time there would be a freeze on settlement expansion. Begin strongly rejected the plan while Labour warmed to it. Four days after the publication of the plan, Begin authorised the establishment of another seven settlements. He argued in a letter to Reagan that the West Bank was part and parcel of Israel's heritage, historically and religiously. Begin threatened to call an early election in 1983 rather than wait until November 1985.

The rising international criticism of the war even muted Israel's friends. In late August, the UN General Assembly voted 120–2 in favour of a Palestinian state, while Arafat had an audience with Pope John Paul II.

Earlier in the year, Begin and Sharon had faced criticism from many West Bank settlers who strongly opposed the evacuation of the settlement of Yamit in Sinai in accordance with the agreement with the Egyptians. Local Arabs facilitated the dismantling of greenhouses and irrigation equipment in the Talmei Yosef region of Yamit.

The residents of Yamit knew that they had to leave by 31 March or forfeit compensation. This did not apply to squatters in Hatzar Adar near Yamit who had arrived from the West Bank. Kach members from Atzmona and yeshiva students from Ophira attempted to block the roads into Yamit. Some attempted to disconnect the water pipeline into Yamit. Kach members threatened a mass suicide amidst booby-trapped shelters.

In Europe, even before the invasion, there had been attacks on Israeli diplomats, synagogues and Jewish community centres. In Berlin, the Mifgash Israel restaurant was attacked, killing a child and injuring several dozen diners. The PFLP was believed to be behind the attack. The attack on the main synagogue in Rome and the killings in the Jo Goldenberg restaurant in Paris had been initiated by the Abu Nidal group. A series of attacks on Israeli premises in Paris, including the consulate and the embassy as well as Israeli-owned banks and companies, had been carried out by the Lebanese Armed Revolutionary Factions (LARF) which had emerged from a faction of the PFLP. They had operated in conjunction with groups on the far Left such as Action Directe and Brigate Rosse. In numerous Latin American countries, there were links with the local far Left and Hezbollah sympathisers.

1983

Begin's resignation as prime minister and retirement from public life marked the end of a lifetime in Zionist politics. This took place after the death of his wife, the catastrophe of the Lebanon war and the verdict of the Kahan Commission on the killings at the camps at Sabra and Shatilla.

Begin is seen here as a wife departing from the 'Likud' home. Her husband is wearing a shirt sporting the face of a crowned Ariel Sharon.

Their screaming baby in a pram entitled 'Tsahal' (Israel Defence Forces) is swaddled in a knotted, overflowing blanket labelled 'Lebanon'.

Ze'ev (*Ha'aretz* 30 August 1983)

10 Feb   Cabinet accepts recommendations of Kahan Commission Report

10 Feb   Emil Grunzweig is killed by a hand grenade thrown at a Peace Now rally

11 Feb   Sharon begrudgingly resigns as minister of defence

24 Feb   Knesset votes 61–51 to approve Moshe Arens as defence minister

6 Mar   Abu Nidal members sentenced in London for shooting Shlomo Argov

21 Mar   Knesset defeats 'Who is a Jew?' amendment to Law of Return, 58–50

23 Mar   Knesset votes 61–57 to appoint Chaim Herzog as sixth president

8 Apr   Alan Goodman sentenced to life for Temple Mount killings

11 Apr   PLO representative Issam Sartawi is assassinated at a conference in Portugal

19 Apr   Moshe Levi appointed IDF Chief of Staff after Raful Eitan

19 Apr   Car bomber enters the US Embassy compound in Beirut and kills more than sixty

20 Apr   Ministerial Settlement Committee approves three new settlements on the West Bank

28 Apr   Argentina condemned after admission that 340 disappeared Jews are no longer alive

16 May   Central Bureau of Statistics places inflation at 160 per cent for 1983 so far

17 May   Peace agreement is signed between Israel and Lebanon

4 June   Peace Now demonstration calls for withdrawal of Israeli forces from Lebanon

15 June   Doctors at Soroka hospital, Beersheba, go on hunger strike

19 June   Simha Erlich, Liberal party leader and former finance minister, dies aged 68

24 June   EEC agreement to allow Israel access to the European Bank

5 July   Strike by 900 X-ray technicians for better safety standards and shorter hours

7 July   Aharon Gross, a student at the Shavei Hevron yeshiva. killed near Hebron's marketplace

26 July   Attack by Jewish Underground on Islamic College in Hebron kills 3, injures 33

11 Aug   Shekel devalued by 7.5 per cent against the dollar

28 Aug   Menahem Begin announces to the cabinet his intention to resign

4 Sept   Israel completes withdrawal to new defence line at Awali River

4 Sept   Mustapha Doudin, head of Village Leagues on West Bank, resigns

12 Sept   Hundreds of Lebanese Christians cross into Israel, escaping conflict

10 Oct   Yitzhak Shamir becomes prime minister

11 Oct   Shamir government approves shekel devaluation and austerity measures

18 Oct   Yigal Cohen-Orgad becomes finance minister, replacing Yoram Aridor

23 Oct   Suicide bombers kill more than 300 members of multinational force in Beirut

30 Oct   Raful Eitan announces formation of far Right party, Tsomet

4 Nov   Suicide bomb attack on base in Tyre, kills 28 Israelis and 32 Lebanese

15 Nov   Government reduces subsidies for basic food products

16 Nov   Meir Shamgar nominated president of Supreme Court after Yitzhak Kahan

6 Dec   No. 18 bus bombing in Jerusalem kills 6 and injures 43

9 Dec   Sharon sues *Time* magazine over cover story about Kahan report findings

21 Dec   Arafat and 4,000 PLO members leave Tripoli under UN auspices

Menahem Begin announced his intention to resign in August and this came as a great surprise to the Israeli cabinet as well as to those close to him. Since the death of his wife at the end of 1982, he had been unable to function properly as prime minister and to provide leadership. The Kahan Commission Report into the killings in the Sabra and Shatilla camps had further called into question his leadership during Operation Peace for Galilee and his judgement in deferring to the approach of the defence minister, Ariel Sharon. The report and the cabinet's decision, by a vote of 16–1, to accept the commission's recommendations finally led to Sharon's resignation despite Begin's support for him. Sharon refused to accept 'indirect responsibility' for the killings in the camps at Sabra and Shatilla and remained in the cabinet as minister without portfolio.

Menahem Begin, the former head of the Irgun, was succeeded by a former leader of Lehi, Yitzhak Shamir, who had defeated David Levi to become Herut's nominee for prime minister. As Israel's foreign minister, Shamir too had been heavily criticised in the Kahan Commission Report.

Shamir was faced with an urgent economic problem. In 1982, the GDP had failed to increase, the balance of payments deficit increased, inflation was in triple digits and real salaries had decreased by 3 per cent on average. The Central Bureau of Statistics report for April indicated that the cost-of-living index rose by 13.3 per cent – the highest monthly increase since the establishment of the state in 1948. Inflation was running at an annual rate of 160 per cent.

This situation provoked a wave of strikes amongst hospital staff including one by doctors. In June, doctors in Beersheba, Safed and Nahariya staged a hunger strike while relaxing the strictures on admissions to already overcrowded hospitals. X-ray technicians wanted shorter hours to lessen the time exposed to radiation.

In August, the shekel was devalued by 7.5 per cent relative to the US dollar. Further devaluations followed with the swearing-in of Shamir's cabinet in October. The cabinet introduced 50 per cent increases in the price of basic foods including bread and dairy produce. This prompted a threat from Tami to leave the coalition – they represented the Mizrahi working class. The Tel Aviv Stock Exchange closed and the sale of bank shares was suspended. The crisis forced the resignation of the finance minister, Yoram Aridor, specifically because he intended to link the shekel to the dollar. With inflation running at 131.3 per cent, Israel had the highest rate in the world with the exceptions of Bolivia and Argentina. This situation induced a two-hour walk-out of Israel's entire labour force. Despite this, the coalition survived a Knesset vote of no confidence in the government's economic policies by 61–54. Labour further failed to capitalise on Israel's economic woes in the municipal and mayoral elections.

The presence of UNIFIL forces, the Israeli military and Major Saad Haddad's Christian militia in south Lebanon and the ongoing civil conflict in the country catalysed the involvement of Iran and Syria in assisting the Shi'ite community and in general to oppose any foreign presence. The coalescence of Shi'ite resistance into the embryonic Hezbollah coincided, first, with negotiations, then a fragile peace agreement in May to normalise relations between Amin Gemayel's Phalangist-led administration and Begin's government. Israel also agreed to the redeployment of its troops in Lebanon, contingent on the departure of both PLO and Syrian forces from the country.

Yet, within Israel, it was becoming increasingly clear that the normalisation of relations with Lebanon was in name only. In the face of Syria's refusal to leave, there was increased pressure for a unilateral withdrawal of troops from Lebanon. In the Shouf mountains, which were occupied by Israeli forces, there was still fighting between the Druze and the Phalangists. Peace Now organised a protest march from Rosh Hanikra on the Lebanese border to Tel Aviv.

President Reagan had stated in April that he would delay the delivery of seventy-five F-16 fighter bombers if Israeli forces remained in Lebanon. In July, the head of the IDF, Moshe Levi, confirmed that Israel would withdraw to the Awali River, 28 miles north of the border with Lebanon.

The much-vaunted Reagan Plan was stalled when Begin denounced its proposed freeze on settlement building. Reagan had also suggested 'something in the nature of a national home' for the Palestinians. The Palestine National Council meeting in Algiers also declared the plan to be unacceptable. King Hussein abandoned any possibility of negotiations with Israel when such a move found disfavour with both the Saudis and the PLO. Former President Carter met two PLO officials in Cairo while Henry Kissinger met one in Morocco. The USA further protested when a ministerial committee authorised the construction of three new settlements including Bracha, overlooking Nablus.

The involvement of Iran and Syria also promoted the introduction of suicide bombing. In April, the US Embassy in Beirut was bombed, killing more than sixty, including Robert Ames, the CIA's Near East and South Asia director. In October, suicide bombers targeted housing complexes for both US and French members of the multinational peacekeeping forces and killed more than three hundred people. In November, Israeli and Lebanese forces were targeted by suicide bombers in Tyre, killing more than sixty. The Soviet Union was reportedly delivering SS-21 ground-to-ground ballistic missiles to Syria. In November, an Israeli aircraft was shot down by a Soviet missile over Lebanon.

The Abu Nidal group continued its campaign of assassination against the PLO, Jordan, Saudi Arabia and the Gulf States. In April, Issam Sartawi, who with Arafat's unspoken agreement had floated ideas about a two-state solution and reconciliation with Israel, was gunned down at a Socialist International meeting in Portugal. There were several attacks in Jordan and attempts on the lives of Jordanian ambassadors in New Delhi and Rome.

Negotiations took place between Palestinian groups and Israel in an attempt to secure a prisoner exchange under the auspices of the Red Cross and the Austrian government. Israeli prisoners were being held by Fatah, the PFLP-GC and Syria.

Negotiations also took place to secure the evacuation of PLO fighters from Tripoli where they were under fire from both the Syrian-backed dissident Abu Musa group and from the Israeli navy. In December, Arafat and his forces sailed to Tunis and to Yemen in hired Greek ferries, escorted by French naval vessels.

The US administration strongly promoted the Reagan Plan of September 1982 despite the fact that it had been rejected by both Begin and Arafat. Washington continued to protest about Jewish settlements on the West Bank. In July, a nineteen-year-old yeshiva student, Aharon Gross, was stabbed near the marketplace in Hebron. The commander of Israeli forces on the West Bank responded to Gross's death by dismissing the mayor of the city, Mustafa Natshe. This followed the burning of an Arab bus by the inhabitants of Kiriat Arba in retaliation for a grenade thrown at a passing Israeli vehicle. In this tit-for-tat state of heightened tension, a curfew was imposed.

The Jewish Underground, which followed the example of Lehi forty years before, had previously maimed Palestinian mayors. Led by key figures in Gush Emunim, the Underground retaliated for the killing of Gross. Three days after the curfew was lifted and under the supervision of the Underground's Menahem Livni, masked men attacked students and teachers who were taking summer courses in the courtyard of Hebron's Islamic College, killing three and wounding thirty-three.

211

1984

The Israeli police came under pressure to prevent incidents from a number of assailants.

Here chickens in the pen look nervously on as a seemingly confident policeman is carrying rows of eggs. His hat bears broken eggs labelled 'oversight' and 'intelligence'.

Carrying the eggs in an ultra-orthodox hat, the top layer refers to an attempt to blow up the Dome of the Rock by nationalist Israelis. One egg sports a lighted fuse. The middle layer refers to Palestinian attacks on buses. This cartoon appeared one day before the attack on Bus 300. The bottom tier is labelled in Hebrew 'TNT' or 'Terror against Terror'. This refers to revenge attacks, often by the Jewish Underground on the West Bank as reprisals against Palestinians.

Ze'ev (*Ha'aretz* 11 April 1984)

3 Jan Foreign trade deficit stands at $3.47 billion, a 17 per cent increase over 1982

14 Jan Sa'ad Haddad, commander of Christian militia in south Lebanon, dies aged 47

23 Feb Former Bank Hapoalim head Ya'akov Levinson commits suicide

11 Feb In Amman King Hussein and Arafat agree a reconciliation agreement on future action

5 Mar Under Syrian pressure, Lebanon cancels peace agreement with Israel

2 Apr Grenade and gun attack on shoppers in King George Street, Jerusalem

12 Apr PFLP hijacks Bus 300 in Ashdod and demands release of 500 prisoners

13 Apr Shamir defeats Sharon 407–306 in Herut central committee in leadership contest

26 Apr MKs demand inquiry into the killing of four Palestinians in the Bus 300 affair

27 Apr Jewish Underground members held after attempt to blow up Arab buses

16 May Central Statistics Office states cost-of-living index had risen 263 per cent in past year

5 June Israeli attaché in Cairo shot in hand by assailant in passing car

10 June Tel Aviv Peace Now demonstration against Jewish Underground

17 June Trial begins of Jewish Underground members in Jerusalem

19 June Kahane's Kach party barred from standing in July election

20 June Shekel devalued by 2.6 per cent

22 June Reserve officer Gilad Peli sentenced to ten years on charges of terrorism

29 June Prisoner exchange between Syrians and Israelis in Quneitra

29 June Supreme Court rules that Kach can participate in election

19 July Jewish Agency formally confirms the presence of Ethiopian Jews in Israel

23 July Labour emerges as the largest party in the election for eleventh Knesset

27 July Israel closes its liaison office in Beirut

5 Aug Protest against newly elected MK Meir Kahane in Umm al-Fahm

22 Aug Unemployment at three-year high, having increased by 45 per cent since January

13 Sept Peres presents rotational government with Likud to the Knesset

14 Sept Abdul-Hamid Kishta, mayor of Rafah, killed after Friday prayers

16 Sept Benjamin Netanyahu appointed Israel's ambassador to the UN

17 Sept Shekel devalued by 9 per cent as hyperinflation nears 400 per cent

20 Sept Hezbollah bombs US Embassy annex in Beirut, killing 24

24 Sept Price of fuel raised by 30 per cent

5 Oct East Jerusalem business strike supporting Arab inmates in Nablus prison

22 Oct University students Ron Levi and Revital Seri killed near Beit Jala

29 Oct Ben-Gurion University does not open through lack of funds

29 Oct Rocket attack on Arab bus en route to Hebron kills one and injures ten

1 Nov Rabin authorises establishment of a Palestinian bank on the West Bank

2 Nov Government, Histadrut, Manufacturers Association agree three-month wage and price freeze

6 Nov Ronald Reagan defeats Walter Mondale in US election

4 Dec Hussein and Mubarak endorse PLO as a full partner in negotiations

213

The election at the end of July resulted in an effective equal split whereby neither the Labour Alignment nor the Likud could form a workable coalition. Both lost seats. A national coalition government was therefore established whereby Labour, the largest party, would take the premiership for the first two years and Likud for the second two years. By September, Shimon Peres had established the largest coalition in Israeli history, constituting eight parties and 97 of the 120 MKs. Shas, the party of the Mizrahi ultra-orthodox established by Ovadia Yosef, gained representation for the first time and subsequently held ministerial posts. Peres became prime minister and Rabin minister of defence.

Both Meir Kahane's Kach and Mohammed Miari's Progressive List for Peace secured representation in the Knesset, having been initially banned by the Central Elections Committee and then reinstated through appeals to the Supreme Court. Kahane's list was originally banned 18–10, with 7 abstentions. The chairman of the committee, Judge Gavriel Bach, argued that Kahane's list undermined the principles of democracy. Kahane's election to the Knesset led to several protest rallies and demonstrations.

Kahane called for the release of the members of the Jewish Underground who had been arrested at the end of April, following a failed attempt to blow up several buses during the rush hour in East Jerusalem. The buses would have been carrying Arab worshippers, returning from commemorating the Isra Wal Meeraj holiday. This, in turn, followed the discovery of explosives, grenades and detonators on the Temple Mount when an Arab guard had interrupted a carefully planned operation to cause maximum damage to Muslim holy places. Most of those arrested were associated with the leadership of Gush Emunim. They had been active for several years and moved from a stance of individual terror in maiming Palestinian mayors to indiscriminate mass violence in this planned attack against customers of the Kalandiya-Atarot Bus Company. The arrests further highlighted the ideological gap between the Left and the Right. President Chaim Herzog called them 'unbalanced men', whereas Shamir implied that they were unrepresentative of the settler movement. In June, Gilad Peli, an IDF reserve captain, was sentenced to ten years despite a plea bargain. He was accused of stealing large amounts of explosives from an army base in the Golan Heights and subsequently taking fifty landmines.

Moshe Levinger of Hebron was seen as the spiritual mentor behind the Jewish Underground. He was called in for questioning for forty-eight hours about the activities of his son-in-law, Menahem Livni, who had been arrested. In the Knesset, some twenty MKs campaigned on behalf of the Jewish Underground. In November, twenty-five MKs wrote to Shimon Peres complaining about the conditions in which the prisoners were held.

Yasser Arafat's diplomacy effected a gradual rapprochement with King Hussein. West Bank Palestinians were included in this process and several dozen travelled to Amman. Both Hussein and Arafat had rejected the idea of confederation as delineated by the Reagan Plan. The question of whether Jordan should be the dominant partner was a point of dispute. Arafat refused to endorse UNR 242 as a basis for opening a dialogue with the Americans. By December, Hussein and Mubarak endorsed the PLO as a full partner in negotiations with Israel. Shamir attacked Egypt's move as a retreat from the principles of Camp David.

Attorney-General Yitzhak Zamir warned that any member of the Knesset who either entered an enemy country or met a member of the PLO would be open to criminal proceedings. Such a felony would merit a sentence of up to fifteen years.

In parallel, there were numerous attacks against civilians in Jerusalem. In early April, there was a gun and grenade attack by members of the DFLP on shoppers in King George Street. There was an attack on a bus south of Beersheba, bound for Kiriat Arba. A few weeks later, there was an attack on a bus with Arab passengers en route to Hebron in Jerusalem, with an IDF-issue missile fired at it.

In mid-April, four Palestinians from Gaza hijacked a no. 300 bus in Ashdod en route from Tel Aviv to Ashkelon. The bus was stopped near the Deir el-Balah camp in Gaza and eventually stormed by Israeli commandos who secured all the passengers, bar one. Two hijackers were killed in the operation and two captured. While both the government and the military proclaimed that all the assailants had been killed during the rescue operation, the daily *Hadashot* published a photograph of one of the Palestinians being led off the bus. The Likud's Ehud Olmert and Mapam's Victor Shemtov called for an investigation despite an official denial stating that normal procedure had been followed. Further revelations by the Israeli and international press forced the defence minister, Moshe Arens, to establish an inquiry, headed by Meir Zorea. When this was leaked by *Hadashot*, the newspaper was instructed not to appear for several days. Zorea's report was delivered to the Knesset's Foreign Affairs Committee. This subsequently led to the trial of the commanding officer, Yitzhak Mordechai, and several of his associates.

Israeli troops still remained in southern Lebanon despite repeated promises to withdraw. Their presence was accompanied by attacks by Shi'ite militia. Two years after the invasion of Lebanon, Israeli casualties stood at 584 dead and almost 4,000 injured. The visit of Amin Gemayel, the Lebanese president, to Damascus was the symbolic acceptance that the May 1983 treaty with Israel was now defunct. In July, the Lebanese government withdrew its personnel from the Liaison Commission at Dbayeh, north of Beirut, leaving only its Israeli officials. The thirty diplomats and attachés were then flown back to Israel. In September, the IDF handed over its responsibility for security in the area to the essentially Christian South Lebanon Army (SLA) under the command of Antoine Lahad. Repeated negotiations between the Lebanese and the Israelis under the auspices of the United Nations Interim Force in Lebanon (UNIFIL) at the village of Nakura made no progress towards a withdrawal of Israeli troops. The Israelis insisted that the SLA take control of the area north of Israel's border with Lebanon.

In the Knesset in January, the government defeated three motions of no confidence in their handling of the economy. Shimon Peres stated that the national debt had increased from 30 billion to 3 trillion shekels and the annual inflation rate had risen from 30 per cent to more than 190 per cent in 1983. The three-member Mizrahi party, Tami, by threatening to withhold its support for the government, had managed to obtain an increase in child care allowance and to raise the income tax threshold for impoverished families. The finance minister also promised to introduce a minimum wage bill.

By mid-year inflation was averaging 350–400 per cent per year. The Central Bureau of Statistics released figures that indicated a 3 per cent drop in exports and a 4.5 per cent increase in imports. In September, panic purchasing of the dollar forced the devaluation of the shekel by 9 per cent. In response to the general economic situation, the government introduced austerity measures involving public spending cuts and a reduction in subsidies. It then implemented a six-month ban on importing and purchasing luxury goods such as cars, televisions and refrigerators to stem the flow of the country's foreign currency reserves. This was followed by a three-month wage freeze. By the end of the year, nearly a hundred thousand people were unemployed, some 6 per cent of the labour force.

215

1985

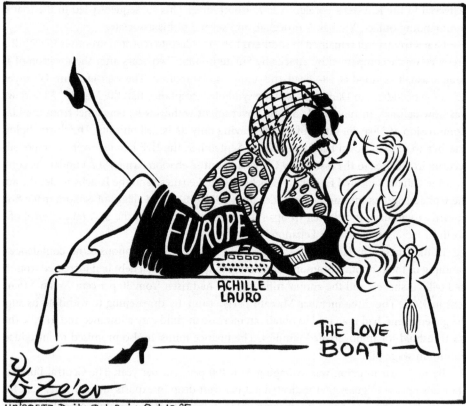

ACHILLE
LAURO

EUROPE

THE LOVE
BOAT

Ze'ev

HA'ARETZ, Daily, Tel-Aviv, Oct. 10. 85

A wheelchair-bound retired American Jew, Leon Klinghoffer, was executed on board a hijacked Italian cruise ship, the *Achille Lauro*, by a pro-PLO faction of the Palestine Liberation Front. Klinghoffer was on holiday with his wife to celebrate their wedding anniversary. The Italians throughout this saga played an ambivalent role. Here 'Europe' is being seduced – almost 'Italian-style' – by a stereotypical Palestinian hijacker who bears a clear resemblance to Yasser Arafat. All this is taking place on a couch on 'The Love Boat', presumably the *Achille Lauro. The Love Boat* was a popular television programme where romance always blossomed.

Ze'ev (*Ha'aretz* 10 October 1985)

5 Jan   Ethiopian Jews' flights halted after Peres's revelation of Operation Moses

15 Jan   Egyptians and Israelis meet to discuss the future of Taba

24 Jan   Jury finds *Time* magazine guilty of faulty reporting, but not libel against Sharon

9 Feb   Uri Avnery and five other Israelis meet Arafat in Tunis

11 Feb   Arafat and Hussein sign accord in attempt to find common ground

19 Feb   IDF withdraws from the Awali River to new positions in Lebanon

10 Mar   Truck bomb kills 12 Israeli soldiers in southern Lebanon

25 Mar   Ethiopians protest outside Knesset at treatment by Chief Rabbinate

4 Apr   Ansar detention camp in south Lebanon demolished

30 Apr   IDF leaves Tyre

8 May   Government and WZO offer $1 million for information on Josef Mengele

13 May   President Mobutu Sese Seko of Zaire arrives in Israel

13 May   5 per cent swing from Likud to Labour in Histadrut election

20 May   Three Israeli prisoners, held since 1982 in Damascus, swapped for 1,150 Arabs

20 May   Government cuts subsidies on essentials in new austerity programme

27 May   Japan protests about Israel's release of Kōzō Okamoto, involved in 1972 airport killings

11 June   Last IDF units leave Lebanon three years after Operation Peace for Galilee

11 June   Schoolchildren killed near Moshav HaBonim when train hits stalled bus on a crossing

1 July   Peres announces economic stabilisation plan and Israel's embrace of capitalism

3 July   Knesset votes 70–17 to approve emergency economic programme

3 July   1.5 million people stage 24-hour general strike

3 July   Three hundred Shi'ites, released from Atlit camp, transferred to the Red Cross in Lebanon

11 July   Fifteen members of Jewish Underground found guilty by Jerusalem court

22 July   Livni, Sharabaf and Nir sentenced to life for attack on Hebron Islamic College

1 Aug   Knesset votes 60–0 to ban racist and anti-democratic parties

20 Aug   Israel Embassy attaché Albert Atrakchi killed by gunmen in Cairo

24 Aug   Andre Aloush of Netanya killed in Tulkarem jewellery shop

4 Sept   New shekel goes into circulation

19 Sept   Israel's population stands at 4.255 million

25 Sept   Three Israelis killed in Yom Kippur attack on yacht moored in Larnaca

1 Oct   Israeli F-15s attack and destroy PLO headquarters at Hammam Chott, Tunisia

7 Oct   *Achille Lauro* hijacked by a PLF faction, killing Leon Klinghoffer

21 Nov   Jonathan Pollard arrested by FBI on suspicion of passing US classified information to Israel

4 Dec   Herzog appearance at a Rakah conference, first time for an Israeli president

5 Dec   Liberal Centre party breaks away from the Likud

27 Dec   Rome and Vienna airports attacked by Abu Nidal group

31 Dec   Journalist Amnon Kapeliuk fined 1.6 million shekels for visiting Jordan

In early January, the ten-member inner cabinet met to discuss the stalemate in the talks in Nakura between the Israelis and the Lebanese on Israel's withdrawal from Lebanon, following the invasion of 1982. Israel argued that UNIFIL should take over responsibility for security between the Zahrani and Awali rivers, while the South Lebanon Army (SLA) would patrol the area between the Litani River and the Israeli border. Lebanon did not recognise the Israeli-backed Christian militia, the SLA, and insisted on a more limited role for UNIFIL.

The Israelis then presented a three-stage unilateral withdrawal plan. The first redeployment was to leave Sidon and move to the region of the Litani. The IDF took with them the last Jewish family in Sidon, Yaffa Levi plus her four children and aunt. The evacuation of Sidon was followed by pro-Iranian Shi'ite demonstrations, demanding an Islamic republic in Lebanon. Some 1,500 members of the Iranian Revolutionary Guards were believed to be in Lebanon.

The Israeli withdrawal was accompanied by attacks on Shi'ite villages, Salim, Bazouriye, Maarake, Abbassieh and Bedyass. The Israeli liaison office in Nabatiyeh was also attacked several times. In addition, there were skirmishes between rival Shi'ite factions, Amal and Hezbollah. In March, a suicide truck bombing killed twelve Israeli soldiers and wounded fourteen less than a mile from the Israeli border town of Metulla. Further attacks on convoys took place – in particular one at the Palestinian refugee camp at Rashidieh. Such attacks provoked demands in Israel by the Left for a speedier withdrawal and an end to the 'iron fist' policy towards the Shi'ites.

The second stage of the withdrawal averted a potential clash with Syrian forces stationed in the Bekaa Valley. By the end of April, the IDF evacuated Tyre. The Ansar detention camp, north of the Litani River, released the last of its prisoners who were captured during the advance into Lebanon in 1982. The camp was then demolished by IDF bulldozers.

In a complex prisoner exchange, three Israeli soldiers, captured during the early days of the Lebanon war by the PFLP-GC, were flown from Damascus to Geneva and then returned to Israel. One of the hundreds of prisoners exchanged was Kōzō Okamoto, the sole surviving member of the Japanese Red Army unit which was involved in the killing of Puerto Rican pilgrims at Lod airport in 1972. This release provoked both Shamir and Sharon to request the release of members of the Jewish Underground. Former Austrian chancellor, Bruno Kreisky, who had been instrumental in facilitating the prisoner exchange, cancelled his visit to Israel for security reasons, for fear of attack from the Right.

The last IDF units left Lebanon on 11 June, a few days after the third anniversary of the invasion of Lebanon. A small group of advisers remained behind to liaise with the SLA. On 12 June, Shimon Peres commented that the war had been a huge mistake: it had gone far beyond the stated limits of Operation Peace for Galilee in June 1982.

The Likud faced challenges at the beginning of the year when King Hussein and Yasser Arafat signed an agreement which implied any movement towards peace negotiations would involve a joint Jordanian–Palestinian delegation. When Mubarak proposed talks between Israel and such a joint delegation, Shamir opposed any discussion while Peres welcomed it, providing that there was no PLO involvement. Shamir claimed that this was an attempt to bring about USA–PLO negotiations. This was followed shortly afterwards by a meeting between six Israelis and Arafat in Tunis – a meeting denounced by the Likud and Tehiya which demanded that the individuals involved be put on trial.

In April, Shamir and other right-wing ministers vetoed a visit to Cairo by Ezer Weizman, a former leading figure in the Likud. The Likud was also opposed to any Labour initiative to hold an international peace conference. In early November, Arafat agreed to the 'Cairo Declaration'. He stated that he was 'opposed to all forms of terrorism', but resolved at the same time to carry on the armed struggle only on territory which had been occupied by Israel.

Following the prisoner exchange in which more than a thousand Palestinians were freed, Shamir and Sharon called for the release of the members of the Jewish Underground who were on trial in the Jerusalem District Court.

In May, King Hussein held talks with Reagan on a proposal that the PLO would recognise Israel's right to exist in return for the USA recognising the right of the Palestinians to self-determination. This would lay the basis for an international conference. Peres instead called for direct negotiations with Jordan 'under conditions of equality' within the context of the framework of a five-stage timetable. He also spoke about an 'authentic Palestinian representation' which would be acceptable to all sides.

At the end of September, three Israeli tourists were killed by Force 17, originally a unit of personal bodyguards for Arafat, on board a yacht at Larnaca, Cyprus. This was followed a few days later by an Israeli air force attack on the PLO headquarters in Tunis – a flight of more than 2,000 km from Tel Aviv.

In July, three members of the Jewish Underground were sentenced to life imprisonment for murder, while twelve others received terms of between four months and seven years. Haim Kaufman, head of the Likud in the Knesset, lobbied for a bill that would grant an early release to those sentenced.

A pro-Iraqi faction of the Palestine Liberation Front (PLF) hijacked the *Achille Lauro* cruise ship and killed a wheelchair-bound passenger, Leon Klinghoffer. An Egyptian flight on which the PLF leader, Abu Abbas, was travelling was intercepted by four US navy F-14s and forced to land at a NATO base in Sicily. The Italians refused to hand over Abbas – as did the Yugoslavs when Abbas was allowed to travel to Belgrade. While Abbas went free, four hijackers and a Syrian involved in the attack were tried in Genoa on firearms charges and sentenced to between four and nine years.

219

Yonah Avrushmi was sentenced to life imprisonment for throwing a hand grenade into a Peace Now demonstration in 1983 and killing Emil Grunzweig.

Foreign Minister Shamir also faced growing criticism from within Herut when he supported the incorporation of the La'am faction, led by Ehud Olmert, into the Likud. Some members of the Likud supported a ban on demonstrations by Meir Kahane's Kach party. A breakaway Centre Party, led by Tel Aviv mayor Shlomo Lahat, further complicated Likud's status as an umbrella for the Right.

Following a nineteen-hour cabinet meeting, Israel turned away from a socialist economy and adopted a stabilisation plan to deal with the huge inflation. This turn towards a capitalist society involved not only austerity but also a shrinking of government's role in providing services and lower taxes. It pitted the Treasury against the Central Bank and excluded prominent economists from involvement in forging the plan. The USA had offered a $1.5 billion grant if Israel overhauled its economy and this was overseen by professionals from both countries.

President Mobutu Sese Seko of Zaire visited Israel after re-establishing diplomatic relations between the two countries in 1983. Mobutu was believed to have forfeited a $120 million grant from the Saudis by doing so. This was viewed as a further step in renewing ties with African nations which had been broken off in the aftermath of the Yom Kippur War. Nigeria, Ghana, Kenya, Togo and the Ivory Coast, which did not have diplomatic relations, were now extensively trading with Israel.

1986

Anatoly Shcharansky (Natan Sharansky), a seminal figure in the Soviet human rights and Jewish emigration movement, was released after nine years in a strict regime labour camp in the USSR, in exchange for Eastern bloc spies imprisoned in the USA and West Germany.

A gleeful bird, sporting the Star of David and labelled 'Shcharansky', flies to freedom from an onion-domed, snow-covered building where a multitude of doleful birds are imprisoned.

A blackbird labelled 'Mandela' is also taking flight – an indication of the relaxation of his incarceration by the apartheid regime in South Africa.

Ze'ev (*Ha'aretz* 12 February 1986)

1 Jan Second Lebanese Jew kidnapped by Shi'ite militants found dead in Beirut

15 Jan Visit of right-wing MKs to Temple Mount causes Arab disturbances

23 Jan Sharon and *Time* magazine reach out of court agreement in libel case

8 Feb Israel Galili, Ahdut Ha'Avoda politician, dies aged 74

11 Feb Exchanged for a Czech spy, refusenik Natan Sharansky arrives in Israel

12 Feb Diplomatic relations with Ivory Coast, broken off in 1973, resumed

19 Feb King Hussein ends negotiations seeking a joint approach with the PLO

2 Mar Zafer al-Masri, mayor of Nablus, assassinated by Palestinian militants

9 Mar Fifteenth convention of Herut opens, displaying divisions and disarray

21 Mar Golan Druze demonstrate against harassment at Majdal Shams

27 Mar Katyusha hits schoolyard in Kiriat Shemona, injuring teacher and pupils

28 Mar First Israeli test tube baby born at Tel Hashomer hospital

15 Apr US attack on Libya after attack on West Berlin nightclub

17 Apr Plot to blow up El Al flight from London by Nezar Hindawi foiled

11 May Head of Bank Leumi resigns over shares scandal

24 May Margaret Thatcher becomes the first British prime minister to visit Israel

9 June Israeli ambassador to Vienna recalled after election of Kurt Waldheim

11 June Secularist attack on Tel Aviv synagogue after Jerusalem arson by religious Jews

15 June Michael Bruno appointed next governor of Bank of Israel

24 June Strike by 11,000 hospital nurses over right to form a union

25 June Shin Bet head, Avraham Shalom, resigns over Bus 300 controversy

26 June El Al guard discovers handbag bomb at Madrid airport

7 July Jordanian government orders closure of all Fatah offices in Jordan

10 July PFLP seaborne attack on Nahariya foiled

21 July Peres arrives in Morocco to negotiate with King Hassan

10 Aug Israel and Egypt sign arbitration agreement over possession of Taba

26 Aug Cameroon re-establishes diplomatic relations during Peres visit

6 Sept Istanbul synagogue attacked during Shabbat service, killing 22

11 Sept Peres and Mubarak meet in Alexandria for first summit in five years

22 Sept Peres meets Soviet foreign minister in diplomatic relations thaw

28 Sept Cabinet approves the establishment of a commercial television channel

20 Oct Shamir takes over as prime minister as part of the rotation agreement

8 Nov Israel's first liver transplant patient dies at Rambam hospital

9 Nov Government confirms that Mordechai Vanunu is imprisoned in Gedera

15 Nov Breslav hasid killed in knife attack in Muslim quarter of Jerusalem

26 Nov Trial begins in Jerusalem of John Demjanjuk, accused of being a guard at Treblinka

28 Dec Akram Haniya, editor of East Jerusalem daily *A-Shaab*, deported

Yitzhak Shamir struggled on several fronts in order to retain the possibility of the premiership – to be vacated by Shimon Peres in October, according to the terms of the rotation agreement. In mid-January, a new Liberal Centre party was formed by former members of the Liberal party, now integrated into the Likud. Led by Tel Aviv mayor, Shlomo Lahat, and Jewish Agency head, Leon Dulzin, its appeal was to the middle class with calls for lower income tax and religious pluralism.

In May, the fifteenth convention of Herut opened in Jerusalem amidst a three-way split between Shamir, Sharon and the housing minister, David Levy. It reflected not only a generational conflict but also one between Ashkenazim and Mizrahim. There was also a determination at all costs to stop Sharon from becoming party leader. Shamir's candidate, Moshe Katsav, narrowly won the contest to become chairman of the party presidium by 940 votes to 900. Sharon, however, decisively defeated Binyamin Begin to become chairman of the Mandates committee. The conference was marred by violence, intimidation and verbal abuse before disintegrating towards the end.

The Likud was also at odds with its Labour party partner in government. It took a different approach towards negotiations with Egypt over Taba. During Passover, Shamir promised Gush Emunim in Hebron to place greater emphasis on settling the West Bank. Shamir was also considering the appointment of Otniel Schneller, the secretary of the Council of Jewish Settlements, as an adviser on settlement activity.

Shamir's most difficult problem was the implication that he had given approval to the execution by the Shin Bet of the two Palestinians in the immediate aftermath of the Bus 300 hijacking in April 1984.

The secret Zorea committee had exonerated the Shin Bet's head, Avraham Shalom, while testimonies by operatives had pointed the finger of suspicion at Yitzhak Mordechai, who had led the Sayeret Matkal storming of the bus. In 1985, the trial of Mordechai – together with eleven others – had led to an acquittal. The unravelling of this cover-up led to Reuven Hazak, the deputy head of the Shin Bet, and two other senior officials approaching Peres and informing him of their suspicions about Shalom. The three were dismissed from their posts. Attorney-General Yitzhak Zamir wanted to instigate an investigation, but he too was forced to resign.

Avraham Shalom's resignation in June and President Herzog's subsequent pardoning of him aroused the ire of many in the Labour party and others who demanded transparency in the affair. Herzog compared the pardon to that given to Richard Nixon following the Watergate controversy. His predecessor, Yitzhak Navon, now a Labour minister, called for a further investigation.

Yitzhak Shamir, waiting quietly to succeed Peres in October, became embroiled in this deepening controversy since he had been prime minister at the time of the Bus 300 affair and the head of the Shin Bet reported directly to him. Despite the endorsement of the lack of transparency by numerous Labour figures, it also presented the possibility of unseating Shamir before he could attain the premiership. Motti Gur, the former head of the IDF and now the minister of health, called upon Shamir to resign.

When the presidential pardon was challenged in the Supreme Court, Avraham Shalom stated that his actions were 'authorised and approved'. Shamir therefore opposed any investigation of Shalom's actions. It was only in July, when Shamir was forced to speak publicly, that he contradicted Shalom's assertion that he had acted with official sanction. Shamir pleaded that he did not know about the killing of the two Palestinians until after the incident and that it was therefore a local initiative. His version also differed from that of Peres, who had made a statement that the head of the Shin Bet had 'general backing'. In July, the cabinet discussed the possibility of a full judicial inquiry and was evenly split between Labour and the Likud. The proposal was eventually voted down 14–11 owing to the vote of the three NRP ministers. Instead the Attorney-General would now proceed with a general police inquiry.

The Abu Nidal group had been responsible for attacks on El Al facilities at both Vienna and Rome airports. It also claimed responsibility for the attack on the Neve Shalom synagogue in Istanbul. Nezar Hindawi was believed to be a member of the Abu Nidal group, but it is more likely that he was employed by Syrian intelligence in attempting to smuggle semtex explosives aboard an El Al flight at Heathrow airport in London. The destruction of the aircraft was due to take place on Syria's National Day. His unaware, pregnant girlfriend, Anne-Marie Murphy, was given the semtex, but this was discovered during a security check. Hindawi had already booked a flight to Damascus for later that day. He was sentenced to forty-five years. During his trial, he implicated the Syrian ambassador, with the result that Margaret Thatcher broke off diplomatic relations with Syria.

King Hussein broke off cooperation with the PLO during a long broadcast on television. He spoke about the PLO's lack of 'commitment, credibility and constancy'. Arafat refused to accept a written agreement in support of UNR 242. Hussein closed down the Fatah offices in Amman and accused the PLO of involvement in Jordan's internal affairs, such as the clashes at Yarmuk University in Irbid.

Since 1983 Jordanian diplomats had been assassinated or been the targets of failed attempts to kill them in Delhi, Athens and Madrid. The facilities of Royal Jordanian Airlines had been bombed in Rome, Athens and Nicosia. On the West Bank, the newly appointed mayor of Nablus, Zafer al-Masri, who had pro-Jordanian sympathies, was assassinated. Al-Masri's appointment was to be the first in restoring mayors to Ramallah, El Bireh and Hebron.

The Foreign Ministry under Shamir did have success in re-establishing diplomatic relations with several African nations, after twenty-nine had severed official contact under Arab economic pressure in the aftermath of the Yom Kippur War. However, the Camp David Agreement between Israel and Egypt and the withdrawal from the Sinai had removed obstacles to the resumption of diplomatic relations. Egypt was a full member of the Organisation of African States. The Ivory Coast and Cameroon had followed Zaire and Liberia in re-establishing formal relations, while there was a general improvement with states who had unofficial and semi-official ties with Israel. This was accompanied by a stronger condemnation by Israel of apartheid in South Africa. In June, the Foreign Ministry condemned the state of emergency proclaimed by the South African government in response to the proposed demonstrations to mark the tenth anniversary of the Soweto protests.

Senior figures in the four major banks in Israel resigned following the findings of the Bejski inquiry. They were accused of manipulating bank shares and thereby contributing to the crash on the Tel Aviv Stock Exchange in October 1983.

In early November the Iran–Contra story broke in the press and questions began to be asked about Israel's role in the transaction of arms.

The accession of Mikhail Gorbachev began to indicate a thaw in the frostiness between the USSR and Israel. Although diplomatic relations had been broken off after the Six Day War, Shamir had met Andrei Gromyko for an official discussion at the UN in 1984. In September, Shimon Peres met the Soviet foreign minister, Eduard Shevardnadze, to discuss the normalisation of relations between Israel and the USSR. This followed the release of the leading refusenik and human rights activist Natan Sharansky (Anatoly Shcharansky) after nine years' internment in Soviet camps and prisons and his emigration to Israel.

1987

The costs involved in developing the Lavi fighter jet soared astronomically. The launching of a prototype was seen as a means of securing independence from the Americans by developing a homegrown arms industry.

The cabinet was divided along Left–Right lines. A vote at the end of August resulted in a 12–11 vote to cancel the Lavi with one abstention. The fight to retain the Lavi was led by Moshe Arens, but Prime Minister Shamir had miscalculated the level of support. Labour was joined by the Likud finance minister who was unable to justify the cost.

The tree here is titled 'Lavi', and 'Israel' is seen as being pulled in opposite directions.

Shmuel Katz (*Ma'ariv* 18 August 1987)

4 Jan	Interior minister Yitzhak Peretz submits resignation to cabinet over Reform convert
4 Jan	Vanunu goes on hunger strike over conditions in Ramla prison
26 Jan	Head of Fatah Youth, Mohammad Yusuf Dahlan, deported from Gaza
1 Feb	Cabinet approves Dan Shomron as next IDF Chief of Staff
6 Feb	Navy intercepts ship from Cyprus carrying 50 members of Fatah
21 Feb	Meir Ya'ari, founder of Mapam, leader of Kibbutz Artzi, dies aged 89
22 Feb	Jerusalem bomb injures 17 people outside Damascus Gate
4 Mar	Jonathan Pollard sentenced to life imprisonment for espionage in USA
18 Mar	Inner cabinet decides to stop military and technology sales to South Africa
11 Apr	Shimon Peres and King Hussein sign London Agreement
5 May	Israel interests section opened in Warsaw
11 May	Inner cabinet rejects Peres's plan for an international conference
14 May	Fatah activists Khalil Ashour and Marwan Barghouti deported to Jordan
24 May	Supreme Court overturns espionage conviction of Izat Nafsu and orders release
26 May	Shinui's Amnon Rubinstein resigns as minister of communications
1 June	Bomb in helicopter kills Lebanese premier Rashid Karami
7 June	Armed Jewish settlers attack Daheisha refugee camp near Bethlehem
9 June	Togo renews diplomatic relations, broken off in 1973
11 June	USA cancels sale of 1,600 Maverick air-to-ground missiles to Saudi Arabia
7 July	Oliver North tells US court that Israel knew about Iran–Contra affair
8 July	MKs prevent Chief Rabbinate having the sole right to approve conversions abroad
19 July	Rabin turns back Sharon's bulldozers preparing for West Bank settlement
30 Aug	Vanunu trial opens *in camera* in Jerusalem District Court
30 Aug	Lavi project discontinued by cabinet vote 12–11, with one abstention
1 Sept	Workers block Jerusalem–Tel Aviv highway over Lavi cancellation
2 Sept	Moshe Arens resigns from cabinet over Lavi cancellation
11 Sept	Amiram Nir, implicated in Iran–Contra affair, sacked as Shamir adviser
14 Sept	Israel and Hungary to set up interest sections in respective countries
15 Sept	US administration closes Washington PLO information office
16 Sept	Inner cabinet decides to impose far-reaching sanctions on South Africa
25 Sept	Abba Kovner, poet and Vilna partisan, dies at Kibbutz Ein HaHoresh aged 79
30 Sept	Peres meets foreign minister of China, Wu Xueqian, at UN
15 Oct	Refusenik Ida Nudel arrives in Israel after 17 years' refusal
26 Oct	Vladimir and Masha Slepak, long-time refuseniks, arrive in Israel
25 Nov	Hang-gliding Palestinian from Lebanon kills six soldiers near Kiriat Shemona
2 Dec	William Nakash extradited to France following in-absentia murder conviction
9 Dec	First Intifada begins after motor accident in Jabalia refugee camp

225

In April, Shimon Peres and King Hussein signed the London Agreement which embellished the Jordanian option in the form of an international conference, to be attended by the five permanent members of the UN Security Council and the main actors in the Middle East conflict. Signed in the presence of Zaid al-Rifai and Yossi Beilin, it represented almost two years of discussion between then Prime Minister Peres and King Hussein.

As prime minister, Peres had fashioned the possibility of such a conference in an address to the United Nations General Assembly in September 1986 and had secured Mubarak's agreement to establish a joint preparatory group with the Egyptians. He argued that there should be no imposed solution. The format would be an opening ceremony, followed by bilateral committees which would hammer out the specifics of such regional disputes. Peres had stipulated that any Palestinian participation should only take place as part of the Jordanian delegation and that such participants should not be members of the PLO. The conference was based on acceptance of UN resolutions 242 and 338 which the PLO rejected.

With a political thaw taking place with Gorbachev's leadership of the USSR, Peres insisted that Moscow's participation would be predicated on its lifting of restrictions preventing Jewish emigration from the Soviet Union. He also demanded that diplomatic relations between the USSR and Israel should be restored. While leading refuseniks such as Natan Sharansky, the Slepaks and Ida Nudel were allowed to leave for Israel, the Kremlin only offered the proposition of establishing 'interest offices' in Tel Aviv and Moscow.

Yitzhak Shamir strongly opposed the idea of an international conference. He believed that France, China and the USSR would enforce a return to the 1967 borders and a reversal of the settlement drive on the West Bank and Gaza.

Unofficial meetings between Israeli and Chinese diplomats in Europe were often positive, with the promise of recognition in the event of an international conference. Shamir argued that Peres's plan would leave Israel isolated and instead called for direct negotiations with the Jordanians on the model of the Camp David Agreement of 1979. King Hussein, however, refused to negotiate with Israel outside the framework of an international conference. This stand-off became more pronounced once Shamir had become prime minister in October 1986 while Peres became foreign minister.

While the Likud was deliberately kept out of the picture and Shamir not even shown the text of the London Agreement, both sides tried to cultivate outside actors, in particular the USA. Peres had tried to persuade the United States that it should present the London Agreement as purely an American initiative.

By May, both the London Agreement and Shamir's own plan were presented to the inner cabinet, which split along party lines. Although no vote was taken, the division was 5–5. While many in Labour called for the dissolution of the government and a general election, Peres discovered that the party did not have sufficient votes to ensure the dissolution of the Knesset. The other choice of going into opposition meant handing over power to figures such as Sharon.

The stalemate persuaded the initially enthusiastic Americans not to interfere. Despite an address to the UN General Assembly and Peres's appeal to the Palestinians that 'the time for recrimination and blame is past', the London Agreement was stillborn.

The Palestine National Council, meeting in Algiers, moved towards a harder line. The PFLP was welcomed back into the PLO while both Egypt and Jordan distanced themselves from Arafat. Even so, Israel's approach towards cultivating pro-Jordanian Palestinians made hardly any advances. In June, there was an assassination attempt on Abdullah Lahluh, the mayor of Jenin.

Many Israeli leftists were willing to meet members of the PLO. Four Israelis met PLO representatives in Romania and were promptly put on trial on their return to Israel. At their trial, an intelligence official testified that they had met with the PLO with government approval in the hope of finding a pathway to secure the release of Israelis held by Arab states.

Ezer Weizman was the sole Israeli politician who was willing to propose talks with the PLO. The Likud attacked anyone who argued for a dialogue with the Palestinians. Abba Eban, the chairman of the Knesset Foreign Affairs and Security Committee, was attacked for giving an interview on Amman television. In contrast, Ariel Sharon moved into his apartment in the Muslim quarter of Jerusalem in December and held a housewarming party there.

At the end of 1986, details of the Iran–Contra affair appeared in the Lebanese press. Senior officials in the Reagan administration were prepared to circumvent the arms embargo of Iran in order to secure the release of American hostages held in Lebanon by Shi'ite militants. Several Lebanese Jews had been kidnapped and murdered as 'spies for the Mossad' by 'the Organisation of the Oppressed of the Earth' – a Shi'ite group with connections to Hezbollah. In addition, thousands of Iranian Jews were allowed to leave their country. The operation would be facilitated by using Israel as an intermediary and building on the transfer of PLO arms, captured in the Lebanon war in 1982, to Iran. The plan was modified to divert funds from the sale of the arms to the Contra rebels in Nicaragua.

In April, three Israeli citizens were indicted for their role in selling American arms to Iran. Amiram Nir, a counter-terrorism adviser to both Peres and Shamir, resigned from his post. Following the revelations of the Pollard case, American Jews and their organisations were critical of the Shamir government, viewing the USA–Israel relationship as undermined. Moreover, in testifying to the House–Senate select committee on the affair, Lt. Col. Oliver North further described 'the ineptness' of the Israelis in supplying the wrong type of Hawk missiles to the Iranians.

The Comprehensive Anti-Apartheid Act in the USA forced Israel to terminate its role as a supplier of arms and weapons systems to South Africa. These included Saar-class boats, Gabriel surface-to-surface missiles and components of the Kfir jet fighter-bomber. Israel feared the loss of jobs and quantities of coal imported from South Africa. The South African Jewish Board of Deputies and the Zionist Federation opposed the imposition of sanctions, while the Afrikaaner press was critical of Israel's actions. In contrast, many Black African states began to strengthen their ties with Israel which had been broken off after the Yom Kippur War in 1973. In September the inner cabinet approved moves to freeze government loans, the import of iron and steel and the purchase of Krugerrands.

After he was abducted from Rome in a honey-trap operation in October 1986, the trial of Mordechai Vanunu began at the end of August in the Jerusalem District Court. Despite a determined attempt by Vanunu, his family and supporters to have an open trial, it took place behind closed doors. Vanunu was charged with treason, espionage and the acquiring of classified information regarding Israel's nuclear programme during his time as a technician at Dimona. Vanunu's revelations had been published by the *Sunday Times* in the UK in October 1986 and his incarceration was confirmed by Israel a few weeks later. He revealed that Israel had the ability to produce the isotope tritium and could process plutonium. The *Sunday Times* suggested that Israel had stockpiled up to a hundred nuclear devices and was the world's sixth largest nuclear power. While Vanunu was regarded as a disarmament hero within the international peace movement, he was looked upon as a traitor in Israel.

227

1988

At the end of July, King Hussein divested himself of the West Bank and all its troubles. He bequeathed all responsibility – including the payment of salaries to officials – to Yasser Arafat and the PLO.

Hussein is seen here swiftly walking away from Jordan's self-proclaimed rapport with 'the Territories'. An armed, sweating Arafat is left unexpectedly in control. His forehead is stamped 'Palestinian independence' and he carries a flag labelled 'Intifada'. The first Intifada had started in December 1987.

Shmuel Katz (*Ma'ariv* 9 August 1988)

6 Jan   Rabin states that 1,978 arrests were made, but 900 released during the Intifada

6 Jan   Shimon Peres takes the stand in the Vanunu trial

7 Jan   Hanna Seniora, editor of *Al-Fajr*, announces civil disobedience campaign

20 Jan   Iosif Begun, refusenik for seventeen years, arrives in Israel

26 Jan   Judges Harafai, Arbel and Cohen to stand trial on corruption charges

14 Feb   Druze protest on the anniversary of the Golan Heights annexation

16 Feb   Explosion cripples the PLO *Voyage of Return* ship in Limassol

7 Mar   Fatah members hijack a Dimona working mothers' bus, three killed

11 Mar   Seventy MKs ask for presidential pardon for Pollard

12 Mar   Demonstration in Tel Aviv in support of Shultz plan

22 Mar   Knesset legalises homosexuality and raises the penalty for rape

27 Mar   Vanunu is sentenced to 18 years for treason and espionage

30 Mar   Netanyahu resigns as UN ambassador to run for election for the Likud

1 Apr   President Herzog pardons two members of the Jewish Underground

6 Apr   Fifteen-year-old Tirza Porat accidentally killed by an Elon Moreh guard at Beita

16 Apr   Fatah leader Abu Jihad assassinated in Tunis by Sayeret Matkal

25 Apr   John Demjanjuk sentenced to death by Jerusalem District Court

2 June   Strike by 130,000 public sector workers

2 June   Four Israelis, tried for meeting PLO in Romania, are found guilty

7 June   Bassam Abu Sharif floats two-state solution at Algiers conference

13 June   Palestinian non-violence advocate Mubarak Awad deported to USA

14 June   Knesset defeat for bill proposing validity only for orthodox conversions

15 June   Abba Eban omitted from the list of Labour's election candidates

17 June   Britain orders expulsion of Aryeh Regev, Mossad head in London

28 July   Israeli consular delegation arrives in Moscow

31 July   King Hussein announces moves to separate West Bank from Jordan

31 July   Faisal Husseini placed in administrative detention for six months

14 Aug   Abu Iyad ready to recognise Israel on the basis of UNR 181

18 Aug   Rabin outlaws popular committees on the West Bank and Gaza

1 Sept   Teachers go on strike over pay at the beginning of the school year

19 Sept   Ofek-1, first Israeli satellite, is launched by Shavit 3 rocket

20 Sept   Mass vaccination programme against polio in Hadera area

29 Sept   International arbitration panel awards Taba to Egypt

5 Oct   Kahane's Kach barred from running in the national election

1 Nov   Likud (40) defeats Labour (39) in the national election

15 Nov   Arafat proclaims Palestinian state at PNC meeting in Algiers

14 Dec   US prepared to open 'substantive dialogue' with PLO

19 Dec   Labour and Likud agree to form a coalition government

229

The proclamation of a state of Palestine at the Palestinian National Council (PNC) in Algiers in November was the culmination of a series of historic events. The Intifada that had erupted on the West Bank and Gaza during the previous December intensified with little abatement. The IDF announced in June that it had claimed the lives of 156 Arabs, while 8,000 had been arrested, 5,300 detained and another 2,500 placed in administrative detention.

While stone-throwing proliferated, it was essentially a revolt without guns by the mainstream organisations. Hanna Siniora, the editor of *Al-Fajr*, advocated a civil disobedience campaign including such actions as non-payment of taxes and a boycott of Israeli goods. He was joined by Mubarak Awad, the head of the Centre for the Study of Non-Violence in East Jerusalem – who was under threat of immediate deportation to the USA as he possessed dual citizenship. Although Shamir implied that the PLO was controlling the uprising, it proved more of an indigenous revolt. Faisal Husseini, a leading supporter of the Palestinian peace camp, was placed in administrative detention for the fourth time and 'popular committees' began to organise protests.

Fewer Arab workers turned up for work in Israel. There were short-term curfews in A-Tur and Shuafat in Jerusalem, barricades in Jaber Mukabar and a mass rally of Israeli Arabs in Nazareth. There were confrontations with Israeli police on the Temple Mount. Arab mayors and councillors on the West Bank resigned en masse. General strikes proliferated. Even the Druze demonstrated in Majdal Shams amidst demands that the Golan Heights should be returned to Syria. Member of the Knesset Abdel Wahab Darousha resigned from the Labour party in protest against Rabin's 'Iron Fist' policy. Although there was a common view that stability had to be restored, there were clear differences within the Labour party. Abba Eban termed Rabin's approach 'an insult to intellect and morality'.

In the political arena, right-wing parties pushed for a harder line in suppressing the revolt while the Left protested against the deportation of Palestinian activists and accused the IDF of contravening the 1949 Geneva Convention.

The use of 'beating' rather than 'shooting' led to protests at home and abroad. The Foreign Press Association accused the police of assaulting journalists. The photographer Sven Hackstrand, working for *Agence France Presse*, was severely beaten. The European Community and the USA strongly opposed the deportation of Palestinian activists and were able to inhibit immediate action taken against figures such as Mubarak Awad. Diaspora Jews began to state their opinion – some two hundred French Jews signed an advertisement in *Le Monde*. In the USA, the American Jewish Congress was critical while the Presidents' Conference was supportive.

In Israel, Peace Now mounted an ongoing campaign with regular rallies in Tel Aviv. Organisations such as Yesh Gvul assisted those reservists who refused to serve in the occupied territories and who were often sentenced to twenty-eight days' imprisonment. By July, 126 IDF reservists had been sentenced and another 600 had signed a commitment not to serve in the territories. A network of senior IDF officers, doctors and civilians was uncovered by whom bribes were accepted to allow citizens to escape military service.

The Reagan administration attempted to utilise the Intifada to resurrect negotiations between Israel and its neighbours. The US Middle East envoy, Richard Murphy, visited Israel in February, with a view to launching permanent status negotiations once the national election had taken place. While Labour was generally sympathetic, the Likud was not. Shamir pointed out that according to the terms of the Camp David Agreement, a transitional agreement between the parties should be arrived at first of all. This laid the basis for shuttle diplomacy by US secretary of state, George Shultz, a few weeks later. Shultz sent a letter to Shamir in early March in which he suggested bilateral negotiations between Israel and its neighbours, based on UNR 242 and 338, by as early as May. There would be further negotiations between Israel and a joint Jordanian–Palestinian delegation which would take place over a six-month period, followed by final status negotiations. All this would be completed within a year. Peres agreed; both Shamir and the PLO did not. Polls suggested that a majority of US Jews supported the Shultz initiative.

In June, an aide to Arafat, Bassam Abu Sharif, floated the idea of negotiations with Israel and implied its recognition. This was followed two months later by Salah Khalaf (Abu Iyad), ostensibly number two in the PLO, similarly suggesting negotiations, based on the original UNR 181 of 1947 which proposed a two-state solution. While this promoted a sympathetic reticence on the part of the Labour party and liberal mainstream Diaspora organisations, such proposals were dismissed by the Right as public relations. The Israeli Left, however, took a different approach in contacting the PLO despite questions of legality. Four Israelis who met PLO representatives in Romania in November 1986 were tried and sentenced to six months' imprisonment. The Israeli restaurateur Abie Nathan travelled to Tunis to meet Arafat.

In the USA, Shultz met American Palestinian academics Edward Said and Ibrahim Abu-Lughod. The Israeli Right argued that such meetings were a violation of a 1975 memorandum of understanding in which Washington pledged to have no contact with the PLO. In Europe, an invitation was extended to Arafat to address the European Parliament in Strasbourg. In September, the French foreign minister, Roland Dumas, met Arafat.

At the end of July, King Hussein detached the West Bank from Jordan and effectively put an end to the Israeli Labour party's Jordanian option. A five-year, $1.3 billion development plan for the West Bank was cancelled and the lower House of Parliament – members of which represented West Bank interests – was dissolved. Economic aid to the West Bank ceased, including the $70 million annual payment to West Bank civil servants, of whom more than 16,000 were now not paid for the month of August.

While Sharon argued for extending Israeli law to the West Bank and Gaza, Peres was relatively muted in his condemnation of the PLO. Many in Labour followed the Yariv–Shemtov formula to open a dialogue with the PLO if it renounced terrorism.

Thirty countries including Egypt recognised a Palestinian state. The Soviet bloc and the European Community welcomed the declaration of independence, but did not accord it diplomatic recognition. In December, the USA announced its intention to open a dialogue with the PLO.

The election returned the Likud as the largest party with one more seat than Labour, which lost seats to Ratz and Mapam. It allowed Shamir to become prime minister once again, but without the disadvantage of being in a rotational government with Labour. Herut itself was divided into three factions, led by Levy, Sharon and Arens – all of whom were positioning themselves to become Shamir's successor. Benjamin Netanyahu entered the Knesset for the first time. There was also a split in Agudat Yisrael between hasidim and their opponents, the mitnagdim, led by Eliezer Schach and his Degel HaTorah faction.

With Gorbachev in charge, there was a thaw in relations with the Communist bloc. Peres visited Hungary in May, with Shamir following in September. In August, a five-member Israeli consular delegation visited Moscow – the first Israeli diplomats to be recognised since the breaking of relations in 1967. This was followed by consular exchanges with Czechoslovakia and Yugoslavia and an invitation to an Israeli chess coach to lecture in East Germany. There was a further easing of restrictions on Jewish cultural life in the USSR and emigration to Israel. Despite this, Shabtai Kalmanovich, who had immigrated from the USSR in 1971, was sentenced in December to nine years for spying for the KGB.

231

1989

Following the Palestinian declaration of independence in Algiers and implicit recognition of a two-state solution, Yasser Arafat tried hard to cultivate the Americans, but earned the opposition of groups both within the PLO and outside it. The Bush administration was pulled in different directions by the right-wing government of Yitzhak Shamir and the PLO's Yasser Arafat, who was adept at using ambiguous language to keep both the Americans and his opponents happy.

Here Shamir is pulling at the coattails of a sweating Uncle Sam and pointing at the accoutrements that a worried Arafat is carrying in addition to an olive branch. They are labelled with the names of Palestinian rejectionist groups – Ahmed Jibril (PFLP-GC), Nawef Hawatmeh (DFLP) and the Abu Nidal Group.

Shmuel Katz (*Ma'ariv* 7 March 1989)

8 Jan   Arens and Shevardnadze agree to upgrade consular relations

29 Jan   Faisal Husseini released from Kfar Yona prison

31 Jan   Peres presents $30 billion austerity budget to Knesset

31 Jan   Shamir reveals his own peace plan in a *Le Monde* interview

12 Feb   Jewish Cultural Centre opened in Moscow amidst Soviet goodwill

16 Feb   Avi Sasportas abducted and killed by Hamas operatives disguised as haredim

21 Feb   Ultra-orthodox Jews oppose publication of *The Satanic Verses* in Hebrew

11 Mar   Yuli Kosharovsky arrives in Israel after 18 years a refusenik

5 Apr   Release of 434 Palestinians, many from administrative detention

17 Apr   Shamir opposes participation by East Jerusalem Arabs in territories' vote

28 Apr   Hollinger Inc. buys *Jerusalem Post* from Koor for $17.8 million

2 May   Arafat declares the PLO Charter 'caduque' (obsolete) on Paris visit

14 May   Cabinet votes 20–6 to support Shamir plan for Palestinian self-rule

16 May   Large-scale disturbances in Hebron by Kiriat Arba residents

21 May   Ahmed Yassin and 150 Hamas activists arrested in Gaza

22 May   James Baker warns Israel about 'unrealistic vision' of a Greater Israel

25 May   Supreme Court interim order protecting Women of the Wall's right to pray

19 June   Arafat rejects Israeli plan for Palestinian elections

22 June   Shekel devalued by Bank of Israel for third time in as many weeks

22 June   Israel Prize professor, Menahem Stern, killed in Intifada attack

5 July   Likud central committee imposes restraints on Shamir plan

6 July   Bus attack by Islamic Jihad kills 14, injures 27

10 July   Labour's executive votes 41–2 to end coalition with Likud

24 July   Supreme Court rules Interior Ministry must register non-orthodox converts

28 July   Islamist leader Abdel Karim Obeid kidnapped from Lebanese village

28 Aug   Moshe Levinger goes on trial in Jerusalem for the killing of a Palestinian in Hebron

18 Sept   Hungary resumes diplomatic relations with Israel

18 Sept   Austria reduces its diplomatic representation as a result of Waldheim criticism

24 Sept   China agrees to open tourism bureau in Tel Aviv

3 Oct   Abie Nathan receives six-month sentence for meeting Arafat

11 Oct   IDF raids Beit Sahour near Bethlehem to break Palestinian tax revolt

20 Oct   Dahn Ben-Amotz, writer and playwright, dies in Jaffa aged 65

30 Oct   Hunger strike staged by 1,600 prisoners seeking better conditions

5 Nov   Inner cabinet votes 9–3 to accept Baker's five-point proposal

9 Nov   Berlin Wall falls, heralding the collapse of the Eastern bloc

14 Dec   Andrei Sakharov dies in Moscow of a heart attack aged 68

26 Dec   Erwin Frenkel, *Jerusalem Post* editor, resigns over editorial independence

233

Following Arafat's renunciation of terrorism in Geneva at the end of 1988, accompanied by a discussion about its actual meaning, Robert Pelletreau, the US ambassador in Tunis, was instructed to formally commence a dialogue with local PLO representatives. Arafat simultaneously instructed the Intifada on the West Bank and Gaza to continue. This sparked division both in Israel and within the PLO.

In Israel, the Likud rejected any contact with the PLO while Labour wished to explore the possibility. Shamir stated that he opposed a Palestinian state regardless of the method pursued to achieve it, either through negotiation or through violence. Thirty-two right wing MKs appealed to the police to prevent MKs Ora Namir, Yair Tsaban, Arieh Eliav and Shulamit Aloni from attending a conference in Paris where PLO members would also participate. The MKs responded that they would not be negotiating, but only attending an international conference. In Amsterdam, Abba Eban shared a platform with Bassam Abu Sharif, and a dinner for him which was to be hosted by the Israeli ambassador was suddenly cancelled on orders from the Foreign Ministry. There were also attempts to bar Chava Alberstein, one of Israel's best-known singers, from participating in the official celebrations for Israel's Independence Day because of her dovish views. The far Right Sicarii carried out attacks on the homes and vehicles of Mina Tsemah, Dan Almagor, Dan Margalit and Amos Schoken, dovish professionals often featured in the media.

Diaspora leaders and organisations were divided in their response to these new developments. The American Jewish Congress was critical of Shamir's approach while the Anti-Defamation League was supportive. Intellectuals, academics and writers such as Arthur Miller, Philip Roth and Sir Isaiah Berlin issued critical statements or signed collective letters. In March, a 'Conference on Jewish Solidarity with Israel' was called by Shamir, designed to bolster the coalition government. Large numbers of Diaspora leaders did not attend.

234

A campaign against the dialogue was launched by the foreign minister, Moshe Arens, and his deputy, Benjamin Netanyahu. Both wanted to win over, in particular, the leadership of American Jewry. There were also official rebukes for the Canadians, the French and the Belgians who engaged with PLO representatives.

While Fatah ceased cross-border attacks, the PFLP, DFLP and other Palestinian groups continued. Netanyahu blurred the differences between these groups and initially attributed the bombing of Pan Am flight 103 over Lockerbie in December to the PLO. He campaigned strongly to persuade US Jewish leaders to support the Likud's approach towards the PLO. Dealing with the PLO was often invoked in apocalyptic terms and the Munich Agreement of 1938 was often cited.

The Intifada continued apace, with periodic deportations of Palestinian activists to Lebanon. In January, sixty Palestinian defence lawyers went on strike, accusing the military authorities of employing tactics that made it impossible to stage a fair trial.

The Muslim Brotherhood, operating as Hamas, kidnapped two Israeli soldiers, Avi Sasportas in February and Ilan Saadon in May, and subsequently killed them.

Peres, now minister of finance, devalued the shekel twice within a few days at the beginning of the year – first by 5 per cent and then by another 8 per cent.

Peres further introduced austerity measures to make up a 1.14 billion shekel shortfall. These included reduced subsidies on a wide range of goods and on public transport. Subsidised goods increased by 20 per cent while inflation was expected to erode wages by 7 per cent. Education was hit through registration costs for high school students, increased university tuition fees and a reduction in funding for yeshiva students. Maternity grants were halved and free education for toddlers was abolished in several development towns. There was a cut of 120 million shekels in the defence budget. A visitor's fee of 4 shekels was introduced at doctors' surgeries. Some four thousand civil servants – 10 per cent of the government's workforce – would be laid off.

Police found themselves overloaded in terms of work because of the Intifada. There was a 28 per cent increase in serious crime. Car theft and drugs offences also increased. There was a 42 per cent decline in exports during the previous year and trade with the West Bank and Gaza was down by 40 per cent. Arson destroyed tens of thousands of trees.

Yitzhak Rabin, the minister of defence, attempted to quell the violence while simultaneously putting forward a plan for local elections in the West Bank and Gaza. He authorised Shmuel Goren, the coordinator of activities in the territories, to sound out local Palestinian leaders sympathetic to the PLO about the prospect of elections. Goren's visit to Faisal Husseini's prison cell resulted in his release after some discussion. This dialogue was followed by meetings between members of the Israeli Left and figures such as Husseini. Labour and Mapam MKs met Palestinian activists at venues such as the Notre Dame Hotel, situated on the 'seam' between Jewish and Arab Jerusalem. More than four hundred Palestinian prisoners were released although six thousand remained in prison.

Shamir put forward his own plan on the basis of the Camp David Agreement of 1979, which stipulated extensive autonomy which would be followed by detailed negotiations on the final status of the territories. He opposed the idea of a Palestinian state and advocated no contact with the PLO. He rejected any notion of land for peace and initially opposed local elections for the Palestinians.

Shamir then merged his ideas with those of Rabin and began to support the idea of local elections, but he also rejected the possibility of East Jerusalemites voting. This move brought him into confrontation with his opponents within the Likud, Sharon, Levy and Modai'i. While the cabinet voted 20–6 to support the Shamir–Rabin plan, the Likud central committee voted overwhelmingly to place constraints on it. Sharon demanded an end to the uprising before discussions, a rejection of any cessation of settlement expansion and no consideration of a Palestinian state.

Mubarak put forward his own ten-point proposal which was followed by a five-point plan from US secretary of state, James Baker. This was rejected by Shamir. The relationship between the new Bush administration and Shamir's government declined rapidly owing to US irritation at lack of progress. The USA refused to block a UN Security Council Resolution which condemned deportation. At the end of May, Baker addressed the American Israel Public Affairs Committee (AIPAC) conference and attacked 'the vision of a Greater Israel' and settlement activity.

235

Glasnost, perestroika and détente with the USA improved relations with the USSR. An Israeli consular mission had operated out of the Dutch Embassy in Moscow since the summer of 1988. Israeli athletes were allowed to compete in a basketball match in Moscow and a Soviet ship docked at Ashdod to pick up relief supplies for victims of the Armenian earthquake, organised by Abie Nathan. This was the first time since 1967 that Israel had had contacts with Soviet citizens. The Solomon Mikhoels Cultural Centre was opened in Moscow and attacks on anti-Zionism and anti-Semitism appeared in the Soviet press. Members of the Jewish Anti-Fascist Committee executed under Stalin were rehabilitated and Hebrew was taught openly. Soviet Jews working in both the religious and cultural spheres were allowed to study in both the USA and Israel. A Zionist group was allowed to be established in Moscow. Yitzhak Shamir predicted that a million Soviet Jews would now emigrate to Israel.

Hungary agreed to resume diplomatic relations and allowed Hebrew to be taught in schools. The East German minister of religious affairs visited Yad Vashem in Jerusalem.

The forthcoming publication of Salman Rushdie's *The Satanic Verses* by Keter was criticised by both Muslim and Jewish clerics. Degel HaTorah's Avraham Ravitz condemned the work's publication. Eliezer Schach, the spiritual leader of Degel HaTorah, disparaged the Jewish status of the Habad hasidim and accused the Lubavitcher Rebbe of being a false messiah.

The 1990s

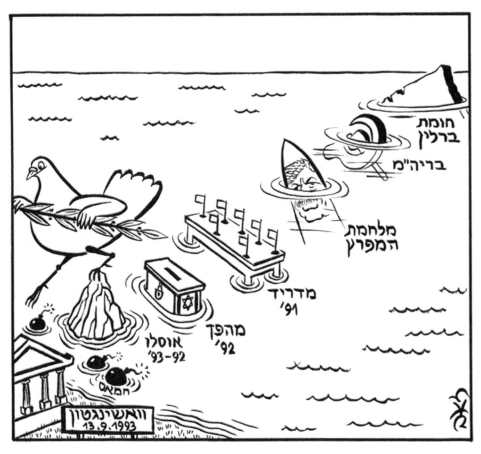

The 1990s was a decade of great hope amongst some Israelis that a final peace agreement with the Palestinians was in sight. The signing of the Declaration of Principles on the White House lawn with Yasser Arafat was opposed by the new leader of the Likud, Benjamin Netanyahu. An agreement with King Hussein in the Arava in 1994 created further enthusiasm – although negotiations with the Syrians achieved very little. A second agreement was signed between Israel and the Palestinians just a few weeks before the assassination of Yitzhak Rabin by a member of the far Right in November 1995.

Here the dove of peace is seen precariously proceeding from one momentous event to the next, starting from the demolition of the Berlin Wall and the collapse of the Soviet Union. Next Saddam Hussein's face is seen inscribed on a Scud missile, aimed at Tel Aviv during the Gulf War. Then comes the Madrid Conference, which took place in 1991, with Shamir reluctantly taking part before being defeated in the 'earthquake' election of 1992 when Rabin was returned as prime minister. This, in turn, was followed by the clandestine negotiations between Israelis and Palestinians in Oslo, leading to the signing of the Accord in September 1993. The bomb in the water at this stage is labelled 'Hamas'.

Ze'ev (*Ha'aretz* 14 September 1993)

1990

A consequence of perestroika and glasnost during the Gorbachev era together with a rapprochement with the United States was the mass emigration of Soviet Jews. This became accentuated as the USSR's economic woes worsened.

Here multitudes of Soviet Jews are queuing to board a Moscow–Tel Aviv flight amidst other flights flying to Israel. The billboard reads: 'Last one out – please turn off the light...'

Ze'ev (*Ha'aretz* 1 October 1990)

2 Jan Mass resignations at the *Jerusalem Post* over the actions of the new publisher

3 Jan Italians protest about police attack on human chain protesters around Jerusalem walls

8 Jan Communist veteran Meir Vilner resigns from Knesset

14 Jan Shamir tells Likud rally that Soviet emigration will produce 'a greater Israel'

22 Jan Vaclav Havel states that Czechoslovakia will resume diplomatic relations

4 Feb Attack on tour bus near Cairo kills nine Israeli civilians

19 Feb Sharon resigns from cabinet and is replaced by Moshe Nissim

2 Mar USA will provide housing loan guarantees if there is no settlement in the West Bank

13 Mar Shamir dismisses deputy prime minister Shimon Peres

15 Mar Knesset no-confidence vote, 60–55, brings down Shamir's government

20 Mar Sri Lanka government orders closure of the Israeli interests' office in Colombo

26 Mar Rav Schach attacks secular Jews and kibbutzniks at Tel Aviv rally

11 Apr Lubavitch MKs defect from Agudat Yisrael and stop Peres from forming a coalition

1 May Moshe Levinger sentenced to five months in prison for killing a Palestinian shopkeeper

3 May Bulgaria re-establishes diplomatic relations with Israel

20 May Ami Popper kills seven Palestinian labourers at bus stop at Rishon l'Zion

21 May Greece establishes full diplomatic relations with Israel

28 May Pipe bomb in Mahaneh Yehuda market in Jerusalem kills pensioner

30 May Seaborne attacks on two beaches by Palestine Liberation Front

7 June Labour defection permits Shamir to form a Likud–far Right coalition

14 June Histadrut calls out one million workers in a general strike

20 June White House suspends dialogue with the PLO

22 July Peres beats Rabin 54 to 46 per cent for party leadership in central committee vote

28 July Seventeen-year-old Canadian tourist killed in Tel Aviv beach bombing

2 Aug Iraqi Republican Guard lead the invasion of Kuwait

9 Aug Israel successfully tests the Arrow ballistic missile

4 Sept Interior Minister Deri questioned by the police on corruption allegations

11 Sept One hundred thousandth immigrant in 1990 arrives in Israel

30 Sept Israel and USSR establish full consular relations

1 Oct Bush offers Patriot missiles to Israel in order to meet any Iraqi attack

2 Oct White House and Israel agree $400 million US loan guarantees

3 Oct Shamir congratulates Helmut Kohl on German reunification

8 Oct Twenty Palestinians are killed during disturbances on the Temple Mount

14 Oct Sharon announces plan to build 15,000 new apartments in Arab East Jerusalem

15 Oct Israel distributes gas masks to its citizens

28 Oct Rami Dotan, head of air force procurement, arrested on suspicion of embezzlement

5 Nov Meir Kahane assassinated during New York talk

26 Dec Underground members are freed after less than seven years' imprisonment

With the fall of the Berlin Wall and the collapse of Communist regimes in Eastern Europe, huge numbers of Soviet Jews were allowed to emigrate from the USSR. From an original estimate of 40,000 in January, the revised figure by April was 230,000. It was estimated that well over 40 per cent of all immigrants since 1948 came during the Soviet wave of the 1990s. Such an influx severely tested Israel's resources such that there was talk of re-establishing ma'abarot – the tent cities of the early emigration after 1948.

With inflation running at 21.7 per cent during the previous year, this placed a heavy financial burden on the state. Prime Minister Shamir, however, had inferred that the immigrants would settle in 'a greater Israel' – the West Bank and Gaza. This alarmed the Palestinians, which further fuelled the Intifada, even though there was little actual desire on the part of the immigrants, mainly from the USSR and Ethiopia, to settle beyond the Green Line. Settler tours of locations such as Gush Katif in Gaza failed to entice. The Jewish Agency produced figures to indicate that only 45 of 9,980 families who had arrived between April and December 1989 had actually settled in the territories. However, immigrants could obtain a thirty-year interest-free mortgage on a $40,000 home in the territories, whilst the maximum term within the Green Line was around twenty years.

The idea that Soviet Jews preferred the stability and certainty offered by settling in urban areas in Israel failed to placate the Palestinians who staged a general strike over the issue in February. In addition, the Israeli government asserted that no funds from either US administration sources or philanthropic donations would be used beyond the Green Line.

In the spring, the US Congress supported the granting of $400 million in loan guarantees to Israel to ameliorate the situation. The USA had previously provided $25 million annually since 1973 to provide for the absorption of new immigrants. The Bush administration, however, tied any approval of this new loan to a pledge not to settle the immigrants in new settlements or expanded ones in the West Bank and Gaza. This accentuated the division within the Likud – with Shamir and Arens on one side, and a more hardline approach from Sharon, Levy and Modai'i. It also emphasised the ideological gap between the Likud and Labour which preferred settling the new immigrants in development towns. Shamir was under pressure from his opponents within the Likud, his Labour party colleagues in the coalition and the US secretary of state, James Baker.

Shamir's red-line revolved around any solution involving the PLO. He dismissed Ezer Weizman, the science minister, for 'maintaining contact with the PLO', then reinstated him, but ousted him from the inner cabinet. There were attempts to crack down on the political activities of local Palestinian leaders, several of whom were deported. Faisal Husseini was first prohibited from travelling abroad, then arrested, then released. Sari Nusseibeh was prevented from crossing into Jordan. All this provoked not only Palestinian protests, but many from Israeli and Diaspora groups as well as the White House.

Netanyahu, now deputy foreign minister, had conducted a campaign designed to disrupt and then terminate the USA–PLO dialogue – mainly by equating Fatah, which refrained from conducting cross-border raids from Lebanon, with those that did, the PFLP and DFLP. The dialogue came to an end when the Iraqi-sponsored Palestine Liberation Front (PLF) mounted a seaborne attack on Nitzanim beach, situated between Ashkelon and Ashdod. Arafat, however, refused to jettison Abul Abbas, the PLF representative on the PLO Executive, and asserted that it was the responsibility of the Palestine National Council (PNC). This, coupled with the PLF's taking of the *Achille Lauro* in October 1985 and the killing of the American invalid Leon Klinghoffer, persuaded President Bush to end the dialogue.

Sharon openly opposed Shamir's peace proposals and in particular elections for the Palestinians. At a meeting of the 2,600-strong Likud central committee, he publicly resigned. He then wrote a public letter which accused Shamir of 'cowardice and incompetence'.

Arafat then aligned the PLO with Saddam Hussein in the wake of the Iraqi invasion of Kuwait in early August. This proved disastrous eventually for the tens of thousands of Palestinians who worked in Kuwait and sent back money to their families, but more immediately it produced a cutting off of funds to the PLO from Saudi Arabia and the Gulf States. Mokassed Hospital in East Jerusalem depended on Kuwait for 75 per cent of its funds. The crisis did, however, bring about an improvement in the poor relationship between Shamir and the Bush administration. The USA provided Israel with Patriot missiles and a pledge to come to Israel's aid in the event of an Iraqi attack. Leading figures such as Faisal Husseini and Abdel Wahab Darousha MK identified with the local Palestinian enthusiasm for Saddam's action. This, in turn, earned the disdain of the Israeli peace camp.

The slow collapse of the coalition was due in part to the rivalry between Peres and Rabin. Peres attempted to cultivate the ultra-orthodox in an attempt to form an alternative government, while Rabin preferred Labour to remain in Shamir's administration and to modify its positions. Labour was far more sympathetic to Baker's five-point proposal and was prepared to allow East Jerusalem Arabs to vote in any Palestinian election.

Labour began to play an increasing role in foreign affairs at the expense of Likud's Moshe Arens. Finance Minister Peres visited Czechoslovakia to meet its new president, Vaclav Havel, while Ezer Weizman met the Soviet foreign minister, Eduard Shevardnadze, in the Kremlin. In March, Shamir dismissed the deputy prime minister, Shimon Peres, but the Likud lost a subsequent vote of no confidence when Agudat Yisrael sided with Labour. All but one of the Shas MKs stayed away on the instruction of Ovadia Yosef. Peres was on the verge of forming a government several times, but ultra-orthodox representatives repeatedly changed their positions, reflecting the views of their rabbis as well as the rivalry of different groups such as between the hasidic Lubavitcher Rebbe, Menahem Mendel Schneerson, and the spiritual leader of his Lithuanian opponents, Eliezer Schach. The Gerer Rebbe's son favoured Labour, his brother the Likud. The Vishnitzer Rebbe wanted an alliance with the Likud, the Sadagora Rebbe one with Labour. Rabin later referred to Peres's approach as 'this stinking manoeuvre'. Even so, he was defeated by Peres in a contest for the Labour party leadership.

Shamir unexpectedly could now form a new centre Right–far Right coalition with the defection of Ephraim Gur of Ashdod from Labour to the Likud. The new government now included the far Right parties Tsomet and Tehiya and won Knesset approval by 62 votes to 57. Levy was appointed foreign minister and was able to conclude an agreement with Baker which implicitly restricted the use of the loan guarantees to within the Green Line. Sharon, now housing minister, immediately announced his intention to build fifteen thousand apartments in East Jerusalem, arguing that it was within the terms of the agreement since it was inside the Green Line.

The dire economic situation was further reflected in the problems within the Histadrut's Koor Industries, which accounted for a third of Israel's industrial output. In mid-January, thousands of its employees went on strike. This resulted in the sale of the *Jerusalem Post* to the Hollinger chain which was solely profit-oriented. Its preference for the Likud and the desire of its new management to interfere in editorial matters caused the mass resignation of senior staff.

241

1991

The Madrid Conference, organised by the superpowers, was attended by neighbouring Arab states, Syria, Lebanon and Jordan. The Israel government would allow only Palestinians who were not members of the PLO to attend as part of the Jordanian delegation.

Here Prime Minister Shamir is dressing, about to leave his home 'Government of Israel' with his suitcase, labelled 'Madrid'.

A sweating Shamir was the head of a centre Right–far Right government. In the doorway is a bed of nails entitled 'Extreme Right', who opposed the very idea of a peace conference.

Shmuel Katz (*Ma'ariv* n.d. 1991)

14 Jan Moshe Levinger sentenced to four months for attack on Hebron Arab family

14 Jan Abu Iyad assassinated in Carthage by gunmen connected to Abu Nidal

18 Jan Iraqi Scud attacks on Tel Aviv and Haifa after start of Operation Desert Storm

19 Jan US manned Patriot missiles operational in Israel

22 Jan Israel asks USA for extra $10 billion in aid over five years

29 Jan Germany to supply poison gas detection system to Israel

3 Feb Cabinet approves Moledet leader Rehavam Ze'evi as minister without portfolio

8 Feb Holland loans Patriots to Israel, gives food and gas masks to Palestinians

20 Feb Sharon calls for attack on Scud missile launchers in western Iraq

20 Feb USA releases $400 million in loan guarantees

27 Feb Women of the Wall sue government, rabbinate and police over no access

10 Mar Four Jewish women stabbed to death at bus stop at Kiriat Yovel in Jerusalem

11 Mar Shekel devalued by almost 7 per cent

17 Mar Ami Popper receives life sentences for seven Arabs killed in Rishon Le-Zion

9 Apr Kurdish Jews protest to Baker in Tel Aviv about plight of Iraqi Kurds

11 Apr Last of 300 Albanian Jews arrive in Israel after secret airlift

16 Apr New West Bank settlement, Revava, coincides with Baker's visit

23 Apr New West Bank settlement, Talmon B, started with eight mobile homes

21 May Mengistu regime collapses as 17,000 Ethiopian Jews await flights to Israel

24 May Operation Solomon brings 14,000 Ethiopian Jews to Israel

4 June $500 million French loan for 10,000 immigrant homes in Beersheba

18 June Hamas beats PLO candidates in Hebron Chamber of Commerce election

11 July Oil and gas discovered in exploration near Ashdod

11 July Tel Aviv Stock Exchange crash trial opens in Jerusalem District Court

31 July Bush and Gorbachev announce Middle East peace conference for October

4 Aug Far Right parties in cabinet vote against participation in peace conference

5 Aug Defence Ministry allows military post, Eshkolot, to become a settlement

20 Aug PLO activists welcome coup by hardliners against Gorbachev

4 Sept Israel recognises independence of Latvia, Lithuania and Estonia

12 Sept Threatening veto, Bush demands 120 day extension of $10 billion loan

21 Sept Peace Now calls upon PNC in Algiers to endorse peace conference

6 Oct Abie Nathan sentenced to 18 months in prison for meeting Arafat

16 Oct Hamas spiritual mentor Sheikh Yassin sentenced to life imprisonment

18 Oct USSR establishes full diplomatic relations with Israel

23 Oct Hamas general strike over delegation composition to Madrid conference

30 Oct Middle East peace conference opens in Madrid's Royal Palace

16 Dec UN repeals 'Zionism is Racism' resolution 111–25

24 Dec Tsomet leaves coalition government

243

Following the invasion of Kuwait, Saddam Hussein publicly promised that if Baghdad was attacked, then Tel Aviv would be also. Despite a French diplomatic initiative to avert war, many airlines stopped flying to Tel Aviv or operated a reduced service. There was an exodus of foreign nationals from Israel and foreign embassies moved their headquarters out of Tel Aviv. El Al continued to fly normally and Soviet Jews arrived on Malev flights, whose charter aircraft had been hired by the Jewish Agency.

Before the 15 January UN deadline for Iraqi withdrawal from Kuwait, Shamir publicly refused to rule out retaliation if Israel was attacked. Operation Desert Storm commenced shortly after the UN deadline had passed. Between 18 January and 25 February, some forty-three modified Scud missiles were launched in eighteen attacks mainly on Tel Aviv and Haifa from the area around Qaim in the western reaches of Iraq. In all, there were seventy-seven Israeli fatalities, the vast majority due to heart attacks and only three to missile strikes. Three Scuds were aimed at the nuclear facility in Dimona, but fell into the surrounding desert.

Although several hundred people were injured in the attacks and more than four thousand buildings were damaged with several hundred apartments completely destroyed, the relatively low number of casualties was essentially owing to the inaccuracy of the missile. Some Scuds fell into the sea, others broke up on re-entry and the explosive payload of still others failed to detonate on impact.

Gas masks were distributed to most of the population and citizens were requested to remain in gas-proof sealed rooms in their homes rather than evacuate to underground bomb shelters. In the event, the Iraqi missiles were not loaded with chemical or biological weapons, but instead each warhead possessed the equivalent of 250 kg of TNT destructive power.

Under pressure from George Bush and Dick Cheney, Israel did not join the US–Arab military coalition. The Israeli cabinet also decided against a pre-emptive strike. While Arens, Sharon and Barak were keen to retaliate, Shamir agreed not to, for fear of collapsing the thirty-five-nation coalition and uniting the Arab nations around the question of the Israel–Palestine conflict instead. Both Syria and Saudi Arabia threatened to leave the coalition if Israel retaliated. This brought public criticism from Ariel Sharon and the far Right parties in the government coalition.

Shamir brought Rehavam Ze'evi's Moledet into the coalition and he was appointed a minister without portfolio, approved by a vote of 61–54 in the Knesset. Moshe Arens opposed the appointment because of Moledet's policy of voluntary transfer of the Palestinians, while Benny Begin termed it 'political pollution'.

An intensification of the Intifada was expected. There was increased infiltration from Jordan, random stabbings and a failed attack on a crowded pizzeria in central Tel Aviv. Palestinian euphoria on the West Bank soon dissipated once it became evident that Iraq was taking a severe pounding. Faisal Husseini initially supported Iraq and then qualified his remarks. In Hebron, there was an attack on the Avraham Avinu synagogue and in Nablus there were street demonstrations.

Arafat's support for Saddam brought a cutting off of funds from Saudi Arabia and the Gulf States. The PLO came out of the conflict in a weakened state: the Americans did not renew dialogue, the Europeans refused any contact and the Israeli peace camp kept its distance. King Hussein supported Saddam, given that Iraq was Jordan's powerful neighbour.

While the USA brought Patriot missile batteries to Israel from their store in Germany, they did not become operational until after twelve Scuds had already fallen. Moreover, the Patriots were only 40 per cent effective.

There was a boost in domestic tourism, with Israelis escaping Tel Aviv and Haifa for Jerusalem and Eilat. $1 billion was lost in reduced international tourism with the same amount lost in worker production.

244

Operation Solomon brought fourteen thousand Ethiopian Jews to Israel at the end of May as the regime of Mengistu Haile Mariam collapsed. Two-thirds of the immigrants were under the age of eighteen. Following the abrupt cessation of emigration with the end of Operation Moses in 1985, the Mengistu regime re-established diplomatic relations with Israel in November 1989. This took place when both the USSR and East Germany informed Ethiopia that they could no longer help the country. Jews were now allowed to emigrate at roughly two hundred a week, but many thousands had made the journey to Addis Ababa in anticipation. By early 1991, some seventeen thousand were living in the Israeli Embassy compound in the Shola district of Addis Ababa or near it. Living in extremely basic conditions, they were given $50 a month; rudimentary schooling was provided for children and a health clinic was operated by the Joint Distribution Committee.

As the rebels closed in on Addis Ababa, Mengistu stopped emigration in an attempt to secure arms from Israel. American pressure and Mengistu's eventual flight from Ethiopia gave way to Operation Solomon, whereby forty flights brought thousands to Israel on board overcrowded jumbo jets and Hercules transport planes. This took place over forty-eight hours amidst a news blackout and was led by the deputy head of the IDF, Amnon Shahak.

The ongoing saga of an international peace conference reached its apogee at the end of October when it finally took place in Madrid under the sponsorship of Bush and Gorbachev. It was the culmination of eight visits to the region by US secretary of state, James Baker. Shamir stood firm on 'maintaining the enthusiastic intensity of settlement building', the barring of the PLO and the demand for the USSR to re-establish diplomatic relations with Israel. Shamir was under pressure from Sharon, Ne'eman and Ze'evi, representatives of the far Right in government, to reject all possibilities that would allow either the Soviets or Palestinian nationalists the possibility of participation.

245

The decision of a dying USSR to re-establish diplomatic relations after nearly a quarter of a century finally allowed the conference to go ahead. Bilateral negotiations began in early November and symbolically brought the parties to the conflict together. It also catalysed the revocation of UNR 3379, the 'Zionism is Racism' resolution.

In a much weakened state after the Iraqi defeat, the PLO eventually agreed to the idea of a joint Jordanian–Palestinian delegation, but indirectly ensured it controlled the choice of Palestinians. It maintained a presence behind the scenes at the conference.

On Shamir's departure for Madrid, the 'Peace for Peace' organisation held a rally and called upon him not to make any concessions. Shamir attempted to balance the different ideological forces within the Likud whose candidates were also positioning themselves to succeed him. Levy and Sharon did not attend the conference while Netanyahu operated in a public relations role in Madrid. Tehiya, Moledet and Tsomet all opposed the conference and eventually began to resign from the government coalition by the end of the year.

The relationship between the USA and Israel sank to a new low. Every visit to Israel by James Baker was greeted with the establishment of new settlements such as Revava, and Talmon B. Baker viewed the settlement drive as an obstacle to peace and floated the idea of a settlement freeze in return for an end to the Arab League boycott of Israel. He was able to achieve agreement from Assad for Syria to conduct direct negotiations.

In March, General Rami Dotan, head of procurement for the Israeli air force, was found guilty of corruption, bribery and embezzling millions of dollars and sentenced to thirteen years' imprisonment.

1992

The national election returned Labour to power – without the Likud in government – for the first time since 1977. Rabin had displaced Peres as leader and then defeated Shamir in a decisive poll.

Here Shamir tells Rabin that 'the country is in a good state', but hands him a spiked relay baton in the shape of Israel.

Ze'ev (*Ha'aretz* 16 July 1992)

5 Jan   One-day strike by public health services over the privatisation of six hospitals

15 Jan   Labour and Welfare Ministry states that unemployment highest since 1966

21 Jan   Tehiya and Moledet leave government over Shamir's attendance at Madrid Conference

24 Jan   Israel and China establish diplomatic relations

27 Jan   Israel participates in a multilateral conference on Middle East in Moscow

29 Jan   Israel and India establish diplomatic relations

2 Feb   Mapam, Ratz and Shinui agree to run as a peace bloc in general election

14 Feb   Three IDF recruits hacked to death at training camp next to Kibbutz Gal'ed

16 Feb   Abbas Musawi, founder and secretary-general of Hezbollah, assassinated by Israel

19 Feb   Rabin defeats Peres, 40 to 34 per cent, in Labour primary

20 Feb   Shamir defeats Levy and Sharon in Likud leadership vote

7 Mar   Ehud Sadan, Istanbul Embassy's security chief, killed by car bomb

9 Mar   Menahem Begin dies of a heart attack aged 78

17 Mar   Suicide bombing of Israeli Embassy in Argentina kills 29

18 Mar   Knesset passes reform bill providing for direct election of the prime minister, 55–32

7 Apr   Arafat survives air crash in the Libyan desert

25 Apr   Syria lifts restrictions on travel for its Jewish community

30 Apr   Degel HaTorah and Agudat Yisrael agree to fight election together

3 May   Two-day strike by 20,000 high school teachers over wages

10 May   Emil Habibi awarded Israel Prize for Arabic Literature

12 May   Islamic Movement agrees to take part in Israeli elections for first time

3 June   Elections Committee vote 25–5 to ban Kahane Chai from running

8 June   Atef Bseiso, PLO contact with foreign intelligence agencies, gunned down in Paris

14 June   Former Soviet president Mikhail Gorbachev arrives in Israel for four-day visit

23 June   Yitzhak Rabin's Labour defeats Likud 44–32 seats in general election

24 June   Nineteen settler families establish new settlement outside Kfar Adumim

13 July   Shulamit Aloni appointed education minister, provoking haredi outrage

22 July   Ya'akov Hazan, founder of Mapam, dies at Mishmar Ha'Emek aged 93

26 July   Cabinet establishes committee to investigate settler benefits

29 July   Permanent working commission established by Israel and the Vatican

12 Aug   Ministry of Justice moves to decriminalise meetings with PLO members

24 Aug   Ministry of Defence cancels deportation orders against 11 Palestinians

31 Aug   First of 600 Palestinians released from Ketziot prison in Negev

4 Oct   El Al Flight 1862 crashes into Amsterdam suburb with loss of 43 people

4 Nov   Yitzhak Rabin congratulates Bill Clinton on his election victory

5 Nov   Accidental killing of five Sayeret Matkal members at Tze'elim training base

10 Nov   Supreme Court building inaugurated in Jerusalem

17 Dec   415 Palestinian Islamists deported to Lebanon after killing of policeman

The question of $10 billion in loan guarantees over a five-year period proved to be a central bone of contention between the Bush White House and the Shamir coalition of the Right and far Right in an election year for both regimes. There was initially an unspoken linkage between the loan guarantees and the building of new settlements in the West Bank and Gaza which the Bush administration believed to be an obstacle to peace in the area. This linkage became more public when the US secretary of state, James Baker, called for a settlement freeze in return for the release of the loan guarantees which were needed to secure loans from commercial banks. The White House wanted to review the loan guarantees scheme annually.

Many Jewish organisations in the USA campaigned for the loan guarantees on 'humanitarian' grounds in that huge numbers of Soviet immigrants were without housing and jobs. Shamir, however, repeated several times his ideological pledge to build in all areas of the Land of Israel so as to stop any leakage from settler supporters in an election year. Construction plans were allegedly formulated to allow for an influx of fifty thousand immigrants into the territories.

Bush, however, refused to budge, even after a 120-day delay that he had called for. He further rejected a compromise that several US senators had formulated. Bush's hard line had been predicated on the earlier experience of US loan guarantees of $400 million. Baker argued that promises given then had been broken and the General Accounting Office stated that there had been a lack of full disclosure. There had been a tripling of settlement starts in the aftermath of assurances given in 1991.

The standoff came to an end with Yitzhak Rabin's election in June and his desire to differentiate between security settlements and ideological ones. Within a few weeks of taking power, the Rabin government cut $410 million in funding for housing in the territories. Contracts and plans for 5,364 housing units in the West Bank and Gaza were cancelled. A cabinet committee was established to investigate tax breaks, discount mortgages and subsidised utilities in the territories.

This led to an announcement by Bush that he now supported the giving of loan guarantees – in part because he felt that his stand might have antagonised Jewish Republican voters in swing states during a lacklustre campaign. His opponent, Bill Clinton, had come out in support of granting loan guarantees as well as opposing the formation of a Palestinian state.

The departure of both Moledet and Tehiya from the coalition because they disagreed with the very idea of autonomy for the Palestinians resulted in the dissolution of the Knesset in early February and the moving of the election from November to June. The parties believed that the 300,000 new immigrants would be the key to victory. Each party therefore had its own 'Russian' to cultivate the newcomers. The Soviet immigrants came from a Communist society and therefore were highly critical of any vestige of their Soviet past being on display. Labour quickly divested itself of the Red Flag and assumed a more patriotic blue and white symbol.

There were also internal party struggles. Within the Likud, David Levy came a creditable second to Shamir in a vote by the party's central committee. However, Levy was displaced by Moshe Arens from the number two position in the electoral list, thus decreasing his chances of succeeding Shamir. Of the twenty-nine names on the Likud candidate list, only three were Levy supporters. Levy threatened to resign from the Likud and to form his own party. Shamir was worried about the prospect of defections since several had already left to form the New Liberal party. Levy was therefore restored to a senior position.

In Labour, Peres was viewed as having accumulated too many political failures. Rabin just crossed the 40 per cent mark to Peres's 34 per cent and thereby avoided a run-off for the leadership. A quarter of the vote, however, went to Yisrael Kessar and Ora Namir whose participation may have deprived Peres of victory.

In both the secular and the haredi camps, there were new alignments. The Zionist Left of Ratz, Mapam and Shinui formed Meretz, while the mitnaged Degel HaTorah united with the hasidic Agudat Yisrael to establish United Torah Judaism.

The three Arab parties, the Arab Democratic party, the Progressive List for Peace and Hadash, were joined for the first time by the participation of the Islamic Movement.

The Likud played on Rabin's fondness for drink and trumpeted his 'breakdown' in 1967. Rabin's meetings were often interrupted by hecklers such that Labour purchased a consignment of whistles to do the same at Shamir's rallies.

The victory of Yitzhak Rabin as leader of the Labour party in the June election was a by-product of the fragility of the centre Right–far Right coalition. Raful Eitan had pulled Tsomet out of the coalition because of Shamir's prevarication over the reform bill. This promoted the idea of a separate ballot for a prime minister in addition to the one electing the rest of the Knesset from party lists. This system, it was argued, would liberate any prime minister from small-party pressure. It was passed by the Knesset 52–23 in March.

The victory of Labour (forty-four seats) over the Likud (thirty-two) in the *mahapakh* (earthquake) was marked by the inability of Tehiya and the New Liberal party to pass the new electoral threshold of 1.5 per cent, whereas the other far Right parties, Moledet and Tsomet, increased their number of seats. Among the new immigrants, 47 per cent voted for Rabin – a greater percentage than among normal Israeli voters. Labour, Meretz and the silent backing of the Arab parties accounted for sixty-one seats.

The economic situation persuaded many new Russian immigrants to vote for Labour's Rabin and to discard any purely ideological motivations. The unemployment rate had been at its highest rate since the economic crisis of 1966. At the end of 1991, 10.9 per cent of the labour force were unemployed and inflation was at 18 per cent. Housing costs rose 29 per cent and health care by 19.5 per cent.

249

Shamir, who commented that he had intended to drag out the autonomy negotiations for ten years, stepped down as party leader and Moshe Arens, his one-time successor, announced that he was leaving politics.

Shulamit Aloni, Meretz's devout secularist, was appointed minister of education in Rabin's government, much to haredi outrage. Yet Shas, guided by its dovish spiritual mentor, Ovadia Yosef, did join the government coalition – and was strongly criticised for this move. In part, this was a reaction to the comment of Degel HaTorah's Eliezer Schach that the Mizrahim were 'not mature enough to lead either state or religion'.

The assassination of Hezbollah's secretary-general, Abbas Musawi, in Lebanon and Iran's opposition to the Madrid Conference led to several attacks on Israeli civilians and military personnel and to an increase in border attacks in southern Lebanon. The killing of Ehud Sadawi, the security chief at the Istanbul Embassy, two days after the formal establishment of diplomatic relations with Turkey and the bombing of the Israeli Embassy in Buenos Aires were believed to have been linked to Hezbollah and to the broad rejectionists of the peace process.

In the wake of the disintegration of the USSR and the Madrid Conference, diplomatic relations were established with China. There had previously been an academic and scientific liaison office in Beijing and a Chinese government tourist office in Tel Aviv. Ties were also established with India despite its Muslim minority. In March, a trade delegation of Israeli businesspeople visited Hanoi and agreements were subsequently struck.

1993

Yitzhak Rabin smokes the pipe of peace with Yasser Arafat on the agreement of the Declaration of Principles – the Oslo Accord between Israel and the Palestinians.

The smoke is depicted as a dove. The pipe is embellished with an olive branch.

Arafat is seen as throwing away his stereotypical dark glasses – often viewed symbolically as a cover for subterfuge and the armed struggle.

Ze'ev (*Ha'aretz* 10 September 1993)

3 Jan   Shin Bet agent Haim Nahmani killed in apartment in Rehavia, Jerusalem

4 Jan   First official visit of an ANC delegation to Israel

14 Jan   Netanyahu confesses on television to 'Bibigate' extramarital affair

19 Jan   Knesset overturns ban on contact with PLO members

21 Jan   First interview on Israel Television with Arafat in Tunis

24 Jan   Yeshayahu Leibowitz declines Israel Prize after strong cabinet protest

27 Jan   Haredi protest over court decision to allow motorway near burial caves

1 Feb   Rabin agrees to take back a hundred Islamists deported to Lebanon

21 Feb   Yisrael Meir Lau and Eliahu Bakshi-Doron elected Chief Rabbis

2 Mar   Israeli gas worker killed after accidental entry into Rafah refugee camp

24 Mar   Ezer Weizman elected president in Knesset vote, 66–53

25 Mar   Netanyahu receives 52.5 per cent of vote to beat Levy to become Likud leader

30 Mar   West Bank and Gaza sealed off from Israel

18 Apr   Ian Feinberg, Israeli lawyer working on EU project in Gaza, killed by PFLP 'Red Eagles'

30 Apr   First 15 Palestinian exiles including mayors and a university president return to West Bank

11 May   Shulamit Aloni resigns as education minister due to clash with Shas

16 May   Annual Likud conference takes place in Katzrin in the Golan Heights

13 June   New IDF regulations ban discrimination against gay people in the army

16 June   Israel participates in ceremonies to mark Soweto Day

20 June   Attorney-General indicts interior minister, Arieh Deri, on multiple charges

24 June   Petition to stop Pinochet from visiting Israel signed by 28 MKs

1 July   Two women killed by armed Palestinians on no. 25 bus near French Hill

12 July   Israel and Vietnam agree to establish diplomatic relations

29 July   Demjanjuk guilty verdict overturned by Supreme Court

4 Sept   Tel Aviv rally in support of autonomy plan for Palestinians

7 Sept   Jerusalem rally opposing peace agreement with Palestinians

9 Sept   Shas withdraws from government, leaving 56 MKs supporting Rabin

10 Sept   Government recognises PLO as representative of Palestinian people

13 Sept   Rabin and Arafat sign peace accord on the White House lawn

23 Sept   Knesset votes 61–50 to approve accord signed with the PLO

1 Oct   Peres negotiates with Crown Prince Hassan of Jordan at the White House

4 Oct   USA will deduct $437 million for settlements from loan guarantees

9 Oct   Two Israeli hikers killed at Wadi Kelt near Jericho

2 Nov   Ehud Olmert defeats Teddy Kollek to become mayor of Jerusalem

8 Nov   King Juan Carlos of Spain visits Israel

29 Nov   Israeli daily *Hadashot* closes

9 Dec   Histadrut organises general strike to protest against privatisation

12 Dec   Rabin delays withdrawal from Jericho and Gaza

The repeated rumours of a rapprochement with the PLO put the government coalition under tremendous strain. Many parties were split regarding a possible deal with the Palestinians. Seventeen hawkish members of the Labour party wanted to bring Tsomet and the NRP into government. Both Shas, the Mizrahi haredi party, and Meretz, a devoutly secular one led by the outspoken Shulamit Aloni, sat in the same cabinet and their constant clashes threatened a collapse of Rabin's government and a challenge to his policies.

While Shas's spiritual mentor, Ovadia Yosef, was perceived as a political moderate, the party's voters were seen as far more hawkish. Shas was also beset by accusations of corruption. Yair Levy, a former MK, was sentenced to five years for embezzlement while the youthful leader of the party, Arieh Deri, was part of an ongoing police investigation into his financial affairs. Six Shas supporters were tried and convicted for wiretapping both a former police chief and the *Yediot Aharanot* journalist whose story had initiated the police investigation into Deri's affairs.

Haredi rage at Shulamit Aloni's repeated comments boiled over when she referred to the two Chief Rabbis as 'the two popes'. Ovadia Yosef was reluctant to allow Shas to leave the coalition and lose a source of funding and political power. Rabin and Meretz's ministers were similarly reluctant since it would weaken any movement towards a peace agreement with the Palestinians, leaving the government with only fifty-six MKs in support and reliant on Arab parties outside the coalition.

In May, Aloni criticised Rabin for saying the daily 'Shema' prayer at a commemoration to remember the Warsaw ghetto uprising. Deri consequently resigned as minister of the interior. United Torah Judaism, however, was split over joining the government as a replacement for Shas. Aloni was shifted to the Ministries of Science and Communication while Meretz held on to Education. Deri then returned to his ministerial position and to the possibility that he would be charged with fraud, breach of public trust and accepting bribes, following a legal hearing. The Shas deputy minister of religious affairs, Rafael Pinhasi, was further accused of making misleading and false declarations. In September, the Supreme Court ruled that both men should step down from their ministerial positions. On the eve of Rabin and Arafat signing the Declaration of Principles, Shas withdrew from the coalition.

The fall of the Soviet Union and the growing rapprochement with the PLO brought about the establishment of diplomatic relations with Vietnam, Laos, Turkmenistan, Cambodia, Gabon and Burkina Faso. At the end of the year Rabin visited China, which had already established diplomatic relations. An ANC delegation from South Africa visited Israel.

While Rabin had replaced Shamir on the Israeli side, the move towards mutual recognition was in part stimulated by political vulnerability on the Palestinian side. Arafat's defence of Saddam Hussein's invasion of Kuwait had led to a wholesale cutting of funds to the PLO from Saudi Arabia and the Gulf States. This had led to austerity measures and to the selling off of PLO assets. Arafat's authoritarian nature further produced resignation threats from central Palestinian notables such as Hanan Ashrawi, Saeb Erekat and Faisal Husseini. The periodic statements of warmth towards the Israelis induced dire threats from the PFLP and the DFLP. The Islamist groups Hamas and Islamic Jihad, which had aligned themselves with Iran – they already had attended a rival conference to the superpower-sponsored one in Madrid in 1991 – were similarly hostile. Farouk Kaddoumi, the PLO foreign minister, and the USA-based intellectual Edward Said were also critical.

The dropping of the PLO-contact law of 1986 and the evolution of the back-channel with the academics Yair Hirschfeld and Ron Pundak in London gradually brought on board official figures such as Uri Savir, the director-general of the Foreign Ministry, and then Peres himself. Rabin was finally informed as the bilateral talks in the USA, following the Madrid Conference, procrastinated and went around in circles. The agreement to implement self-rule, 'Gaza and Jericho First', and a broad outline of a 'Declaration of Principles' solidified during the summer.

Abie Nathan and Yael Dayan visited Arafat in Tunis who gave an interview for the first time to Israel TV. The environment minister, Yossi Sarid, met Nabil Sha'ath in Cairo as some of the 415 Palestinians deported to Lebanon were gradually allowed to return.

As rumours about the impending agreements between Israelis and Palestinians began to surface in the media, those involved in the bilateral talks in the USA were irritated because they had known nothing of the back-channel negotiations. The cabinet secretary, Elyakim Rubinstein, who had headed the Israeli team, tendered his resignation. The poet Mahmoud Darwish resigned from the PLO Executive.

At the end of August, the cabinet approved the tentative agreement outlining limited Palestinian self-rule by 16–2. The agreement provoked annoyance from King Hussein who had similarly been kept in the dark, while President Assad of Syria was aggrieved that the agreement was 'not coordinated with Arab brethren'. Rejectionists carried out reprisals in order to stymie the negotiations. In Gaza, Fatah activists were killed by Islamists. In the north, the PFLP attempted military operations from Lebanon. At Wadi Kelt in the Judaean desert, two hikers were killed and Islamic Jihad claimed responsibility.

At the end of July, the IDF launched a military operation against Hezbollah, 'Din v'Heshbon', amidst continuing attacks in the north of Israel.

Benjamin Netanyahu was elected the new leader of the Likud, winning 52.5 per cent of the vote on a 68 per cent turnout of party members. This came in spite of the revelation that he had had an extramarital affair with a married woman 'several months ago'. Netanyahu's victory created many foes, in particular David Levy. Netanyahu's move to present a new constitution for the party which would devolve more powers to its head earned the enmity of Sharon and other veterans in the Likud. Levy actually boycotted the Likud conference in Katzrin because of this.

Netanyahu pursued an Americanisation of Israeli politics in his projection of a new Likud. When the Oslo Accords arose, he spoke of 'a mini-Libya' in Israel's backyard and disparaged Rabin as a new Chamberlain – someone who had sold out his country to the forces of evil. Likud was initially viewed as being left behind by the rapprochement with the Palestinians. This produced further criticism within a divided party.

Netanyahu was blamed by his rivals, Sharon and Levy, as well as by the 'princes' of the Likud. Sharon wanted an abandonment of the Camp David Agreement of 1979 and of any kind of autonomy for the Palestinians. Roni Milo wanted a 'Gaza First' policy and a withdrawal from Gaza. He and two other Likud MKs refused to oppose the Declaration of Principles in the Knesset and instead abstained. Netanyahu had argued for an extension of the autonomy granted to Gaza for another twenty years.

Yehoshua Matza argued that the Likud should incite the public against the agreement. Right-wing rallies were held in which it was argued that Rabin had no mandate to return territory. Soldiers who opposed the agreement refused to serve in the West Bank and Gaza, while settlers attempted to establish a new settlement outside Tekoah.

By early winter, there was talk of deposing Netanyahu as leader of the Likud. Sharon called for 'a collective leadership of experienced men'.

Despite the euphoria about the Declaration of Principles and the handshake on the White House lawn, Rabin and Arafat were unable to agree the dimensions of the Jericho district and the Israeli withdrawal in December was postponed.

253

1994

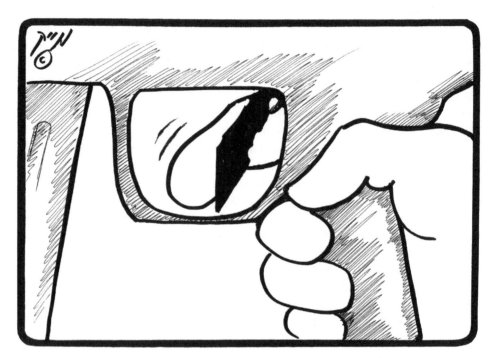

Baruch Goldstein's finger is on the trigger of the gun which killed Muslim worshippers at the al-Ibrahimi mosque in the Cave of Makhpela in Hebron during the festival of Purim.

Prime Minister Rabin called the American Goldstein, a follower of Meir Kahane, 'a foreign implant'. Here the trigger is depicted in the shape of Israel and the West Bank (Judaea and Samaria) – signifying Goldstein's ideological motivation as a settler.

Mike (*Yediot Aharanot* 1 March 1994)

9 Jan   University lecturers go on strike for increased wages

16 Jan President Clinton meets Syrian President Assad in Geneva

17 Jan Rabin wants a national referendum before any Golan Heights withdrawal

25 Feb Baruch Goldstein kills 29 Muslim worshippers in Hebron mosque

28 Feb Syria, Lebanon, Jordan suspend bilateral negotiations in Washington

13 Mar Cabinet unanimously bans Kach and Kahane Chai

6 Apr   Hamas suicide bomber kills eight on bus no. 348 in Afula

13 Apr Hamas suicide bomber kills six at Hadera central bus station

22 Apr Fatah and Hamas declare a month-long truce between themselves

4 May   Rabin and Arafat sign Gaza–Jericho self-rule accord in Cairo

10 May Newly established Palestinian police force enters Gaza

10 May Labour defeated in Histadrut elections by Haim Ramon's list

18 May Former chairman, Ernst Japhet, sentenced to 11 months in Bank Leumi scandal

15 June Israel and the Vatican agree to establish full diplomatic relations

19 June Israel lifts embargo on arms sales to South Africa

26 June Shamgar Commission finds that Baruch Goldstein acted alone

1 July   Yasser Arafat visits Gaza for the first time in 27 years

18 July Suicide bombing of communal AMIA building in Buenos Aires kills 85

19 July Internal flight from Colón to Panama City explodes

25 July Rabin and King Hussein meet for White House peace ceremony

28 July Car bomb explodes outside Israel Embassy in London

1 Aug   Arafat orders closure of pro-Jordanian Arabic daily, *An-Nahar*

16 Aug US Jewish leaders meet Assad in Damascus

17 Aug PLO to receive 75 per cent income tax earned by Palestinians working in Israel

18 Aug Yeshayahu Leibowitz, critical defender of Jewish humanist values, dies aged 91

28 Aug Cabinet agrees transfer of civilian affairs to Palestinians

1 Sept Morocco and Israel establish economic liaison offices

5 Sept Israeli Consulate opened in Shanghai

9 Oct   Amnon Shahak appointed next IDF Chief of Staff

14 Oct Nachshon Waxman killed by kidnappers during failed rescue attempt

19 Oct Hamas bus bomb kills 22 in Dizengoff Street, central Tel Aviv

26 Oct Rabin and Hussein sign peace treaty in the Arava desert

30 Oct Prince Philip visits his mother's grave on a personal visit to Israel

30 Oct Rabin attends a Middle East economic summit in Casablanca

7 Nov   National Insurance Institute states that 12 per cent of Israelis are below poverty line

10 Nov King Hussein pays first public visit to Israel

29 Nov Supreme Court orders El Al to treat gay couples the same as heterosexual ones

10 Dec Nobel Peace Prize is awarded to Rabin, Peres and Arafat in Oslo

The Oslo Accord of September 1993 came close to collapse because of the attacks on Israelis by Hamas during 1994. The killing of twenty-nine worshippers in the al-Ibrahimi mosque within the Cave of the Patriarchs in Hebron caused a profound reaction within the Arab and Muslim worlds. Its perpetrator, Baruch (Benjamin) Goldstein, originally from Brooklyn's Bensenhurst neighbourhood, was associated with Meir Kahane's Kach. His action was widely condemned by Israeli Jews including both the Ashkenazi and Sephardi Chief Rabbis. There were demonstrations in Arab population centres in Israel such as Jaffa and Nazareth. There were also disturbances in East Jerusalem and on the Temple Mount. Syria, Lebanon and Jordan suspended the bilateral negotiations in Washington.

In response to the action of Baruch Goldstein, seven of the nine ministers in the Israeli cabinet advocated the removal of the four hundred settlers in Hebron. Rabin promoted instead a Supreme Court inquiry, chaired by its president, Meir Shamgar. The 350-page report, submitted in June, revealed that Goldstein had acted alone.

The Islamists took Goldstein's action as a green light to accelerate the development of suicide bombing within the Green Line and to further undermine the ongoing peace process between Rabin and Arafat. Attacks took place at a bus stop in Afula and as a bus was leaving the central bus station in Hadera on the eve of Israel's Independence Day. There were killings of hitchhikers near the Ashdod–Tel Aviv highway and stabbings in Gush Katif. There was an attack on diners at a restaurant in Jerusalem's fashionable Yoel Salomon Street. Two Israeli workmen installing a lift in Ramla were killed. A nineteen-year-old soldier, Nachshon Waxman, was kidnapped and held in the village of Bir Nabala near Jerusalem. A rescue attempt initially failed to break through a fortified entrance and Waxman was shot by his Hamas captors. They had wanted to exchange him for Hamas's spiritual mentor, Sheikh Yassin, incarcerated in an Israeli prison.

Arafat at first prevaricated in taking action for fear of strengthening his Islamist opponents as well as the PFLP and DFLP. Ten Palestinian organisations had formed a rejectionist front in Damascus and began a campaign of attacks on Israeli civilians. Arafat eventually condemned such attacks and then arrested several Hamas activists. There were clashes between the supporters of Arafat and those of Hamas, sometimes breaking out into armed warfare in Gaza. Perceived collaborators were executed by Hamas. This was fuelled by a 60 per cent unemployment rate in Gaza.

The question of Palestinian autonomy in Gaza and the area around Jericho was agreed in early February and signed in May. During protracted negotiations, questions regarding cross-border security, the actual size of the Jericho enclave and the transfer to civilian authority were sorted out. There were also four 'safe passage' routes from Gaza to Jericho which were delineated.

Joint patrols of Israelis and Palestinians in both Jericho and Gaza were agreed, as was a nine thousand-strong police force in Jericho and Gaza. Some two thousand Palestinian prisoners were released. The release of some seven hundred more was held back because the prisoners refused to sign a document which stated that they supported the peace process. Arafat visited Jericho following his return to Gaza after twenty-seven years.

Rabin was similarly under siege by the opponents of Oslo. New organisations such as Zo Artzeinu and Women in Green appeared. Zo Artzeinu launched 'Operation Duplication' in which new settlements on the West Bank would be established – each one named after a victim of terror attacks. There were mass rallies in Jerusalem while the Bnei Akiva youth group staged a sit-in in the ancient synagogue in Jericho as the IDF handed over control of the city to the Palestinians. The cabinet had agreed to transfer the taxation, education, health, social welfare and tourism portfolios to the PLO. Newly arrived Soviet Jewish activists such as Ida Nudel, Iosif Mendelevitch and Yosef Begun aligned themselves with the opposition to Oslo.

The bus bombing by Hamas in Dizengoff Street in central Tel Aviv further undermined the peace process in the minds of many Israelis. There was growing dissent within Rabin's Labour party and a dramatic drop in the party's standing in opinion polls. Rabin effectively operated a minority government with fewer than sixty-one Knesset seats and depended upon the votes of the Arab parties which were outside government. A two-person breakaway from Tsomet, Yi'ud, aligned itself with Rabin, who in turn made concessions to Shas's religious agenda such as the cessation of archaeological excavations in Modi'in in return for a promise to return to the government coalition.

The new leader of the Likud, Benjamin Netanyahu, led protests on the West Bank and signed a pledge together with fifteen Likud MKs to do whatever was allowed under the law to prevent the return of territory to the Palestinians.

Netanyahu wanted to stage a walkout when the Jericho–Gaza Agreement was placed before the Knesset for a vote. Shamir, Levy, Meridor and Benny Begin disagreed and were not present for the vote. Netanyahu had been criticised for his actions by his many opponents in the party. Sharon called for a new leadership election and put himself forward as a candidate. Benny Begin resigned from the party's leadership over Netanyahu's approach, while Moshe Katsav came out in support of the autonomy agreement. Netanyahu took a centrist position in opposing some measures while supporting others. He supported the treaty with Jordan whereas Sharon and the far Right party, Moledet, opposed it. In the wake of the Hamas bombings, Netanyahu addressed large rallies of Israel's far Right and blamed Rabin's policies.

Yasser Arafat also opposed Jordan's involvement in that it continued its historic role as the guardian of the Muslim holy sites in Jerusalem. There were Palestinian demonstrations against King Hussein.

In July, there were several attacks on Diaspora Jews, probably ultimately under the aegis of Hezbollah and Iran – and designed to bring the peace process to an end. The AMIA Jewish community headquarters in Buenos Aires was bombed on 18 July. The day after, Alas Chiricanas Flight 901, carrying many Jewish passengers, exploded after take-off in Panama. On 28 July, a suicide car bomb exploded outside the London Israeli Embassy while another bomb went off outside Balfour House, the headquarters of Zionist activity in the British capital.

There were ongoing negotiations with the Syrians, a visit by President Clinton to Damascus and shuttle diplomacy by the US secretary of state, Warren Christopher, but with little resolution. Syria wanted Israel to withdraw to the 4 June 1967 line, whereas Israel wanted to retain its foothold around the Sea of Galilee in accordance with the international demarcation under the British Mandate. Yet Assad had met American Jewish leaders and since April 1992 had allowed the vast majority of Syria's four thousand Jews to emigrate to New York. From there, many travelled on to Israel.

In the aftermath of the Declaration of Principles, Yitzhak Rabin visited Oman, and Peres was deeply involved in economic conferences in Jordan and Morocco. Several African countries such as Rwanda re-established diplomatic relations with Israel. The emerging states of the former Soviet Union also did so and numerous countries in the Arab world established economic liaison offices in Tel Aviv. This was paralleled when Israel opened a consulate in Shanghai, China's economic hub.

Yasser Arafat, Yitzhak Rabin and Shimon Peres were all awarded the Nobel Peace Prize for 1994.

257

1995

זה ארצנו

In the months before the assassination of Yitzhak Rabin, several far Right groups staged protests and demonstrations against Rabin and the Oslo Accords.

One group was Zo Artzeinu (This is our Land), which blocked major roads, causing massive traffic jams, depicted here in the shape of Israel.

This cartoon's title plays on the double meaning of 'This is our Land' as both an exasperated comment by gridlocked citizens and the groups' interpretation. It indicates the burning of books – one of which is entitled 'The Law'. Another is the parliamentary symbol of the Knesset.

Ze'ev (*Ha'aretz* 11 August 1995)

1 Jan Cabinet halts settlement construction at Givat HaTamar hilltop near Efrat

8 Jan Cohen–Kedmi Commission to investigate the 'disappeared' Yemenite children

22 Jan Two suicide bombers at Beit Lid kill 20 soldiers returning from weekend leave

22 Jan Cabinet establishes a committee to monitor settlement construction

6 Feb DFLP Red Star Brigade attacks civilian convoy delivering petrol to Gaza

21 Feb Religious Affairs and Tourism Ministry given to Labour in the absence of Shas

1 Mar Carmi Gillon appointed head of the Shin Bet

3 Mar Martin Indyk appointed first Jewish US ambassador to Israel

31 Mar *Al Hamishmar*, Mapam daily, closes down

5 Apr Ofek-3 surveillance satellite launched

6 Apr Government agrees a bailout plan for debt-ridden kibbutzim

9 Apr Islamic Jihad suicide bombing of a Kfar Darom bus kills eight

30 Apr Cabinet agrees the expropriation of Arab land around Jerusalem

7 May Greenpeace surround Haifa trawler to prevent dumping of toxic waste into the sea

10 May Report criticises Religious Affairs Ministry funding of ineligible institutions

22 May Knesset Arab parties force abandonment of the expropriation of Jerusalem land

2 June Haredim launch boycott of companies that advertise on Shabbat and holidays

7 June Natan Sharansky announces the formation of the Yisrael B'Aliya party

18 June Levy leaves Likud and sets up new party, to run for prime minister

16 July Deputy defence minister, Motta Gur, commits suicide after cancer diagnosis

17 July Supreme Court annuls Health Ministry rule banning surrogate mothers

18 July Ehud Barak becomes minister of the interior

18 July Two Israeli hikers killed at Wadi Kelt

24 July Suicide bombing of no. 20 bus at Ramat Gan kills 6 and injures 33

30 July Arrow-2 anti-ballistic missile successfully launched

31 July Right-wing pirate radio station ship boarded and shut down by police

11 Aug Peres and Arafat agree outline of agreement for autonomy next phase

13 Aug Aharon Barak sworn in as president of the Supreme Court

16 Aug *Ma'ariv* editor-in-chief, Ofer Nimrodi, charged with wiretapping

21 Aug Ramat Eshkol suicide bombing kills 5 and injures 100

10 Sept Israel transfers seven areas of responsibility to Palestinians

28 Sept Oslo II Accord signed by Arafat and Rabin in Washington

5 Oct Knesset ratifies Oslo II Interim Agreement 61–59

26 Oct Islamic Jihad head Fathi Shakaki assassinated in Malta

4 Nov Yitzhak Rabin assassinated by Yigal Amir after Tel Aviv peace rally

8 Nov Shamgar Commission of Inquiry into Rabin assassination appointed

12 Nov Leah Rabin addresses mass rally in renamed 'Yitzhak Rabin Square'

22 Nov Shimon Peres becomes prime minister and forms new government

The assassination of Yitzhak Rabin in November was the culmination of a year of incitement and an undermining of the peace process by both the protests of the far Right and the suicide bombers of the Palestinian Islamists. Shimon Peres became prime minister and formed a new government which included Rabbi Yehuda Amital of the dovish religious party Meimad as minister without portfolio.

The settlers on the West Bank and Gaza had mounted an ongoing campaign against Rabin by establishing new settlements, often portrayed as extensions of existing ones. In January, the cabinet halted construction of five hundred housing units at Givat HaTamar, a hilltop near Efrat. Both the settlers and the inhabitants of the village of al-Khader claimed ownership of the land. The settlers were given the possibility of moving to Givat HaZayit which was nearer to Efrat. The conflict produced no-confidence motions from the NRP and from Tsomet in the Knesset.

The ongoing negotiations with Arafat and the PLO and the subsequent redeployment of the IDF from Palestinian population centres brought about a campaign of civil disobedience from the settlers. Embryonic hilltop settlements were initiated at Givat HaDagan near Efrat, but also near Beit El, Kedumim, Nebi Samuel, Ofra and Karnei Tsur.

The far Right group Zo Artzeinu started a disruption campaign at intersections of major roads within Israel. Its leader, Moshe Feiglin, was fined $3,300 by a Rehovot court and given a six-month suspended sentence.

The government – which existed on a wafer-thin majority – was divided between those who wanted a controlled settlement drive and those who did not want any. In January, the housing minister, Binyamin Ben-Eliezer, wanted to build thirty thousand units in Jerusalem and the Gush Etzion bloc, but was opposed by the Meretz ministers. A government committee was established to monitor settlement building. It approved the construction of further units within Givat Ze'ev, Ma'ale Adumim and Betar. Plans for 6,500 homes at Har Homa were approved.

Even in the Golan Heights, which were formally annexed by Israel in 1981, there were protests which lasted several weeks in September. There was a fear that Rabin would compromise the position of the 13,500 settlers in thirty-two settlements in return for a deal with Syria. Significantly many of the Golan residents were Labour voters.

The number of Knesset seats of Labour, Meretz and Yi'ud – a breakaway faction of Rafael Eitan's Tsomet – amounted to fifty-nine. Rabin therefore had to rely on the six seats of the Arab parties which remained outside government.

At the end of April, the government ordered the expropriation of 120 acres of land around Jerusalem in order to build new outer Jewish suburbs and thereby encase Arab neighbourhoods within. In May, both Hadash and the Arab Democratic party put forward a no-confidence motion and were supported by the Likud and the Right. This would have undoubtedly caused the downfall of the government. Rabin agreed to freeze the building of these new areas around Jerusalem, with the result that the Arab parties quickly withdrew their motion of no confidence.

Rabin's policies were further undermined by Palestinian Islamists and the ten rejectionist groups domiciled in Damascus. A comparison of the number of Israelis killed before Oslo with the number in the same time period after it indicated a large increase after September 1993. In 1994, more people were killed within Israel than in the territories. This, coupled with a deep fear of suicide bombers, made many Israelis dubious about the veracity of the peace process. It was this that effectively created an unspoken alliance between many Israelis and the Right. A letter in February from Ovadia Yosef to Rabin essentially confirmed that Shas would not return to the coalition because of the deteriorating security situation.

The campaign by Palestinian Islamists against the Accord was carried out through shootings at the occupants of passing cars, random stabbings, ramming of cars and the bombing of buses. The

Beit Lid suicide bombing of teenage recruits was conducted by members of Islamic Jihad which had forged an alliance with Hamas. This incident produced a cabinet debate about building a fence to prevent infiltration into Israel by the bombers. The police minister, Moshe Shahal, put forward a plan for a separation area, 221 miles long, ranging in width from a few hundred feet to greater distances, and guarded by police and border guards on the western side and the IDF on the eastern side. There would also be guard dogs, electronic surveillance and up to ten crossing points.

There were repeated closures of the West Bank as responses to the bombings. After the Beit Lid bombing, the cabinet agreed to bring in another six thousand foreign workers, mainly from Thailand and Romania, to fill the jobs of Palestinians. Doves such as Uzi Baram advocated a permanent closure of the territories.

Within Labour, there were rumours of replacing Rabin, possibly with Peres. Two Labour hawks, Avigdor Kahalani and Emanuel Zismann, voted against Oslo II in September and eventually formed their own party, 'The Third Way', composed mainly of military figures. Natan Sharansky established a new party, Yisrael B'Aliya, to attract the votes of the 400,000 new immigrants from the former Soviet Union. Within the Likud, there was increasing dissent at Netanyahu's leadership. After his candidates were effectively eliminated from the Likud candidates' list, David Levy first formed a movement inside the Likud, then broke away to form a new party. Levy, Eitan and several others announced that they would stand for prime minister in the 1996 elections. This would be the first time under a new system that a prime minister could be elected directly. The second vote would be a normal one for a party.

Despite all the criticism of Netanyahu, the anger directed at Rabin over an inability to stop Islamist suicide bombers, with the resulting casualties, outweighed other considerations. Despite his own difficulties, Netanyahu's standing in the opinion polls was much higher and the prospect loomed of Labour being defeated in the 1996 election.

261

Netanyahu argued that the West Bank should have self-rule apart from foreign policy and questions of security. He also argued for a 'wire fence' and a minefield to stop suicide bombers from entering Israel. Netanyahu modified his approach to the Oslo Accord and accepted it as 'facts on the ground'. If the Palestinians violated its terms, he argued, then Israel would not honour its commitment to it.

At the same time, Netanyahu dallied with the far Right. He had 'an understanding' of Zo Artzeinu's frustrations. The Likud's attacks on Labour's views were predicated on Rabin's 'mental state and weakness' as 'the man who could not say "no" to Yasser Arafat'.

Arafat, too, was undermined by the Islamists, despite the fact that many attempts by Hamas and Islamic Jihad were foiled by the Palestinian police and that arrests of suspects were carried out. In mid-April, Palestinian courts sentenced offenders to prison terms. Although dates for proceeding to the next phases of the Oslo Accord were repeatedly moved back, the arrangements for the redeployment of Israeli troops from six major Palestinian population centres and 450 towns and villages were finally agreed in September as the Oslo II Agreement. This provided for the transfer of authority to the Palestinians. The West Bank was divided into three areas, A, B and C, whereby security was either under the aegis of the Israelis or the Palestinians or there was shared responsibility.

Jerusalem and Damascus continued an ongoing if indirect dialogue, facilitated by the US secretary of state, Warren Christopher.

1996

Benjamin Netanyahu remarkably won the election by a sliver of votes, displacing the experienced veteran, Labour's Shimon Peres. While the electorate never favoured Peres in contrast to Rabin, the repeated suicide bombings by Palestinian Islamists had eroded trust in the Oslo Accords.

Here Netanyahu is depicted as being a master of public relations on a television screen. His political adaptability shows him about to speak to the secular as well as to the national religious, the haredim as well as the Arabs – with seemingly equal conviction.

Mike (*Yediot Aharanot* 4 June 1996)

1 Jan	Supreme Court rules that the non-orthodox can stand for Haifa religious council
5 Jan	Chief Hamas bombmaker, Yehiya Ayash, killed by phone bomb
8 Jan	Shin Bet head, Carmi Gillon, resigns after Rabin assassination
10 Jan	King Hussein pays his first official state visit to Israel
14 Jan	Ami Ayalon appointed head of Shin Bet
20 Jan	Palestinians go to the polls to elect a president and legislative council
22 Jan	Israel Eldad, far Right ideologue and Lehi founder, dies in Jerusalem aged 85
28 Jan	Ethiopian Jews protest about refusal to accept blood donations due to AIDS fear
12 Feb	Moshe Vardi, editor of *Yediot Aharanot*, charged with wiretapping
25 Feb	Hamas suicide bombing of no. 18 bus in Jerusalem kills 26
28 Feb	Supreme Court upholds $300,000 fine on bank shares manipulators
3 Mar	Second Hamas suicide bombing of no. 18 bus in Jerusalem kills 19
3 Mar	Cabinet agrees separation fence between West Bank and Israel
4 Mar	Hamas suicide bombing of Dizengoff Centre kills 13
24 Mar	Danny Yatom appointed head of the Mossad
27 Mar	Yigal Amir sentenced to life in a trial at Tel Aviv District Court
1 Apr	Peres leads a trade mission to Oman with leading industrialists
2 Apr	Israel and Qatar to open trade offices in Tel Aviv and Doha
11 Apr	Operation Grapes of Wrath launched against Hezbollah
18 Apr	Mistaken shelling of UN compound at Qana kills more than 100 Lebanese civilians
24 Apr	PNC votes to amend Palestinian National Covenant 504–54
2 May	Emil Habibi, poet and writer, leader of Palestine Communist party, dies aged 74
16 May	Amos-1 communications satellite launched from French Guiana
21 May	Daily *Davar Rishon*, successor to Histadrut's *Davar*, closes down
29 May	Netanyahu beats Peres in the election by a sliver of 30,000 votes
19 June	Netanyahu announces formation of a National Security Council
30 June	Sara Netanyahu dismisses Tanya Shaw in Nannygate affair
21 July	Bodies of two soldiers returned in prisoner exchange with Hezbollah
29 July	Sharon orders the construction of two roads through Palestinian territory
4 Aug	Cabinet ends the freeze on settlement construction
8 Aug	Justice minister, Ya'akov Ne'eman, resigns after Attorney-General opens investigation
15 Aug	Supreme Court rules that Jerusalem's Bar-Ilan Street be opened to Shabbat traffic
4 Sept	First meeting between Netanyahu and Arafat takes place at Gaza's Erez crossing
8 Sept	Jerusalem mayor, Ehud Olmert, charged with misappropriation of funds
24 Sept	Temple Mount riots take place after a new tunnel entrance is opened
26 Sept	Nablus clashes take the lives of 11 Israelis and 39 Palestinians
3 Oct	Amir brothers and Dror Adani sentenced on Rabin conspiracy charges
13 Dec	Cabinet gives tax breaks and financial benefits to West Bank settlers

In January, more than three thousand international observers led by former US president Jimmy Carter were present during the Palestinian elections for both the president and the eighty-eight-member legislative council. Arafat removed candidates from the Fatah list that he did not care for and several therefore ran as independents. Arafat received almost 90 per cent of the vote and Fatah secured fifty-five mandates. Hamas did not put up any candidates and the turn-out was therefore low in Hebron.

The campaigns of both Arafat and Peres were undermined by a wave of suicide bombings by Palestinian Islamists which were mainly aimed at Israeli civilians. They weakened Peres in the eyes of the Israeli voters, who complained that Oslo had not brought peace, and strengthened by default his younger rival, Netanyahu. Both Arafat and Peres had to demonstrate resolve to their own publics while pushing ahead with implementing the Declaration of Principles. Yahiya Ayash, the chief Hamas bombmaker and head of its armed wing on the West Bank, was killed when a device planted in his telephone was detonated remotely by the Israelis. Although opposed to Hamas, Arafat condemned the killing and spoke to a large gathering of mourners in Hebron.

The repeated closures of the West Bank and Gaza after every suicide bombing within Israel prevented tens of thousands of Palestinians from working in Israel, which in turn produced economic problems for Arafat. Each suicide bombing meant an Israeli search in the territories for the perpetrators. This rendered the idea of self-rule and independence somewhat meaningless. The Peres government in addition resolved to replace Palestinian workers with foreign labourers.

Peres called for an election in the expectation that he would capitalise on the anguish felt after the assassination of Rabin. A Gallup poll at the beginning of February suggested 52 per cent for Peres and 30 per cent for Netanyahu. Like Arafat, Peres had to maintain a balancing act between those in government who wanted further construction in the territories and those who did not. Labour's Binyamin Ben-Eliezer wanted to develop further a ring of suburb settlements around Jerusalem which would effectively expand the city and incorporate Arab East Jerusalem. The Meretz ministers in the cabinet opposed the development of Ma'ale Adumim, Givat Ze'ev and Alfei Menashe to create a Greater Jerusalem.

At the end of February, a suicide bomber attacked a no. 18 bus in Jerusalem's Jaffa Road with a large loss of life and great damage caused to shops. A week later, another Hamas bomber blew up another no. 18 bus carrying many passengers. There was also an attack by a suicide bomber on the Dizengoff Centre in the heart of Tel Aviv. On the same day as the second Jerusalem bomb, an emergency cabinet meeting resolved to implement a plan for a separation fence between Israel and the West Bank with some eighteen crossing points and patrolled by eight hundred security guards. Israel proclaimed its right to enter the territory under Palestinian self-rule to locate militants involved in such hostile acts. A new anti-terror command was established, led by Ami Ayalon, the head of the Shin Bet.

The target of Israeli popular anger was Arafat and the Palestinian Authority, perceived as being reluctant to look for and imprison the Islamists. It was only after the Jerusalem bus bombings that Arafat outlawed the military wings of Hamas and Islamic Jihad and a concerted campaign of arrests and imprisonment was conducted.

Although Netanyahu accepted limited Palestinian autonomy as a fait accompli and was willing to talk to Arafat, he publicly opposed Oslo. The rash of suicide bombings weakened Peres's standing in the election campaign. In April, the IDF embarked on Operation Grapes of Wrath which was designed to halt Hezbollah's attacks on towns such as Kiriat Shemona and Nahariya near the Lebanese border.

Israel had already suspended talks with the Syrians in March because Assad refused to condemn the Islamists. It was also cooperating with the USA in building the Arrow air-defence system and the Nautilus laser system, designed to eliminate Hezbollah's katyusha attacks. However, these defences were not yet ready to prevent injuries to growing numbers of Israelis, damage to apartment blocks, a standstill in economic life and the flight of tourists from northern Israel.

The ports of Tyre, Sidon and Beirut were blockaded, and a UN compound at Qana was erroneously targeted. More than a hundred civilians sheltering there were killed. Some 400,000 Lebanese fled the fighting. The State Comptroller's report indicated that IDF desertions and the number who simply failed to turn up for army service had increased dramatically.

The Labour party dropped its objections to a future Palestinian state. Likud depicted Peres as weak and untrustworthy – someone who would divide Jerusalem. It was also a time of economic troubles. The lending rate of Bank Leumi and Bank Hapoalim was 17 per cent. Many Israeli Arabs refused to vote in the election for prime minister, doing so only for the Knesset. This further diminished Peres's support.

Peres's lacklustre campaign was capped by a poor performance in a televised debate with the more polished Netanyahu. Although the media informed Israelis that Peres had a slight lead on election night, Netanyahu emerged next morning as the winner in the contest for prime minister with a majority of just under 30,000 votes, even though Labour was the largest party.

Labour had lost ten seats and the Likud eight. However, the Likud had formed an electoral alliance with David Levy's new party, Gesher, and with Raful Eitan's Tsomet. The Likud, in fact, had slipped back to only twenty-four seats, but because Netanyahu (50.5 per cent) had gained more votes than Peres (49.5 per cent) in the election for prime minister, it was the Likud that was called upon to form a government.

Netanyahu relied on new parties, Sharansky's Yisrael B'Aliya and Kahalani's Third Way, to form a government with the Likud–Gesher–Tsomet electoral alliance. Both Lubavitch-Habad ('Netanyahu is good for the Jews!') and their religious ideological opponents in Degel HaTorah supported Netanyahu in the vote for prime minister. The religious parties, the NRP, Shas and the United Torah Judaism (UTJ, formed from Agudat Yisrael and Degel HaTorah in 1992), all came into a Netanyahu-led government.

Netanyahu formed a Likud-led government of the Right and the religious, creating a new Ministry of Infrastructure for his rival, Ariel Sharon. Netanyahu prevaricated over meeting Arafat for fear of opposition from within his government and sent his policy adviser, Dore Gold, instead. Netanyahu argued that Arafat had not done enough to stop Islamist terror, Syria was still supplying arms to Hezbollah and that controversial clauses of the Palestinian National Covenant remained even after amendment. Labour's freeze on new settlement construction was abandoned. Sharon ordered an extension of the trans-Samarian motorway in the territories and a building of a road linking Atarot to Jerusalem at a cost of $57 million.

Netanyahu challenged the judiciary in appointing Tsahi Hanegbi as justice minister and the civil service professionals by filling the posts of deputy directors-general of ministries with political appointees. Cuts were made to public sector budgets and the privatisation of state-owned utilities was advanced.

A first meeting with President Clinton indicated the vast gap between them. While an annual State Department report indicated that the PLO was in compliance with US views on terrorism, Netanyahu presented Clinton with a long list of violations. Netanyahu addressed both houses of Congress with his 'Peace with Security' approach.

Netanyahu's 'Lebanon First' plan offered a withdrawal of Israeli troops from south Lebanon in exchange for the disarming of Hezbollah. Syria wanted a withdrawal from the Golan Heights.

1997

Benjamin Netanyahu was extremely reluctant to embrace the Oslo Accords and was strongly opposed to dealing with Arafat and the PLO. Following his election victory, he inherited the path which both Rabin and Peres had followed under American guidance. Netanyahu found himself attempting to please both the Americans and the opponents of Oslo in his own party and those further to the Right.

Here a tired, forlorn Netanyahu, having been pressured to sign the Hebron Accord to effectively divide the city, is now being led by President Clinton into the next boxing ring to deal with the Syrians.

Shmuel Katz (*Ma'ariv* n.d. 1997)

1 Jan   Noam Friedman fires into a crowded Hebron market, wounding seven

16 Jan   Knesset approves Hebron Agreement 87–17

29 Jan   Government agrees to a funding of the Jewish enclaves in Hebron

4 Feb   Two military helicopters collide in southern Lebanon, killing 73

7 Mar   Cabinet votes 10–7 to return 9 per cent rural West Bank to Palestinians

13 Mar   Jordanian soldier kills seven schoolgirls on field trip from Beit Shemesh

16 Mar   King Hussein pays condolence visits to bereaved families of schoolgirls

21 Mar   Hamas suicide bomber kills three women in Café Apropos, north Tel Aviv

1 Apr   First reading of conversion bill passes in the Knesset, 51–32

15 Apr   Police recommend fraud and breach of trust indictment of Netanyahu

13 Apr   Supreme Court rules that Jerusalem's Bar-Ilan Street should be open to traffic on Shabbat

17 Apr   Former president Chaim Herzog dies in Tel Aviv aged 78

20 Apr   Netanyahu and Hanegbi not charged through insufficient evidence

1 May   Israeli press reports that Syria has the ability to make VX nerve gas

15 May   Nahum Manbar on trial for selling chemical weapons components to Iran

15 May   Ya'akov Ne'eman acquitted of perjury and obstruction of justice charges

3 June   Ehud Barak elected head of the Labour party

16 June   Ariel Sharon meets Mahmoud Abbas privately

7 July   Sharon bypassed by Netanyahu as Ne'eman is selected as finance minister

14 July   Five Australians die after Yarkon bridge collapse at Maccabiah Games

24 July   One-day strike against privatisation by workers in public utilities

30 July   Hamas suicide bombings kill 16 civilians in Mahane Yehuda market

5 Aug   Supreme Court rules that Reform woman must sit on Netanya Council

9 Aug   Prisoners protesting about conditions at IDF prison take hostages

11 Aug   Haredim disrupt egalitarian Tisha B'Av prayers at Western Wall

13 Aug   Cabinet approves cuts of $650 million in 1998 budget

20 Aug   Arafat stages unity conference for Islamists in Gaza and Ramallah

21 Aug   Barak dismisses Labour party employees due to $24 million deficit

31 Aug   Mevasseret Zion Reform nursery in private apartment firebombed

2 Sept   Moshe Feiglin and Shmuel Sackett of Zo Artzeinu convicted of sedition

4 Sept   Hamas suicide bombers kill five civilians in Ben-Yehuda pedestrian mall

4 Sept   Israel establishes diplomatic ties with Croatia

24 Sept   Failed Mossad attempt to poison Hamas leader Khaled Mashal

28 Sept   Ehud Olmert cleared of financial irregularities in 1988 election

1 Oct   Sheikh Ahmed Yassin, Hamas spiritual head, released from prison

7 Oct   Jerusalem's Harel Reform synagogue daubed with swastika

4 Nov   Tel Aviv court rules Sharon misled Begin during Lebanon war in 1982

23 Nov   Avigdor Lieberman resigns as director-general of Prime Minister's Office

Despite an unpublicised meeting between Arafat and Netanyahu at the Erez crossing into Gaza, an accord on Hebron initially remained elusive, in part because Netanyahu feared division within his cabinet and dissension amongst his supporters on the Right. There had already been a lone attack by a yeshiva student on the marketplace in Hebron in which several Palestinians had been shot and injured.

In mid-January, an agreement was reached in which the IDF would withdraw within a ten-day period from the H1 area of the city where a majority of Palestinians lived, but would remain to provide security for the several hundred Jews who remained in the H2 enclaves. A buffer cordon would be established around H2 whereby no Palestinian would be allowed to carry arms. A four hundred-strong Palestinian police force would be formed and there would be joint patrols in sensitive areas. It also called for the opening of the main thoroughfare, al-Shuhada Street, known to the Jews as King David Street. A temporary international presence would monitor compliance with the agreement.

It was further agreed that there would be three IDF redeployments between March 1997 and May 1998, with permanent status talks completed by May 1999.

In cabinet, a twelve-hour discussion took place with a final vote of 11–7 in favour of the agreement – and the resignation of the minister of science, Benny Begin. The Knesset voted 87–17 in favour of the agreement. In Hebron, religious Jews sat 'shiva' as if in mourning for a loved one and rended their clothes. The Jewish presence in Hebron was given 'A' status by the government – the equivalent of development towns within Israel – which made it eligible for receiving subsidies for housing and education.

The Hebron Agreement also offered Arafat a means of engaging Hamas and Islamic Jihad in the hope of influencing their supporters and thereby stopping their erosion of the peace process. He visited the city a few days after the Accord had been approved in a Knesset vote and told a rally that Hebron had been liberated and that the next step would be a Palestinian state with Jerusalem as its capital.

Netanyahu, however, responded that he was opposed to a Palestinian state and approval was given for the construction of sixty housing units at Ma'aleh Ephraim in the Jordan Valley. Netanyahu further promised to accelerate settlement building on the West Bank and to expand Jerusalem under pressure from the NRP, Tsomet and the Third Way in government. An announcement was made to implement plans for housing units in Har Homa which would ensure that Jerusalem was encircled by Jewish suburbs.

This was criticised internationally and by the USA, and there was condemnation in the Arab world and protests in Nablus and Jenin. A private initiative to build in Ras al-Amud in a populated Palestinian area was opposed by Netanyahu. Arafat refused to return to talks with the Israelis until all construction work at Har Homa had ceased.

A Hamas suicide bomber entered Café Apropos in Tel Aviv and killed several civilians. Shoppers were killed in the crowded Jerusalem market of Mahaneh Yehuda at the end of July. One continuing demand of Hamas was the release of its spiritual mentor, Sheikh Ahmed Yassin, who had been held in an Israeli prison for almost a decade. This took place at the end of the year, not because of Hamas attacks, but instead through negotiations about a botched attempt by Mossad operatives to poison Khaled Mashal, head of the political bureau of Hamas, in Jordan. Travelling on false Canadian passports, the operatives were captured – leading to an angry response from the Canadian government and a threat by King Hussein to revoke the 1994 peace treaty between the two countries. The head of the Mossad, Danny Yatom, took the antidote to Jordan, Mashal recovered and normal relations were restored. Significantly Arafat was kept out of the exchanges between Israel and Jordan. When Yassin went to Gaza, he received a tremendous welcome.

268

This debacle not only alienated the far Right, but also further antagonised Netanyahu's opponents within the Likud – some with ideological differences such as Yitzhak Shamir, Uzi Landau and Benny Begin, but others such as Dan Meridor, David Magen, Natan Sharansky and Avigdor Lieberman because they felt that Netanyahu had gone back on his word to them. Moreover Ariel Sharon, a long-time opponent, was passed over as minister of finance and he subsequently began to cultivate a less radical, more responsible public image in meeting Mahmoud Abbas.

Netanyahu challenged the status quo in appointing Tsahi Hanegbi as minister of justice and by bypassing foreign office professionals in favour of political appointees such as Dore Gold and Leonard Davis, comparatively recent American immigrants. However, Netanyahu found it difficult to know the boundaries of what was permissible and together with Hanegbi was indicted in the Bar-On affair. The appointment of the long-term Likud stalwart Roni Bar-On as Attorney-General was approved by the cabinet in early January, only to be superseded by his resignation two days later. Dan Avi-Yitzhak, Netanyahu's nominee for the post, was Shas's Arieh Deri's lawyer. He resigned when he was passed over for the job. The suspicion was that Bar-On would be appointed so that a plea bargain could be offered to Deri who had been indicted for bribery. If this transpired, then Shas would support the upcoming Hebron Agreement.

Netanyahu was interviewed for four hours, but not charged by Attorney-General Elyakim Rubinstein, for lack of evidence. The minister of justice, Ya'akov Ne'eman, was acquitted at the end of a trial. Only Deri was charged for breach of trust, fraud and extortion.

Netanyahu was also faced with a bill to ensure that all conversions to Judaism in Israel would be subject to confirmation by the orthodox Chief Rabbinate. Up until then, such conversions had not been sanctioned in law. Reform and Conservative congregations in the USA particularly reacted strongly to this such that their rabbinical representatives in Israel chained themselves in protest to a bench outside the Ministry of the Interior. Netanyahu depended on the twenty-three mandates of the Orthodox parties in the Knesset to keep him in power and therefore disparaged the claims of the Reform and the Conservatives. The Supreme Court, however, instructed the Interior Ministry, controlled by the Orthodox, to allow women and Reform representatives to sit on municipal religious councils. A Conservative synagogue in Kfar Saba, Hod v'Hadar, was vandalised during Yom Kippur. A ceasefire of sorts came about when the Reform and Conservatives withdrew from approaches to the Supreme Court while the Orthodox withdrew their bills from the Knesset.

The annual budget for $58 billion was passed in the Knesset by a vote of 60–42. This included cuts in public spending, but increased funding for the settlements. A plan by Tzipi Livni of the Government Companies Authority and Moshe Lion of the Prime Minister's Office to sell off thirteen state-owned companies provoked several strikes organised by the Histadrut in protest against this mass privatisation of public utilities. The companies included Bezek, United Chemicals, Zim Shipping, Mekorot Water and Rafael Defence Industries.

A Tel Aviv court instructed the IDF to grant full benefits to the male partner of Colonel Doron Meisel of the Medical Corps who had died of cancer in 1991. The IDF was forced to recognise the rights of gay couples.

269

1998

The Wye Plantation Accord to restart the Oslo II Agreement and advance further redeployment of Israeli forces was carried through on the initiative of President Clinton. A hesitant Netanyahu and a reticent Arafat both signed the agreement. Both feared criticism when they returned.

Netanyahu feared the Right and the West Bank settlers while Arafat was concerned about the Islamist reaction from Hamas and Islamic Jihad.

Here Netanyahu looks to a stormy cloud, labelled 'Bibi, Traitor!' while Arafat looks to his cloud, titled 'Arafat, Traitor!' The forecast near the table predicts the political weather: 'Partly cloudy'.

Shmuel Katz (*Ma'ariv* 3 November 1998)

4 Jan   David Levy resigns as foreign minister; Gesher withdraws from the coalition

20 Jan   Zevulun Hammer, NRP leader and deputy prime minister, dies aged 61

4 Feb   Letter of support to resolve the conversions crisis signed by 65 MKs including the NRP

16 Feb   Commission clears Netanyahu of responsibility in the Mashal poisoning

24 Feb   Mossad head Danny Yatom resigns after failed assassination of Mashal

4 Mar   Ephraim Halevi appointed the head of the Mossad

22 Mar   Cabinet rejects the US plan to withdraw from 13.1 per cent of West Bank

28 Apr   Zalman Shoval reappointed ambassador to the USA, replacing Ben-Elissar

13 May   Shaul Mofaz approved by cabinet as the next IDF Chief of Staff

9 June   Amir Peretz defeats Maxim Levy in Histadrut election, winning 77.6 per cent of the vote

26 June   Gay Pride march in Tel Aviv

9 July   Shaul Mofaz takes office as the next IDF Chief of Staff

16 July   Nahum Manbar given 16 years for selling chemical weapons to Iran

22 July   First flight of Iranian Shahab-3 missile

20 Aug   Hebron rabbi Shlomo Ra'anan stabbed to death in Tel Rumeida

25 Aug   Hezbollah fires katyushas at Kiriat Shemona, leaving 14 injured

27 Aug   Pipe bomb explodes on the corner of Allenby Street, Tel Aviv, injuring civilians

10 Sept   Adel Awadallah, Hamas leader in the West Bank, killed in shoot-out

15 Sept $50 million casino opens in Jericho

27 Sept   Clashes over land expropriation in Umm el-Fahm and Muawiyya

28 Sept   Netanyahu and Arafat meet at the White House for the first time in nearly a year

13 Oct   Ariel Sharon takes office as foreign minister

15 Oct   Wye Plantation talks on deployments open in Maryland

19 Oct   Grenade attack on Beersheba central bus station injures 64

23 Oct   Netanyahu and Arafat sign Wye Plantation Agreement

26 Oct   Demonstration outside prime minister's home after Wye signing

6 Nov   Islamic Jihad suicide bombing injures 21 in Jerusalem's Mahane Yehuda market

9 Nov   Netanyahu postpones Wye redeployment timetable after market bombing

10 Nov   Ron Huldai wins election to become mayor of Tel Aviv

17 Nov   Knesset approves Wye Agreement 75–19 with 9 abstentions

18 Nov   Cabinet approves first redeployment 7–5 with 3 abstentions

24 Nov   Arafat airport opened in southern Gaza

7 Dec   Sharon tells Albright that the second redeployment will not be implemented

9 Dec   Supreme Court rules that the army deferral of 30,000 yeshiva students is illegal

14 Dec   Clinton addresses PNC in Gaza

20 Dec   Netanyahu ensures cabinet vote to suspend Wye Agreement

21 Dec   Knesset votes 81–30 to hold new elections

David Levy resigned as foreign minister at the beginning of the year and pulled his Gesher faction out of the coalition. He accused the government of 'stonewalling' on foreign policy and stalling on social policy. He was the third minister to resign from Netanyahu's administration. This left Netanyahu with a majority of two seats in the Knesset, 61 to 59.

This weakness was compounded by many other problems, not least the need to fulfil the pledges in the Oslo II Agreement, to facilitate three redeployments and to proceed to a final status agreement by May 1999.

Netanyahu was beset by two competing pressures. The first was from the Clinton White House to commit to a first redeployment involving a transfer of 13.1 per cent of West Bank territory to the Palestinians. The second was the opposition of many inside the cabinet and outside it to doing so. Ariel Sharon, minister for infrastructure, argued for a maximum of 9 per cent while Rafael Eitan, the minister of agriculture and leader of Tsomet, favoured 7 per cent. The NRP was opposed while the Third Way grew frustrated at the lack of any decision.

Netanyahu suggested a referendum on redeployment and then an international conference. He attempted to shore up his coalition by negotiating first with the far Right, Moledet, and then with the Labour party in the hope of forging a unity government. All such moves came to nothing.

There was further fragmentation within the Likud and on the Right generally. The mayor of Tel Aviv, Roni Milo, was considering breaking away while far Right parties such as Tkuma and Herut were in the process of coalescing. The Land of Israel group of seventeen MKs reflected the views of many West Bank settlers when it stated it would bring down the government if redeployment went ahead.

On the Palestinian side, Hamas and Islamic Jihad, vehemently opposed to the Oslo process, continuously targeted Israeli civilians through suicide bombing such as the attack on the popular Jerusalem market of Mahane Yehuda. This, in turn, brought condemnation of Arafat from Netanyahu and the Right for failing to crack down on his Islamist opponents. Arafat, for his part, was wary of too harsh a criticism as this would encourage his opponents and weaken his authority. He made a distinction between the killing of settlers and the killing of Israelis. He was silent therefore on the killings in the settlement of Yizhar on the West Bank. He also avoided responding to Israeli demands that specific Palestinians, suspected of attacks on civilians, should be handed over.

Yet Hamas's strategy was working in that negotiations were gridlocked, deployments never took place and deadlines were regularly put back. When Adel Awadallah, a leading commander of Hamas's military wing, was discovered by the IDF with his brother, Imad, and killed in a shoot-out near Hebron, there were numerous demonstrations and a call for retaliation from Sheikh Yassin. This process of undermining Israeli–Palestinian dialogue extended to the cancellation of a concert in Nablus by Zehava Ben, an Israeli Mizrahi performer popular in the Arab world.

Arafat's image divided both Diaspora Jews and Israelis. In January, the Holocaust Museum in Washington refused to receive him when acting in an official capacity. Critics raised the issues of terrorism and anti-Semitic caricatures in the Palestinian press. This led to the resignation of the museum's director. In April, Arafat made a 'private visit' to Anne Frank's house in Amsterdam.

President Clinton finally brought together Netanyahu and Arafat for a period of concerted negotiations at the Wye Plantation in Maryland in October, in the hope of resolving the stalemate that had prevailed. Sharon, recently appointed foreign minister, refused to shake Arafat's hand and argued that a 13 per cent transfer of territory was dangerous, but that there was no choice. The week of negotiations produced an agreement in which a timetable for the deployments was set out. The first one was scheduled to take place on 2 November.

There was a promise by the Israelis to release seven hundred Palestinian prisoners, a pledge by the Palestinian police to clamp down on Hamas members and an agreement from Clinton for $500 million to fund the redeployments and to build bypass roads to settlements.

When Netanyahu returned to Israel, despite 70 per cent public support for the agreement, there was strong dissension within the cabinet such that ratification was delayed. The Knesset approved the Wye Plantation Agreement 75–19, but two NRP ministers voted against and five Likud ministers absented themselves. In addition, United Torah Judaism threatened to pull out of the coalition because the Supreme Court had instructed the Ministry of Religious Affairs to allow representatives of both Reform and Conservative Judaism to take their seats on municipal religious councils. The government coalition gradually fell apart despite Netanyahu's retreat on his agreement in order to cultivate the support of the opponents. The dissolution of the Knesset was agreed with a new election to take place in mid-1999.

The haredim also opposed any compromise on the question of conversions. The Ne'eman Committee had spent many months trying to resolve the question of conversions. The solution was a plan in which Orthodox, Conservative and Reform representatives under the auspices of the Jewish Agency would jointly prepare converts and the formal conversion would be conducted by orthodox religious courts. In February, sixty-five MKs, including members of the NRP, wrote to Netanyahu recommending acceptance. It was not endorsed by the Chief Rabbinate Council. The two Chief Rabbis refused to respond directly to the initiative while the religious parties opposed it. Netanyahu needed the votes of the religious parties to ensure that his coalition remained in power, even though he personally supported the Ne'eman Commission's proposals.

Relations with Jordan reached a low point because of the debacle of the botched poisoning of Khaled Mashal in Amman. King Hussein closed down the Mossad office which had operated since 1994. Netanyahu was cleared by the inquiry which looked into the operation, but the head of the Mossad, Danny Yatom, tendered his resignation. The Mashal affair coincided with a failed operation in Switzerland whereby a Mossad team had allegedly attempted to bug telephones in a location outside Berne. In addition, a Mossad operative, Yehuda Gil, was put on trial for supplying misleading information on Syria and taking funds which had been allocated for paying informers. Yatom was replaced by London-born Ephraim Halevi who was tasked with repairing relations with Hussein and overhauling the Mossad.

There was increasing concern about Iran's missile capability and the development of the Shahab-3, based on the North Korean Nodong-1. Reports in the Israeli press suggested that Iran possessed nuclear knowhow which had been obtained from Russia. Scud-3 missiles in Syria were being modified by Russian engineers, while joint Syrian–Russian military exercises were held and President Assad visited Moscow.

The economic situation in Israel began to improve, partly due to a privatisation and deregulation policy: 43 per cent of Bank Hapoalim and 49 per cent of El Al were approved for private sale. Bezek's monopoly of telecommunications was broken such that the price of international calls fell dramatically. The Arab boycott had become less relevant since the Oslo Accords. Technological start-ups by young people, including many recent Soviet immigrants, were becoming crucial to the economic recovery. Firms such as Checkpoint and Mirabilis were sold for hundreds of millions of dollars, automatically turning their young owners into multi-millionaires.

The European Union became more critical of goods manufactured in settlements in the West Bank such as Ahava cosmetics, Barkan wine and Modan bags. This led to accusations of mislabelling of goods as 'Made in Israel'.

273

1999

The victory of Ehud Barak's 'One Israel' over Netanyahu's Likud posed problems for the Mizrahi party, Shas. Although it had made great advances electorally, its young leader in the Knesset, Arieh Deri, had been convicted on bribery charges during his time as minister of the interior.

Its spiritual mentor, Ovadia Yosef, had tried to save the loyal Deri by refusing to endorse Shas's entry into the Barak coalition. Here Yosef is seen as leaving Deri to his fate as his coattails tear. Yosef, with followers in train under his cloak, is entering the government. A sign on the door refers to 'Yossi Sarid', a progressive secularist and opponent of Shas who became minister of education.

Shmuel Katz (*Ma'ariv* n.d. 1999)

3 Jan   Avigdor Lieberman launches a new party, Yisrael Beiteinu

23 Jan   Netanyahu dismisses the defence minister, Yitzhak Mordechai, on television

26 Jan   Knesset votes 50–49 to support the Chief Rabbis' authority over religious councils

27 Jan   Moshe Arens, defeated in the Likud leader primary, becomes defence minister

5 Feb   Knesset passes the budget 48–34, after $135 million goes to orthodox projects

7 Feb   King Hussein of Jordan dies; his son, Abdullah II, succeeds

17 Feb   Four Kurdish demonstrators killed outside the Israeli Consulate in Berlin

2 Mar   Abdel Rahman Zuabi appointed to the Supreme Court as the first Arab judge

8 Mar   Houston's BMC pays $700 million for TA's New Dimensions Software

9 Mar   Herut, Moledet and Tkuma agree to run on a joint election platform

15 Mar   USA instructs retired generals not to visit East Jerusalem and Golan Heights

17 Mar   Deri found guilty of accepting $155,000 in bribes, fraud and breach of trust

25 Mar   Balad's Azmi Bishara becomes the first Arab to run for prime minister

26 Mar   EU recognises the right to Palestinian self-determination including a state

31 Mar   Netanyahu belatedly supports the NATO bombing of Yugoslavia in Kosovo crisis

15 Apr   Former interior minister, Arieh Deri, sentenced to four years' imprisonment

25 Apr   Foreign Minister Sharon meets the Pope to discuss the Nazareth mosque

28 Apr   Palestinians vote to delay a unilateral declaration of independence

16 May   Benny Begin and Yitzhak Mordechai drop out of race for the premiership

17 May   Barak defeats Netanyahu 56 to 44 per cent in the election for prime minister

24 May   Israeli–American team detects the *Dakar* submarine on the seabed near Crete

12 June   Dalai Lama participates in a Jerusalem inter-faith meeting

13 June   Abu Daoud, planner of Olympics hostage-taking, barred from West Bank

14 June   Sharon defeats rivals Olmert and Shitreet in Likud procedural vote

15 June   Deri resigns as leader of Shas, clearing the coalition pathway

17 July   Kibbutz Gan Shmuel shop fined for opening on Shabbat

18 Aug   Hanoch Levin, playwright, poet, satirist, dies in Tel Aviv aged 55

30 Aug   Jordan shuts down Hamas offices in Amman

4 Sept   Wye II Agreement signed at Sharm el-Sheikh

5 Sept   Car bombings in Haifa and Tiberias carried out by Israeli Arabs

10 Oct   Cabinet authorises Barak to examine removal of settlement outposts

13 Oct   Yesha Council agrees to dismantling 12 settlement outposts

15 Oct   Yosef Burg, founder of the NRP, dies in Jerusalem aged 90

18 Oct   Nelson Mandela arrives in Israel after intervening on behalf of 13 Jews arrested in Iran

25 Oct   Safe passage route for Palestinians opened between Gaza and West Bank

7 Nov   Barak agrees to talk to leaders of the disabled after a 37-day strike

8 Nov   Final status talks begin in Ramallah

15 Dec   Barak and Farouk al-Sharaa resume Israeli–Syrian talks in Washington

Two factors dominated Israeli politics in an election year – the deep unpopularity of the prime minister, Benjamin Netanyahu, and the pivotal position of Shas, the Mizrahi party, which held the balance of power in the coalition.

The antagonism towards Netanyahu was occasionally attributed to his lack of experience, but more often to personal feelings against both Netanyahu and his increasingly vocal wife, Sara. Netanyahu attempted to straddle the pressure from the White House to make concessions on the West Bank and from cabinet ministers and from his own party, the Likud, not to. The election had been caused in essence by Netanyahu's willingness to sign the Wye Plantation Agreement which transferred 13 per cent of the territory of the West Bank to the Palestinians.

At the beginning of February, the Knesset voted 48–34 to approve the annual budget of $54 billion. This only came about because Netanyahu had pledged $135 million to projects which had been supported by haredi legislators. Both Shas and United Torah Judaism subsequently endorsed Netanyahu.

Netanyahu's former mentor, Moshe Arens, returned from retirement to stand against him as the unity candidate in the Likud primary – and was heavily defeated, achieving less than 20 per cent on a very low voter turnout. David Levy, who had first formed a faction within the Likud, then broken away, now allied his Gesher party with Barak's 'One Israel'. He accused Netanyahu of following 'Thatcherite policies' with his emphasis on the privatisation of state utilities.

Benny Begin left the Likud and formed a new party, Herut, which soon merged with Moledet and Tkuma to form the far Right National Union. Begin was admired for his honesty across the political spectrum.

Yitzhak Mordechai, Roni Milo and Dan Meridor also left the Likud to form the Centre party with the recently retired IDF head, Amnon Lipkin-Shahak. Many Mizrahim were offended after Mordechai, the minister of defence, was dismissed by Netanyahu on television. The traditional Mordechai, who was of Kurdish origin, then became a candidate for prime minister, visited the Western Wall and was greeted by Ovadia Yosef.

Netanyahu was also at odds with the White House and President Clinton, his wife, Hillary, and Vice-President Al Gore. All avoided meeting the Israeli prime minister. Pollsters close to Clinton, James Carville, Stanley Greenberg and Robert Shrum, all worked for Barak during the election. Their slogan for 'One Israel', imitating Clinton's famous epithet in the 1992 US election, was 'It's about change, stupid!'

In contrast, the Russian prime minister, Yevgeny Primakov, told Netanyahu on a visit to Moscow in March that if he was an Israeli, he would vote for Netanyahu. Assad too had visited Moscow and negotiated an arms deal. It was rumoured that Syria had acquired the technology for the dispersal of chemical agents such as VX gas. While representatives of political parties visited the USA to secure funding from philanthropists, Yisrael B'Aliya appealed to Jewish oligarchs in Russia.

Azmi Bishara of the National Democratic Alliance (Balad) became the first Arab to stand for the post of prime minister. He argued that Israel should be a state of all its citizens and not primarily a Jewish state. The Givat Haviva Centre for Peace indicated that during Netanyahu's tenure, Arab citizens who denied Israel's right to exist increased from 6.8 per cent to 18.4 per cent.

Shas, with ten seats in the Knesset, was in control of the Ministry of the Interior. It had taken a hard line regarding the status of the often secular Russian immigrants and their non-Jewish partners. This led in part to the establishment of new parties which looked to the large number of recent Russian immigrants – Sharansky's Yisrael B'Aliya in 1996 and Avigdor Lieberman's Yisrael Beiteinu in January 1999.

The ministry had also taken a hard line against advocates of religious pluralism and the right of non-orthodox representatives of Reform and Conservative Judaism to take their seats on municipal religious councils which had jurisdiction over the allocation of funds, supervision of kosher food and questions of status such as marriage and burial. The non-orthodox returned time and again to the Supreme Court, which continually ruled in their favour and instructed the Ministry of the Interior to carry out its rulings. When this did not happen, the ire of non-orthodox Jews in the Diaspora was aroused and, unlike in Israel, they were far from being a minority.

Shas's Eli Suissa then formulated the By-Pass Act, which required all members on the religious council in municipalities to abide by the rulings of the orthodox Chief Rabbinate. Suissa further considered reducing the size of such councils as well as delaying their meeting. At the end of January, the By-Pass bill was approved 50–49 on its third reading.

During the election campaign, Barak gave up on attracting the haredi vote and instead integrated the moderate orthodox party Meimad into his 'One Israel' alignment. He also favoured conscripting yeshiva students into the armed forces.

Shas had established a network of schools in poor neighbourhoods and faced a financial black hole in this endeavour. Ovadia Yosef wanted Shas to remain in government. He argued that the views of the Supreme Court were superseded by Jewish law. Shas utilised a 'J'Accuse' video by Deri in its election campaign.

Hundreds of thousands of yeshiva students were called upon to participate in a prayer vigil outside the Supreme Court to protest against the decisions on non-orthodox representation on religious councils and the possibility of a draft. The Supreme Court had also ruled that kibbutzim could open their doors on Shabbat. Barak, Mordechai and Netanyahu were conspicuously absent from the large haredi protest and each candidate avoided any direct comment on the question.

A counter-demonstration of fifty thousand supported the Supreme Court decisions and the writers Amos Oz, David Grossman and A. B. Yehoshua exhorted Israelis to support the Reform and Conservatives by joining their movements.

After Arieh Deri was sentenced to four years, he could formally remain in the Knesset while his appeal was being heard. Apart from the National Union's Benny Begin, no contender for the premiership categorically stated that they would not negotiate with Deri for fear of losing the Shas vote.

The election brought Barak victory, defeating Netanyahu by 56.1 per cent to 43.9 per cent for the office of prime minister. The three other contenders dropped out in the days before the election. However, Barak's 'One Israel' won only twenty-six seats and the Likud was down to nineteen.

New parties, Shinui, National Union, Yisrael Beiteinu and the Centre party, won between four and six seats eavh. Shas expanded to seventeen seats, to become the third largest party. Barak finally refused to accept Shas as a coalition partner unless Deri, who was appealing against his four-year sentence, was effectively ditched as leader. Despite death threats against the judges and the distribution in large numbers of a seventy-two-minute video proclaiming the flaws in the legal process, Deri eventually resigned as the leader of Shas.

Netanyahu resigned thirty minutes after the election results became clear. Barak formed his government, but appointed figures such as Yossi Beilin to inappropriate posts regarding the peace process and refused to establish an inner 'kitchen cabinet'. Barak pursued peace negotiations with Syria rather than with the Palestinians when redeployment became bogged down in disagreement between both sides.

At the end of February, the EU allowed Israel to join its research and development programme, thereby allowing it access to a fund of $15 billion with which to further develop its blossoming hi-tech industry. New Dimensions Software and Oshap were both sold to US firms for hundreds of millions of dollars.

277

The 2000s

https://shlomocohen.com/

The beginning of a new millennium provided Benjamin Netanyahu with a new political opportunity after his heavy defeat at the polls in 1999. Returning as minister of finance under Sharon, he accelerated the trend towards a neo-liberal economy. However, Sharon's plan for disengagement from Gaza led to a split in the Likud. After much hesitation, Netanyahu resigned to take charge of the rump of the Likud. Sharon's stroke and Olmert's legal problems provided the path for a return to power for Netanyahu in early 2009 after leading the Likud back from the lowest ebb in its history.

Netanyahu had learned to do a political pas de deux with his opponents. Inclined towards the US Republicans, Netanyahu is teaching 'a popular Israeli dance' to the new sceptical, Democrat president, Barack Obama. 'One step forward, two steps back'. Understand what is possible and repeat – advance and retreat as necessary.

Shlomo Cohen (*Israel Hayom* 6 September 2009)

2000

The Camp David meeting between Ehud Barak and Yasser Arafat ended in failure and both sides faced a concerted opposition at home.

Here the self-imposed obstacles are already apparent. Both Barak and Arafat are carrying planks, labelled 'red lines'. Many of the parties in Barak's coalition had recently departed. These are depicted as angry people running away from the Israeli delegation who are just about to enter the Camp David compound.

A huge 'standing orders' is lying on the negotiations table, clearly designed to make any agreement impossible.

Shmuel Katz (*Ma'ariv* n.d. 2000)

3 Jan   Talks between Israel and Syria resume in Shepherdstown

5 Jan   IDF withdraws from army bases in Nablus and Jenin

10 Jan   Mass rally opposing a Golan withdrawal takes place in Tel Aviv

27 Jan   State Comptroller fines 'One Israel' $3.2 million for faulty campaign financing

7 Feb   Hamas leader, Abdel Aziz Rantisi, is released from a PA prison

23 Feb   Singer Ofra Hazan dies of AIDS-related pneumonia aged 42

8 Mar   Supreme Court rules that the state cannot allocate land for exclusive use of Jews

20 Mar   Pope John Paul II arrives in Israel

26 Mar   Hafez Assad rejects peace proposals at a meeting with Clinton in Geneva

28 Mar   Police recommend that Netanyahu be charged with fraud and bribery

28 Mar   Y2hacK, an international hackers conference, takes place in Tel Aviv

29 Mar   UTJ oppose a Knesset bill granting equal rights to women in Israeli life

6 Apr   Insufficient evidence to charge President Weizman with bribery

12 Apr   Chinese president Jiang Zemin visits Israel

16 Apr   Police recommend charging Yitzhak Mordechai with sexual assault

7 May   Government approval for 25 per cent capital gains tax on income and interests

14 May   Cabinet votes 15–6 to transfer Abu Dis, Al-Azariya, Sawahara to the Palestinians

15 May   Sharon speaks at a Jerusalem settler rally amidst more West Bank violence

22 May   Supreme Court rules that women's prayer services should proceed at the Western Wall

24 May   Last Israeli troops leave southern Lebanon

29 May   Supreme Court rules that a lesbian couple can register as their child's mothers

5 June   Four are given prison terms for bridge collapse at 1997 Maccabiah Games

10 June   President Hafez Assad of Syria dies aged 69

20 June   Shas ministers temporarily resign from Barak's government

21 June   Meretz ministers resign from government, but support Barak coalition

9 July   Yisrael B'Aliya, NRP and Shas all resign from Barak's government

10 July   Ezer Weizman resigns as president

11 July   Barak tells Clinton that Israel has cancelled sale of Phalcon early warning system to China

25 July   Camp David summit ends without agreement between Barak and Arafat

31 July   Likud's Moshe Katsav is elected president after defeating Shimon Peres

3 Sept   Cabinet approves the dismantling of the Religious Affairs Ministry

22 Sept   Yehuda Amichai, Hebrew poet and writer, dies aged 76

28 Sept   Ariel Sharon visits the Temple Mount, triggering Palestinian violence

7 Oct   Joseph's tomb in Nablus is destroyed by a Palestinian mob

8 Oct   Old mosque in Tiberias is attacked by a Jewish mob

12 Oct   Crowd lynches two Israeli soldiers after storming a police station at El Bireh

12 Nov   Leah Rabin, widow of Yitzhak Rabin, dies aged 72

23 Dec   Clinton Parameters are presented to both sides of the conflict

281

Ehud Barak's timetable for the year included a framework agreement with the Palestinians by mid-February, a unilateral withdrawal of Israeli forces from south Lebanon by early July and a peace agreement with Assad's Syria by the summer.

The Israel–Palestine negotiations consequently became secondary to a drive to secure a peace agreement with Syria. Following talks by the US secretary of state, Madeleine Albright, with both Barak and Assad, negotiations were resumed for the first time since 1996 between Barak and the Syrian foreign minister, Farouk al-Sharaa, in Shepherdstown, West Virginia. The talks immediately went around in circles: there was no symbolic, three-way dinner with President Clinton at the very outset of talks.

Barak was primarily interested in security arrangements for the strategically important Golan Heights which looked down on settlements in the Galilee region. Areas would become demilitarised, early warning stations connected to US satellites installed and joint Israeli–Syrian patrols instituted to ensure compliance with the agreement.

Barak was so certain there would be a successful outcome to the talks that he requested $17 billion from the USA to cover the security costs of any withdrawal from the Golan Heights. This would include Apache helicopters, Tomahawk cruise missiles and information from US satellites. Both Yisrael B'Aliya and the NRP were opposed to any withdrawal from the Golan. Shas did not have any reservations since it did not regard the Golan as being part of the biblical Land of Israel and therefore any outcome, based on a land-for-peace formula, would save Israeli lives.

While research into desalination as well as the treatment and recycling of waste water was proceeding apace in Israel, at that time a third of all fresh water used in the country originated from the Sea of Galilee and Israel was concerned that this might fall under Syrian control. Israel focused on a withdrawal to the east of the original international border between Palestine and Syria, agreed by the British and French in 1923. Syria, however, wanted a total withdrawal to the pre-1967 borders.

Shuttle diplomacy to convey ideas and messages between the two countries had already been taking place during Netanyahu's time in office, carried out by intermediaries – the cosmetics magnate Ronald Lauder and the Lebanese-American businessman George Nader.

Syria wanted a clear declaration that Israel would withdraw from the Golan Heights and when this was not met, the Syrians refused to resume any talks. When Barak agreed to publicly state a willingness to withdraw, President Clinton believed that an agreement was now within reach and agreed to meet Assad in Geneva. The meeting was to no avail and negotiations collapsed. There had been press reports that Hafez Assad was seriously ill with cancer and diabetes. In the context of the meeting, his main aim may have been to secure the succession for his son. Within weeks of the abortive meeting, he was dead.

This attempt to negotiate with Syria and Barak's proposal to hold a referendum on any outcome was criticised by Yisrael B'Aliya, the NRP and Shas. The many settlers in the Golan Heights – mostly Labour supporters – mounted a vigorous, public campaign against any withdrawal. All this took place against the backdrop of a unilateral Israeli withdrawal from Lebanon and increased attacks from Hezbollah, whose arsenals were being filled by convoys of Syrian and Iranian armaments.

The unilateral withdrawal from south Lebanon in late May after a period of eighteen years took place six weeks before the specified date. Israel remained in control of the Shaba'a farms. Many members of the South Lebanon Army and their families subsequently fled into northern Israel. Hezbollah militants replaced them.

Barak's 'One Israel' had won only twenty-six seats in the 1999 election. The extra thirty-five seats to attain a blocking majority for any government were secured by enlisting parties that were fundamentally critical of both peace proposals and religious reforms. In particular, the devoutly secular Meretz and the Mizrahi Shas, the third biggest party, were diametrically opposed in their respective world views. The UTJ had opposed a Knesset vote in late March supporting equal rights for women in every sector of Israeli life.

The focus of this clash was the Education Ministry, whose minister was Meretz's Yossi Sarid, and the cash-strapped Shas school system. Sarid insisted that in return for financial aid, the schools would have to meet specific educational criteria and reform their administration. Ovadia Yosef, Shas's spiritual mentor, in frustration suggested that Sarid should be 'obliterated from the Jewish people and surely God would wipe his name out'. In the aftermath of the Rabin assassination, the Attorney-General ordered an investigation. Shas then threatened to withdraw its seventeen MKs from Barak's unwieldy coalition if this happened.

This divergence was accentuated by Shas's indifference to the Melchior Commission to find a resolution to the question of religious pluralism. Rabbi Melchior suggested a five-day week and a greater openness to the secularists. Instead Reform Judaism's Hebrew Union College in Jerusalem was vandalised and Conservative Judaism's Ya'ar Ramot synagogue was set on fire.

The negotiations with the Palestinians also never achieved any final resolution. Redeployments were agreed from specific territory and repeatedly postponed. Barak's proposal to transfer the villages of Anata, Beitunia and Ubeidiya near Jerusalem to Palestinian control brought a threat of resignation from Natan Sharansky and eventually the withdrawal of both Yisrael B'Aliya and the NRP from the coalition. Barak never implemented the proposition and further marginalised the idea that Abu Dis, half a mile from the Old City Walls, should become the legislative centre for the Palestinians.

This idea had emerged from the Beilin–Abu Mazen Agreement which had been completed just before Rabin's assassination, but never actually adopted. In July, all three parties formally resigned from the government. This was capped by Barak's failure to secure an agreement with Arafat at Camp David and David Levy's resignation as foreign minister. Moshe Katsav also unexpectedly defeated Shimon Peres for the presidency.

In response to this collapse, Barak attempted a 'secular revolution'. The interior minister called for the removal of the nationality clause from the identity card and the Religious Affairs Ministry was dismantled. There was support in the polls for the introduction of civil marriage in Israel and permission for El Al to fly on Shabbat. The survival of the government and the ongoing negotiations with the Palestinians was guaranteed by the votes of the Arab parties which remained outside government. All this was dashed with the onset of the polarising violence of the al-Aqsa Intifada. This distanced the Arab parties from Barak's government and extinguished its private support.

The al-Aqsa Intifada began at the end of September when the Likud leader, Ariel Sharon, visited the Temple Mount. This was seen as a provocation by many Palestinians and resulted in the deaths of dozens of people in clashes with the police. Low-level violence now mushroomed into a full-scale uprising. An ancient synagogue was set on fire in Jericho, while Israeli soldiers who had lost their way were lynched by a mob in a Ramallah police station. Israeli Arabs lost their lives in demonstrations while helicopter gunships attacked Ramallah and Gaza in retaliatory actions. Arafat attempted to regain control while the Arab world strongly condemned Israel. Twelve-year-old Mohammed al-Durrah, killed in crossfire, became the iconic symbol of the violence. His death was the subject of a debate in the wider world as to who was actually responsible for the tragedy. Failing to agree a national unity government, Barak and Sharon now agreed to an early election for prime minister, in part to prevent an early political comeback by Netanyahu.

283

2001

ממשלת אחדות

Ariel Sharon, who succeeded Netanyahu in 1999, was originally seen as little more than a caretaker leader of the Likud. Yet the outbreak of violence during the al-Aqsa Intifada undoubtedly helped him to win the national election and defeat Labour's Ehud Barak by a landslide.

Here a smiling Sharon is seen to be having his revenge on the Left's strong opposition to his past actions. A lamb, labelled 'Labour', is being carried to the slaughter. The title is 'Unity Government', subsequently formed with the far Right and religious parties.

Ze'ev (*Ha'aretz* 9 February 2001)

1 Jan   Car bomb in Netanya injures 30

3 Jan   Arafat gives conditional approval to the Clinton Parameters at White House

17 Jan   Hisham Miki, head of Palestinian TV, gunned down in a Gaza hotel

21 Jan   Taba talks commence in a last attempt to resolve Clinton Parameter differences

6 Feb   Sharon wins an overwhelming victory, defeating Barak 62.5 to 37.4 per cent

14 Feb   Palestinian drives a bus into a crowd near Holon, killing 8, injuring 26

19 Feb   Orr Commission inquiry into the deaths of Israeli Arabs opens in Jerusalem

20 Feb   Ehud Barak resigns as Labour leader

26 Feb   Labour's central committee votes to join Sharon in a national unity government

7 Mar   Knesset repeals the legislation for the direct election of a prime minister

26 Mar   Ten-month-old Shalhevet Pass shot dead in Hebron

27 Mar   Suicide bombings in Talpiot and French Hill in Jerusalem

30 Apr   Yitzhak Mordechai given an 18-month suspended sentence for sexual assault

30 Apr   Mitchell Report links the settlements to ongoing violence in West Bank

5 May   Lebanese boat *Santorini*, carrying PFLP-GC weapons, is intercepted

18 May   Hamas suicide bomber kills six in the HaSharon Mall, Netanya

21 May   Sharon announces a unilateral ceasefire

31 May   Faisal Husseini dies of a heart attack in Kuwait aged 60

1 June   Hamas bombing of Dolphinarium discotheque kills 21, mainly teenagers

22 June   Sharon heckled at Likud central committee meeting for self-restraint

9 Aug   Suicide bombing of Sbarro pizza restaurant in Jerusalem, 15 killed

12 Aug   Orient House, PLO headquarters in East Jerusalem, closed down

18 Aug   Hillel Kook (Peter Bergson) dies in Kfar Shmaryahu aged 76

27 Aug   Helicopter missile kills PFLP secretary-general Mustafa Zabri in Ramallah

9 Sept   Suicide bombing of Nahariya station; car bomb near Netanya

9 Sept   Cabinet deadlocked on plan for buffer zone between Israel and West Bank

12 Sept   Israel declares Day of Public Mourning marking 9/11

23 Sept   Sharon proclaims support for a Palestinian state for the first time

26 Sept   Peres and Arafat meet at Gaza airport, proclaiming new ceasefire

17 Oct   Tourism minister, Rehavam Ze'evi, killed by PFLP in a Jerusalem hotel

22 Oct   In Jerusalem, 100,000 people demonstrate for Arafat's removal

28 Oct   Islamic Jihad kill civilians in Hadera and Bethlehem

2 Nov   Eliezer Menaham Schach, mitnaged leader, dies aged 102

1 Dec   Hamas suicide bombing in Ben-Yehuda, Jerusalem kills 13

2 Dec   Hamas suicide bus bombing in Tel Amal, Haifa kills 15

25 Dec   'Fuad' Ben-Eliezer elected Labour party leader

285

The campaign to elect a prime minister – as opposed to voting for political parties – pitched a weakened Barak against an internationally controversial Ariel Sharon. Barak's election campaign referred to Sharon's part in the Lebanon war of 1982 and to the killing of Palestinians in the camps at Sabra and Shatilla, but as his walk on the Temple Mount in September the year before had demonstrated, history had moved on.

Sharon formed a broad coalition of the centre Right, the far Right, the religious and the Russians on a campaigning slogan of 'Only Sharon will bring peace'. He was vague on any political platform apart from promising a long-term interim agreement with the Palestinians, no division of Jerusalem and retaining control of the Jordan Valley.

Barak seemed to have frittered away all his political capital through bad judgement and bad luck. The Arab electorate was disillusioned following the killing of thirteen Israeli Arabs during displays of solidarity with the Palestinians. Barak had taken very little notice of their concerns. On election day only 13 per cent of Israeli Arabs actually turned out to vote – and many of them cast a blank sheet of paper into the voting box. This marked a historic breach with the Israeli Left.

The Russians, who had initially voted for Labour under Rabin, moved to the Right. Sharon was perceived as a strong leader in the Soviet tradition who would quell the Intifada. A Russian-speaker and a secularist, he was also seen as someone who would support them in the face of the demands of Shas, which was in control of the Interior Ministry. Both Sharansky and Lieberman had declared their support for him.

The Clinton Parameters proposed allocating sovereignty over the different components of the Jerusalem conundrum to both Israelis and Palestinians. Both Barak and Arafat expressed acceptance with serious caveats, while the Israeli cabinet voted to approve the Parameters. Even though Barak had spoken about 'unilateral separation', the National Religious had become very anxious about his negotiations with the Palestinians and his general stand on peace-making. His willingness to debate the Temple Mount was regarded as heretical in many religious quarters, despite his comment to the Chief Rabbinical Council and to the Clinton White House that he would not allow the Palestinians to control the site.

In early January, Sharansky and Ehud Olmert, the Likud mayor of Jerusalem, organised a rally to protest against Barak's policies regarding the Temple Mount. It was attended by Diaspora leaders such as Ronald Lauder and rabbis such as Jonathan Sacks who believed that the issue transcended a normal silence on criticism of Israeli government policies.

The rally was also attended by Netanyahu, who had emerged successfully from a series of indictments ranged against him. Since he was no longer a sitting member of the Knesset, he was thereby disqualified from standing as a candidate for prime minister. Opinion polls, however, favoured Netanyahu over both Sharon and Barak.

The increasing violence of the Intifada made many voters query Arafat's ability and willingness to confront his Islamist opponents. At the very beginning of the year, a car bomb injured thirty people in Netanya. The settlers reacted militantly to the increasing number of attacks in the West Bank and Gaza and politically to the Clinton Parameters which proposed the withdrawal of the IDF.

The late Meir Kahane's son and founder of Kahane Chai, , Binyamin Ze'ev, was killed together with his wife in a drive-by shooting near Ofra. Kahane Chai had been banned from standing in previous Israeli elections.

As Clinton's tenure in office began to be measured in days, the peace camp became increasingly fatalistic about the decay of the Oslo process. The talks at Taba were unable to break the impasse between Israelis and Palestinians even though some questions were resolved. The targeted killings of Palestinians divided the peace camp. Questions were raised when Thabet

Thabet, Fatah's representative in Tulkarem, was killed. He had previously worked with Israeli peace activists. Barak's efforts were perceived as erratic, while Arafat was unable to contain the suicide bombers. Now aged seventy-two, Arafat was seen as ailing and dictatorial. His comments about the Israeli use of depleted uranium were viewed as both bizarre and counter-productive.

Sharon distanced himself from the past and projected himself as the avuncular grandfather of the nation. He easily demolished Barak at the polls on a very low turn-out of voters.

The Intifada continued, with drivers shot and killed on the road at Beit Jalla, Rachel's Tomb in Bethlehem coming under gunfire, mortar shells dropping on Netzarim and roadside bombs exploding at Kfar Darom. The IDF retaliated with targeted killings of figures such as Massoud Ayad and Iyad Abu Harb. In April, the IDF entered the Khan Yunis refugee camp to engage militants in Operation Enjoyable Song. In August, a helicopter gunship killed the secretary-general of the PFLP, Mustafa Ali Zibri, in al-Bireh. In response, the PFLP killed the tourism minister, Rehavam Ze'evi, at a hotel in Jerusalem.

Islamist suicide bombers repeatedly attacked civilians in Netanya, Hod Hasharon, Binyamina, Kfar Saba, Hadera and Haifa. In Jerusalem, the neighbourhoods of French Hill, Talpiot, Gilo and Ma'alot Dafna were attacked. Babies were often caught in the crossfire: ten-month-old Shalhevet Pass and five-month-old Iman Hije were killed. Young people were targeted – whether sitting in restaurants or waiting for a bus. Copying the example of Hezbollah, videos of suicide bombers were published afterwards.

Following the bombing of the HaSharon Mall in Netanya in May, F-16 fighters were employed in attacks on strategic sites in the West Bank and Gaza. The use of American-made aircraft also brought US criticism. The bombing of the Dolphinarium disco on the Tel Aviv seafront, killing mainly Russian teenagers, was a watershed. The cabinet was divided on how to implement separation and the idea of a buffer zone was shelved. Municipal councils close to the Green Line constructed barriers to prevent suicide bombers from entering Israel.

The Labour party was divided over joining a national unity government under Sharon, and there was anger that Barak had rescinded his resignation before resigning a second time. Barak wanted to become defence minister, but Benjamin Ben-Eliezer was appointed instead. Shimon Peres joined Sharon's coalition as foreign minister; however, this caused a schism with his long-time dovish supporters. Within weeks, the Knesset abolished the recent practice of one vote for the prime minister plus another for the party – and reverted to the old system.

Although Sharon employed his son, Omri, to act as a back channel to Arafat, his public approach was no negotiations under fire. Peres was grudgingly given permission to meet Arafat, but produced no breakthrough. Proclamations of ceasefires came and went. Peres became increasingly isolated in cabinet, even from his colleagues in the Labour party, as the number of suicide bombings increased.

Arafat was the first leader in the Arab world to condemn 9/11 and Peres perceived this as a possible diplomatic opening with the Palestinians. While both US President George W. Bush and UK Prime Minister Tony Blair pledged support for a future Palestinian state, the Islamist attacks continued. Anthony Zinni and William Burns were sent to the Middle East to act as American mediators to resolve an increasingly polarising situation. Sharon came under pressure from within the Likud, and especially from Netanyahu silently on the sidelines, to be more forceful in confronting the bombers, stopping IDF redeployments and supporting the settlers. In both the USA and Israel, Arafat increasingly came to be seen as irrelevant.

2002

A Hamas bomb was detonated as guests sat down to a Passover recitation of the biblical exodus from Egypt at a hotel in Netanya. The title refers to the search for leaven on the night before Passover. Arafat is offered a pan and brush to make a stand and sweep up weapons of war rather than breadcrumbs. The Israeli navy had captured the Iranian ship the *Karine A*, laden with armaments believed to be destined for Arafat's Fatah at the height of the al-Aqsa Intifada.

The note on the table highlights Arafat's approach in public and implicitly in private. It states: 'Embarking on a ceasefire'.

Shmuel Katz (*Ma'ariv* n.d. 2002)

3 Jan The Israeli navy intercepts the *Karine A*, laden with Iranian arms

14 Jan Raed Karmi, al-Aqsa Martyrs Brigade head, is killed in Tulkarem

17 Jan Al-Aqsa Martyrs Brigade bombing kills six at a barmitzvah in Hadera

24 Jan Senior Hamas commander Bakr Hamadan killed in Gaza

25 Jan Islamic Jihad suicide bomber injures 24 in a Tel Aviv mall

16 Feb PFLP suicide bomber attacks mall in Karnei Shomron settlement

19 Feb Six Israeli soldiers killed by gunmen at a Ramallah roadblock

27 Feb Azmi Bishara's trial resumes in Jerusalem

9 Mar Hamas bomber from Silwan kills 11 at Café Moment after peace demonstration

12 Mar Elon and Lieberman resign from coalition government

27 Mar Passover seder bombing of Park Hotel, Netanya, kills 30

28 Mar Saudi Peace Initiative endorsed by Arab League in Beirut

29 Mar Operation Defensive Shield, Israeli military incursion into West Bank, begins

31 Mar Hamas bombs Israeli Arab-owned Matza restaurant, Haifa, killing 16

2 Apr Palestinian militants seek refuge in the Church of the Nativity in Bethlehem

15 Apr Marwan Bargouti, Tanzim leader, captured in Ramallah

28 Apr Cabinet votes against allowing UN fact-finding mission to visit Jenin

2 May Arafat emerges from the IDF siege of his Ramallah headquarters

7 May Hamas suicide bomber kills 16 at a Rishon l'Zion games club

10 May As IDF leaves Bethlehem church, 13 Palestinian militants go into exile

12 May Likud central committee opposes Sharon and votes against a Palestinian state

5 June Islamic Jihad car bomb blows up bus near Megiddo prison, killing 17

16 June Bulldozers start work on security fence between Israel and West Bank

19 June Petition against suicide bombing signed by 55 Palestinian intellectuals

22 June Operation Determined Path begins a new military incursion into West Bank

24 June Bush gives Rose Garden address, calling for a new Palestinian leadership

22 July Salah Shehade, commander of Hamas's military wing, killed in Gaza

23 July Knesset passes Tal Law, allowing yeshiva students a decision year before their IDF service

31 July Nine killed in bombing of Hebrew University's Frank Sinatra cafeteria

2 Sept Marwan Bargouti's trial begins in Tel Aviv

21 Oct TNT-laden jeep rams bus at Karkur Junction, killing 14

30 Oct Knesset budget vote 67–45 forces Labour to exit from government

17 Nov Abba Eban dies in Tel Aviv aged 87

19 Nov Amram Mitzna defeats Ben-Eliezer for the Labour party leadership

28 Nov Israeli-owned Mombasa hotel attacked by al-Qaeda operatives

28 Nov Sharon defeats Netanyahu for Likud leadership

At the UN, Palestinian representatives pressed for the return of all refugees who had left since 1948 and the restoration of their property. The al-Aqsa Intifada took the lives of large numbers of civilians on both sides of the conflict. It was characterised by the periodic use of Palestinian suicide bombers and Israeli retaliatory action. Attempts by figures on both sides to halt the conflict and return to diplomacy and dialogue were continually thwarted by new outbreaks of violence to interrupt periods of calm and hope.

Palestinian Islamist organisations Hamas and Islamic Jihad, known for their use of suicide bombers, were now joined by nationalist groups the PFLP and the al-Aqsa Martyrs Brigade, which had emerged out of Fatah. They had close ties to the Tanzim, a group of young Palestinian militants originally formed in 1995 to support Arafat who, with the start of the Intifada, were often involved in attacks against Israelis, including suicide bombings. The Islamists who depended on Iranian support opposed the Oslo process in its entirety, while the nationalists opposed Oslo II which postulated a partition of the West Bank. In addition, a new generation of Palestinians, fashioned by the post-Oslo years, opposed the older returnees from Tunis. Many were disillusioned with Arafat's leadership and the lack of good governance and a clear vision of the future.

The al-Aqsa Intifada was far more violent than the first Intifada – and crucially lacked any participation from the Israeli peace camp. It was characterised by suicide bombers, car bombs, gun attacks and knifings. While there were attacks on the inhabitants of the West Bank settlements, there were also bombings of crowds in malls and at bus stops in Tel Aviv, Haifa, Netanya, Hadera and other major cities within Israel itself.

Jerusalem was repeatedly attacked because of its geographical location. In January, a Palestinian militant carrying an M-16 assault rifle began to fire on passers-by in Jaffa Road, a central thoroughfare in Jerusalem. A second attack took place in the same location a few days later. Such incidents often happened when crowds had gathered to mark the beginning or end of festivals. The bombings on the eve of Passover in Netanya and the gatherings in Jerusalem after Shabbat were designed to undermine Israelis psychologically.

Family celebrations in Hadera and Beit Israel in Jerusalem were targeted. In Hadera, a batmitzvah was attacked by the al-Aqsa Martyrs Brigade, killing several guests, in retaliation for the killing of Raed Karmi. The IDF then proceeded to demolish the Palestinian television and radio broadcasting headquarters in Ramallah. Young children on both sides of the conflict were often victims of such attacks.

Tulkarem was temporarily occupied by the IDF and a sweep of the town resulted in fifty people being detained. Israeli assaults on known militants in their homes in Gaza and the West Bank or in their cars often resulted in the killing of their families as well. The IDF's official policy was to avoid civilian casualties.

Unlike the first Intifada, the advent of the suicide bomber eliminated the possibility of cooperation between Israelis and Palestinians. The nihilism of the conflict silenced both the Palestinian intelligentsia and the Israeli peace camp. The bombing of the popular Matza restaurant in Haifa, owned by Israeli Arabs, killed entire families at lunch. The bombing of Café Moment in the Rehavia neighbourhood of Jerusalem occurred 200 yards away from the Prime Minister's Office where a demonstration, demanding withdrawal from the West Bank and Gaza, had just taken place. Several protesters were killed.

During the summer, Sari Nusseibeh, Hanan Ashrawi and several score leaders of Palestinian society signed a letter opposing the use of suicide bombing. It asked the suicide bombers to reconsider their acts because they led to 'more hatred and animosity between the two peoples'. However, opinion polls suggested that given the polarisation between Israelis and Palestinians, they were now in a distinct minority. In Israel, voices for a cessation of violence such as those of Yossi Sarid and Yossi Beilin were marginalised.

Although Sharon had stated on more than one occasion that he would not negotiate under fire, he did maintain contact through back channels. He had to balance criticism from far Right parties in his cabinet, such as National Union and Yisrael Beiteinu, with a desire to end the violence. His rival for the leadership of the Likud, Netanyahu, now outside the Knesset, positioned himself to the right of Sharon as an advocate of tougher action against the Palestinians. Sharon's standing in the opinion polls plummeted as the frequency of the suicide bombings increased.

The bombing of the Park Hotel in Netanya as guests gathered at the beginning of Passover to recite the story of the exodus from Egypt forced Sharon to call up twenty thousand reservists and mount Operation Defensive Shield, a major incursion into the West Bank to seek out militants, to dismantle workshops for manufacturing Qassam missiles and to confiscate arms caches. The building of a security separation barrier commenced.

Cabinet members had begun to describe Arafat as 'irrelevant' after two bomb attacks in Haifa. The implication was that he was impotent to stop the suicide bombings and had no control over militant factions. This co-existed with Netanyahu's accusation that he was responsible and therefore he should be expelled. This was augmented by the belief that Arafat was implicated in the affair of the *Karine A*, a ship on which were found large quantities of Iranian arms and ammunition bound for Palestinian militants. The arms had been loaded on the island of Kish near the Iranian coast.

While the Saudis, China and the Europeans – as well as Foreign Minister Peres – argued that Arafat was the only person who could bring the violence to a halt, the Bush administration became increasingly critical. When former President Clinton and Vice-President Dick Cheney visited Israel on separate occasions, they made no effort to meet or contact Arafat.

When the US envoy to the Middle East, Anthony Zinni, returned to Israel in early January, the IDF withdrew from Nablus and lifted the blockades around Hebron and Qalquilya. Zinni arrived with the intention of getting both sides to agree to a ceasefire plan, drafted by the CIA director, George Tenet. He made no progress in resolving the dispute or implementing the work of his predecessors, George Tenet and George Mitchell. Sharon argued that he wanted a week without violence before making any moves.

At the end of January, the US administration began to criticise Arafat directly and to place such comments in the context of the link with the *Karine A* arms ship. At the end of June, in his Rose Garden declaration, Bush became the first US president to call for a contiguous Palestinian state. He said that 'if Palestinians embrace democracy, confront corruption and firmly reject terror, they can count on American support for the creation of a provisional state of Palestine'. Bush also suggested that a new Palestinian leadership, 'not compromised by terror', be elected. Arafat responded by placing the spiritual leader of Hamas, Sheikh Yassin, under house arrest in Gaza. Sharon welcomed the comments about Arafat whereas Peres was more sceptical.

All this helped Sharon nationally in Israel and in his contest with Netanyahu. The Intifada had damaged Israel's economy, with 300,000 unemployed and a $7 billion budget deficit. Sharon's efforts to cut benefits and welfare spending in order to devote more resources to combating the Intifada were opposed by Shas, UTJ and Labour, which led to the collapse of the government and to new elections.

291

2003

Dry Bones

Ariel Sharon used the term 'occupation' to the shock of many in his party. He then backtracked shortly afterwards, stating that he mis-spoke and should have said 'control over disputed lands'.

However, this was clearly a signal that Sharon was moving towards the political centre and inducing a split within the Likud.

Ya'akov Kirschen (*Jerusalem Post* 1 June 2003)

5 Jan	Al-Aqsa Martyrs Brigade suicide bombers kill 23 at a Tel Aviv bus station
6 Jan	Cyril Kern money laundering affair, implicating Sharon, is leaked to the press
28 Jan	Likud defeats Labour under Amram Mitzna 38 seats to 19 in the election
1 Feb	First Israeli astronaut, Ilan Ramon, dies during the re-entry of the space shuttle *Columbia*
16 Feb	United Torah Judaism's Uri Lupoliansky becomes Jerusalem mayor
16 Feb	Cabinet decides to bring 20,000 Falash Mura from Ethiopia
17 Feb	Hamas military leader Riad Abu Zeid killed in Gaza by undercover unit
18 Feb	Isser Harel, creator of the Shin Bet and the Mossad, dies aged 91
21 Feb	IAEA visits new uranium enrichment plant at Natanz, Iran
5 Mar	Hamas suicide bomber kills 17, mainly students, on Haifa bus
8 Mar	Ibrahim al-Makadmeh, a Hamas founder, killed by helicopter gunship
16 Mar	Rachel Corrie, International Solidarity Movement activist, killed in Gaza by IDF bulldozer
19 Mar	Mahmoud Abbas becomes prime minister of the Palestinian Authority
20 Mar	US-led invasion of Iraq commences
30 Mar	Islamic Jihad bombing of London Café in Netanya injures 54
13 Apr	Public dispute between Arafat and Abbas over candidates for new cabinet
14 Apr	US forces in Iraq capture PLF head, Abul Abbas, hijacker of *Achille Lauro*
30 Apr	British suicide bombers kill 3, injure 50, in Mike's Place, a Tel Aviv bar
13 May	Raed Salah and other northern branch Islamic Movement arrested
18 May	Hamas bus suicide bomber kills seven at French Hill, Jerusalem
25 May	Cabinet approves Road Map 12–7 with 4 abstentions
26 May	Sharon tells Likud MKs that the occupation is bad for Israelis and Palestinians
4 June	Bush meets Sharon, Abbas and Abdullah in Aqaba
11 June	Hamas suicide bus bombing kills 17 in Jerusalem
29 June	Palestinian militant groups declare a *hudna* (ceasefire)
30 June	Israelis and Palestinians resume sharing security responsibility in Gaza
2 July	Vicky Knafo marches 120 miles from Mitzpe Ramon to protest against cuts to welfare
27 July	Black Hebrews are granted permanent residency in Israel
19 Aug	Jerusalem bus suicide bomber kills 24 and injures more than 100
21 Aug	Hamas leader, Ismail Abu Shanab, killed in a missile strike in Gaza
2 Sept	Orr Commission Report on the killing of Israeli Arabs is published
6 Sept	Mahmoud Abbas resigns as prime minister in a dispute with Arafat
9 Sept	Hamas suicide bomber kills seven at Café Hillel in Jerusalem
4 Oct	Islamic Jihad bombs Haifa's Maxim restaurant, owned by Arabs and Jews
1 Dec	Yossi Beilin–Yasser Abed Rabbo Geneva Initiative launched
18 Dec	Sharon announces disengagement plan from Gaza and northern West Bank

293

The election victory of the Likud, which won thirty-eight seats to Labour's nineteen, was a resounding vote of confidence in Ariel Sharon and his handling of the al-Aqsa Intifada. His opponent, Amram Mitzna, the former mayor of Haifa, put forward a dovish platform which featured a willingness to unilaterally withdraw from the West Bank and to engage in negotiations with Arafat. In the midst of an ongoing campaign of suicide bombing, such an approach did not resonate with the Israeli voter and marked the diminution of Labour's centrality in the political arena – even though Mitzna criticised Sharon for not moving faster to construct a security barrier.

In 1992, Labour and Meretz together accounted for fifty-six seats – in 2003, they accounted for twenty-five. The Russians' vote had moved broadly to the Right. Sharon gained 80 per cent of the Russians' vote against Barak as they gradually became part of Israeli society. One-quarter of IDF soldiers were immigrants from the former Soviet Union. This process diminished the attraction for Natan Sharansky's Yisrael B'Aliya, which decided to merge with the Likud.

The advance of Tommy Lapid's Shinui heralded the possibility of a secular coalition of Likud, Labour, Shinui and One Nation, amounting to seventy-five seats. Sharon instead allied himself with the National Religious and the far Right.

This victory overcame several ongoing scandals – an unusual transfer of $1.5 million, front companies to channel election campaign funding, and dubious deals involving Sharon's sons, his long-time friend Cyril Kern, the Austrian businessman Martin Schlaff, the Israeli building contractor Dudi Appel and a US company, Annex Research Ltd, established by his lawyer, Dov Weisglass.

In addition, there were severe economic problems owing to the onset of the Intifada. The economy shrank dramatically and unemployment reached 10.5 per cent. Few tourists now visited Israel and investment in hi-tech companies had fallen by 43 per cent compared with 2001.

Israel waited for the expected US-led invasion of Iraq and wondered what the consequences would be for the country. Twelve thousand reservists were called up in Israel. Batteries of the Arrow anti-ballistic missile system which could fire at six incoming missiles simultaneously were installed. This was backed up by the arrival of US Patriot-3 missiles. While gas masks and sealed rooms were invoked once more for fear of biological and chemical weapons, US forces explored Iraq's western desert to prevent a repeat of Scud missiles falling on Tel Aviv.

The defeat of the Iraqi forces raised the possibility of a reopening of the oil pipeline from Mosul to Haifa. It also opened up the possibility of a push by Iran to gain influence amongst Iraq's Shi'ite communities. Shi'ites made up 60 per cent of the Iraqi population. Shi'ite clerics had rushed from Iran to visit the holy sites in Najaf and Karbala. This coincided with Iran's desire to develop its uranium enrichment facilities at Natanz.

The standing of Yasser Arafat had fallen not only within Israel and the United States, but also within the Palestinian territories. The pattern of suicide bombings and Israeli retaliation continued unabated, interrupted by short periods of calm. Several Israeli cabinet members such as Mofaz, Netanyahu and Silvan Shalom began to advocate the exiling of Arafat, whom they suspected of being unwilling or unable to contain the killing. While Sharon refused to meet Arafat, he preferred to relegate him to a ceremonial figure, a president without political power, by promoting instead the idea of a prime minister. Arafat had left the besieged Muqataa in Ramallah for only one day during the past year. Under intense American pressure, he gave way in March and appointed his long-time colleague Mahmoud Abbas as prime minister. Within weeks, there was a dispute between the two as to the composition of the new Palestinian cabinet. Abbas wished to ditch Arafat stalwarts and bring in Mohammed Dahlan to deal with security. He further believed that greater gains could be obtained through non-violent resistance. Abbas resigned after less than six months in the post.

Talks in Cairo between the Palestinian Authority (PA) and Hamas in January failed to reach any conclusion. Hamas wanted a 40 per cent representation in PA institutions. Under Arafat, elections had been postponed, the draft constitution shelved and reforms delayed. Although the al-Aqsa Martyrs Brigades and the PFLP had participated in suicide bombings, it was Hamas and Islamic Jihad which maintained an increasing influence amongst Palestinians.

Israel responded to attacks on civilians by using helicopter gunships which targeted senior Hamas figures. The firing of Qassam rockets at Sderot near the Gaza border was followed by attempts to kill the military and political leadership of Hamas. In late June, the Islamists declared a *hudna* – a ceasefire – and for six weeks there was little violence. The Jerusalem bus bombing in mid-August ended the *hudna* but initiated attempts to assassinate Ahmed Yassin – often accompanied by the 'collateral damage' of family and neighbours in attacks on apartments.

Such actions brought international condemnation and a public letter from twenty-seven Israeli combat pilots who announced their intention not to carry out such missions.

Palestinian actions began to descend into attacks on their own people. The governor of Jenin was pulled out of a car by masked men and beaten up. Khalil Shikaki's Palestinian Centre for Policy and Survey Research was attacked by a mob because it was about to publish a scientific survey indicating that a majority of refugees did not wish to return, but preferred instead to receive monetary compensation or the possibility of settling in other locations.

The publication of the Road Map – a three-phase peace plan by 'the Quartet' of the USA, Russia, EU and UN – ran into problems straight away when the Israeli cabinet approved it, but rendered it effectively impotent with a plethora of caveats. There was a strong opposition to a settlement freeze and Sharon therefore wanted any discussion of the settlements deferred from the first phase to the last. While it met many Palestinian needs, the Road Map did not meet Sharon's basic demand for an initial cessation of violence. Palestinian militants were not prepared to lay down their arms until they could visualise the shape of any agreement.

295

Sharon shuffled Silvan Shalom and Netanyahu such that the latter unwillingly became finance minister. In 2002, the performance of Israel's economy was the worst since 1953 and 1.3 million people were below the poverty line. The bursting of the dot-com bubble halted the development of Israel's hi-tech industry. Netanyahu therefore began to reduce the $6 billion deficit by a series of free market reforms which would liberalise the economy. He advocated a smaller government and lower taxes, curtailing the welfare state by cutting the public sector, privatising public utilities and promoting an entrepreneurial private enterprise. Education was targeted with a reduction in the number of teachers, and foreign workers were deported. Foreign investors such as the State of South Carolina and Guardian Insurance in the USA began to invest heavily in Israel Bonds.

Sharon intended that the stationing of Palestine Authority patrols on Gaza's northern border would prevent the firing of Qassams so that the IDF could gradually leave the area. Sharon and Ehud Olmert began to publicise their willingness to withdraw from parts of the West Bank and Gaza, signalling that Beit El and Shilo might have to be dispensed with. Sharon now categorically referred to 'the occupation' and told the cabinet that 'controlling 3.5 million Palestinians cannot go on forever'. He proposed a disengagement plan from Gaza and was in favour of the Quartet's Road Map. In May, only twelve ministers among twenty-three had voted in favour of the Road Map; now Netanyahu became increasingly favoured as a replacement for Sharon within the Likud.

2004

The suicide bombing of Maxim's, the Arab–Jewish-owned restaurant in Haifa, was the subject of an artwork at a genocide conference in Stockholm's Museum of National Antiquities. Twenty-one people, Jews and Arabs, were killed. The artwork, entitled 'Snow White and the Madness of Truth', was the subject of a protest by the Israeli ambassador who was escorted out of the museum.

In the midst of attacks on institutions outside the Middle East, Sweden is seen here as the exception.

The handler instructs his bombers: 'Salah, you go to Paris. Mahmud, to Rome. You, Abed, to London. Jamal, you're off to Washington. And Bassam – take these flowers to Stockholm.'

Moshik Lin (n.d. 2004)

29 Jan	Al-Aqsa Martyrs Brigade suicide bus bombing in Jerusalem kills 11
29 Jan	Major prisoner exchange between Israel and Hezbollah
22 Feb	Al-Aqsa Brigade suicide bus bombing near Liberty Bell kills eight
28 Feb	Islamic Jihad commander Mohammad Judah killed in Gaza
14 Mar	Suicide bombing of Ashdod port kills ten
16 Mar	Yossi Beilin elected leader of Meretz
22 Mar	Ahmed Yassin, spiritual mentor of Hamas, killed in Gaza by helicopter gunship
14 Apr	Bush recognises Israeli claim to parts of West Bank in letter to Sharon
17 Apr	Abdel Aziz al-Rantisi, new leader of Hamas, killed in missile strike
21 Apr	Mordechai Vanunu released after 18 years in prison in Ashkelon
2 May	Islamic Jihad kill pregnant woman and four daughters near Kissufim
2 May	In Likud referendum, 60 per cent vote against Gaza disengagement
12 May	Operation Rainbow launched to destroy tunnels between Gaza and Egypt
4 June	Sharon dismisses far Right cabinet ministers Elon and Lieberman
6 June	Cabinet votes to withdraw from Gaza 14–7 but no mention of settlements
6 June	Ehud Olmert orders settlement construction freeze in Gaza
15 June	Bribery charges against Sharon in Greek island affair dropped
26 June	Naomi Shemer, songwriter who penned 'Jerusalem of Gold', dies aged 74
30 June	Supreme Court rules a section of the separation fence not justified on security grounds
9 July	International Court of Justice rules that the separation fence is illegal
11 July	First suicide bombing in Tel Aviv for six months kills one person
25 July	130,000 form human chain protest from Gush Katif to Jerusalem
25 Aug	Windsurfer Gal Friedman wins Israel's first Olympic gold medal
19 Aug	Likud central committee votes against a unity government with Labour
31 Aug	Hamas suicide bombers kill 16 in Beersheba
29 Sept	Operation Days of Repentance launched at northern Gaza
7 Oct	Truck bombing of Taba Hilton, Egypt kills 31 tourists
26 Oct	Knesset votes 67–46 to support Gaza disengagement plan
1 Nov	PFLP suicide bombing of Carmel market, Tel Aviv
2 Nov	George W. Bush returned as president in US election
11 Nov	Yasser Arafat dies in a Paris hospital aged 75
23 Nov	Rafael 'Raful' Eitan, former Chief of Staff, drowns at Ashdod
1 Dec	Sharon dismisses Shinui ministers who voted against 2005 budget
10 Dec	Aaron Ciechanover, Avram Hershko, Israeli Nobel laureates in chemistry
12 Dec	Hamas operatives, emerging from tunnel, destroy IDF Gaza outpost
17 Dec	Sharon and Peres agree to a Likud–Labour unity government

297

Sharon's desire to unilaterally disengage from Gaza manifested itself within the Likud as a conflict between pragmatism and ideology. It proposed the evacuation of twenty-one settlements from Gush Katif in the Gaza area and four in the northern West Bank – Ganim, Homesh, Kadim and Sa-Nur – accompanied by a generous compensation given to its eight thousand inhabitants to resettle within Israel.

The deep split within the Likud was countered by Sharon's campaign to win over the waverers. He did this by taking a tougher approach towards the Islamists in particular and to maintain the isolation of an ailing Arafat in Ramallah. In March, helicopter gunships fired three missiles and killed the founder and spiritual leader of Hamas, Ahmed Yassin, his two sons and two bodyguards. Arafat declared three days of official mourning for Yassin. A few weeks later, his replacement, Abdel Aziz al-Rantisi, was killed in Gaza in a similar fashion.

This, in turn, provoked several instances of suicide bombing with a concentration of attacks at the crossing points into Gaza. The IDF's Operation Rainbow in May was designed to close down smuggling tunnels between Gaza and Egypt which were now being utilised to bring in weapons and parts for arms workshops in Gaza. Operation Rainbow expanded the Philadelphi Route, a buffer zone between Egypt and Gaza, into Gaza itself. The Israelis destroyed several hundred houses – some of which were used as entry points into the tunnels – as well as agricultural land and a zoo.

In retaliation, Islamic Jihad killed an eight-months pregnant woman and her four daughters, aged two to eleven, in her car and attacked a memorial service for them a week later.

In September, Israel launched Operation Days of Repentance which focused on the launch sites of Qassam rockets which were targeting Sderot in Israel and their command chain. More than a hundred Palestinians were killed in a seventeen-day incursion.

Sharon also pushed ahead with a separation barrier which had been agreed by the cabinet in July 2001. By the beginning of the year, 124 miles of the total 500 miles had been completed. It would eventually consist of fences equipped with electronic sensors, ditches, watchtowers, cameras and patrol roads. Sharon also tried to ensure that 'fingers' into the West Bank such as Ariel – 13 miles into the West Bank with a population of 18,000 – would be attached to the security fence and that Ma'aleh Adumim and Gush Etzion would be on the Israeli side. The Palestinian argument was that a loop attaching Ariel to the barrier would break the territorial contiguity of the Palestinian area.

In April, President Bush followed up his Rose Garden speech in 2002 with a letter to Sharon in which he welcomed the disengagement plan. He also argued that in the context of final status negotiations with the Palestinians, a return to the armistice lines of 1949 could not be expected. Israel's claim to parts of the West Bank through Jewish settlements was therefore recognised for the first time. Bush wanted 'a viable, contiguous, sovereign, independent Palestinian state' under a leadership which would act against violence. He further proposed that Palestinian refugees should return to a Palestinian state rather than to Israel.

Bush's letter, the construction of the security barrier and the assassinations of Yassin and Rantisi were in part designed to win over members of the Likud to Sharon's disengagement plan for Gaza.

Even so, in the Likud referendum of 193,000 members at the beginning of May, almost 60 per cent voted against the plan. Moreover there was a concerted campaign against the disengagement by the Right and the settlers in a series of large demonstrations and protests. In July, an estimated 130,000 people formed a human chain from the Gaza settlements of Gush Katif to Jerusalem. Yet all this flew in the face of the fact that a majority of Israelis, some 70 per cent according to opinion polls, supported the plan.

Sharon, who was originally a Mapainik and a follower of Ben-Gurion, was broadly opposed by those whose ideological heritage lay in Menahem Begin's Herut and the Irgun. Even so, the families of figures such as Ehud Olmert and Tzipi Livni who supported Sharon came from similar Irgun backgrounds.

Avigdor Lieberman wrote to ten hawkish ministers in the hope of securing a majority of twelve of the twenty-three ministers in the cabinet who opposed the disengagement plan. Sharon solved his problem by dismissing both Benny Elon (Tourism) and Lieberman (Transportation), representing the far Right ministers of the National Union–Yisrael Beiteinu alliance, in early June. A few days later, a cabinet meeting voted 14–7 to accept a withdrawal in principle, but in order to retain Netanyahu in the government, there was no mention that settlements would have to be dismantled. At the end of October, Sharon won the disengagement vote in the Knesset 67–45 with seven abstentions. His opponents in the cabinet, Netanyahu, Limor Livnat, Danny Naveh and Silvan Shalom, voted in favour, but two Likud ministers who voted against, Uzi Landau and Michael Ratzon, were sacked. Netanyahu and the others remained despite repeated threats to leave unless a national referendum was held.

While it was likely that the NRP MKs would also leave the coalition, Sharon attempted to secure the entry of Labour which would ensure government support of more than the blocking majority of sixty-one. Netanyahu opposed this because, as finance minister, he feared a challenge to his neo-liberal economic policies and his advocacy of privatisation. While the economic situation in Israel had improved with a 5.1 per cent growth in GNP and an increase in exports of 35.6 per cent in the first quarter of 2004, unemployment was at a twelve-year high with 1.3 million Israelis below the poverty line. In addition, both Netanyahu and Shalom feared that they would be replaced by Labour ministers in any deal between Sharon and Peres.

Sharon was also under pressure from the USA to stop settlement expansion and not to compromise on the disengagement strategy. As acting housing minister, Sharon suspended tenders for 1,300 housing units for West Bank settlements in Ariel, Betar Illit, Geva Binyamin, Karnei Shomron and Ma'aleh Adumim.

In October, the Knesset voted in favour of the formal disengagement plan. Netanyahu and other ministers who tried to rally opponents until the very last moment finally capitulated and supported Sharon. During the debate, Sharon symbolised his political volte-face by quoting Begin's assertion that the settlers possessed a messianic complex.

A few weeks later, the government lost the vote on the 2005 budget, 69–43, because Tommy Lapid's party, Shinui, refused to endorse $65 million for religious institutions in the midst of deep austerity cuts. Sharon wrote termination letters to the five Shinui ministers resulting in the government only being able to count on forty MKs. Not wishing to go to new elections, the Likud central committee agreed 62 per cent to 38 per cent to instruct Sharon to enter into talks with Peres to form a unity coalition with Labour which supported disengagement. In this new coalition, Netanyahu justified his decision to remain at his post as minister of finance because of the uncertainty caused by Arafat's death.

In July, the *Sunday Times* in London reported that the Israeli air force had completed military preparations for a pre-emptive strike on the Bushehr nuclear facility in Iran. This report occurred when Russia announced that it intended to supply fuel rods to Tehran in order to enrich uranium.

2005

Sharon's plan to unilaterally leave Gaza and evacuate the settlements there split the Likud. Sharon founded the new Kadima party with those Likudniks who supported him, but it also attracted many from other parties as well as veterans such as Shimon Peres.

Here Sharon is saying that he has no more room in the sheep-pen. This reflected the tremendous support that he had in Israel after halting the al-Aqsa Intifada militarily. It also reflected the centrist character of the new party as well as the opportunism of many wishing to join it.

Shmuel Katz (*Ma'ariv* n.d. 2005)

6 Jan	United Torah Judaism joins the government coalition
9 Jan	Mahmoud Abbas is elected PA president with 62 per cent of the vote
8 Feb	Sharon and Abbas meet at Sharm el-Sheikh and agree ceasefire
9 Feb	Hamas rocket barrage of Gaza settlement, Neve Dekalim
10 Feb	Hamas leader Mahmoud Zahar agrees to ceasefire
25 Feb	Islamic Jihad suicide bombing kills five outside Tel Aviv nightclub
8 Mar	Sasson Report on unauthorised settlement outposts published
29 Mar	Knesset finally agrees $61 billion budget for 2005
24 Apr	Ezer Weizman dies in Caesarea aged 80
2 May	Diaspora minister, Natan Sharansky, resigns due to disengagement plan
1 June	Dan Halutz appointed IDF Chief of Staff
12 July	Islamic Jihad suicide bombing kills five in Netanya mall
4 Aug	Eden Natan-Zada kills four Israeli Arabs in Shefa-Amr
7 Aug	Netanyahu resigns as minister of finance over disengagement
15 Aug	Disengagement from Gaza begins
28 Aug	Omri Sharon indicted on charges of political corruption and perjury
28 Aug	Islamic Jihad suicide bombing injures 50 at Beersheba bus station
12 Sept	IDF withdraws from the Philadelphi Route
12 Sept	Qassams are fired at Sderot after Israeli withdrawal from Gaza
14 Sept	Pakistan's Prime Minister Musharraf meets Sharon at the UN
22 Sept	Four settlements in northern West Bank are evacuated
24 Sept	Qassam barrage at Sderot, Nahal Oz and Kibbutz Raim injures five Israelis
26 Sept	Vote to bring forward Likud primaries is defeated 52–48 per cent
10 Oct	Hebrew University's Robert Aumann is awarded the Nobel Prize for game theory
26 Oct	Islamic Jihad suicide bombing of a Hadera market kills six
9 Nov	Amir Peretz defeats Shimon Peres to become leader of the Labour party
20 Nov	Labour central committee votes to leave government coalition
21 Nov	In a letter to the Likud central committee, Sharon resigns from the party
24 Nov	Sharon establishes a new pro-disengagement party, Kadima
25 Nov	Rafah crossing from Gaza opens for the first time since 1968
30 Nov	Shimon Peres leaves labour movement after lifetime membership
5 Dec	Islamic Jihad suicide bombing kills five in second Netanya mall attack
11 Dec	Rocket fired at Israel for the first time from the West Bank
11 Dec	Defence minister, Shaul Mofaz, leaves Likud for Kadima
18 Dec	Sharon suffers minor stroke
26 Dec	Qassam lands near kindergarten Hanuka party at Kibbutz Sa'ad

301

Sharon's determination to follow through and unilaterally leave Gaza as well as dismantling the settlements there led to a deepening conflict within the Likud. While the move was popular within the country, Sharon found himself in a minority in the Likud and at odds with Netanyahu, his minister of finance.

Following Arafat's death, Mahmoud Abbas was elected president and endorsed a ceasefire a few weeks later at a summit with Sharon. Five hundred Palestinian prisoners were released by the Israelis, followed by another four hundred in June. Some seven thousand were still being held – many of whom the Israelis refused to release because they had 'blood on their hands'. Both Jericho and Tulkarem were handed back to the Palestinians. Abbas further attempted to impose discipline on the plethora of militant groups that had followed their own path when Arafat was alive. Many militants were absorbed into the Palestinian police and armed forces.

Following the assassination of both Yassin and Rantisi in 2004, Hamas agreed to the ceasefire in February. The ongoing construction of the security fence meant that suicide bombing within Israel itself was increasingly inhibited. Hamas concentrated instead on developing the range and sophistication of its Qassam rockets.

Islamic Jihad did not agree to the ceasefire and continued to send suicide bombers into Israel itself, including two attacks on the same mall in Netanya. Crowds were also targeted, such as outside the Stage nightclub in Tel Aviv, the central bus station in Beersheba and the market in Hadera as well as at checkpoints at the crossings from Gaza.

The report of Talia Sasson in March indicated that government bodies had been diverting funding – at least 70 million shekels by the Ministry of Housing – to build unauthorised outposts under both Sharon and Netanyahu. The Sasson Report accused the ministries of Housing, Defence, Education and Energy. The Attorney-General had already ruled on these practices in mid-December 2004. The critics of the report argued that practices such as providing mobile homes and connecting them to the electricity grid were therefore not illegal before the Attorney-General's ruling. Sasson also pointed out that twenty-four illegal outposts had been established since Sharon became prime minister in 2001.

Sharon's unilateral approach with regard to the territories was matched by Netanyahu's doctrine of reciprocity – that nothing should be given away without something in return. Sharon hinted at further withdrawals – a second unilateral disengagement – and evacuating remote settlements while maintaining the large settlement blocs. In a similar vein, Olmert suggested a Palestinian presence in Jerusalem through the nearby villages of Abu Dis and al-Ayzaria.

In mid-February, the Knesset passed the Evacuation and Compensation Act 59–40, but crucially seventeen Likud MKs abstained. A few days later the cabinet agreed to the evacuation 17–5.

Sharon's options narrowed during the course of the year. Two days before the deadline, the Knesset approved the 2005 budget of $61 billion by 58–36, thereby preventing an immediate election. Despite this, it was clear that there was no supportive majority of Likud MKs even if Sharon had won the next national election.

Netanyahu finally resigned from the government on the eve of the evacuation. Yet, confounding all expectations, the evacuation from Gaza was surprisingly easy and it was completed within a week. An overwhelming number of police and military controlled the exit of the settlers. Despite slogans such as 'Jews do not expel Jews' and constant reference to the Shoah, such as the wearing of the yellow star, there was no overt violence, no civil war and no mutiny by the military. Yet there were hunger strikes, petitions and demonstrations as well as the uprooting of trees which had been planted by Palestinians.

While a few rabbis argued that the evacuation was a transgression of the Torah and called upon religious soldiers to disobey their officers, few accepted this ruling. This suggested that further withdrawals could take place without violence. While nearly nine thousand settlers had been evacuated from the Gaza region, the Central Bureau of Statistics revealed that another twelve thousand had moved to the West Bank.

The Palestinian Authority was unable to prevent the vandalism of the deserted settlements and twenty-one synagogues which had been left behind were destroyed. The evacuation did not prevent the firing of Qassams and mortars, but instead brought into range dozens of new targets within Israel. In 2005, more than five hundred mortars and three hundred Qassams were fired into southern Israel. In late November, the Palestinian Authority opened the Rafah crossing which meant that Gaza citizens could now move in and out of the area without Israeli checkpoints.

The Egyptians agreed to patrol the Philadelphi route and to provide checkpoint police for the Rafah border. The crossing from Gaza into Egypt opened for the first time in thirty-seven years without Israeli border guards. Even so, Netanyahu argued that the withdrawal from Gaza would be disastrous for Israel's security and that it would become a base for terrorism. Although he had been strongly criticised for not resigning earlier, he was now able to project himself as 'the real voice of the Likud' by taking a position to the right of Sharon. He accused Sharon of taking 'the leftist route' and presiding over increasing corruption. Netanyahu further rejected an open borders policy, while his supporter Danny Naveh, the minister of health, opposed prisoner release. Natan Sharansky resigned as minister for the Diaspora because he disagreed with the disengagement and stood for election to become head of the Jewish Agency against Sharon's candidate, Ze'ev Bielski – and won. The split in the Likud was further demonstrated when Sharon defeated a move to bring forward the Likud primaries by 52 to 48 per cent at a central committee meeting of the party.

When Netanyahu resigned, the MAOF Stock Market Index fell by 5.25 per cent. In contrast, Sharon's main partner in the coalition, the Labour party, strongly opposed Netanyahu's sharp turn to neo-liberalism when he was minister of finance. This influenced the election of a new leader of the party in November when Amir Peretz unexpectedly defeated the 82-year-old Shimon Peres by 42.3 to 40 per cent. Peretz had been extremely vocal about Netanyahu's economic policies and criticised Sharon for permitting this change to take place. Peretz wanted to take the party out of the coalition and to pose a genuine ideological alternative to the Likud.

A week later, Labour's central committee voted to leave the coalition. This triggered Sharon to finally break with the Likud, write to Tsahi Hanegbi, the head of the party's central committee, and to establish a centrist party, dedicated to securing a solution to the conflict. Originally called the party of 'national responsibility', it emerged as Kadima. It secured the allegiance of fourteen Likud MKs, five Likud ministers, including Ehud Olmert, Tsahi Hanegbi, Tzipi Livni and Meir Shitreet, and six deputy ministers. They were joined by the minister of defence, Shaul Mofaz. Kadima remarkably also attracted Shimon Peres from Labour after almost sixty years' membership of the broad labour movement.

Sharon also called upon President Katsav to dissolve the Knesset and to authorise new elections in 2006. Opinion polls suggested that Kadima, with Sharon and Peres at the helm, would do very well in the electoral contest. Both men, however, were in advanced old age. The obese 77-year-old Sharon suffered a minor stroke in mid-December.

303

2006

Hezbollah's barrage of missiles during the second Lebanon war forced a depopulation of northern Israel.

Here rockets are seen flying over the fortified northern border with Lebanon. Israelis are seen taking the moveable 'confrontation line' further south and out of the range of the missiles.

Shmuel Katz (*Ma'ariv* n.d. 2006)

4 Jan   Sharon suffers a major stroke, Olmert takes over as acting prime minister

25 Jan   Hamas wins a majority of seats in the Palestinian legislature election

1 Feb   Israel suspends the transfer of tax revenues to Palestinian Authority

14 Feb   Singer Shoshana Damari dies in Tel Aviv aged 82

14 Feb   Omri Sharon is given nine months for illegal 1999 election contributions

18 Feb   Israel imposes sanctions on the PA and travel restrictions on leading Hamas figures

14 Mar   IDF raids Jericho prison, apprehends Rehavam Ze'evi assassins

28 Mar   Kadima wins the election with 28 seats, Likud is reduced to 12

28 Mar   Katyusha fired for the first time from Gaza

17 Apr   Second Islamic Jihad suicide bombing of Tel Aviv takeaway kills 11

4 May   Olmert presents his convergence plan to the Knesset

4 May   Navy stops a boat carrying components for Qassam rockets from Egypt

10 May   Prisoners from five Palestinian factions call for a state within 1967 borders

11 May   Yossi Banai, singer and actor, dies in Tel Aviv aged 74

14 May   Supreme Court reaffirms stopping Palestinian spouses of Israeli Arabs living in Israel

19 May   Socialist Zionist pioneer Yitzhak Ben-Aharon dies aged 99

26 May   Islamic Jihad leader, Mahmoud al-Majzoub, killed by car bomb in Sidon

30 May   Al Aqsa Martyrs Brigade suicide bombing in Kedumim kills four

8 June   Popular Resistance Committees leader Jamal Abu Samhadana killed in Gaza

10 June   Hamas ends ceasefire

12 June   Five killed as train hits car at crossing near Beit Yehoshua

17 June   Quartet supplies funds directly to Palestinians, bypassing Hamas PA government

25 June   Hamas tunnel kidnap attempt, kills two, takes Gilad Shalit

25 June   Eliyahu Asheri, kidnapped and killed by Popular Resistance Committees

28 June   IDF Ground Operation Summer Rains launched at Gaza

5 July   Ashkelon hit for the first time by a long-range Qassam

12 July   Second Lebanon war starts with the abduction of Israeli soldiers

13 July   Beirut's Rafik Hariri airport bombed, Haifa shelled

3 Aug   Hugo Chávez recalls Venezuelan chargé d'affaires from Israel

11 Aug   UNSCR 1701 unanimously calls for ceasefire

14 Aug   Ceasefire brings Lebanon war to a close

21 Aug   Writer Yizhar Smilansky (S. Yizhar) dies aged 89

23 Aug   President Katsav questioned under caution about rape allegations

18 Sept   Winograd Commission into the second Lebanon war begins its work

1 Nov   IDF Operation Autumn Clouds launched against Beit Hanoun

21 Nov   Supreme Court recognises same-sex marriages performed abroad

305

At the very beginning of the year, Prime Minister Sharon had a major stroke – this time ruling him out of the political equation completely. Ehud Olmert stepped in as acting prime minister and as head of the new party, Kadima.

At exactly the same time, Sharon's son, Omri, had pleaded guilty to violating the law about party funding and lying to the State Comptroller. He had received more than six million shekels from donors within Israel and abroad to fund his father's campaign to become leader of the Likud and its candidate for prime minister.

Within weeks, Mahmoud Abbas, while credited with the calming down of the situation, also inherited the chaos, confusion and corruption of the Arafat era. Splinter groups from Fatah such as the Popular Resistance Committees and the Mujaheddin Brigade gained in popularity. Salafist groups such as Jaish al-Islam emerged from Hamas and Islamic Jihad. Kidnappings proliferated, including that of Israeli soldier Gilad Shalit, taken near the Kerem Shalom border crossing in June.

The chaotic situation in Gaza was exacerbated by the comments of Mahmoud Ahmadinejad, the Iranian president, which appeared to portray the Holocaust as no more than a myth. His periodic comments about both Israel and Zionism were often coloured by traditional anti-Semitic tropes. This was apparent when a Holocaust cartoon exhibition opened in Tehran in August, in which both Holocaust denial and its trivialising were dominant themes. This was the result of a competition in which cartoonists from several European countries such as Belgium, Greece, Italy, Poland and Sweden submitted entries. A few months afterwards, a conference about the Holocaust was organised by the Iranian Foreign Ministry's Institute for Political and International Studies.

In January, Palestinians voted for a legislative council and returned Hamas. The old guard who had returned from Tunis in 1993 were now seen as corrupt and inefficient. Hamas attained 76 seats of a total of 132, while Fatah only gained 43. Many Palestinians viewed Hamas's resistance as the reason why Israel unilaterally withdrew from its Gaza settlements. Hamas, however, was unable to recognise Israel ideologically and its new leader, Ismail Haniya, vowed to follow both the parliamentary path and the armed struggle.

The Prisoners' Document, calling for a Palestinian state within the 1967 borders, was signed by leaders of Fatah, Hamas, Islamic Jihad, the PFLP and the DFLP in Israeli prisons. While Israel rejected it, Hamas similarly was unable to accept it because it implied a recognition of Israel and the loss of a Greater Palestine.

Israel responded to Hamas's election by refusing to transfer funds to the Palestinian Authority. Ten thousand Fatah security personnel demonstrated in Gaza because of the non-payment of salary. While Russian President Vladimir Putin argued that the supply of aid to the Palestinian Authority should be unaffected, both the USA and the EU thought differently. The USA withheld $411 million in aid to be distributed over several years and asked for the return of $30 million already given.

Hamas concentrated on the development of more sophisticated Qassams with a longer range. The number of Qassam firings quadrupled in 2006 to 1,247 compared with the year before, while the use of mortars and suicide bombers diminished. More Qassams fell on kibbutzim and towns in locations just over the Israeli border. In July, a Qassam reached Ashkelon. The Israelis put in place a Tseva Adom (Red Colour) which provided a two-minute early warning system. Educational institutions were now equipped with bomb-proof shelters.

Kadima under Ehud Olmert easily won the national election, but the predicted number of seats decreased in the absence of Sharon. The Likud, once again led by Netanyahu, was reduced from thirty-eight to a rump of twelve seats. This was the first time that a centrist party – as opposed to Labour or Likud – had won an election in Israel. The Pensioners' Party and Yisrael Beiteinu also made sizeable inroads.

Olmert formed a government with Labour, the Pensioners and Shas. The Labour leader, Amir Peretz, who had little military experience, was appointed minister of defence. Olmert pursued Sharon's objective of withdrawing from part of the West Bank by following a convergence plan. Several settlements would be evacuated and some of the inhabitants resettled in Area C of the West Bank where there was a growing Jewish population. This would be annexed at some point and separation between the two peoples would be achieved with the establishment of new borders. Such plans fell into disuse with the outbreak of the second Lebanon war in July.

In March, firms such as Coca-Cola and Western Union withdrew their advertisements from Lebanon's al-Manor television station from where Hezbollah's programmes were broadcast. US pressure was similarly placed upon satellite companies such as the Saudi-owned Arabsat and the Egyptian-owned Nilesat which facilitated Hezbollah's broadcasts.

On Israel's northern border, Hezbollah had set the pattern for the abduction and killing of Israeli soldiers which Hamas and other groups tried to imitate on Israel's southern border. Hezbollah wanted the release of Lebanese prisoners held in Israeli prisons and in particular, the Druze, Sami Kuntar, who was held responsible for the killing of a family in Nahariya in 1979.

Hezbollah had won 23 seats out of 128 in the Lebanese election in June 2005, but it also pursued the armed struggle on Israel's northern border while facilitating the smuggling of Iranian arms to Hamas and Islamic Jihad on Israel's southern border.

Hezbollah had already attempted to kidnap soldiers in November 2005, but in July the seizure of soldiers and the killing of others on the Israeli side of the border brought a military response which lasted an unexpected thirty-four days in which 18,000 reservists were called up. It also saw a naval blockade of Lebanon which lasted until the beginning of September.

The Israelis attacked Beirut airport, a transfer point of weapons to Hezbollah, the Beirut–Damascus highway, and the Rayak airbase and Baalbek in the Beka'a Valley. The new Chief of Staff, Dan Halutz, placed his trust in air power, which led to a large number of Lebanese casualties and a flight of civilians. More than 120 Israeli soldiers were killed. Many were ground troops in the Litani Offensive.

Although UNSCR 1559 of September 2004 required all Lebanese militias to disarm, Hezbollah remained well-armed and well-trained, often by Iranian military personnel. North Korean engineers with the expertise to drill below the DMZ built arms stores, food reserves, underground tunnels and bunkers on the border with Israel.

The firing of four thousand katyushas into Israel from underground positions killed forty-three people and almost depopulated northern Israel. Many Israelis fled southwards while others spent nights in bomb shelters. Arab villages such as Majdal el-Krum, Sasa, Fassuta and Hurfeish, which possessed no shelters, came under Hezbollah bombardment. The katyushas also set fire to woodlands including the Naftali forest near Kiriat Shemona and the Birya forest near Safed. The war cost Israel $3.5 billion and damaged Ehud Olmert and Kadima politically. It also led to criticism of Dan Halutz.

Hezbollah was supported by Iran, Syria and Yemen, but was criticised by the Sunni states. It won broad popular support within the Arab world for its resistance to Israeli forces. Unlike the first Lebanon war in 1982, there was a consensus in Israel to confront Hezbollah. It suggested to Israelis that unilateral withdrawal both from Lebanon (May 2000) and from Gaza (August 2005) had not brought about a cessation of hostilities.

2007

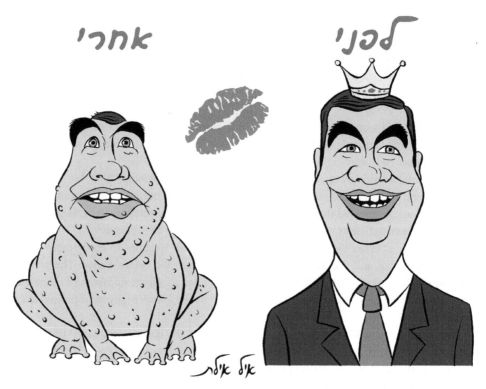

אחרי   לפני

אייל אילת

Haim Ramon, a member of the Labour party who had joined Kadima, was found guilty of a sexual assault and sentenced to one hundred hours of community service. He was also minister of justice and was reinstated as deputy prime minister later in the year. This was indicative of the increasing number of scandals affecting public figures in Israel.

From right to left, the minister is depicted here as a prince who is transformed into a frog by a kiss. This 'before' and 'after' reverses the traditional fairy tale.

Eyal Eilat (*Walla News* 3 February 2007)

2 Jan	Teddy Kollek, mayor of Jerusalem 1964–93, dies aged 95
2 Jan	Shula Zaken, head of Ehud Olmert's office, is placed under house arrest
6 Jan	Abbas outlaws the Hamas-controlled Executive Force
15 Jan	Olmert is investigated for influencing the sale of his stake in Bank Leumi
17 Jan	Dan Halutz resigns as head of IDF after a much-criticised performance in the Lebanon war
19 Jan	President Katsav takes 'leave of absence' after rape allegation
28 Jan	Labour's Raleb Majadele is appointed the first Muslim minister
29 Jan	Islamic Jihad suicide bombing of Eilat bakery
31 Jan	Former justice minister, Haim Ramon, convicted of sexual harassment
8 Feb	Hamas–Fatah sign agreement in Mecca to form a unity government
14 Feb	Gabi Ashkenazi is appointed IDF Chief of Staff
18 Feb	Jacky Matza, Tax Authority head, accused of taking bribes, resigns
25 Feb	IDF discovers three arms factories in Nablus
12 Mar	Jaish al-Islam kidnaps BBC journalist Alan Johnston in Gaza
18 Mar	Israeli cabinet vote to continue boycott of PA government
20 Mar	Israel refuses to see Norwegian deputy foreign minister after his meeting with Haniyeh
24 Mar	Ban Ki-moon arrives on his first visit to Israel and will not meet Hamas officials
20 Apr	Mohammed el-Attar given 15 years in Cairo court for spying for Israel
30 Apr	Initial Winograd Report criticises political and military leaders
2 May	Foreign Minister Tzipi Livni calls upon Ehud Olmert to resign
20 May	Cabinet broadens the range of Gaza militants to be targeted in airstrikes
28 May	Amir Peretz is ousted as Labour leader
13 June	Ehud Barak returns as Labour leader, narrowly beating Ami Ayalon
14 June	Abbas dismisses his government and declares a state of emergency
15 June	Hamas defeats Fatah militarily and completes a takeover in Gaza
15 June	Abbas appoints Salam Fayyad as prime minister
16 June	USA lifts its embargo on aid to the new Palestinian Authority government
1 July	Moshe Katsav resigns as president
1 July	Finance minister, Avraham Hirschson, resigns due to police investigation
4 July	Jaish al-Islam releases Johnston to Hamas's custody after a worldwide campaign
15 July	Shimon Peres is elected president of Israel at the age of almost 84
5 Sept	Security cabinet decides to bomb nuclear facility in northern Syria
6 Sept	Israeli air attack on Syrian nuclear site al-Kibar at Deir ez-Zur
7 Oct	Katyusha, fired from Gaza, reaches outskirts of Netivot
12 Nov	Gaza Fatah rally, commemorating Arafat, dispersed by Hamas gunmen
27 Nov	Olmert, Abbas and Bush meet for peace conference in Annapolis

309

Following the growing criticism of Ehud Olmert's handling of the second Lebanon war, his government found itself mired in a series of police investigations. This followed rape and sexual harassment allegations directed at President Katsav in 2006. Katsav took a leave of absence and resigned two weeks before his seven-year term of office officially came to an end in July. Haim Ramon, the deputy prime minister, was convicted of sexual assault and sentenced to one hundred hours of community service and a fine of $3,600.

A police investigation into the conduct of the prime minister, Ehud Olmert, was ordered when he temporarily became the minister of finance after Netanyahu's resignation from the post. This related to the tender offered to the public in November 2005, following the privatisation of Bank Leumi.

Avraham Hirschson, the new minister of finance from May 2006, was accused of laundering more than five million shekels in a sick fund deception when he was head of the National Workers Labour Federation. He resigned from office in July. Hirschson, originally a member of the Likud, had continued Netanyahu's economic policies in removing any financial safety net from the public. This included the elimination of food subsidies, a decrease in child allowance, reducing the eligibility for welfare payments and cuts for pensioners and the elderly.

Shula Zaken, who had worked for Olmert for decades and was now head of the Prime Minister's Office, was detained in early January, then placed under house arrest. She was being investigated for breach of trust and influencing decisions within the Tax Authority. Her brother, Yoram Karshi, was accused of soliciting public servants. Zaken was placed on leave along with several officials from the Tax Authority. The head of the Tax Authority, Jacky Matza, was investigated for taking bribes and resigned from his post in February.

The initial findings of the Winograd inquiry into the second Lebanon war were harshly critical, listing political haste and lack of military preparedness. The Chief of Staff, Dan Halutz, who relied primarily on air power, resigned months before this preliminary report was published. Opinion polls suggested that Olmert and Amir Peretz, the minister of defence, should follow in his footsteps. In May, 150,000 people attended a demonstration in Tel Aviv and called upon them to step down. Amir Peretz attained only 22 per cent in the primary for Labour leader and was replaced in June by Ehud Barak, who returned as party leader and was subsequently appointed minister of defence. Olmert, however, refused to resign despite a call from Foreign Minister Livni that he should go. Opinion polls reported that Likud's Netanyahu would return to power if elections were held.

More than twice as many Qassams were fired at Israel from Gaza in 2007 compared with 2006. It replaced the suicide bomber as a weapon of choice, following the building of the separation fence. In February, Amir Peretz initiated the production of the Iron Dome anti-missile system. It would become an integral part of a multi-layered missile defence system in order to prevent a reoccurrence of the barrage of Hezbollah missiles during the second Lebanon war and to stop the Qassams fired from Gaza, which were increasing in both range and sophistication.

In addition to the Qassams used by Hamas, the armed wings of other Palestinian groups, such as Islamic Jihad, the Popular Resistance Committees and the Fatah-affiliated al-Aqsa Martyrs Brigade, also developed their own versions of the Qassams. The range of most rockets was short and they fell just inside the Israeli border. The town of Sderot and nearby kibbutzim were heavily targeted. Several individuals were killed and many were injured. However, it was the psychological damage and the disruption of normal life by living in shelters that caused a dramatic increase in mental illness in Sderot. Qassams landed near Sapir College, next to a kindergarten and damaged a synagogue in the town.

The unilateral disengagement from Gaza and the evacuation of settlements brought the rocket launchers nearer to Israel. The IDF responded by targeting militants, often within civilian locations and based on intelligence from Gaza, by using helicopter gunships. In September, Qassams were fired at the Zikim army base from Beit Hanun in Gaza.

The ideological rivalry between Fatah and Hamas was played out in a series of repeated broken ceasefires amidst diplomatic efforts by the Saudis and the Egyptians to bring the two sides together. Fatah and Hamas finally agreed to establish a unity government in February which was subsequently boycotted by the USA and the EU, but was welcomed by Russia and China. Hamas's Ismail Haniyeh became prime minister, but despite agreeing to stop the firing of rockets from Gaza, the barrage continued. Fatah's Mahmoud Abbas controlled the Presidential Guard and the National Security Forces. Sayed Seyam, a member of Hamas's collective leadership after the demise of Yassin and Rantisi, was appointed minister of the interior and he was in charge of the police and preventative security services.

Israel boycotted the new government while the Americans and the Europeans started to work out ways of delivering funds to the PA, but, crucially, bypassing the Hamas leadership. Following the abduction of Gilad Shalit, Israel detained a quarter of the members of the Palestinian Legislative Council.

Olmert entertained the possibility of reviving the Saudi initiative of 2002, but Haniyeh told a summit in Riyadh a few weeks later that it would compromise the Palestinian right of return.

In June, Hamas's Sayed Seyam created the Executive Force to rival the forces of Fatah's Mohammed Dahlan. In mid-June, Abbas declared a state of emergency and dismissed the unity government under Haniyeh. He appointed Salam Fayyed instead as prime minister.

The Executive Force subsequently played a crucial role in the takeover of Gaza. Open hostilities between the two Palestinian groups broke out with multiple killings and executions. It ended with a Hamas victory. More than a hundred Palestinians had been killed. It gave control of Gaza to Hamas on the one hand, but allowed the USA, the EU and Israel to end the embargo on the PA now solely under Mahmoud Abbas on the West Bank. The Bush White House stated that it would provide funding to train those security forces which were loyal to Mahmoud Abbas.

Many Palestinian Authority employees lost their jobs. At a rally in Gaza in November to commemorate the passing of Yasser Arafat, Hamas forcibly dispersed the mass gathering – seven were killed and eighty injured. Russia parted company with the Quartet's policy of isolating Hamas.

Russia started to deliver Pantsir S-1 missile systems to the Assad regime in August – with some of this cargo being delivered to Tehran. Israel was concerned that such missiles would also reach Hezbollah on Israel's northern border and subsequently be forwarded to Hamas in the south. Syria studied the approach of the Israeli air force during the Lebanon war and proceeded with the construction of a nuclear facility, al-Kabir, at Deir ez-Zur in the remoter northern part of the country, close to the Turkish border. This was also where chemical weapons and Scud-D missiles were being manufactured. North Korean experts had advised on the construction of al-Kabir and based it on the Yongbyon facility. The White House declined to bomb it. Olmert and the security cabinet voted to attack the facility, citing the precedent of the destruction of the Osirak reactor in Iraq in 1981.

2008

The bribery charges against Ehud Olmert in the Talansky affair were compounded by the highly critical findings of the Winograd Commission into the second Lebanon war.

A snappy dresser, Olmert is pictured here with a cigar and a brown envelope – perhaps containing illicit funds – in his breast pocket. He is tying the noose as if it was a tie. His downfall was perceived widely as being of his own making.

Dudy Shamai (*Ma'ariv* n.d. May 2008)

9 Jan   Outgoing President Bush visits Israel for the first time

22 Jan   Breach at the Rafah crossing and an exodus of Gazans into Egypt to buy essentials

30 Jan   Winograd Commission Report into the second Lebanon war is published

4 Feb   Hamas suicide bombing of Dimona mall kills one and injures nine

12 Feb   Imad Mughniyeh, Hezbollah's no. 2, killed by a car bomb in Damascus

27 Feb   Qassam kills a student at Sapir College in Sderot

28 Feb   IDF Operation Hot Winter begins in Gaza to stop the launch of Qassam rockets

6 Mar   East Jerusalem Arab kills eight students at Merkaz HaRav yeshiva

9 Mar   Olmert agrees to the construction of 750 homes in Givat Ze'ev

16 Mar   German Chancellor Angela Merkel visits Israel

21 Mar   Russian Foreign Minister Lavrov advocates an international peace conference

27 Apr   Shas MK Shlomo Benizri sentenced to 18 months for moral turpitude

30 Apr   Palestinian factions agree to ceasefire

8 May   Olmert promises to resign if he is indicted in the Talansky affair

9 May   Shmuel Katz, Irgun member, Herut MK and Jabotinsky biographer, dies aged 93

12 May   Police raid Jerusalem City Hall in connection with Olmert's tenure as mayor

14 May   PFLP-GC Grad katyusha hits Hutzot mall in southern Ashkelon

21 May   Israel and Syria announce talks under Turkish auspices in Ankara

25 May   Jimmy Carter states that Israel has more than 150 nuclear weapons

1 June   Tommy Lapid, journalist, TV debater, deputy PM, Shinui founder, dies aged 76

4 June   Former finance minister Avraham Hirschson charged with embezzlement

16 June   Nahariya killer Samir Kuntar exchanged for the bodies of kidnapped soldiers

19 June   Hamas and Israel agree to a six-month ceasefire, mediated by Egypt

29 June   Cabinet agrees to a prisoner swap with Hezbollah

2 July   Lone ramming attack by East Jerusalem Arab kills three

4 July   Hamas suspends Egypt-mediated talks about Gilad Shalit

13 July   Israel and Syria both participate in the launch of the Union for the Mediterranean

20 July   Gabriella Shalev is appointed the first female Israeli ambassador to the UN

24 Aug   Budget for 2009 passed by the cabinet 13–12

27 Aug   Abie Nathan, peace activist, dies in Tel Aviv aged 81

17 Sept   Tzipi Livni narrowly defeats Shaul Mofaz 43 to 42 per cent to become leader of Kadima

21 Sept   Olmert resigns, Livni attempts to form a new coalition government

28 Nov   Lashkar-e-Taiba attack on Habad house in Mumbai kills six

1 Dec   Libyan vessel carrying supplies for Gaza tries to break Israeli naval blockade

20 Dec   Hamas announces end of its ceasefire

27 Dec   Operation Cast Lead begins

The political fallout from the second Lebanon war continued when a judgement of Olmert's conduct was published in the Winograd Commission Report at the end of January. The Commission found that while he had acted in good faith, the military operation failed in achieving its goal to inflict a decisive defeat on Hezbollah. Within a few weeks, the head of Hezbollah's military activities, Imad Mughniyeh, was killed by a car bomb in Damascus. He was wanted by the Argentinian authorities for the attack on the Israeli Embassy in Buenos Aires in 1992. In June, Samir Kuntar was released in exchange for the bodies of Regev and Goldwasser whose abduction and killing had sparked off the war. In 1979, Kuntar had left Tyre, sailed down the coast to Nahariya and been involved in the killing of members of the Haran family in their apartment.

Although Yisrael Beiteinu had left the coalition before the publication of the Winograd Report over the future status of Jerusalem, Olmert was still able to continue in office with a workable majority – Ehud Barak's threat to withdraw Labour from the government coalition proved to be an empty one. An alliance of Netanyahu's Likud, bereaved parents and angry reserve soldiers was also unable to force his resignation.

Olmert was eventually brought down because of the Talansky affair in which an American orthodox businessman, Morris Talansky, had passed funds to Olmert for his political campaigns, including the one to become mayor of Jerusalem. The US billionaire Sheldon Adelson was questioned by police while Talansky was investigated by the National Fraud Unit. Talansky was asked about $150,000 which he had given to Olmert in cash handouts over a period of fifteen years.

Given the investigations into Olmert's predecessors as well, corruption began to feature in citizens' concerns. In June, Avraham Hirschson, a former minister of finance, was charged with embezzlement, breach of trust and fraud with regard to a $750,000 sum which was missing from the National Workers Fund.

Olmert's ongoing legal difficulties proved to be political fodder for his rivals in Kadima, Tzipi Livni and Shaul Mofaz, and for Labour's Ehud Barak in his attempts to reclaim the premiership. In the summer, Olmert finally indicated that he would step down. In September, Livni narrowly defeated Mofaz in an election for the leadership of Kadima.

Although Livni was perceived as 'clean', she proved unable to form a coalition government – in part because she would not easily submit to the economic demands of the haredi parties, Shas and United Torah Judaism, and also because the fact that she was a woman did not find favour in haredi eyes. An election was then called for early 2009.

Olmert pursued his negotiations with Mahmoud Abbas until the day of his resignation. The Annapolis conference aimed at reviving the peace process at the end of 2007 had not produced any real breakthrough, despite good intentions. In 2008, there was a concerted effort to reach an outline of a final status agreement before both Olmert and Bush stepped down. The Olmert plan of mid-September was based on the Clinton Parameters. It suggested a non-militarisation of the West Bank while permitting a police force. An international force would be stationed in the Jordan Valley, with Israel granted access to Palestinian airspace. Israel would annex 6.5 per cent of the West Bank with land swaps of 5.8 per cent. A tunnel would connect the West Bank and Gaza. Palestinians would only be able to relocate to Palestine, but Israel would take in five thousand refugees over five years. The Holy Basin consisting of the Old City of Jerusalem, the City of David and Mount Scopus would come under the jurisdiction of an international body. While some points were agreed, Abbas wanted Israel to accept full responsibility for the events of 1948 and the removal of Ariel in the West Bank. No final agreement was reached.

Hamas continued to shy away from suicide bombings and to concentrate instead on developing both homemade rockets and smuggling new types of missile into Gaza. In addition

314

to developing longer-range and more accurate Qassams, Grads, often of Russian or Iranian origin, now reached much further and could hit northern Ashkelon, Netivot, Kibbutz Shaar Hanegev and the Sdot Negev region. The Grads had been smuggled through tunnels from Egypt into Gaza.

In January, a hole was blown in the security fence separating Gaza from Egypt. Released from their state of siege, huge numbers of Gaza residents streamed into Egypt, keen to buy food and other necessities before the reimposition of the fence. Under the provisions of the Camp David Agreement, Egypt was allowed to station 750 troops to safeguard the border; this figure was now doubled.

The breach in the fence also allowed new weapons to be brought into Gaza. The suicide bombing of a shopping mall in Dimona, some 40 miles from Gaza and 20 miles from the West Bank, was believed to be a consequence of this breach of the border.

The firing of mortars and rockets more than doubled in 2008 compared with the year before. The predictable pattern was the firing of rockets from Gaza followed by an Israeli retaliation by aircraft and artillery and a ground incursion. The possibility of reaching a mediated ceasefire became more difficult as different Palestinian factions were now able to manufacture rockets and to gain the expertise to fire them. In June, a six-month ceasefire was agreed between Israel and Hamas, with the Egyptians acting as intermediaries. However, Islamic Jihad continued to fire rockets for several days afterwards. The Iron Dome anti-missile system was not ready for production even though rabbis had given dispensation to its builders to work on Shabbat. Although Olmert differed from Sharon in that he was willing to evacuate settlements under fire, he still had to react strongly to the increased firing of rockets and mortars into Israel. This induced demonstrations by the citizens of Sderot outside the prime minister's residence in Jerusalem.

President Bush paid a visit to Israel and criticised the proliferation of outposts of Jewish settlements on the West Bank. He visited Mahmoud Abbas in Ramallah and said that the establishment of a Palestinian state was overdue.

In November, the IDF launched an attack to destroy a tunnel in Gaza which the Israelis believed was to be utilised for abducting Israeli soldiers beyond the border. A rocket barrage followed, after which the IDF closed border crossings, limited the delivery of provisions, stopped the delivery of fuel and prevented journalists from entering Gaza. While some restrictions were later alleviated and a delivery of $25.5 million from the West Bank was permitted in order to pay the salaries of 70,000 employees in Gaza, this was a repeating pattern. It came to a climax with a dispute between the military and political wings of Hamas over whether to renew the ceasefire. This led to Operation Cast Lead by the IDF at the end of the year.

A ship from Libya containing food supplies attempted to break the naval blockade, failed and was forced to dock in Egypt. The Iranian Red Crescent promised to send food and medical supplies, while the *Dignity*, which had sailed from Cyprus and was sponsored by the Free Gaza Campaign, similarly failed to breach the naval blockade and finally docked in Lebanon.

Israeli retaliation influenced an outbreak of several lone ramming attacks in Jerusalem from inhabitants of local Arab villages, Sur Baher, Umm Tuba and Jubal Mukaber.

315

2009

Operation Cast Lead, a military offensive against Gaza, was in response to the continual firing of missiles into Israel. A central target of the Qassam rockets was the Israeli border town of Sderot.

Here a family in Sderot is seen sheltering from a missile barrage.

The front page of the newspaper informs the reader that Imad Mugniyeh, a Hezbollah military leader, has been 'eliminated'. The father's cynical comment is: 'Thank goodness, we have once again proved our power of deterrence!'

Guy Morad (*Yediot Aharanot* 14 February 2008)

1 Jan Nizar Rayyan, leading Hamas spiritual leader, is killed with his family in Gaza

3 Jan Ground invasion of Gaza begins

5 Jan Long-range Grad attacks on Beersheba, Yavne, Ashdod and Ashkelon

6 Jan Chávez's Venezuela expels the Israeli ambassador and his diplomats

17 Jan Tamar-1 gasfield discovered in the Mediterranean near Haifa

17 Jan IDF unilateral withdrawal from Gaza ends Operation Cast Lead

10 Feb Kadima defeats Likud 28–27 seats in the national election

20 Feb Netanyahu has the greatest support from other parties and is invited to form a government

19 Mar Former president Moshe Katsav is charged with rape and other sexual offences

24 Mar Labour central committee votes 680–570 to join the Netanyahu government

5 May US Vice-President Joe Biden calls for a settlement freeze

11 May Pope Benedict XVI visits Israel

25 May Former president Ephraim Katzir-Katchalski dies aged 93

1 June Netanyahu tells a Knesset committee that no new settlements will be built

4 June Obama proposes 'a new beginning' to the Arab world in a speech in Cairo

14 June Netanyahu accepts a Palestinian state with several conditions attached

17 July Former Mossad head and intelligence innovator, Meir Amit, dies aged 88

24 July Netanyahu praises the Arab Peace Initiative for the first time

1 Aug Two killed in an attack on a Tel Aviv LGBT centre

4 Aug Amos Kenan, journalist, sculptor and political activist, dies in Tel Aviv aged 82

4 Aug Fatah General Assembly meets for the first time in 20 years in Bethlehem

20 Aug Entertainer Dudu Topaz hangs himself in a Ramla detention centre

30 Aug Olmert is charged with fraud, breach of trust and fraudulent earnings

31 Aug Barak tells Yesha that 31 unauthorised outposts will be evacuated

7 Sept Barak announces 455 West Bank housing units to be constructed, 2,500 to be completed

9 Sept Tenders are published for the construction of 486 housing units in Pisgat Ze'ev

15 Sept UN fact-finding Goldstone Report on the Israel–Gaza conflict is published

22 Sept Obama, Abbas, Netanyahu meet in an attempt to restart talks

24 Sept Netanyahu attacks Ahmadinejad's Holocaust denial at the UN

25 Sept Ehud Olmert's trial begins in Jerusalem

25 Sept Writer Amos Elon dies in Italy aged 82

4 Nov 300 tons of Iranian arms for Hezbollah on MV *Frankop* seized at sea

25 Nov Cabinet votes for a 10-month freeze on settlement construction

1 Dec Inspectors inspecting a freeze on construction are turned away at West Bank settlements

10 Dec Ribosomal crystallographer Ada Yonath awarded the Nobel Prize for Chemistry

28 Dec Plan to build in Pisgat Ze'ev, Har Homa, Neve Ya'akov announced

Operation Cast Lead began at the very end of 2008, lasted twenty-two days and took a heavy toll in Palestinian civilian casualties. The conflict had broken out after a failure by Hamas to renew the six-month ceasefire – in part due to internal differences between its political and military wings. At the beginning of January, the minister of defence, Ehud Barak, ordered a ground invasion and fighting took place in the built-up areas of Gaza.

Civilians had nowhere to run to. Hamas hid weaponry in civilian buildings – apartments, schools, mosques, hospitals. Israel was unsparing in its use of F-16 fighter aircraft and helicopter gunships. There was a belief that Hamas could be 'bombed into moderation'. The senior leaders of Hamas were attacked in government offices, police stations and in their homes. Israel lost thirteen soldiers, while Hamas lost in the region of 500–700 police officers and combatants.

The Israelis argued that the killing of so many bystanders in Gaza was due to the fact that Hamas had embedded themselves in civilian areas. Even so, the dramatic destruction and civilian loss of life brought international criticism and a UN fact-finding investigation into the fighting, chaired by Judge Richard Goldstone. His findings were published in September.

Unlike previous conflicts, the vast majority of Israelis supported the war. This was due in part to the continuous bombardment of Israeli settlements near the border with Gaza. Short-range Qassams hit Sderot and longer-range Grads were fired at Beersheba, Ashkelon, Yavne, Gedera and Ashdod. Other missiles were of Russian and Chinese origin. Many missiles were manufactured in Gaza workshops, but parts and blueprints were smuggled in through tunnels under the border with Egypt. Five tunnels under the Egyptian border which brought supplies and arms into Gaza were destroyed.

At the end of hostilities in mid-January, Hamas vowed to rearm. Even so, the number of missiles fired in 2009 was approximately a quarter of those fired in 2008. Moreover 60 per cent of those fired in 2009 were launched during the Gaza conflict.

In October, an armaments factory manufacturing pipe bombs and short-range rockets was discovered in Abu Dis just outside Jerusalem.

In mid-January, a Hamas unit trained by Iran's Revolutionary Guards in Iran and in the Hezbollah camps in the Beka'a Valley was decimated by the fighting in Gaza's Zeytun area. Members of the al-Qassam Brigades had been trained by the Iranians as far back as 1999. In March, the Iranian defence minister signed several military cooperation agreements with Sudan which then permitted Iran and Hezbollah to operate in the country. A convoy of trucks believed to be carrying Iranian Fajr-3 missiles which were destined for delivery to Hezbollah and eventually for transportation to Gaza was attacked by aircraft. A unit of the Iranian Revolutionary Guards, travelling on Iraqi passports in Egypt, was also apprehended.

The election campaign resumed and in contrast to many poll predictions, Tzipi Livni's Kadima defeated Netanyahu's Likud by twenty-nine seats to twenty-eight. Her candidature had been damaged by the international economic crisis which contrasted the global failure with Netanyahu's success as finance minister under Sharon. Moreover, she was not an incumbent prime minister because of Olmert's refusal to step down as acting premier. Shas and the UTJ baulked at the idea of serving under a woman. Labour, once the dominant party in power, could now only achieve single-figure mandates. Kadima, Labour, Meretz and the Arab parties could now only account for fifty-five seats – far short of the blocking majority of sixty-one.

Netanyahu had made a political comeback after the wilderness years and Likud gained fifteen seats, returning it to its usual representation. Yisrael Beiteinu, which advocated civil marriage, gained another four in a clear swing to the Right.

For the first time, the largest party was not called upon to form a government because Netanyahu had more endorsements from other parties and could therefore forge a coalition of more than sixty-one seats. Even though Labour had lost a third of its seats, its central committee voted narrowly to join the government.

Netanyahu could thereby form a coalition consisting of the Likud, Yisrael Beiteinu, Labour, Shas and HaBayit Hayehudi – the last, a far Right party that had evolved from the National Religious party.

Netanyahu had come to power at a time when the US Republicans had lost their mandate to govern. This put Netanyahu, whose sympathies lay with neo-conservatism and the Republican party, at ideological odds with Barack Obama who led the Democrats. Their first formal meeting in May lasted two and a half hours, but there was no public comment on contentious issues such as Palestinian statehood or the settlement drive. Netanyahu found that members of Congress only wanted to talk about a settlement freeze and not about the nuclear threat from Iran.

The new US administration strongly advocated a blanket freeze on settlements. Secretary of State Hillary Clinton was clear: 'not some settlements, not outposts, not natural growth exceptions'. Netanyahu viewed settlement activity not only in ideological terms, but also in security ones. He had to contend with the views of the settlers themselves and the far Right, including many within the Likud itself. Netanyahu therefore argued for a partial freeze: no new settlements, but a natural growth within the municipal boundaries of legal settlements. At the end of September, Netanyahu discussed ways to restart the peace process with Obama and Mahmoud Abbas at the White House.

In April, Obama addressed the Arab world from Cairo University, called for 'a new beginning' and proclaimed the 'unbreakable' bond between the USA and Israel. Ten days later, Netanyahu responded in a speech from Bar-Ilan University in which he called for a Palestinian state for the first time. The caveats applied were a demilitarised state, Jerusalem as a united capital, a dropping of the right of return and a reiteration of the natural growth of settlements. This did not find favour either within the Israeli Right or amongst the Palestinians.

Netanyahu also spoke favourably for the first time about the Arab Peace Initiative while rejecting American demands on the question of the settlements. In August, Fatah held its first Congress in twenty years and produced a series of hardline resolutions while the settlers, through Yesha, mounted an ongoing campaign. While the minister of defence, Ehud Barak, announced that thirty-one unauthorised outposts would be evacuated, two soldiers from the Kfir Infantry Brigade held up placards stating: 'We did not enlist to evacuate Jews!' They were sentenced to twenty days' imprisonment.

At the end of November, the Israeli cabinet voted for a ten-month freeze, with only Uzi Landau from Yisrael Beiteinu in opposition. Netanyahu's caveats included the completion of already authorised and semi-completed construction projects. The Israel Lands Authority put out public tenders for the construction of 486 apartments in Pisgat Ze'ev; this was regarded as part of Jerusalem and therefore not seen as subject to any restrictions. The White House continued to dispute building in and near East Jerusalem, such as in Neve Ya'akov and in Har Homa.

Civil Administration inspectors who had come to ensure that settlement activity had ceased were turned away from Kiriat Arba, Karnei Shomron, Shavei Shomron, Elon Moreh, Talmonim, Kedumim and Revava. School pupils blocked roads into the settlement of Maleh Levona while 'price tag' retaliation by West Bank settler youths against Palestinians and perceived opponents took place in a rampage through the village of Einbus. The IDF and police became involved in protecting inspectors.

319

The 2010s

The 2010s was the decade of Netanyahu's mastery of the black arts of political manipulation and manoeuvring. Despite charges of bribery, fraud and breach of trust, despite weekly demonstrations in Jerusalem, despite his wife's loose understanding of the difference between state responsibility and domestic aggrandisement, Netanyahu saw off one opponent after another. He won successive elections from the beginning of 2009 through to the beginning of 2021 – the fourth election in two years of political stalemate. He was finally displaced by Naftali Bennett in the summer of 2021.

Netanyahu's antagonism to President Obama was matched by his closeness to Trump, who willingly transferred the US Embassy to Jerusalem. The 'deal of the century' to annex part of the West Bank was displaced by the establishment of diplomatic relations with the UAE, Bahrain and Morocco. Despite opposition to the settlement drive on the West Bank and a broad disdain for his conduct in public office, Netanyahu was seen as a safe pair of hands – someone who could be trusted with providing security for family and friends.

Here a self-satisfied Netanyahu, smoking a favoured cigar, sits at his desk. Behind him are the heads of his defeated opponents, displayed like the trophies of a big game hunter in times past. Above him directly is the head of Benny Gantz (Kahol v'Lavan). To the left are Benny Begin (Likud) and Avi Gabbay (Labour). On the upper right are Shaul Mofraz (Kadima) and Tzipi Livni (Kadima). On the lower right are David Levi (Likud) and Isaac Herzog (Labour).

Yonatan Wachsmann (*Calcalist* 3 December 2020)

2010

The Israeli commando attack on the *Mavi Marmara* resulted in a fracas in which nine Turkish militants were killed. The boat belonged to a flotilla of ships which intended to break the blockade of Gaza. Netanyahu, egg/paintball on his face, is seen descending into the shark-infested waters. His weapon is a paintball gun, the barrel of which is turned backwards to face the firer. The original interception plan was non-lethal and to splash any resistors on the ship with paintball for later identification. Pistols were carried instead of assault rifles.

Avi Katz (*Jerusalem Report* June 2010)

19 Jan	Head of Hamas weapons procurement is killed in a Dubai hotel
20 Jan	Avraham Sutzkever, Yiddish poet of the Shoah, dies in Tel Aviv aged 96
1 Feb	Barrel bombs washed up on Ashdod and Ashkelon beaches
24 Feb	Palestinian militants kill a Zikhron Ya'akov teacher near Beit Shemesh
10 Mar	Municipality approves construction of 1,200 units in Ramat Shlomo
18 Mar	Thai worker in a Netiv Ha'asara greenhouse is killed by a Gaza rocket
23 Mar	UK Foreign Office announces the expulsion of the head of the Mossad in London
22 Apr	Three Grads fired at Eilat from Sinai
20 May	US House of Representatives approves $205 million for Iron Dome
30 May	Liova Eliav, leading Israeli dove, dies in Tel Aviv aged 88
31 May	Free Gaza flotilla boarded, nine Turkish activists killed
2 June	3D seismic survey reveals the existence of the Leviathan gasfield
22 Jun	Ofek-9 satellite launched from the Palmachim airbase
9 July	Yeshiva head and leader of Meimad, Yehuda Amital, dies aged 85
12 July	Giora Eiland reports to the IDF on the *Mavi Marmara* incident
27 July	Unrecognised bedouin village, al-Arakib, demolished
30 July	Grad hits residential area in Ashkelon
2 Aug	Five Grads hit Eilat and Aqaba, killing one
19 Aug	Elon Lindenstrauss wins global mathematical award, the Fields Medal
31 Aug	Four settlers killed by Hamas near Kiriat Arba
2 Sept	Israeli–Palestinian direct talks finally resume in Washington
8 Sept	Israel Tal, father of Israeli tank warfare, dies in Rehovot aged 85
15 Sept	Phosphorous shells fired from Gaza into Israel
23 Sept	Obama tells the UN that a Palestinian state is possible within a year
27 Sept	Islamic Jihad members launching rockets are killed in Israeli drone strike
28 Sept	Navy intercepts activists' ship trying to break the Gaza blockade
3 Nov	Army of Islam senior leader, Mohammed Namnam, is killed in Gaza
10 Nov	Israeli F-16 crashes into Makhtesh Ramon
14 Nov	Cabinet allows 8,000 Falash Mura to enter Israel
22 Nov	Knesset passes a referendum law for any withdrawal from the Golan and East Jerusalem
23 Nov	Ali Akbar Salehi announces that malware had affected Iranian centrifuges
30 Nov	Carmel Tunnels opened in Haifa, cutting down the journey time across the city
2 Dec	Fire kills 44 and destroys many acres of the Carmel forest
6 Dec	Kornet anti-tank missile fired from Gaza penetrates Merkava tank
17 Dec	Christian missionary killed by Palestinian militants in the Beit Shemesh forest
30 Dec	Former president Moshe Katsav convicted on two counts of rape

The rockets from Gaza decreased to just over a quarter of the number fired in 2009. In part, this was due to the growing difficulty of smuggling arms into Gaza. In addition, the mobile Iron Dome anti-missile system had tested successfully at the beginning of the year and was ready to be deployed. In May, the US House of Representative had voted 410–4 to approve $205 million to support the Iron Dome project. Even so, at the year's end, the Shin Bet released information that a thousand mortar shells, hundreds of short-range rockets and several dozen anti-tank missiles had been smuggled into Gaza, often through tunnels from Egypt.

Arms from Iran were often unloaded in Sudan and made their way up through Egypt and Sinai before finding a passage into Gaza. Grad missiles were utilised to attack Eilat twice, in April and in August, when one missile also reached Aqaba in Jordan and killed an inhabitant. In early December, Chief of Staff Gabi Ashkenazi revealed that a Russian-made Kornet missile, fired from Gaza, had penetrated a Merkava tank.

The Army of Islam, a Salafist group, had fired rockets which landed near a kindergarten in a kibbutz in the western Negev. In early November, a senior commander of the Army of Islam, Mohammed Namnam, was killed. Two weeks later two more leaders of the group were killed. The Army of Islam retaliated by firing a Grad towards Ofakim. In view of this, after a period of relative inaction in attacking Hamas targets, the Israeli air force abandoned its assault on smugglers' tunnels, arms workshops and rocket launchers. It struck instead at Hamas's military bases.

Sinai provided the hinterland for long-range rockets which were fired at Eilat with a couple landing accidentally in Aqaba in Jordan instead.

Numerous isolated settlements were located alongside Route 60 which connected Jerusalem to Beersheba, but bypassed nearby Bethlehem and Hebron. Sharon and Olmert had probably planned to evacuate such isolated settlements in the event of any peace agreement. However, there were several attacks and killings of travellers along Route 60 in August and September.

In addition, a Zikhron Ya'akov teacher, Neta Sorek, was killed by Palestinians near Beit Shemesh. A police officer, Yehoshua Sofer, was shot dead by members of the al-Aqsa Martyrs Brigade in a drive-by shooting. An American missionary, Kristine Luken, was stabbed to death in a forest near Beit Shemesh. Four settlers were killed near Kiriat Arba. There were arrests after attempts to run down border policemen in Jerusalem.

In January, Mahmoud al-Mabhouh was killed in a Dubai hotel. Wanted by several Arab governments, he was a founder of the al-Qassam Brigades, Hamas's military wing, but crucially the head of Hamas's weapons procurement programme. He was the middleman between Hamas and its Iranian arms supplier, the al-Quds Force of the Revolutionary Guards.

He had arrived from Damascus and booked into a Dubai hotel under an assumed name and without bodyguards. Many assumed that the killing was a Mossad operation, involving some twenty-six operatives. Several fake foreign passports from the UK, Australia, Ireland, Germany and France were utilised by these operatives. They were based on the passports of real people, often dual nationals who were living in Israel, but using different photographs and false details. Mossad agents in Israeli embassies in the UK, Ireland and Australia were subsequently expelled.

This coincided with Tehran's problems at its nuclear facilities. At the beginning of the year, it was reported that Iran had decommissioned and replaced a thousand IR-1 centrifuges in the fuel enrichment plant at Natanz. In February, there were reports that some centrifuges were not functioning. In September, the International Atomic Energy Agency reported that there had been a 30 per cent drop in the number of working centrifuges. Many postulated that this was a result of the 500 kilobyte Stuxnet virus and the work of Israel's military intelligence Unit 8200.

At the end of November, Ali Akbar Salehi, the head of Iran's Atomic Energy Authority, reported that more than a year ago 'westerners sent a virus to our country's nuclear sites'. At the same time there were assassination attempts on two Iranian nuclear scientists.

Although there had been reports that the Stuxnet virus was the product of cooperation between Israel and the USA, Netanyahu's relations with the Obama White House did not improve. As Vice-President Biden arrived in Israel, approval was given by the Jerusalem municipality for the building of 1,200 apartments in Ramat Shlomo in East Jerusalem. In a tense telephone exchange with Hillary Clinton, Netanyahu explained that he had known nothing about these plans until they were announced and promised that no further construction would take place in Ramat Shlomo for at least two years.

At the end of November, the Knesset passed 65–33 a ruling that any withdrawal from East Jerusalem, the Golan Heights and land swaps from within Israel's 1967 borders, but not the West Bank, would be subject to a national referendum or the approval of at least two-thirds of the 120 Knesset members. This made it far more difficult for any prime minister to make territorial concessions in the future.

The Free Gaza Movement had been founded in 2006 and had made several minor attempts to break the Israeli blockade around Gaza. These attempts reached their apex with a flotilla at the end of May 2010, when eight Free Gaza Movement ships were scheduled to leave Cyprus carrying several hundred foreign individuals sympathetic to the Palestinian cause. Two ships were unable to leave, but six did and were intercepted by the Israeli navy in international waters. Three were carrying passengers while three cargo vessels carried humanitarian supplies. Some individuals were also bringing in money.

The flotilla was asked to dock in Ashdod and informed that any non-blockade goods would be delivered to Gaza by the Israelis. This request was rejected and Israeli commandos boarded several ships. There was little or no resistance on most ships, but the *Mavi Marmara*, the flagship of the flotilla, was an exception. It had been purchased by the IHH, a Turkish Islamist aid group, in 2008 for $800,000 and was able to carry more than a thousand passengers.

Members of the IHH armed with knives and clubs attacked the outnumbered Israelis on the *Mavi Marmara*. Firearms were introduced into the melée, with the result that nine Turks were killed and ten Israelis injured. Seven hundred passengers disembarked at Ashdod and were subsequently deported.

Israel rejected an inquiry from the UN, and the Israeli cabinet instituted instead the Turkel Commission to investigate the incident. The international criticism about the incident persuaded the Prime Minister's Office to announce that the blockade would be relaxed and that all non-military items could enter Gaza after docking in Ashdod. Haneen Zoabi, a Balad MK, a passenger on the flotilla, attempted to address a hostile Knesset and was partially stripped of her parliamentary privilege.

Two ships were moored in Haifa with a third in Ashdod. The *Mavi Marmara* was brought back to Turkey by tugboats.

An IDF inquiry by Major-General Giora Eiland was published six weeks after the incident on board the *Mavi Marmara*. It concluded that no choice was left, but only a full boarding of the vessel. It did suggest that not all possible intelligence-gathering operations were fully implemented. It also emphasised lack of coordination between naval intelligence and general military defence intelligence.

325

2011

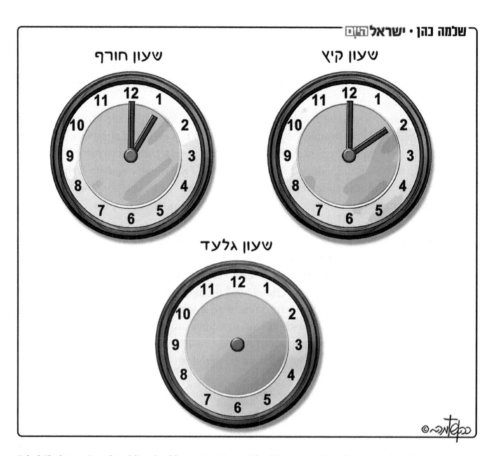

Gilad Shalit, an Israeli soldier, had been imprisoned by Hamas in Gaza for more than five years. He had been denied access to the Red Cross. At the end of 2011, a deal was finalised and Shalit was released in exchange for more than a thousand Palestinian prisoners.

The uncertainty about Shalit's condition is depicted here though clocks. A clock for the time during the winter is seen here at one o'clock. During the summer, the clock shows the time at two o'clock. 'Shalit time', however, is endless.

Shlomo Cohen (*Israel Hayom* 13 September 2010)

17 Jan   Barak and four MKs defect from Labour to form Atzmaut

23 Jan   'The Palestine Papers' from Saeb Erekat's office are leaked by al-Jazeera

25 Jan   Arab Spring protests in Cairo begin

1 Feb   Yoav Gallant's appointment as IDF head is cancelled on the Attorney-General's advice

11 Feb   Hosni Mubarak resigns as president of Egypt

13 Feb   Cabinet appoints Benny Gantz as IDF Chief of Staff

11 Mar   Fogel family, parents and three children, knifed to death by PFLP in Itamar

12 Mar   Tawfiq Toubi, Communist MK during twelve Knessets, dies aged 88

15 Mar   The *Victoria*, intercepted by Israeli navy, was carrying Iranian arms

23 Mar   Jerusalem bus bomb kills Christian Bible translator

28 Mar   Knesset agrees that citizenship be revoked for terrorism, espionage, treason

4 Apr   Dirar Abu Sisi charged in Beersheba as being a developer of Hamas rockets

4 Apr   Juliano Mer-Khamis, peace activist, filmmaker, actor, shot dead in Jenin

6 Apr   Israeli Peace Initiative launched by former ministers and generals

7 Apr   Iron Dome eliminates an incoming Grad missile outside Ashkelon

17 Apr   Cabinet approves Israel's membership of CERN in Switzerland

24 Apr   Breslov hasids attacked en route to Joseph's Tomb near Nablus, one killed

27 Apr   Fatah and Hamas agree to form a transitional government of technocrats

1 May   Israel withholds $100 million in taxes from the Palestinian Authority

29 June   Oil pipeline damage creates an ecological disaster at Nahal Zin nature reserve

10 July   Israel recognises South Sudan the day after it declares independence

11 July   Knesset passes anti-boycott act 47–38, targeted at Israelis and foreigners

14 July   Housing tent protest, Habima Square (Tel Aviv), Zion Square (Jerusalem)

19 July   The *Dignité-al Karama* attempts to break Gaza blockade, but is taken to Ashdod

8 Aug   Trajtenberg Committee appointed to deal with socio-economic questions

18 Aug   Kfar Saba family killed on Highway 12 by infiltrators from Egypt

19 Aug   Jerusalem Light Rail opens, initially free of charge for passengers

29 Aug   Hijacked car crashes into Tel Aviv nightclub, driver stabs civilians

2 Sept   Turkey expels Israeli ambassador, reduces ties, after flotilla incident

9 Sept   Israeli Embassy in Cairo besieged by thousands of demonstrators

21 Sept   Shelly Yachimovich elected Labour party leader

22 Sept   Former president, Moshe Katsav, given seven years for rape and sexual offences

23 Sept   Abbas addresses UN, requests membership for the state of Palestine

4 Oct   Hanan Porat, National Religious MK, advocate for the settlements, dies aged 67

5 Oct   Dan Shechtman awarded the Nobel Prize for Chemistry for his discovery of quasi-crystals

18 Oct   Gilad Shalit returned to Israel in exchange for 1,027 Palestinian prisoners

327

The Netanyahu coalition of the centre Right and far Right utilised its majority in the Knesset to pass measures which limited the freedom of action and of speech of both its political opponents and its enemies.

In March, the Knesset subcommittee on public diplomacy, chaired by Danny Danon, a critic of Netanyahu and aspirant to the premiership, voted to convene hearings on the American Jewish organisation J-Street, which proclaimed itself as 'pro-Israel, pro-peace'. This persuaded several major US Jewish organisations to criticise this unprecedented move as an intrusion into the internal affairs of the Jewish community. During the discussion, Shas's Nissim Ze'ev spoke of J-Street's 'sheer hatred towards Israel' and suggested that the organisation was far worse than any of Israel's actual enemies.

The Knesset also voted 37–25 to fine citizens who disagreed with the founding of the state of Israel in 1948. This, in itself, was a lessening in the penalty of the original version of the Nakba Law in July 2009 which called for three years' imprisonment.

Yisrael Beiteinu make good on its election pledge of 'No loyalty, no citizenship!' The Knesset passed a law 37–11 which allowed for the revoking of Israeli citizenship if an individual had been convicted of terrorism, espionage or treason.

In an op-ed in the *Washington Post*, Judge Richard Goldstone withdrew his allegation which featured in the Goldstone Report that Israeli forces had deliberately targeted civilians during Operation Cast Lead in 2009. He claimed that there was insufficient evidence at the time and that the Israeli government refused to share any such information. Danny Danon then launched a lawsuit in New York against Goldstone.

In July, an anti-boycott law was passed in the Knesset 47–38. This instigated financial sanctions against anyone who encouraged a boycott of the state of Israel – and of territory under its control. Alex Miller MK stated that he would sue Ahmad Tibi MK of Ta'al for suggesting a boycott of Ariel in the West Bank – where Miller lived. The bill was supported by the Likud, Yisrael Beiteinu, Shas, United Torah Judaism and the National Union. It was opposed by Tzipi Livni and MKs from Kadima. However, it was also criticised by those who would normally be in support of strongly combating boycotts, such as NGO Monitor and the Zionist Organisation of America, together with most US Jewish organisations.

In November, the Ministerial Committee for Legislation considered two bills which essentially challenged access to foreign funding by organisations that opposed government policy and those that had provided information to the Goldstone Inquiry. The Likud's Ofir Akunis put forward a bill which would ban any political group which received more than $5,500 from foreign governments and organisations. A second bill by Yisrael Beiteinu's Fania Kirshenbaum suggested a tax of 45 per cent on foreign donations. Both bills were supported by Netanyahu.

The first reading of a libel law passed in the Knesset 42–31. It relaxed criteria for slander and libel – and tripled fines for such offences. This too had been backed by Netanyahu.

In July, mass protests about the lack of housing broke out. Tent encampments were erected initially outside the Habima Theatre in Tel Aviv and in Zion Square in Jerusalem. These protests spread to major cities in Israel and were accompanied by mass demonstrations every Saturday night for many weeks running. At the end of July, 150,000 demonstrated in twelve cities. Netanyahu's ratings in polls dropped dramatically and he blamed 'insane bureaucracies' for the shortage of apartments.

The protests were in support of social justice and a resurrection of the welfare state – a path contrary to Netanyahu's ideological belief in private enterprise and in privatisation. For many Israeli citizens, the trickle-down economy had failed them. There was a profound resentment against several figures who had become extremely wealthy, such that banks, energy companies, supermarket chains and media establishments were all under the control of the few and not the many.

Israel had just joined the Organisation for Economic Cooperation and Development, but was shown to have the largest gap between rich and poor of all its members. The demonstrations, however, were almost apolitical, gaining support right across the political spectrum, including the settlers' movement. Israeli singers such as Shlomo Artzi, Rita and Yehudit Ravitz attended the protests.

Netanyahu's response was to build further apartments in Ramat Shlomo and Har Homa. Ehud Barak, who had defected from Labour to form a new party, Atzmaut, in order to remain as minister of defence in Netanyahu's government, approved the construction of 277 units in Ariel – a third of which would go to those evicted from Netzarim in Gush Katif during the unilateral withdrawal from Gaza in 2005.

The complainants targeted the paucity of social services, excess support for the haredi sector and the settlers, and tax concessions for the very well-to-do. A committee of economists headed by Manuel Trajtenberg was appointed by Netanyahu and it reported in November. It recommended free education for three- and four-year-olds and a reduction in the taxes on fuel, foodstuffs and electrical goods. It proposed cuts in the defence budget and benefits for working mothers, and argued for steeper taxes on high earners and corporations. It also proposed a freeze on tax cuts planned for the middle class.

With Qassams and Grads now reaching more distant targets such as Ashdod, the Iron Dome went into service in April and began to eliminate a majority of missiles fired into Israel from Gaza. Israel still strongly opposed any reconciliation between the Palestinian Authority in the West Bank and Hamas in Gaza. Even when agreements were signed, they were never long-lasting because the ideological gap between the nationalists and the Islamists could not be bridged. Israel's leverage was the repeated withholding of tax revenues destined for the Palestinian Authority.

329

The flotilla campaign to bring publicity to the siege of Gaza continued with the Spanish ship *Dignité-al Karama* being towed to Gaza, the Greek coastguard seizing the Canadian vessel *Tahrir*, while the Irish *Saoirse* and the Scandinavian *Juliano* proved unable to sail. A 'flytilla' was partially prevented when up to two hundred people were stopped from boarding aircraft in European capitals. Of the 118 who arrived in Tel Aviv, 36 were deported and the rest allowed to go on to the West Bank.

The Arab Spring brought about Hosni Mubarak's fall after thirty years in power. Israelis were concerned about who would replace him as Mubarak had preserved the 1979 peace accord between Begin and Sadat. The Egyptian pipeline to Israel was attacked ten times. The demonstrations in Tahrir Square in Cairo worried many authoritarian rulers in the Arab world. Bashar Assad in Damascus described the demonstrators as 'enemies with an Israeli agenda'. The Muslim Brotherhood now openly stepped into the political arena and, as the Freedom and Justice party, led in the first round of elections at the very end of the year.

The Israeli Embassy in Cairo was besieged by demonstrators and its diplomats rescued by Egyptian commandos who had moved in following President Obama's request. In Amman, the Israeli Embassy was temporarily evacuated because of protests.

Palestinian diplomats continued their campaign for support for admission to the UN and thereby recognition of the state of Palestine. Seventeen countries, including several Latin American states, recognised Palestine during the year, but the Obama White House opposed such a move. In September, Mahmoud Abbas submitted an application to join the UN on behalf of the PLO.

2012

The lack of decent housing erupted in the 'tent protests' in several Israeli cities during 2011. Netanyahu's promises and the establishment and recommendations of the Trajtenberg Committee to rectify the situation provided a temporary respite. Such pledges halted the demonstrations and divided the demonstrators. Attempts to resurrect the protests descended into almost a social event.

Here the man asks 'where are you from?' The woman replies that she usually 'tents' in Beit Shemesh, but now she 'tents' in Rothschild Street – one of the most salubrious in Tel Aviv. Written on her tent entrance is the comment that Netanyahu will provide her with a home, whereas the slogan on the man's home is 'The people demand justice!'

Arnon Avni (n.d. [2011])

1 Jan Yaffa Yarkoni, Israel's iconic singer, dies in Tel Aviv aged 86

5 Jan Ehud Olmert is charged with bribery in the Holyland Towers development scheme

16 Jan Tel Aviv Stock Exchange and El Al sites are hacked after Hamas pledge

29 Jan Supreme Court rules that the Tal Law on haredim army service is illegal

31 Jan Netanyahu defeats Moshe Feiglin with 77 per cent vote for Likud leadership

6 Feb Fatah and Hamas sign an agreement in Qatar to form unity government

22 Feb Knesset votes 55–27 to defeat bills requiring national service for all

28 Feb Asher Grunis becomes president of the Supreme Court

4 Mar Ramat Gan court recognises a lesbian couple as both the mothers of their child

9 Mar PRC head Zuhair al-Qaissi killed in IDF Operation Returning Echo

11 Mar Former Mossad head Meir Dagan publicly opposes Israeli attack on Iran

27 Mar Shaul Mofaz defeats Tzipi Livni for Kadima leadership 62 to 38 per cent

5 Apr Grads fired from Sinai hit Eilat

17 Apr In Israeli jails 1,400 Palestinian prisoners begin hunger strike

30 Apr Benzion Netanyahu, academic and Revisionist Zionist, dies in Jerusalem aged 102

8 May Kadima agrees to join government, Mofaz becomes deputy prime minister

17 June Cabinet establishes ministerial Settlement Affairs Committee

24 June Muslim Brotherhood's Mohamed Morsi elected president of Egypt

27 June Hamas commander Ibrahim Hamed convicted on 46 charges of murder

30 June Yitzhak Shamir, Lehi leader and prime minister, dies in Tel Aviv aged 96

4 July Plesner Report recommends army service for all citizens from 2016

10 July Ehud Olmert acquitted on Talansky and Rishon Tours charges

17 July Kadima leaves the coalition over its refusal to fully implement the Plesner Report

18 July Coach bomb in Burgas, Bulgaria, kills 7 and injures 30 tourists

26 July Miriam Ben-Porat, first female Supreme Court head, dies aged 94

18 Sept Haim Hefer, songwriter and poet, dies in Tel Aviv aged 86

6 Oct Iranian drone sent by Hezbollah towards Dimona shot down

23 Oct Air attack on Yarmouk munitions factory in south Khartoum, Sudan

14 Nov Hamas leader, Ahmed Jabari, killed in IDF Operation Pillar of Defence

14 Nov Three Grads target nuclear facility at Dimona

15 Nov Three killed in rocket attack on Kiriat Malachi

16 Nov Rocket from Gaza reaches Gush Etzion region

18 Nov Iron Dome intercepts two Fajr-5 missiles fired at Tel Aviv

21 Nov Bus bomb injures 28 in Tel Aviv's business district

29 Nov Palestine Authority granted non-member observer status at UN

13 Dec Foreign Minister Lieberman charged with fraud and breach of trust

Ehud Olmert was acquitted of the corruption charges that had prompted his resignation as prime minister and leader of Kadima. He was originally charged with fraud, breach of trust, tax evasion and falsifying corporate records in the Talansky and Rishon Tours cases, but was found guilty only of breach of trust in the Investment Centre case. Olmert's long-time office chief, Shula Zaken, was convicted on two counts of fraudulently obtaining benefits, fraud and breach of trust in the Rishon Tours case.

Tzipi Livni, Israel's 'Mrs Clean', was defeated by Shaul Mofaz in a contest for the leadership of Kadima in March. A few weeks later, Kadima joined the Netanyahu government, but two months after that, it left the government. Livni, the leader of the biggest party in the 2009 election, proved unable then to form a coalition because she refused to compromise on her views regarding the religious parties.

At the end of January, the Supreme Court ruled that the Tal Law of 2002 was unconstitutional because it favoured one section of the population over the others. This originally allowed full-time yeshiva students to delay their army service until aged twenty-three, whereupon they would choose between civilian national service or a shortened time in the armed forces. However, in the nine years since it came into force, only 898 haredim had enlisted out of a total group of 61,877. The Tal Law was renewed every five years, but on this occasion it would not be renewed in August. The Supreme Court ruled that the state had failed to implement the law and to come up with a solution to satisfy the ideal of study with service to the state.

Yohanan Plesner MK continued the work of Judge Tal. The Plesner Committee Report called for universal service in the armed forces from 2016. This meant that 80 per cent of haredim would have to serve, apart from 1,500 yeshiva students. The committee recommended sanctions against those who refused to enlist. An individual would lose any allowance from the yeshiva, student status in respect of National Insurance and state support for housing mortgages. There would be no discount permitted on property tax.

While there were demonstrations by yeshiva students in support of the recommendations – 'One People, One Draft!', supported by Mofaz and Kadima – there was also considerable opposition from the religious parties. HaBayit Hayehudi had already left the committee at the beginning of July, while Shas threatened to leave the coalition. Two days before the publication of the report, Netanyahu dissolved the committee. He further rejected Mofaz's suggestion of deferring conscription until age twenty-six. Kadima voted 24–3 to leave the coalition, which resulted in four MKs leaving Kadima. This, in turn, paved the way for new elections.

There was also a proliferation of militant groups in Gaza gaining expertise in rocket warfare, in addition to Hamas. Iranian missile parts were smuggled in from Egypt. While Qassams could hit targets 10 km away, Grads now covered distances twice as far, and four times with upgraded Grads. The Fajr-5 could reach locations 45 km from Gaza. While the deployment of the Iron Dome neutralised many incoming missiles, Operation Returning Echo in March and Operation Pillar of Defence in November targeted military commanders in Gaza.

In March, the Israelis attacked a car carrying Zuhir al-Qaisi (Abu Ibrahim), the secretary-general of the Popular Resistance Committees (PRC). It also killed his passenger, Mohammed Ahmad al-Hannani, a PRC operative in Nablus. This was believed to be in response to a series of attacks on civilians in their cars and on buses in southern Israel during the previous August. Israeli troops entered Sinai and conducted a search for the assailants, in which Egyptian soldiers were also mistakenly killed. This led to a diplomatic argument between Egypt and Israel.

The killings of al-Qaisi and several Hamas commanders provoked a tremendous surge in the firing of missiles, with 2,221 rockets fired during the course of the year, and 1,734 in November alone. In March, 300 Grads were fired in response to Operation Returning Echo. The targets now included Tel Aviv, Kiriat Gat, Beersheba, Kiriat Malachi, Ofakim and Gan Yavne. Schools and universities were periodically closed.

In November, Ahmed Jabari, the second-in-command of Hamas's al-Qassam Brigades, was killed by an Israeli drone. This resulted in several Grads being fired at the nuclear facility at Dimona.

The enhanced military capability of Hamas and other Islamist groups in Gaza was predicated on the delivery of Iranian missile parts and technological know-how. The route for the delivery of Iranian weapons was via Sudan and Egypt. At the beginning of 2009, there had been two attacks on convoys carrying arms northwards towards Egypt. In May, a car bomb destroyed a truck in Port Sudan and killed its driver who was a member of the Ababda tribe which had a reputation for arms smuggling. In October, the Yarmouk munitions factory in south Khartoum was attacked by four aircraft. The factory was believed to be owned and run by the Iranian Revolutionary Guards.

With the fall of Mubarak and the growing power of the Muslim Brotherhood and Salafist groups in Egypt, security had become lax in Sinai. A gas pipeline from Egypt to Israel was attacked near al-Arish in northern Sinai. In August, an attack on an Egyptian base in Sinai resulted in the deaths of sixteen Egyptian soldiers. The assailants took two armoured vehicles and attacked Israeli soldiers at the Kerem Shalom border crossing into Gaza. Tourists were warned about travelling to Egypt.

In May, following his White House visit, Netanyahu rejected claims that Israel could not fight a war against such a major power as Iran. It reflected the difference of views with the intelligence agencies. Even so, the quiet war between Israel and Iran continued. Since 2010, several nuclear scientists in Iran had been assassinated. In mid-January, Mostafa Ahmadi Roshan was killed by a car bomb in Tehran. A few weeks later, a bomb attached to a car in Delhi injured the wife of an Israeli diplomat. In Tbilisi, Georgia, a similar bomb was discovered before detonation. In Thailand, four hundred boxes of bomb-making material were discovered, following the arrest of a Lebanese national. Police in Baku arrested several men who were in possession of 15 kg of C-4 explosives and uncovered a plan to kill the Israeli ambassador. In Mombasa, the police arrested several Iranians and discovered 15 kg of RDX explosives hidden on a golf course. In July, police in Cyprus arrested several Hezbollah operatives.

In July, a suicide bomber killed seven Israeli tourists and a Bulgarian bus driver and injured thirty at Burgas airport in Bulgaria. The bomber was a French-Lebanese national and suspicion fell on Hezbollah as being responsible for the attack.

In September 2011, the Supreme Court had ruled that an outpost in the Ulpana area on the outskirts of Beit El on the West Bank should be demolished because it was built on private land. Netanyahu instead ordered the transfer of the five apartments in Ulpana to Beit El which was several hundred yards away. In addition, Netanyahu pledged to expand Beit El by building ten apartments for every one that had to be moved, totalling another three hundred extra units. The housing minister, Ariel Atias, also promised to build another 550 apartments in Ariel, Maale Adumim, Adam, Efrat and Kiriat Arba.

Three hundred residents of Ulpana marched to Jerusalem before a Knesset vote which was designed to retroactively legalise the buildings in Ulpana. The vote was lost 69–22 after Netanyahu enforced government and party collective responsibility.

333

2013

President Obama's visit to Israel spelled out a different vision for the state. While his speech was well received, little changed after his departure. Obama is seen here as a visionary, imitating the famous photograph of Herzl at the first Zionist Congress in Basel in 1897 – pondering the future. Under this challenge, Netanyahu is depicted as an irritated prime minister hanging on aimlessly with no direction.

Michel Kichka (*Regards* 27 March 2013)

16 Jan	US businessman Donald Trump endorses Netanyahu in YouTube video
22 Jan	Likud emerges as the largest party, but with fewer seats, in the national election
30 Jan	Convoy carrying arms to Hezbollah hit near Damascus–Beirut highway
6 Feb	Menahem Elon, Supreme Court Judge, dies in Jerusalem aged 89
17 Feb	Trial of Avigdor Lieberman, charged with fraud and breach of trust, opens
19 Feb	Tzipi Livni to be in charge of negotiations with Palestinians in new coalition
4 Mar	Menahem Froman, rabbi of Tekoa and peace activist, dies aged 67
5 Mar	Plague of locusts reaches the agricultural areas of Kadesh Barnea
20 Mar	President Obama visits Israel and views the Iron Dome
22 Mar	Netanyahu apologises to Turkish Prime Minister Erdoğan over *Mavi Marmara* incident
31 Mar	First natural gas flows to Ashdod from the Tamar field in the Mediterranean
17 Apr	Majlis Shura al-Mujahidin fires two Grads at Eilat
25 Apr	Air force shoots down Hezbollah drone 8 km off the Haifa coast
3 May	Iranian Fateh-110 missiles in Damascus airport destroyed in air attack
5 May	Syrian military research centre hit at Mount Qassioun, north of Damascus
14 May	Netanyahu visits Putin in Sochi to discuss sale of S-300 missiles to Syria
2 June	Rami Hamdallah to succeed Salam Fayyad as Palestinian prime minister
8 June	Yoram Kaniuk, Hebrew writer and theatre critic, dies in Tel Aviv aged 83
18 June	Visiting international dignitaries celebrate Shimon Peres's 90th birthday
23 June	Cabinet votes to export 40 per cent natural gas while reserving 25 years' domestic supply
30 June	Netanyahu's rival, Danny Danon, becomes the head of the Likud central committee
3 July	President Morsi removed from office in Egyptian army coup
5 July	Russian P-800 Yakhont anti-ship missile targeted in attack on Latakia
7 July	Cabinet agrees reforms to the military conscription bill to conscript haredim
3 Aug	Hassan Rouhani becomes president of Iran
20 Aug	Karnit Flug becomes the first female governor of the Bank of Israel
21 Aug	Assad chemical weapons attack in Damascus creates a rush in Israel for gas masks
26 Aug	Metronit bus rapid system begins operation in Haifa
1 Oct	Netanyahu tells UN that Israel is prepared to attack Iran on its own
7 Oct	Funeral of Ovadia Yosef, Talmudic scholar, Shas mentor, attended by 800,000
30 Oct	Air defence site at Snawbar, south of Latakia, attacked
6 Nov	Lieberman is acquitted by a Jerusalem court and resumes post of foreign minister
22 Nov	Isaac Herzog elected Labour party leader
26 Nov	Singer-songwriter Arik Einstein dies in Tel Aviv aged 74
12 Dec	Government plan to resettle Negev bedouin shelved
22 Dec	Passengers leave before Islamic Jihad pressure-cooker bus bomb explodes

335

Netanyahu was returned to office in January in the highest turnout of voters since 1999. His Likud and Lieberman's Yisrael Beiteinu had formed an electoral alliance at the end of October 2012. The Likud, however, lost seven seats overall and Yisrael Beiteinu another four. Likud critics of the alliance had warned that Yisrael Beiteinu's anti-religious coercion policy and its disproportionate number of Russian supporters would drive away both religious and Mizrahi voters.

Kadima under Shaul Mofaz was decimated. It lost all its seats bar two. Voters switched to new centrist parties – Yair Lapid's Yesh Atid (nineteen seats) and Tzipi Livni's HaTenuah (six seats). Lapid was well known since he had worked as a television journalist for Channel 2.

Labour too recovered under its new leader, Shelly Yakhimovich. It had benefited from Ehud Barak's decision to retire from politics and the decision of his breakaway party, Atzmaut, not to run in the election.

There was also a swing to a rebranded, National Religious party, HaBayit Hayehudi, under Naftali Bennett. During the previous five years, it had consisted of a core of the NRP with different far Right factions joining and departing. The party had criticised Netanyahu for not being sufficiently tough in targeting the Islamists in Gaza during Operation Pillar of Defence. HaBayit Hayehudi increased its number of seats from three to twelve.

The election also marked the formal return of Arieh Deri to Shas. He had been given a three-year sentence in 2000 for bribery and served just less than two years. He had threatened to run independently and this persuaded Shas to give him the number two position on the candidate list. He effectively became the joint leader of the party with Eli Yishai.

A coalition was formed in which Netanyahu, Lapid, Livni and Bennett were the central actors – a government which did not include the haredi parties, United Torah Judaism and Shas. Bennett had a veto over any change in the religious status quo. He stopped a proposal to give equal tax benefits to gay parents.

Yair Lapid had campaigned to secure the conscription of all haredim into the armed forces. At the beginning of July, the cabinet voted 14–4 for reforms to Israel's military conscription law, exempting only 1,800 yeshiva students. Demonstrations of haredi young men in Jerusalem subsequently followed on a regular basis.

While there was an alliance between elements of the far Right, National Religious and secular centrists on this issue, they were divided on other questions. There was pressure from Bennett to ensure that a referendum would be required for any withdrawal from territory conquered in 1967 as well as to prevent the release of Palestinian prisoners, which was a factor in the attempt by the US secretary of state, John Kerry, to reignite Israeli–Palestinian negotiations.

Even though Kerry shuttled back and forth between Netanyahu and Abbas, the talks between Tzipi Livni and Saeb Erekat floundered. Despite a release of almost eighty Palestinian prisoners, the right of return became a subject of discussion. Likud MKs, opposed to the talks, proposed annexing the Jordan Valley.

In parallel, there was an attempt to institute a Jewish State law as a Basic Law. In August 2011, forty MKs had framed a Basic Law proposal which depicted Israel as the nation-state of the Jewish people. In late June, Yesh Atid's Ruth Calderon proposed that Israel's founding declaration be transformed into law. It was argued that religion was a private matter. At the same time, Likud, Yisrael Beiteinu and HaBayit Hayehudi proposed that 'the Land of Israel is the historic homeland of the Jewish people and the place where the state of Israel is founded'.

Yesh Atid understood 'Jewish' in a national sense and promoted the idea of equality. A rival proposal promoted the idea that only Jews in a personal sense had the right to an expression of nationality historically. Arabic was stripped of its equal status in earlier proposals.

A few weeks later, Tzipi Livni, the minister of justice, appointed Professor Ruth Gavison to draft a constitutional framework that would integrate both the Jewish and the democratic nature of the state.

A fence was constructed on the Egyptian border at a cost of $430 million. It was built to prevent the smuggling of Iranian arms and missile parts into Gaza. Although the Muslim Brotherhood's President Morsi had been removed in a military coup in Egypt, Hamas was depicted by Netanyahu as 'a third base of Iranian terrorism'. With Iranian forces and Hezbollah participating in the Syrian civil war, Netanyahu argued for the construction of a fence along the Syrian border. During Obama's visit to Israel in March, Netanyahu warned him about the growing presence of Iranian forces in Syria and the US president was shown the Iron Dome anti-missile system. President Peres drew Obama's attention to the possibility of a chemical weapons attack by Assad's forces.

In early May, the Israeli air force attacked several targets in Syria which housed Iranian arms and missiles. These were stored in warehouses before being transported to Hezbollah. A few days later, Netanyahu travelled to Sochi to speak to Vladimir Putin in an attempt to prevent the sale of missiles to both Iran and Syria.

In March and April, Sarin was probably used in chemical attacks by Assad's forces on Khan al-Assal and on Saraqib. In August, there were several more attacks – on Ghouta, Jobar and Ashrafiyat Sahnaya. This awoke the international community with a jolt to the use of chemical weapons. Obama threatened an American intervention.

It also worried many citizens in northern Israel in that they could now be subjected to Syrian and Iranian attacks using chemical weapons, in response to any US attack. The Iron Dome and Patriot missiles were moved to Haifa while reservists were called up for civil defence units. There was an immediate rush to buy gas masks.

In the shadow of the consequences of the invasion of Iraq in 2003, Obama postponed any attack by referring the matter for approval in Congress. In the UK House of Commons, the Cameron government was unexpectedly defeated in its intention to intervene in Syria. In the end, a deal was brokered with the Russians, Assad's ally, to eliminate chemical weapons from Syria by 2014.

Netanyahu spent some considerable time drawing attention to the growing danger of Iran despite the election of a more moderate candidate, Hassan Rouhani, in the August election. Tehran's progress towards manufacturing nuclear weapons preoccupied Netanyahu. At a speech to the UN in early October, he said that Israel was prepared to go it alone if necessary and to attack Iran's nuclear facilities. Within Israel, there was a determined opposition from the intelligence community to such a move.

In November, Obama revealed that the major powers had reached an interim deal with Iran to limit the enrichment of uranium to 5 per cent and to provide sanctions relief of only $7 billion when $100 billion was being requested. Sanctions on oil and banking were to remain in place. Netanyahu termed it 'a historic mistake' during a speech in Geneva and was supported by Tzipi Livni. Shimon Peres and the new head of the Labour party, Isaac Herzog, were more conciliatory. Despite ongoing monitoring by the International Atomic Energy Agency, Netanyahu argued that a breakout capacity could allow Iran to enrich uranium to a weapons grade 90 per cent within weeks.

337

2014

שלמה כהן • ישראל היום

סיבוב עסף

The kidnapping and killing of three Israeli teenagers led to a military clash between the IDF and Hamas and its allies in Gaza in which a large number of Palestinian civilians died. A central aim of Operation Protective Edge was to prevent the firing of missiles by Palestinian militants into mainland Israel.

Here the conflict is depicted as a war game conducted on a chessboard. A road map of Israel is superimposed on the chessboard. On one side, Palestinian missiles are lined up, ready to fire. On the other, the Iron Dome of the Israelis is in place ready to eliminate airborne missiles. 'Another round' of warfare is depicted as 'another game' of chess.

Shlomo Cohen (*Israel Hayom* 12 March 2012)

10 Jan After John Kerry's departure, a tender is published for 800 homes in West Bank

11 Jan Ariel Sharon dies aged 85 after eight years in a coma

24 Jan Shulamit Aloni, peace activist and education minister, dies aged 85

26 Jan Attack on missile warehouse in the Sheikh Daher area of Latakia

13 Feb Likud ministers march along E-1 corridor to highlight settlement building

24 Feb Attack on Hezbollah facilities at Nabi Chit, Lebanon

2 Mar 'Million man' haredi protest in Jerusalem against conscription

3 Mar Netanyahu conveys to Obama opposition to any Iran deal

5 Mar Red Sea intercept of the vessel *Klos C* carrying Iranian arms

8 Mar Teenagers refuse to serve in the West Bank in a letter to Netanyahu

11 Mar Knesset raises party election threshold from 2 per cent to 3.25 per cent

12 Mar Knesset passes conscription law for haredim 65–1

13 Mar Knesset passes referendum law 68–0 and it becomes part of Basic Law

30 Mar Diplomats go on strike in 103 Israeli embassies worldwide

31 Mar Ehud Olmert is convicted of bribery in the Holyland affair

23 Apr Fatah and Hamas agree once more to form a unity government

29 Apr Kerry's deadline for Israel–Palestine negotiations expires

30 Apr Anti-Trust Authority approves the sale of *Makor Rishon* to Sheldon Adelson

24 May Pope Francis arrives in Israel for a visit

10 June Reuven Rivlin beats Meir Sheetrit 63–53 in the Knesset vote to become president

12 June Three teenagers are kidnapped in Alon Shvut

30 June Bodies of three teenagers are discovered

2 July Teenager Mohammed Abu Khdeir is kidnapped and murdered

7 July Yisrael Beiteinu breaks away from the Likud partnership

8 July Gaza rocket reaches Givat Ze'ev in the environs of Jerusalem

8 July Operation Protective Edge begins with a ground war in Gaza

20 July Israelis enter the Shuja'iyyaa built-up area of Gaza

22 July Americans and Europeans cancel their flights to Ben-Gurion airport

8 Aug Menahem Golan, film producer and director, dies aged 85

21 Sept Cyber Defence Authority is established to stop attacks on civilian sites

29 Sept Netanyahu tells UN that Hamas is similar to ISIS, al-Qaeda and Boko Haram

1 Oct Shlomo Lahat, Tel Aviv mayor 1974–93, dies aged 86

2 Nov Cabinet approves conversion reform allowing local rabbis to implement it

18 Nov Four rabbis and a Druze policeman killed in attack on a Har Nof synagogue

2 Dec Netanyahu dismisses Lapid and Livni and calls a new election

14 Dec Gadi Eisenkot is appointed IDF Chief of Staff

339

The increase in number and sophistication of rockets fired at Israel was a dominant feature of attacks both in the north and in the south of the country. Several missiles were now being manufactured in local Gaza workshops, such as the M-75 which could reach Tel Aviv, while missile sections were being smuggled in via tunnels from Egypt or being transported by sea.

In early March, an Israeli naval force initiated Operation Full Disclosure and boarded the vessel *Klos C* in the Red Sea some 1,500 km from Israel en route to Port Sudan. It had sailed from Iran, docked at Umm Qasr in Iraq and was laden with M-302 long-range missiles of Chinese design, mortars and 400,000 rounds of ammunition suitable for Kalashnikovs. The missiles were concealed in bags of cement. Much of this material had been manufactured in Syria, transported to an Iranian air force base and loaded on to the ship at Bandar Abbas.

There had been attacks earlier in the year on a warehouse housing Russian S-300 missiles in Latakia and at Hezbollah facilities at Nabi Chit. During Operation Protective Edge, the Iron Dome was deployed to intercept missiles approaching Tel Aviv and there were Code Red warnings in central Israel in Netanya, Kfar Saba and Ra'anana. One missile reached Givat Ze'ev in the environs of Jerusalem.

Netanyahu utilised the *Klos C* incident to criticise the Obama administration's approach to Iran and he hoped to thwart any potential agreement with the ayatollahs. Tension between Tel Aviv and Washington increased to such an extent that Netanyahu felt the need to criticise 'American values'.

A central bone of contention was the expansion of settlements on the West Bank and the construction of new neighbourhoods in East Jerusalem. In part, this was done to appease Naftali Bennett, the leader of HaBayit HaYehudi, now positioned to the right of the Likud. Bennett held three ministerial portfolios in Netanyahu's government. those of economy, religious affairs and Diaspora affairs.

An announcement approving plans for eight hundred homes in West Bank locations such as Alfei Menashe, Karnei Shomron, Geva Binyamin and Eliana and six hundred in East Jerusalem was made in early January. Netanyahu stipulated that it should only be made after the departure of the US secretary of state, John Kerry, following his tenth visit to Israel. In 2010, a similar announcement coincided with Vice-President Biden's arrival in Israel and evoked much criticism from the White House. This symbolised the difficulty for Netanyahu's coalition – on one side, HaBayit HaYehudi, which strongly supported the settlement drive in the West Bank, and HaTenuah and Yesh Atid, supported by the Obama White House, on the other.

The coalition had originally been formed because the central issue for Bennett as well as for his opponents, Lapid and Livni, had been the conscription of the haredim into the IDF. A vast demonstration of haredim – adhering to Agudat Yisrael, Degel HaTorah, Shas and the conservative wing of the National Religious – took place in Jerusalem in early March. The protest was compared by its leaders to resistance to the Nazis, political uprisings in Ukraine and the struggle against Persian anti-Semites which is celebrated during the festival of Purim. Conscription was depicted as a means to prevent yeshiva students from studying Torah. Images of Bennett and Lapid dressed as members of the Gestapo were sent to the local media. Both Ashkenazi and Sephardi Chief Rabbis attended. The Belz hasidim threatened to leave Israel en masse.

As differences deepened with Mahmoud Abbas, Netanyahu became more determined to develop settlements on the West Bank and in East Jerusalem. At the end of August, 1,000 acres were taken near the Etzion region. A few weeks later, a plan was published for building 2,610 units at Givat HaMatos in East Jerusalem – some two hours before Netanyahu was due to meet Obama at the White House. There were also plans to build 185 miles of roads which would connect West Bank settlements with Israel. Some 6,000 acres of land would have to be expropriated for this. In

November, Netanyahu approved plans to build in Ramat Shlomo and Har Homa. Yair Lapid, the leader of Yesh Atid and minister of finance, blocked many of these initiatives by delaying the provision of funds. Netanyahu dismissed Yair Lapid and Tzipi Livni in early December.

At the instigation of John Kerry, Israeli–Palestinian negotiations ambled along but with no progress. Netanyahu wanted Palestinian recognition of Israel as a Jewish state and promoted acceptance of this principle as a Basic Law.

Netanyahu baulked at the release of a fourth tranche of prisoners in late March and continually published plans for further construction in the West Bank. Even so, he wanted a continuation of negotiations after the deadline of the end of April had expired. A few days previously Fatah and Hamas had signed an agreement to establish a unity government – whereupon Netanyahu broke off all negotiations.

The increased tension was ratcheted up further by the kidnapping of three teenagers, Naftali Frenkel, Gilad Shaer and Eyal Yifrah, in Alon Shvut. This sparked off a police campaign to find them, a military operation on the West Bank to apprehend militants and a public outpouring of emotion in Israel and the Diaspora. However, a police recording of Gilad Shaer calling a hotline in which shots were heard was not released to the public.

The killers of the teenagers were a lone cell of members of the Hamas-supporting Qawasmeh family, but it was not a direct operation ordered by Hamas itself. Within a few days of the kidnapping, Netanyahu had laid the blame on Hamas, which denied any responsibility. The IDF began arresting Islamists on the West Bank, including nine members of the Palestinian Legislative Council. Hassan Qawasmeh was arrested at the beginning of August and two members of the group were killed in a shootout in September.

A few days later, Mohammed Abu Khdeir was kidnapped by Yosef Chaim Ben-David of Geva Binyamin with two minors. They killed the Palestinian youth and burned his body. Two were on medication and suffered from mental illness. Mohammed Abu Khdeir's family rejected Netanyahu's apology and rebuffed a visit from Shimon Peres, but requested instead that the homes of the killers should be demolished as in the case of Palestinian terrorists.

These events erupted into Operation Protective Edge and a ground invasion of Gaza in early July. By its end in early August, when Israeli forces withdrew, more than two thousand Palestinians had been killed and some ten thousand injured. Sixty-seven Israeli soldiers and six Israeli civilians were also killed. Huge damage was inflicted on Gaza including water supplies, power stations, sewage disposal and factories in industrial zones. Hamas militants attacked protesters in Gaza who complained about the Palestinian leadership in the wake of such destruction.

Many Islamist militants, including leading commanders such as Salah Abu Hassanein of Islamic Jihad, were killed. More than 4,500 rockets and mortars were fired into Israel with more than 700 shot down by the Iron Dome. Some thirty-two tunnels were destroyed.

At the beginning of the year, there was a three-day strike by African immigrants from mainly Eritrea and Somalia, who wanted to be recognised as immigrants rather than labelled as infiltrators. It concluded with a rally in Rabin Square in Tel Aviv. Netanyahu condemned the protests and vowed to 'continue to deport the illegal migrants from our cities'.

341

2015

The killing of the *Charlie Hebdo* cartoonists and the attack on the Hypercacher kosher supermarket in Paris by Islamists demonstrated an inability to accept difference – whether it was offensive cartoons in a satirical periodical or Jews who were out shopping.

The four people killed in the supermarket, François-Michel Saada, Philippe Braham, Yohan Cohen and Yoav Hattab, were buried in Jerusalem.

Here Voltaire is stating his often-quoted comment that 'I do not agree with what you have said, but I am prepared to defend to the death your right to say it.'

The armed assailants, standing in front of a blood-stained bust of Voltaire and a copy of *Charlie Hebdo*, are amazed at Voltaire's comment about the right to a different opinion, and one laughs sarcastically: 'He is prepared!'

Shay Charka (*Makor Rishon* 9 January 2015)

2 Jan Israel freezes $125 million tax transfer to the Palestinian Authority

9 Jan Four killed in Islamist attack on the Hypercacher supermarket in Paris

18 Jan Helicopter attack kills Iranian Revolutionary Guards general

21 Jan Multiple stabbings of passengers on a Tel Aviv bus

28 Jan Hezbollah anti-tank missile kills two Israelis at the Shebaa Farms

10 Feb Six judges resign from the Israel Prize awards over Netanyahu's interference

15 Feb Islamist attack on a Copenhagen synagogue during a batmitzvah kills one

17 Feb Comptroller criticises the Netanyahu household for excessive spending

3 Mar Netanyahu gives a controversially arranged speech on Iran to the US Congress

17 Mar Netanyahu tells voters that Arabs are heading to the polling stations 'in droves'

17 Mar Likud emerges as the largest party in the national election with 30 seats

26 Mar Islamic movement's Raed Salah is given 11 months for incitement

30 Mar Olmert is found guilty in a retrial of the cash-in-envelopes Talansky affair

15 Apr Car attack in French Hill, Jerusalem kills two

25 Apr Attack on Hezbollah and Syrian bases near Kteife and Yabrud

8 May Menashe Kadishman, painter and sculptor, dies in Ramat Gan aged 82

16 May Moshe Levinger, early settler in Hebron, dies in Jerusalem aged 80

26 May Islamic Jihad Grad fired from Gaza lands near Gan Yavne

21 June Border policeman is stabbed in the neck at the Damascus Gate, Jerusalem

29 June Flotilla boat *Marianne of Gothenburg* tries to break the Gaza blockade

14 July P5+1 and Iran sign the JCPOA to restrict the Iranian nuclear programme

15 July Knesset rejects a death penalty bill 94–6

30 July Haredi Yishai Schlissel stabs a 16-year-old to death at a Gay Pride parade

31 July Settler firebomb attack on home in the village of Duma kills parents and a baby

7 Sept Knesset approves a natural gas deal with a consortium of companies

21 Sept Netanyahu and Eisenkot meet Putin in Moscow in order to avoid clashes in Syria

13 Oct Three Israelis are killed in attacks in East Talpiot and Geula in Jerusalem

18 Oct Eritrean asylum seeker, seen wrongly as an assailant, is shot dead in Beersheba

31 Oct Bomb brings down a Russian flight over Sinai, killing 224

6 Nov Yitzhak Navon, fifth Israeli president, education minister, dies aged 94

17 Nov Security cabinet outlaws the northern branch of the Islamic Movement

19 Nov Two congregants killed in a synagogue stabbing in Tel Aviv

19 Nov Three killed, five injured, in attacks on travellers at the Alon Shvut crossroads

20 Nov Jonathan Pollard is released after 30 years in US prisons

4 Dec Yossi Sarid, peace camp leader and writer, dies in Tel Aviv aged 75

19 Dec Samir Kuntar killed in airstrike on Damascus suburb

343

The complexities of the Syrian civil war brought both Iranian and Russian forces to Israel's northern border. While both wished to assist Bashar Assad and ensure the survival of his regime, only Iran expressed hostile intentions towards Israel and supported its ally, Hezbollah, in Lebanon with arms supplies.

Hezbollah's task in mid-January was to block the advance of the al-Nusra Front near the Syrian side of the Golan Heights. An Israeli helicopter attack killed an Iranian Revolutionary Guards Corps general, Muhammed Ali Allah-Dadi, and a Hezbollah commander, Abu Ali Tabatabai, at the village of Mazra'at Amal near the Golan Heights. This provoked an attack on an Israeli military convoy at the Shebaa Farms on the Lebanese–Syrian border ten days later.

Many Syrian rebels including ISIS sought refuge in the Qalamoun Mountains, north of Damascus. It was also the location of military convoys whose task was to supply Hezbollah. At the end of April, there were Israeli attacks on Syrian and Hezbollah bases in the area of Kteife and Yabrud where Scud missile depots were located.

Samir Kuntar who had been given five life sentences for the killing of members of an Israeli family in Nahariya in 1979 and then exchanged for the bodies of two Israeli soldiers in 2008, was killed in an airstrike. He had become a senior official in Hezbollah after his release and been honoured by both Iran and Syria.

Members of Iran's Revolutionary Guard had increased their representation in Syria and included Pakistani, Iraqi and Afghani Shi'ites as well as other foreign fighters. They arrived at Latakia and Tartus. In October, a senior Iranian commander, Brigadier-General Hossein Hamadani, was killed by ISIS in Aleppo. A few days later, two more senior Iranian commanders were killed.

Despite the viciousness of the Syrian civil war and the Assad regime's willingness to use chemical weapons, the North Americans and the Europeans were reticent to intervene with boots on the ground, given their experience following the invasion of Iraq in 2003. Russia possessed no such qualms. Historically it had always sought an outlet in the Mediterranean and during Soviet times had proved a valued ally of Hafez Assad and the Ba'athists in Syria.

Putin agreed to the delivery of S-300 missiles to Iran in 2010. In April, this $800 million sale was abandoned on the eve of delivery as Russia, China, the UK, the USA, France, Germany and the EU were finalising the Joint Comprehensive Plan of Action (JCPOA) to limit Iranian development of its nuclear programme. This was endorsed by the P5+1, the five permanent members of the UN Security Council plus Germany. Ten days after the signing of the JCPOA agreement to limit uranium enrichment at Iranian nuclear facilities, Qassem Soleimani, the commander of the al-Quds Force, visited Moscow. A few weeks later, in August, Russia began to send aircraft, tanks and advisers from Sebastopol for disembarkation at Latakia. The broad division of labour was for Iran to lead ground operations to attack Syrian rebel forces while Russia would use its air power. Russian forces utilised the Sukhoi SU-24 and SU-25 attack fighter aircraft, helicopter gunships and the SU-34 fighter bomber. An information and coordination centre for Russia, Iran, Syria, Iraq and Hezbollah was established at the end of September.

In September, Netanyahu met Putin in Moscow to ensure that Russian and Israeli aircraft did not clash above Syrian skies. The two sides agreed to supply flight information to avoid any confrontation. Gadi Eisenkot, the Chief of Staff of the IDF, met his opposite number, Valery Gerasimov, and agreed to set up a working group to coordinate activities in Syria.

Netanyahu had tried to limit the sale of Russian missiles to both the Iranians and the Syrians. Putin had asked the Israelis not to sell arms to the Ukrainians. Israel, in turn, had not supported a resolution at the UN General Assembly which condemned the Russian annexation of Crimea in 2014. Russia subsequently toned down its criticism of Israeli conduct in Gaza.

In November, Putin visited Iran's Supreme Leader Khamenei in Tehran, By the end of the year, Russian forces had flown five thousand sorties against the Syrian rebels, opened a military airbase at Shayrat near Homs and was attacking the ISIS headquarters at Raqqa from submarines.

Netanyahu waged a public campaign against the JCPOA by attacking Obama's policy once a provisional framework had been agreed with the Iranians. He bypassed both the White House, leaders of the Democrats and traditional US Jewish organisations in securing an address to the US Congress. Netanyahu relied more on Republican allies and evangelical Christians instead. He argued for a total dismantling of Iran's nuclear programme and suggested that the JCPOA would permit an unreformed, hardline, wealthier regime in Tehran to enhance its ability to produce nuclear weapons. He linked Obama's approach on Iran to the failure to stop the nuclear programme of the North Koreans despite a previous agreement and understanding. He found allies for this approach in India, Italy and the Czech Republic – and quietly with the Saudis and the Gulf States. Obama attempted to respond by speaking directly to the Israeli public via the Channel 2 programme *Uvda* and also found allies within the American Jewish community.

There had been car-rammings in Jerusalem and a knife stabbing which killed two in a Tel Aviv synagogue. Shootings took place at a row of cars near Alon Shvut and at Beersheba bus station. A Bedouin from Hura in the Negev was the assailant in Beersheba, but an Eritrean asylum seeker, Haftom Zarhum, was mistakenly identified as a second attacker. He was beaten by onlookers and shot eight times by the police. Four were charged.

Settlers on the West Bank uprooted and burned olive trees. There was also an attack on a Palestinian family in the village of Duma which resulted in the deaths of both the parents and their eighteen-month-old toddler. Although a Grad was fired by Islamic Jihad from Gaza at the end of May, very few missiles were fired after the military confrontation in 2014.

At the beginning of the year, a $225 million tax transfer to the Palestinian Authority was frozen by the Israelis in response to the PA's application to join the International Criminal Court and other organisations. In November, the Israeli Foreign Ministry broke off a dialogue with the European Union which wanted a different labelling system of goods produced in the settlements from those produced in Israel.

In March, the Likud unexpectedly secured thirty seats in the national election. Numerous opinion polls had indicated that the Zionist Union – Isaac Herzog's Labour and Tzipi Livni's HaTenuah – were running neck and neck with the Likud. Netanyahu's coalition with the haredi parties, United Torah Judaism and Shas, was conditional on the dismantling of a raft of legislation dealing with issues such as the military conscription of the haredim, the teaching of English and mathematics in schools, and questions of conversion. All this was instigated in the previous Knesset by Yair Lapid and Tzipi Livni who were now out of office.

Although Netanyahu attempted to form a coalition with the Zionist Union, the new government consisted of the centre Right, far Right and haredim.

In November, Jonathan Pollard was finally released after spending almost thirty years in prison for passing US classified information to Israel. Despite many appeals and pleas from both Israeli and American public figures over decades for the granting of clemency, he was only granted release by the US Parole Commission at the end of July.

345

2016

The unexpected election of Donald Trump delighted the Israeli Right. Unlike traditional Republican administrations, Trump identified strongly with Netanyahu's positions on Jerusalem and the West Bank settlements. This marked a polar opposite in terms of Netanyahu's relations with the Obama administration and his differences with Hillary Clinton. Trump's appointment of his bankruptcy lawyer, David Friedman, a devoted supporter of the settlement of Beit El, as ambassador to Israel caused great consternation amongst American Jews as more than 70 per cent had voted for Hillary Clinton.

This image is based on a photograph of Netanyahu resting his head on the lap of his wife, Sara. It implies Netanyahu's contentment with the new occupant of the White House.

Itamar Daube (*Yediot Aharanot* 12 November 2016)

1 Jan Gun attack on Dizengoff restaurant in Tel Aviv kills two, injures seven

3 Jan New Egyptian ambassador arrives in Israel, the first in three years

5 Jan Planning Council agrees to the first Druze town to be built since 1948

17 Jan Dafna Meir, mother of six, stabbed to death in Otniel

31 Jan Cabinet agrees to a non-orthodox presence extension at Western Wall

2 Feb Three Arab MKs meet attackers' families to secure Israeli release of bodies

7 Feb Brazil refuses to accept settler leader Dani Dayan as its Israeli ambassador

11 Feb Nadav Argaman appointed as head of Shin Bet

8 Mar Stabbing spree in Tel Aviv kills one, injures 13

24 Mar Elor Azaria shoots a wounded Palestinian in the head on the ground in Hebron

18 Apr Hamas bus bombing in Talpiot injures 21

18 Apr Concrete-lined Gaza tunnel leading to Kibbutz Holit is discovered

21 Apr Netanyahu meets Putin in Moscow to avoid military errors in Syria

25 May Avigdor Lieberman and Yisrael Beiteinu join the government

31 May Jerusalem Labour Court rules against Sara Netanyahu in job abuse case

8 June ISIS-inspired attack in the Sarona market, Tel Aviv, kills eight

28 June Israel and Turkey sign a reconciliation agreement in Jerusalem and Ankara

30 June 13-year-old Israeli stabbed to death by 17-year-old Palestinian in Kiriat Arba

4 July Netanyahu visits Entebbe on the fortieth anniversary of the raid which killed his brother

10 July Attorney-General orders a money-laundering investigation of Netanyahu

19 July Knesset amends Basic Law 62–45, to allow for the expulsion of MKs

20 July Diplomatic ties with Guinea re-established after 49 years

1 Aug Knesset votes to exempt haredi schools from teaching the core curriculum

28 Aug Binyamin Ben-Eliezer dies in Tel Aviv aged 80

14 Sept USA and Israel agree a 10-year defence assistance pact

19 Sept Two policemen are stabbed in an attack near Herod's Gate

28 Sept Shimon Peres dies in Ramat Gan aged 93

30 Sept Israel pays $20 million to the families of Turks killed on the *Mavi Marmara*

26 Oct Security cabinet approves submarine purchase from Thyssen-Krupps

9 Nov Donald J. Trump elected US president

24 Nov Beit Samueli, Reform Synagogue in Ra'anana, daubed with graffiti

12 Dec Two F-35 stealth fighters, ordered by air force, arrive in Israel

13 Dec Netanyahu visits Azerbaijan

14 Dec Netanyahu visits Kazakhstan

15 Dec Trump's bankruptcy lawyer nominated as US ambassador to Israel

23 Dec USA abstains in UN Security Council vote condemning the West Bank settlements

347

The new government, elected in 2015, took a turn to the Right when Yisrael Beiteinu joined the government rather than Isaac Herzog's Zionist Union. Two ministers resigned, the defence minister Moshe Yaalon (Likud) and environment minister Avi Gabai (Kulanu). Avigdor Lieberman was appointed in Yaalon's place.

This encouraged a spate of Knesset bills designed to dismantle the more liberal measures passed under the last Netanyahu administration when Yesh Atid was part of the government coalition. In August, the Knesset voted to exempt haredi schools from teaching the core curriculum of maths, English and science to its 440,000 student population.

At the end of January, the cabinet agreed 15–5 to the extension of the non-orthodox prayer section in the Western Wall area. The agreement provided for an area of 9,700 sq.ft, running along a 31 ft segment of the wall, and located in the area of Robinson's Arch. This would accommodate 1,200 people and the government promised to fund the cost of $8.8 million. However, the changing political complexion of the government meant a delay in implementing this. In late November, the small Reform synagogue of eighty families in Ra'anana, Beit Samueli, was daubed with sayings from the Book of Obadiah as well as bullets left in envelopes, addressed to Reform leaders. A few days after this incident, Shas, which did not condemn the attack on the synagogue, proposed a bill in the Knesset which would prevent non-orthodox worshippers in the area of the Western Wall. It proposed a fine of $2,500 or a six-month prison sentence to be levied on participants in egalitarian services and on women who would put on a talit (prayer shawl) or tefillin (phylacteries).

There were also Knesset bills to extinguish liberal opposition to the coalition. In July, the Basic Law was amended 62–45 to permit the expulsion of a colleague from the Knesset. A majority of ninety MKs would have to agree. This came in response to a visit by three Balad MKs to ten families – all of whom wanted the return of the body of a family member who had been killed during attacks on mainly civilians. They all stood for a minute's silence to honour the Palestinian dead. The Ethics Committee suspended Hanin Zoabi and Basel Ghattas from the Knesset for three months and Jamal Zahalka for two months.

Netanyahu also began to run into legal problems. He was associated with the French businessman Arnaud Mimran who was sentenced in July to eight years' imprisonment and a million euro fine for a carbon-tax fraud. Six of the co-defendants were French Jews who had fled to Israel before the trial. Netanyahu had received $40,000 from Mimran in 2001 and often used his apartment in the Avenue Victor Hugo in Paris. Mimran invited Netanyahu to go on holiday with him in Monaco and at Courchavel in the French Alps. Attorney-General Mendelblit subsequently initiated an investigation. In July, Mendelblit ordered a further inquiry into an accusation about money laundering as well as questions about the purchase of three submarines from the firm of Thyssen-Krupps.

Netanyahu's lifestyle also came under scrutiny. A reporter filed a Freedom of Information request to seek the list of expenses from a trip to New York in the autumn of 2015. The Jerusalem District Prosecutor's Office supplied this list and the expenses included a haircut ($1,600), a meal for himself and his wife ($1,860) and the use of a make-up artist ($1,750).

The Netanyahu household also came in for criticism when Sara Netanyahu was twice called to attend the Jerusalem District Labour Court to answer charges of employment abuse. In each case, the judge awarded damages to the complainants, Guy Eliahu ($31,000) and Menny Naftali ($43,735).

Netanyahu's relationship with the Kremlin proved crucial in avoiding a clash with Russian military forces stationed in Syria. While Israel attacked Iranian bases and Hezbollah convoys in Syria, Netanyahu met Putin in Moscow in April to ensure a separation of forces. In June, he visited Moscow for the fourth time in a year to mark the twenty-fifth anniversary of the re-establishment of diplomatic relations. Netanyahu agreed to allow Russian firms to participate in energy projects in Israel.

At the end of June, Israel and Turkey signed reconciliation agreements in Jerusalem and Ankara, following the *Mavi Marmara* incident in 2010. In September, Israel paid $20 million in compensation to the families of those killed on board the vessel.

Netanyahu's relationship with Obama over the expansion of settlements, the Iran deal and many other issues worsened as the US election neared. Netanyahu's relationship with both Bill and Hillary Clinton was similarly historically difficult. Donald Trump's unexpected victory surprised, but delighted Netanyahu who was close ideologically to the US Republican party. He had cultivated many Republican Jewish donors over the years. David Friedman, Trump's bankruptcy lawyer, a strong supporter of the settlement drive and president of the American Friends of Beit El, was nominated for the post of next US ambassador to Israel.

At the very end of the year, Resolution 2334 was placed before the United Nations Security Council. This condemned settlement expansion on the West Bank. Although Obama had agreed a $38 billion award of assistance to Israel in the dying days of his administration, he also indicated his long-term dislike of the settlement policy by instructing the USA to abstain rather than veto the UN resolution. This produced an attack on Obama from president-elect Trump who called it 'a sign of disrespect for Israel' and a call from Naftali Bennett to formally annex the West Bank.

At this point, Netanyahu also felt free to act as he wished and called in the outgoing American ambassador as well the ambassadors of ten states that had voted against Israel. He ordered the return of Israeli ambassadors from Senegal and New Zealand for consultation – and hinted at withholding aid to Senegal. He also cancelled a meeting with the Ukrainian prime minister, Volodymyr Groysman. Israeli officials were unable to find the time to meet the Swedish foreign minister, Margot Wallstrom.

349

The year saw a decrease in attacks on civilians. While few Qassams were fired from Gaza and there was a solitary Hamas bus bombing in Talpiot in Jerusalem, random stabbings both within Israel and on the West Bank took place regularly. A pregnant woman was stabbed in Tekoa in the Gush Etzion bloc. Some attacks were inspired by ISIS such as the gun attacks on the Benedict and Max Brenner restaurants in the Sarona market in Tel Aviv. The noted academic Michael Feige of Ben-Gurion University was killed here.

In March, Abdel Fattah al-Sharif stabbed an Israeli soldier in Hebron. He was subsequently shot and stopped from taking any further action. An IDF soldier, Elor Azaria, then shot him in the head three minutes later as he lay on the ground and killed him. Azaria was charged with manslaughter and conduct unbecoming of a non-commissioned officer. His trial started in May and concluded at the end of November.

In July, Netanyahu visited Uganda to commemorate the fortieth anniversary of the Israeli rescue of hostages at Entebbe airport. The commander of the Israeli force, Netanyahu's brother Yonatan, was killed in the firefight. Netanyahu also visited Rwanda, Kenya and Ethiopia. He visited the remembrance site in Kigali, commemorating the Rwandan genocide in 1994. A few weeks later, diplomatic relations with Guinea were re-established after almost half a century.

2017

The scandals surrounding Netanyahu began to mount up, accompanied by the whiff of corruption. Netanyahu's dismissal of the charges and a general indifference as to how a public servant should conduct himself brought the crowds on to the streets in an ongoing protest.

Here the employee asks the virtually submerged policeman where he should place the latest piece of evidence to add to those relating to the submarine scandal and the hospitality abuse. The door is marked '433' – this refers to the investigative unit of the Israeli police that looks into corruption, bribery and fraud in the national arena.

Yoni Wachsmann (*Calcalist* 6 September 2017)

4 Jan	Elor Azaria convicted of the manslaughter of a disarmed, wounded Palestinian
8 Jan	Truck attack in East Talpiot, Jerusalem kills 4 and injures 15
2 Feb	Evacuation takes place of 42 families at a West Bank outpost at Amona
6 Feb	Knesset votes 60–52 to retroactively legalise settlements in Area C
8 Feb	Iron Dome intercepts missiles targeting Eilat
20 Feb	Netanyahu becomes the first Israeli prime minister to visit Singapore
5 Mar	Cabinet votes to decriminalise recreational use of marijuana
13 Mar	Intel agrees the purchase of Mobileye for $14.7 billion
17 Mar	Incoming Syrian S-200 missiles shot down by the Arrow-2 system
19 Mar	Netanyahu visits China to raise funds from technology investors
2 Apr	David's Sling missile defence system goes into service
6 Apr	US Tomahawk missiles fired at a Syrian base after use of chemical weapons
6 Apr	$2.6 billion arms contract is signed with India
14 Apr	English research student stabbed to death on the Jerusalem Light Railway
17 Apr	Hunger strike by 1,100 Palestinian prisoners seeking better conditions
25 Apr	Netanyahu cancels German foreign minister meeting after 'Breaking the Silence' talk
2 May	UNESCO resolution condemns Israeli sovereignty in Jerusalem
10 May	Knesset first reading of Nation-State Bill passes 48–41
15 May	Makan 33 Arabic TV channel starts broadcasting
22 May	President Trump visits Western Wall in Jerusalem
25 June	Cabinet suspends agreement to create an egalitarian area at Western Wall
4 July	Narendra Modi arrives, first visit of an Indian prime minister to Israel
10 July	Avi Gabbay is elected leader of the Labour party
14 July	Two Druze policemen are killed near Temple Mount
21 July	Father, son and daughter are stabbed to death at Halamish on West Bank
23 July	Attack on security man at the Israeli Embassy in Amman
23 Aug	Netanyahu meets Putin in Sochi to discuss the Iranian presence in Syria
8 Sept	Sara Netanyahu charged with fraud and diverting public funds for family use
26 Sept	Three security guards are killed at the entrance to the Har Adar settlement
3 Oct	Palestinian Authority and Hamas publicly meet for the first time in several years
12 Oct	Israel and USA announce their intention to withdraw from UNESCO
13 Oct	Trump refuses to certify Iran's compliance with JCPOA
28 Nov	Israel announces the opening of its embassy in Rwanda
6 Dec	White House announces that the USA will recognise Jerusalem as Israel's capital
9 Dec	Mass demonstration in Tel Aviv against public corruption
28 Dec	Refusal of 63 school students to be conscripted for service on West Bank

351

The election of Donald Trump brought unexpected opportunities for Benjamin Netanyahu and for the Israeli Right in general. Trump was an admirer of Netanyahu and had endorsed him for prime minister in 2013. The Transition Team had wanted him to attend Trump's inauguration. Netanyahu, through his American network, had been friendly with Jared Kushner and his family for many years. But most important, the restrictions of the Obama White House were lifted and the personal acrimony dissipated.

Netanyahu publicly supported the building of a wall along the USA–Mexico border and compared it to the Israeli fence which had prevented infiltrators from entering Gaza from Egypt. This approach was strongly opposed by US Jewish organisations such as the American Jewish Committee and the Anti-Defamation League. The Israeli ambassador to Mexico was called in by the country's foreign minister.

The year was then marked by two events which demonstrated the closeness of the two administrations. Trump visited Israel in May, flying in straight from Saudi Arabia. At the beginning of December, Trump endorsed the Congressional Jerusalem Embassy Act of 1995 and recognised Jerusalem as Israel's capital. This, however, did not pre-empt the final status of the city. The word 'undivided' did not appear in any statement.

The leaders of thirteen Jerusalem churches urged Trump to withdraw from this recognition. In Gaza, there were demonstrations and many rockets were fired towards Ashkelon which were intercepted by the Iron Dome. The Hamas leader, Ismail Haniyeh, called for a third Intifada. At the UN General Assembly, the vote was 128–9 in condemning Trump's move with 35 abstentions. Both the UK and the Netherlands did not support the recognition.

Netanyahu's opposition to the JCPOA and the Iranian presence in Syria found a resonance in the Trump White House. Although the USA had certified the agreement in April and July, Trump refused to agree that there had been Iranian compliance with the Iran Nuclear Agreement Review Act in October. Many in the Israeli intelligence community opposed Netanyahu's position on the JCPOA for fear that it would encourage Tehran to recommence its nuclear programme.

The advance of Iran during the past couple of years had led to regular contact with Vladimir Putin. In August, Netanyahu travelled to Sochi where he discussed the expanding Iranian presence in Syria with Putin. As ISIS was being defeated in Syria and pushed out, the Iranians were taking their place. Netanyahu opposed the ceasefire with anti-government forces in south-west Syria which had been brokered by both Russia and the USA. He argued that it brought Iranian forces closer to the Golan Heights.

The conflict in Syrian skies was another reason for a closer Israeli–Russian liaison. Following an Israeli attack on Hezbollah locations, Syrian anti-aircraft missiles were launched, which were intercepted by the Arrow-2 anti-missile system. The Israeli ambassador in Moscow was called in by its Foreign Ministry.

In April, Netanyahu supported the firing of US Tomahawk missiles at Shayrat airbase in northern Syria. This was in retaliation for the use of chemical weapons by the Assad regime in Idlib province. In Israel itself, only thirty-five rockets were launched from Gaza – most of which were fired in December after the Trump White House's recognition of Jerusalem as the capital of Israel.

In March, Netanyahu visited China. He then went on to lay a wreath at the Monument to the People's Heroes in Tiananmen Square and studiously avoided any mention of the mass killing of students there in 1989. In the United Nations, China had recognised Palestine, voted for UN Resolution 2334 and condemned the settlements. However, it was the passage of missiles and arms to Iran that concerned Netanyahu. He also requested Xi Jinping exempt Israeli technology companies from currency restrictions so that Chinese investors could operate more freely.

The Israeli Right took advantage of Trump's election to pass acts in the Knesset that solidified Israel's hold on the West Bank. The Regulation Law in early February allowed for the retroactive legalisation of Jewish settlements which had been built on private Palestinian land in Area C. It permitted the implementation of Israeli law in these locations. While US Jewish organisations criticised the move, the White House would not comment. Netanyahu's relations with American Jews worsened when the cabinet decided to suspend its decision to create an egalitarian prayer section at the Western Wall. This was the result of pressure from United Torah Judaism and Shas.

Trump, however, did voice criticism about settlement building. Netanyahu adapted his comments to Trump to suit his moods. He told the security cabinet a few days after the presidential inauguration that all restrictions on construction in East Jerusalem would now be lifted. At the end of March, the cabinet agreed that any future building should take place within or adjacent to existing settlements.

In July, the Ministerial Committee for Legislation approved an amendment to the Basic Law such that any attempt to cede land in the Jerusalem area would now require the agreement of eighty MKs instead of a minimum of sixty-one as previously. This has been pushed by the far Right to prevent a repetition of Barak's attempt to negotiate over Jerusalem in 2001.

Despite warnings from the Attorney-General that legislative acts might be struck down eventually by the Supreme Court, there were numerous attempts by the Right and far Right to pass symbolic legislation. In May, the first reading of a bill which defined Israel as a Jewish state was passed 48–41. Both Yesh Atid and the Zionist Union voted against. Similar bills had been proposed in 2011 and 2015. Arabic was demoted from being an official language to being one of special status.

There were also an increasing number of attacks on the press, academia and the judiciary as well as on dissident Israelis. Breaking the Silence and B'tselem, Israeli organisations that monitor violations of Palestinian human rights, met the Belgian prime minister and were criticised by Netanyahu's office. When the German foreign minister, Sigmar Gabriel, met with Breaking the Silence in Israel, Netanyahu cancelled a meeting with him. The vice-president of the New Israel Fund, which fundraises in the Diaspora for liberal causes in Israel and Palestine, was held and questioned for ninety minutes at Ben-Gurion airport on the basis that she might have contravened Israeli law.

Netanyahu felt further emboldened to withhold Israel's payments to the UN in March and its donation to UNESCO in May for their political stand on Israel.

The Government Press Office revoked the press card of a senior reporter for al-Jazeera in Israel before backing down. This coincided with Saudi Arabia's campaign to isolate Qatar which housed the headquarters of al-Jazeera.

Given the increasing number of charges and accusations against the prime minister and his wife, his close supporter, the US billionaire Sheldon Adelson, was also questioned by the Israeli police. Netanyahu's cousin David Shimron was placed under house arrest in connection with allegations of bribery, money laundering and breach of trust in the 2016 purchase of Thyssen-Krupps submarines.

Elor Azaria was found guilty of manslaughter for killing a wounded Palestinian assailant in Hebron in 2016 and sentenced to eighteen months' imprisonment and a further twelve-month probation period afterwards. This was later reduced by four months. The Azaria case did become a cause célèbre for the Right. Netanyahu telephoned to commiserate with Azaria's father while Bennett called for his release from prison. A rally in support of Azaria took place in Ramla. President Rivlin rejected Azaria's plea for a pardon.

2018

The mounting criticism of Netanyahu as a shady practitioner of the black arts of Israeli politics was compounded by his extravagant lifestyle – particularly in the realm of haute cuisine and gourmet restaurants. The behaviour of his wife, Sara, in this context became a recurring feature of public criticism.

Here Netanyahu states: 'We are the Silver Platter!' and this is a play on Natan Alterman's famous poem about the fighting youth who selflessly established the state. In the poem, the youth responds to the question 'Who are you?' with the answer, 'We are the silver platter upon which the state was given.' The comparison strikes at Netanyahu's sense of entitlement and his sense of indispensability.

Amos Biderman (*Ha'aretz* 25 June 2018)

4 Jan   Aharon Appelfeld, Israel Prize winner for literature, dies aged 85

1 Feb   Work begins on the egalitarian prayer section at Western Wall

4 Feb   Deportation notices are served on refugees from Eritrea and Sudan

5 Feb   Rabbi Itamar Ben-Gal from Har Brakha is stabbed to death near Ariel

10 Feb   Iranian stealth drone is shot down near Beit She'an

12 Feb   Malka Leifer, accused of 74 child abuse charges in Melbourne, arrested

13 Feb   Police recommend charging Netanyahu with bribery and breach of trust

15 Mar   Supreme Court issues restraining order on the deportation of asylum seekers

30 Mar   Palestinian March of Return protests begin at the Gaza border on Land Day

3 Apr   Netanyahu cancels an agreement with UN High Commission for Refugees

26 Apr   Ten youths are killed in a flash flood in Tzafit

30 Apr   Netanyahu presents a cache of Iranian nuclear documentation in Tel Aviv

8 May   Trump White House abandons the JCPOA on the issue of Iran's nuclear policy

12 May   Netta Barzilai wins Eurovision Song Contest with 'Toy'

14 May   US Embassy opens in Jerusalem

14 May   Sixty Palestinians including Hamas members are killed at the border with Gaza

15 May   Turkey expels the Israeli ambassador following the violence in Gaza

2 June   Incendiary balloons are flown from Gaza into Israel

21 June   Sara Netanyahu is charged with fraud and breach of trust

25 June   Prince William, first British royal to officially visit Israel, arrives

19 July   Knesset votes 62–55 to incorporate the Nation-State Law as a Basic Law

22 July   Attack on an Iranian chemical weapons site near Masyaf in Syria

4 Aug   Druze protest against the Nation-State Law in Rabin Square, Tel Aviv

20 Aug   Uri Avnery, political activist and writer, dies in Tel Aviv aged 94

2 Sept   Philippines president, Rodrigo Duerte, visits Israel

17 Sept   Russian aircraft hit by Syrian missile after Israeli raid

28 Sept   Jerusalem–Tel Aviv railway opened

22 Oct   Chinese vice-president, Wang Qishan, visits Israel

26 Oct   Netanyahu visits Oman

30 Oct   Einat Kalisch-Rotem becomes first female mayor of Haifa

13 Nov   Moshe Lion elected mayor of Jerusalem

14 Nov   Defence Minister Lieberman resigns because of the ceasefire in Gaza

2 Dec   Police recommend charging Netanyahu with bribery in Case 4000

4 Dec   Operation Northern Shield to destroy Hezbollah tunnels commences

24 Dec   Knesset dissolved, new elections in 2019

28 Dec   Amos Oz, writer and liberal political voice, dies in Jerusalem aged 79

The style of the Trump White House in promoting its policies encouraged Benjamin Netanyahu to embark on promoting more adversarial politics. At the end of the year, Israel formally left UNESCO.

During the first few days of the year, the cabinet approved a plan to deport tens of thousands of African migrants. Many had entered Israel from Egypt before an effective border barrier was erected. If the migrants left before 31 March, they would be given $3,500 and a free flight. In early February, deportation notices began to be served on refugees from Eritrea and Sudan. This provoked strong protests from several prominent US Jews, Alan Dershowitz, Abe Foxman, Avi Weiss, Marvin Hier and Yitz Greenberg, who asked Natan Sharansky, chair of the Jewish Agency, to head a committee to seek a resolution of the question. Visiting US Democrats in Congress, Nancy Pelosi and Adam Schiff, made a point of meeting asylum seekers. In mid-March, the Supreme Court issued a restraining order to prevent any deportations.

In early April, Netanyahu struck a deal with the UN Commissioner for Refugees that 16,000 would go to Canada, Italy, Germany and other Western countries and another 24,000 could remain in Israel for up to five years. Under attack from HaBayit HaYehudi, Shas and from within the Likud, Netanyahu reversed his position within hours and cancelled the agreement a day later. The language used went from 'infiltrators' to 'migrants' and back again. A plan to deport two hundred to Rwanda fell through.

The passing of the Nation-State Law and integrating it as a Basic Law also aroused the opposition of major Jewish organisations such as the Jewish Federations of North America and the International Fellowship of Christians and Jews. Long-time Netanyahu supporters such as Ronald Lauder were also critical. Zouheir Bahloul of the Zionist Union resigned his seat in the Knesset. Forty former Israeli diplomats signed a collective letter stating that they were 'embarrassed' and 'pained', and 180 writers and artists also signed a letter, including Amos Oz, David Grossman, A. B. Yehoshua, Etgar Keret, Orly Castel-Bloom and Zeruya Shalev. Even President Rivlin announced his opposition because of the absence of symbolic words such as 'equality' and 'democracy'.

The implication that non-Jews were lower in the hierarchy and that Arabic was being demoted to a language of 'special status' provoked the ire of the normally loyal Druze community whose members served in the armed forces and police. Two Druze army officers resigned their commissions and a mass protest by the Druze and their leaders took place in Rabin Square in Tel Aviv.

Netanyahu found himself beset by police recommendations that he be charged with fraud, bribery and breach of trust in three different cases: 1000, 2000 and 4000. A close associate, the suspended director-general of the Ministry of Communications, Shlomo Filber, turned state's evidence in Case 4000, while a former media adviser, Nir Hefetz, under house arrest, turned state's witness. In June, Sara Netanyahu was charged with fraud and breach of trust for ordering $96,000 worth of gourmet meals from high-class restaurants between 2010 and 2013 instead of using the state residence's cook.

Case 2000, the bid to win a favourable coverage in the media, indicated Netanyahu's irritation with criticism in the Israeli press about his policies and in particular coverage of his wife, Sara, and his son, Yair. He resorted to accusations of 'fake news' and even older epithets of labelling journalists as 'Bolsheviks'.

There was a widening gap between US Jewry and the Netanyahu government, not least because there appeared to be a prevarication over the agreement to allow a section of the Western Wall to be used for egalitarian and non-orthodox prayer. Yuval Steinitz, Netanyahu's candidate for running the Jewish Agency, was surprisingly defeated by Labour's former leader, Isaac Herzog.

This was the first time in twenty-three years that such a vote had gone against the choice of an Israeli prime minister.

The Trump White House, which favoured a strong pro-Netanyahu policy, oversaw the US Embassy's move to Jerusalem and recognition of the city as the capital of Israel. This provoked a refusal by Mahmoud Abbas to meet Vice-President Mike Pence when he visited Israel in January. At the end of March, a weekly 'March of Return' protest began at the Gaza border. Some thirty thousand participated and tent camps were set up. While most held back, others approached the Israeli side of the border and were killed. This reached a climax when the protest coincided with the opening of the Jerusalem Embassy. More than sixty people were killed including many members of Hamas. Periodically rockets and mortars were fired from Gaza, but at the beginning of June incendiary balloons were flown from Gaza towards Israel, causing many fires.

There were numerous attacks on Syrian storage warehouses for imported Iranian weapons. An Apache helicopter shot down an Iranian drone near Beit She'an. This was followed by an Israeli attack on the Syrian Tiryas military base in which an F-16 was shot down by an S-200 missile. Another attack on the base followed in April.

A leading Syrian rocket scientist, Aziz Asbar, who was working with the al-Quds Force to develop precision-guided weapons, was killed by a car bomb in Masyaf, north-west Syria. A chemical weapons plant in the same area was also attacked.

At the end of April, Netanyahu presented a cache of Iranian documents, relating to the nuclear issue, at the Ministry of Defence. It amounted to 55,000 pages and 183 CDs. Netanyahu said that Iran stored its documents detailing its Project Amad nuclear programme in a warehouse in the Shorabad district in southern Tehran. Although Project Amad had been halted in 2003, Netanyahu's aim during his presentation was to imply that in fact it had continued after that year. Tehran dismissed the exercise as rehashing old material. Netanyahu's presentation occurred several weeks before President Trump announced the US withdrawal from the JCPOA.

357

In September, during an Israeli raid, a Russian reconnaissance plane was shot down by a Russian S-200 missile which had been supplied to Syrian forces. Vladimir Putin suggested to Netanyahu that Iranian forces could be withdrawn to 60 miles from the Golan Heights – an offer which was rejected. Although Israel was blamed for the incident by the Russian Ministry of Defence, there was now an even closer liaison between Putin and Netanyahu.

In early December, Operation Northern Shield began, designed to destroy Hezbollah's tunnels into Israel itself.

Controversial leaders such as Hungary's Viktor Orban, the Philippines' Rodrigo Duerte and China's Wang Qishan all visited Israel, while Netanyahu attended the inauguration of the new Brazilian leader, Jair Bolsonaro. Guatemala and Paraguay opened embassies in Jerusalem, with the latter moving back to Tel Aviv when a new government was elected in Asunción. Netanyahu visited Sultan Qaboos in Oman, while Idriss Deby became the first president of Chad to visit Israel.

In November, Avigdor Lieberman's resignation as minister of defence forced the dissolution of the Knesset and new elections, to be held in 2019. He had opposed a ceasefire with Hamas, following the firing of 460 missiles into Israel. Benny Gantz registered a new party, Hosen L'Yisrael. HaBayit HaYehudi split with the leadership of Naftali Bennett, and Ayelet Shaked departed to form HaYamin HeHadash. This represented a schism between the NRP and Tkuma, the original components of HaBayit HaYehudi.

2019

BREAKING: IMMUNIZATION SHORTAGE

Netanyahu was formally charged in November by the Attorney-General Avigdor Mendelblit on three counts of fraud, bribery and breach of trust. This took place after years of prevarication.

Netanyahu requested that the Knesset grant him immunity from prosecution.

The notice on the wall reads: 'Warning: Vaccinations Running Out'. Netanyahu's political allies from other parties look on, with a certain measure of dismay while waiting for their own jabs. Can they benefit from Netanyahu's immunity or are they sailing into uncharted waters which will cause them problems further down the road?

Amos Biderman (*Ha'aretz* 31 December 2019)

1 Jan   Avi Gabbay announces end of Zionist Union and partnership with Tzipi Livni

7 Jan   Moshe Arens, Likud defence and foreign minister, dies in Saviyon aged 93

11 Jan   Iranian arms warehouse hit at Damascus airport

20 Jan   Netanyahu visits N'Djamena for resumption of ties with Chad

22 Jan   Arrow-3 missile system is tested successfully at Palmachim base

27 Jan   Israel recognises Juan Guaido as the president of Venezuela

27 Jan   Cabinet approves the export of medicinal marijuana

28 Jan   Netanyahu discontinues Temporary International Presence in Hebron

3 Feb   Construction of a 40 mile long steel barrier around Gaza begins

20 Feb   Otzma Yehudit agrees to a joint election run with HaBayit HaYehudi

21 Feb   Gantz, Lapid, Yaalon and Ashkenazi form the Blue and White party

11 Mar   Regev rules that no Diaspora representative be present at Independence Day celebration

17 Mar   Rabbi Achiad Ettinger, father of 12, killed near Ariel junction

25 Mar   USA recognises Israeli sovereignty over the Golan Heights

25 Mar   Gaza rocket hits Moshav Mishmeret near Netanya

31 Mar   Brazilian president Jair Bolsonaro arrives in Israel

3 Apr   Remains of Zachary Baumel, soldier missing since 1982, returned with Putin's help

9 Apr   Likud just wins national election 26.4 to 26.13 per cent

11 Apr   No soft landing for the satellite Beresheet as it crashes into the lunar surface

14 May   Eurovision Song Contest opens in Tel Aviv

16 June   Sara Netanyahu admits to misuse of public funds, fined $15,210

16 June   Ramat Trump is inaugurated on the site of Bruchim in the Golan Heights

25 June   Bahrain conference to discuss investment in Palestinian areas

3 July   Amir Peretz returns as leader of the Labour party

4 July   Trump Square, next to City Hall, is dedicated in Petah Tiqva

19 July   Israel attacks Iranian targets in Iraq, north of Baghdad

20 July   Netanyahu becomes the longest-serving Israeli prime minister at 4,876 days

25 July   Ehud Barak, Stav Shaffir and Meretz form the 'Democratic Camp' for the election

15 Sept   Cabinet approves new Jordan Valley settlement of Mevo'ot Yericho

17 Sept   Blue and White win second national election by 0.85 per cent of vote

10 Oct   Netanyahu condemns the Turkish invasion of Kurdish areas in Syria

11 Oct   Naama Issachar is sentenced to seven and a half years in a Russian prison

23 Oct   Australian prime minister calls for the extradition of Malka Leifer

12 Nov   Islamic Jihad leader, Baha Abu al-Ata, is killed in Gaza by missile

21 Nov   Netanyahu is charged in three corruption cases

31 Dec   Israel begins gas extraction from the Leviathan field off Haifa

In July, Netanyahu became Israel's longest-serving prime minister – outstripping Ben-Gurion's term in office. He was, however, unable to form a government that would ensure a majority in the Knesset.

Two national elections were held in April and in September which produced a virtual dead heat between Netanyahu's Likud and the newly formed Blue and White alliance of Benny Gantz and Yair Lapid. Avigdor Lieberman refused to join any coalition unless Netanyahu removed legislation which permitted the exemption of haredim from the armed forces. Both United Torah Judaism and Shas refused to join any government which endorsed this.

In the April election, Likud and Blue and White both attained thirty-five seats, but the former led by 0.35 per cent of the vote. Naftali Bennett and Ayelet Shaked left HaBayit HaYehudi at the end of 2018 to form a far Right party, HaYamin HeHadash, which attempted to forge a right-wing alignment of both religious and secular Zionists. HaBayit HaYehudi elected Rafi Peretz as its head and moved further to the Right in cementing an alliance with smaller parties, Tkuma and Otzma Yehudit (Jewish Power), which promoted Kahanist ideas. Moshe Feiglin, who had left the Likud, also formed a far Right party, Zehut.

While the haredi parties gained seats, the far Right lost seats to the Likud. Netanyahu had relied on every right-wing vote being utilised so that he could form a coalition even if Blue and White emerged as the largest party. He therefore persuaded the Kahanist Otzma Yehudit to run as part of the ticket with HaBayit HaYehudi and Tkuma. He cancelled a conversation with Putin in late February to concentrate on creating this arrangement. However, both HaYamin HeHadash and Zehut just failed to cross the threshold of 3.25 per cent which together totalled more than a quarter of a million votes. This prevented Netanyahu from forming a stable coalition.

The inclusion of Otzma Yehudit, which had attracted the support of many Habad hasidim in the April election, provoked a lot of criticism in the Diaspora. At the end of August, Baruch Marzel and Bentzi Gopstein, the leaders of Otzma Yehudit, were both disqualified from standing in the second election. At the end of November, Gopstein was charged with incitement to violence and racism.

The new Blue and White coalition consisted of several military men, together with Yair Lapid of Yesh Atid and the head of the Histadrut, Avi Nissenkorn. Their common aim was to appeal to the many who wished to see an end to the Netanyahu era. During the Trump presidency, Netanyahu had become emboldened to articulate often incendiary, more right-wing policies than in the past. In 2017, there had been a 39 per cent increase in spending on a wide range of facilities on the West Bank. During the election campaign, Trump's face featured prominently on posters. Trump and US secretary of state, Mike Pompeo, did their best to support Netanyahu's re-election bids.

A few weeks before the April election, Netanyahu responded to a comment by the actress Rotem Sela that 'all people are born equal'. He argued that Israel was not a country of all its citizens, but 'the nation-state of the Jewish people'. Netanyahu's comment was condemned by President Rivlin, while Gal Gadot wrote that 'the responsibility to sow hope and light for a better future for our children is on us' .

In an interview with Channel 12's 'Meet the Press', Netanyahu said that he was considering, if re-elected, the annexation of the West Bank after the US recognition of Israel's sovereignty over the Golan Heights. He further made the point that he did not distinguish between settlement blocs and isolated ones.

In January, Netanyahu discontinued the Temporary International Presence in Hebron of sixty observers from European countries which had been operating for twenty years. He argued that there would be no evacuation of settlements and no division of Jerusalem. In an interview with Army Radio, he said that he would annex Hebron and Kiriat Arba.

Despite such promises and the much-criticised planting by Likud activists of 1,200 cameras in polling stations which were located in Arab communities, Netanyahu was unable to form a government with either the ultra-orthodox haredim or their opponents, the devoutly secular followers of Avigdor Lieberman. This stalemate was repeated once more in the September election, even though there was a swing back from the far Right and the election of Bennett's new party, Yamina, which had evolved out of HaYamin HeHadash. Netanyahu persuaded Moshe Feiglin's party, Zehut, to withdraw from the contest in return for a ministerial position. Once again, Netanyahu tried to galvanise support though a unified Right. He was determined not to waste a single right-wing vote through not clearing the 3.25 per cent electoral threshold.

In an interview with Galei Tzahal, he promised to annex both Hebron and Kiriat Arba. He further made his first visit to Hebron since 1998 and spoke to settlers in Elkana. In addition, Pompeo suggested that the USA no longer regarded the West Bank settlements as illegal.

Blue and White similarly was unable to form a government because it did not have sufficient seats. Coalition talks foundered between the Likud and Blue and White such that a third election was scheduled for 2020. Blue and White, in particular, refused to support an immunity law which would protect Netanyahu from being placed on trial.

In November, Netanyahu was formally charged in three corruption cases. This provoked rallies in support of him, even though he was challenged for the Likud leadership by his rival, Gideon Saar. However, as Netanyahu was the head of a caretaker government until the next election, Avigdor Mendelblit, the Attorney-General, also ruled that he was not obliged to resign.

While there were periodic clashes and the firing of rockets from Gaza, it was the presence of Iranian forces in Syria that caused concern. In mid-January, the retiring IDF Chief of Staff, Gadi Eisenkot, revealed that Israel had provided arms to Syrian rebels in order to hinder the Iranian advance in the country. There were ongoing attacks on Iranian storehouses in Syria, including an attack on the T4 airbase in the north. In July, Israel attacked Iranian positions in Iraq, north of Baghdad.

361

In October, in the wake of Trump's desire to withdraw American personnel and effectively desert the Kurds, Netanyahu condemned the invasion of Kurdish areas in Syria by Turkish forces three days later and promised humanitarian assistance to them.

In July, a medical committee of the Jerusalem District Court found that Malka Leifer had faked mental illness in order to avoid extradition to Australia to stand trial on multiple charges of sexual abuse while heading the Adass Israel school in Melbourne. She had left Australia suddenly in 2008 and been arrested in Israel in 2014. However, despite the protests of leaders of both the Jewish community and the government of Australia, the extradition proceedings had stalled.

A few months prior to the ruling of the Jerusalem court, Ya'akov Litzman, the deputy minister of health, had been questioned by the police on the basis that he might have pressured doctors to provide an erroneous psychiatric appraisal of Leifer's condition in 2016. This subsequently prevented the evaluation of the demand for extradition. Both Leifer and Litzman adhered to the Ger hasidim.

2020

Israel led the world in establishing a major vaccination programme against the Covid-19 virus which was causing a global pandemic.

It also led initially to a frenzy of disobeying government and medical expert guidelines as the situation improved and the hospitalisation rate and deaths decreased.

In particular, sections of the ultra-orthodox community proved unable to give up large gatherings such as weddings. Their spiritual leaders appeared indecisive and often ill-informed. This widened the gap between the ultra-orthodox and other members of Israeli society. This was followed by a second lockdown.

Here the desire to get out and normalise life is seen as multitudes riding an escalator to shop. The supermarket or apartment store is replaced by a giant virus holding a 'Sale!' sign.

Zach Cohen (*Calcalist* 2 December 2020)

1 Jan Netanyahu requests parliamentary immunity from prosecution

3 Jan Iranian al-Quds commander Qasem Soleimani killed in a US airstrike

6 Jan Leviathan gasfields start pumping

14 Jan T4 airbase near Homs in northern Syria is attacked

28 Jan Netanyahu is charged on three counts in the Jerusalem District Court

28 Jan Political section of Trump Plan is unveiled at the White House

29 Jan Naama Issachar is pardoned by Putin

4 Feb Israeli air attack on a Hamas weapons facility in Gaza

10 Feb Vered Noam becomes the first woman to be awarded the Israel Prize for Talmudic Studies

21 Feb First case of Covid-19 discovered in Israel

25 Feb Hosni Mubarak, former president of Egypt, dies in Cairo aged 91

2 Mar Likud emerges as largest party in a third national election

26 Mar Yesh Atid breaks away from Blue and White

12 Apr Former Sephardi Chief Rabbi Bakshi-Doron dies of Covid-19

20 Apr Netanyahu and Gantz agree to form a rotational 'emergency' coalition

24 May Netanyahu's trial opens in room 317 of the Jerusalem District Court

26 May IDE Technologies to build Sorek-2 water-desalination plant

30 May Autistic Palestinian Iyad Halak shot dead in Jerusalem

363

5 July Reconnaissance satellite Ofek-16 is launched

7 July Public Health Director, Siegel Sadetzki, resigns over early reopening during a pandemic

7 Aug Adin Steinsaltz, Talmudic scholar and translator, dies aged 83

13 Aug Peace and diplomatic relations with UAE

15 Aug Ruth Gavison, academic and human rights expert, dies aged 75

31 Aug Israel and Hamas agree a ceasefire after the firing of rockets and incendiary balloons

2 Sept Supreme Court rules that Malka Leifer must be extradited to Australia

8 Sept Ministerial committee declares a nightly curfew in 40 Israeli locations

11 Sept Bahrain agrees to establish diplomatic relations with Israel

18 Sept Israel goes into its second lockdown

22 Oct Sudan and Israel agree to proceed towards normalisation of ties

10 Nov Saeb Erekat, the veteran Palestinian negotiator, dies of Covid-19 aged 65

19 Nov Mike Pompeo becomes the first US secretary of state to visit a West Bank settlement

27 Nov Mohsen Fakhrizadeh, Iranian nuclear programme official, is assassinated near Tehran

10 Dec Morocco and Israel agree to establish diplomatic relations

12 Dec Bhutan establishes diplomatic relations with Israel

14 Dec US president-elect, Joe Biden, confirmed by electoral college

20 Dec Mass vaccination against Covid-19 begins in Israel

The establishment of diplomatic relations first with the UAE and then with Bahrain in the Gulf displaced the much-heralded Trump Plan which would have removed numerous obstacles to annexing 30 per cent of the West Bank. The economic part of the Trump Plan envisaged $50 billion for the Palestinian Authority to propel its development, while no mention was made of a two-state solution. The Palestinians rejected both the economic and political aspects of the Trump Plan.

Netanyahu's cabinet meeting to formalise this annexation in February did not take place because the USA opposed any immediate and unilateral action. Instead, a joint committee of Israelis and Americans was established to delineate the actual areas to be annexed. No deadline for the delivery of its conclusions was given.

The proposal to annex part of the West Bank met with widespread opposition in the Diaspora and from those West Bank settlements which suspected that they would be left outside the areas to be annexed and marooned in Palestinian territory.

Several believed that this was a ploy to energise the Right to vote for the Likud and thereby break the electoral deadlock. This was the third election, yet although the Likud did advance and gain four seats, it came at the expense of the far Right.

Despite the fact that Blue and White had not increased its tally of thirty-three seats, Benny Gantz did have the backing of sixty-one MKs including the Joint List and he was therefore asked by President Rivlin to form a government. However, this possibility dissipated when several MKs opposed a reliance on the fifteen seats of the Arab Joint List for political survival.

The sudden onset of the Covid-19 pandemic created a different political agenda. Netanyahu's trial was postponed until May and a state of national emergency was declared. Despite his previous opposition to joining a Netanyahu administration, Gantz agreed to form a rotational unity government. Netanyahu would become prime minister for the first eighteen months, followed by Gantz for the second. This development fragmented the Blue and White alliance with Yair Lapid's Yesh Atid. The new Netanyahu government came into existence in mid-May, with Benny Gantz serving as minister of defence.

Gantz had reservations about the Trump Plan and preferred not to abandon talks with the Palestinians. In the US Congress, there was mounting opposition to unilateral annexation. Of the 233 House Democrats, 191 opposed annexation. Presidential nominee Joe Biden had a long history of supporting Israel while opposing the settlement drive on the West Bank, and his running mate, Kamala Harris, publicly stated her opposition to annexation. In an article in the Israeli press, the UK's newly elected prime minister, Boris Johnson, argued that such a move would be 'contrary to Israel's interests'. In Petah Tiqva, protesters turned the water gushing from the fountain in Donald Trump Square a blood-red colour.

The government was eager to open up and proceeded to relax lockdown restrictions as soon as the first wave of the virus infection began to subside. It did so with the result that serious cases doubled. At the beginning of July, the death toll stood at 338 with more than 30,000 cases of infection. The director of public health, Siegel Sadetzki, tendered his resignation in protest at the government's hasty action. Israel went into its second lockdown in mid-September. There was a nightly curfew in forty cities and towns.

The haredi public liked to gather in large numbers to celebrate occasions such as barmitzvahs and weddings, to congregate for daily prayers and festivals, and to listen to lectures by learned rabbis in normal times – and continued initially to do so in the age of Covid-19. In addition, many haredim lived in overcrowded conditions and there was a long-time suspicion of secular authority.

Although the virus had claimed the lives of several eminent rabbis such as Eliiyahu Bakshi-Doron, there were mixed and confusing signals given by rabbinical leaders. Later in the year, vaccine hesitancy became an issue. The UTJ threatened to leave the coalition if the yeshivot were closed because of the pandemic. All this created a fierce criticism of the haredi sector by the broader population.

In mid-July Israel's unemployment rate reached 21 per cent and there were demonstrations against the economic crisis.

The vaccination campaign itself began at the very end of the year, with 280,000 people vaccinated with the Pfizer BioN-Tech vaccine during the first week of rollout in late December in a public 'Give a Shoulder' campaign. Netanyahu was amongst the first, in an attempt to persuade the vaccine sceptics.

In mid-June, the UAE's ambassador to Washington, Yousef al-Otaiba, had warned in an article in the Israeli press against extending Israeli law to sections of the West Bank. Two months later, the UAE and Israel announced that they would normalise diplomatic relations between the two countries.

There had already been ongoing relations between Israel and the UAE for more than a decade. In September 2012, Netanyahu had met the UAE's foreign minister in New York and there was a quiet Israeli presence in Dubai. The Sunni Gulf monarchies – with the exception of Qatar – sided with the traditionalists in the Middle East and were united in their opposition to Shi'ite Iran.

The relationship between Israel and the UAE was further strengthened by an apprehension at and an opposition to Iran's developing nuclear programme. There was cooperation between the embassies of Israel and the UAE in Washington in an attempt to thwart the signing of the JCPOA by the USA and Iran. The formal signing in Washington of the Abraham Accords, which normalised relations between Israel, the UAE and Bahrain, effectively relegated the Palestinian question to the periphery.

The ongoing military, albeit unattributed, conflict with Iran continued with attacks on Iranian arms warehouses and Hezbollah convoys in Syria. At the beginning of the year, the commander of the al-Quds Force of the Revolutionary Guards Corps, Qassem Soleimani, was killed by a US drone strike near Damascus airport.

Amidst all the concern about the pandemic, a shadow cyberwar between Israel and Iran was taking place. At the end of April, Israel's water distribution and sewerage system was disrupted by a cyberattack. Just over a week later, Iran's Shahid Rajaee port at Bandar Abbas suffered a cyberattack which resulted in disruption and holdups.

Saudi Arabia, which had led the Gulf States in opposition to Iran, did not establish ties with Israel, but was reputed to have ongoing and extensive contacts. In February, members of the US Conference of Major Jewish Organisations visited Saudi Arabia. Both states were concerned about Iran's development of missile technology. A Quds-1 missile had struck the Saudi Abqaiq oil-processing facility in September 2019. A second attack, on a facility in the port city of Jiddah in Saudi Arabia, utilising the Quds-2, took place in late November. This occured after a meeting had allegedly taken place between Crown Prince Mohammed bin Salman, Netanyahu and the head of the Mossad, Yossi Cohen, in the Saudi city of Neom.

The agreement with the UAE effectively derailed the Trump Plan and any annexation was placed in abeyance. While sovereignty was still said to be 'on the table', Jared Kushner remarked that US approval for annexation would not come for some time. This was followed by the establishment of diplomatic ties with Bahrain, Morocco, Bhutan and Sudan. Both Malawi and Serbia agreed to move their embassies to Jerusalem.

In mid-December, Joe Biden was confirmed as US president-elect by the electoral college. His election posed many problems for Netanyahu who had gradually abandoned Israel's traditional bi-partisan approach in Congress during his decade in power.

365

Collections of Works of Early Israeli Cartoonists

Yehoshua Adari
Kav l'Kav (Tel Aviv 1939)
Laughter and Tears (Jerusalem 1945)
Without Embellishment (Tel Aviv 1960)

Noah Bee
The Faces of Tel Aviv in Cartoons (Tel Aviv 1939)

Yaakov Farkash
*'We are searching for Peace': From the Six Day War until the Political Earthquake in Israel,
    1968–1977*
Curator: Nissim (Nusko) Hezkiyahu (Museum of Cartoons, Holon 2008)
*How Ze'ev Saw Them: the Images of David Ben-Gurion and Menahem Begin in Ze'ev's
    Sketches*
Curator: Liat Margolit (Museum of Cartoons, Holon 2013)
Ze'ev: Eyewitness with a Smile
Curator: Daphna Naor (National Museum of Cartoon Art, London 1994)

Kariel Gardosh
Dosh at srulik.co.il

Shmuel Katz
From Dan to Sinai: a Cartoonist's Diary (Tel Aviv 1957)
The Harp Has 10 Strings (Tel Aviv 1958)

Dani Levkovitz
Against the Mainstream: the Communist Party of Israel (CPI), 1919–2009
Eds. Tamar Gozansky and Angelika Timm (Tel Aviv 2009)

Arie Navon
In Black and White (Tel Aviv 1938)
Mr Israel (Tel Aviv 1956)
Drawings (Tel Aviv 1982)

Friedel Stern
Friedel: Humor and More (Haifa 1999)
'I was a Tourist in the Land'
Curator: Yirmi Pinkus (Museum of Cartoons, Holon 2012)

Index

379